Data Science, Machine Intelligence, and Law

Volume 6

Data-driven technologies, such as AI systems and robotics, have the potential to improve our lives, our society and our economy. At the same time, the development and use of these technologies raise unresolved legal and ethical issues. Our new peer reviewed book series brings together works from different legal fields, dealing with the legal, social and economic impact of these technologies, exploring on the one hand the opportunities for law and legal practice, and on the other hand, the ethical and legal frameworks they require. The series especially welcomes book proposals dealing with the legal and/or ethical aspects of data science and the emerging discipline of machine intelligence, which encompasses perception (sensing), AI (planning) and robotics (acting). In this way, our book series aims to contribute to an informed dialogue across the various disciplines about the chances and risks of data-driven systems.

Marton Varju · Kitti Mezei
Editors

The Challenges of Artificial Intelligence for Law in Europe

Springer

Editors
Marton Varju
Institute for Legal Studies
HUN-REN Center for Social Sciences
Budapest, Hungary

Kitti Mezei
Institute for Legal Studies
HUN-REN Centre for Social Sciences
Budapest, Hungary

ISSN 2730-5899 ISSN 2730-5902 (electronic)
Data Science, Machine Intelligence, and Law
ISBN 978-3-031-86812-2 ISBN 978-3-031-86813-9 (eBook)
https://doi.org/10.1007/978-3-031-86813-9

This Springer imprint is published by the registered company Springer Nature Switzerland AG
The registered company address is: Gewerbestrasse 11, 6330 Cham, Switzerland

Preface and Acknowledgments

This book analyses the regulatory and other legal developments that are taking place in Europe to shape and control the technology that is artificial intelligence, as well as the social and economic environment surrounding its development and use. It appears that the need for legal regulation has now been acknowledged, and there is a broad consensus on the priorities and the targets of regulation. Europe now seems committed to a human-focused regulation of the technology, which somehow finds a working linkage between the fundamental rights to be protected and the technological risks to be addressed, and which also maintains a favourable environment for innovation and economic activity from both a domestic and an international perspective. By 2024, the European Union has managed to deliver the majority of regulatory measures, which a few years ago—when the project leading to this publication started—were mere bullet points in a generically formulated industrial and technology policy strategy. Europe now has or is planning to introduce common or harmonised rules on the major risks posed by artificial intelligence systems, liability for damages caused by such systems, as well as rules on data protection and governance, and rules regulating the behaviour of operators in the data economy.

However, amidst the current roll-out of European regulation, there remain significant issues of policy and regulatory strategy, regulatory design and implementation, as well as questions of hard law, which require further investigation and clarification. The contributions in this volume strive to accomplish just this, from multiple perspectives. The number of parallel developments in different arenas of technology regulation raise questions about regulatory coherence, and about the relative virtues and benefits of individual regulatory projects, especially when the general goals pursued are overlapping, or in fact different. The multiple objectives associated with the regulation of artificial intelligence also require scrutiny, so that we understand where the particular model came from and what it aims to achieve, and what problems it may pose for every actor involved in the compliance side of regulation. There are also dilemmas and already visible problems in particular areas of technology use, such as policing, immigration or criminal justice, which provide a fertile ground for regulatory and legal analysis. The concerns of technology actors—for example whether they are able to implement their regulatory obligations in the complex processes of technology development and deployment—present a further problem for law and regulation. These are the main, although not the only, angles, from which the chapters of this book examine the emerging European (and international) law of artificial intelligence.

The editors express their gratitude to all those who have contributed to this volume and to the international conference organised at the HUN-REN Centre for Social Sciences in Budapest, where the first versions of the chapters published here were presented. The work of the Budapest team was generously supported by the HUN-REN Hungarian Research Network, which is the umbrella organisation of the Centre for Social Sciences, and by the Hungarian National Laboratory on Artificial Intelligence (MILAB), of which the Centre for Social Sciences is a member. Our special thanks goes to János Rékasi for his dedication and organisational assistance and to George Seel for language editing the manuscripts.

Budapest, Hungary

Marton Varju
Kitti Mezei

Contents

Contributors

Konrad Burdziak Faculty of Law and Administration, University of Szczecin, Szczecin, Poland

Dániel Eszteri Hungarian National Authority for Data Protection and Freedom of Information, Budapest, Hungary;
Artificial Intelligence National Laboratory, HUN-REN Centre for Social Sciences, Budapest, Hungary

Anikó Grad-Gyenge Faculty of Economic and Social Sciences, Budapest University of Technology and Economics, Budapest, Hungary

Ljupcho Grozdanovski FNRS/University of Liège, Liège, Belgium

Adam Harkens Strathclyde Law School, University of Strathclyde, Glasgow, UK

András Hárs Department of International Law, Faculty of Public Governance and International Studies, Ludovika University of Public Service, Budapest, Hungary

Pin Lean Lau Brunel Law School, Brunel University of London, London, UK

Kitti Mezei Institute for Legal Studies, HUN-REN Centre for Social Sciences, Budapest, Hungary

Tamás Molnár EU Agency for Fundamental Rights, Vienna, Austria;
Department of International Relations, Corvinus University of Budapest, Budapest, Hungary;
Institute for Law and Governance, WU Vienna University of Economics and Business, Vienna, Austria

András Pünkösty Pázmány Péter Catholic University, Budapest, Hungary;
Ludovika University of Public Service, Budapest, Hungary

Judit Sándor Central European University (CEU-PU), Vienna, Austria

Béatrice Schütte University of Lapland, Rovaniemi, Finland;
Information Society Law Center (ISLC), University of Milan, Milan, Italy

Zoltán Turbék Permanent Mission of Hungary to the UN in Geneva, Geneva, Switzerland

Marton Varju Institute for Legal Studies, HUN-REN Centre for Social Sciences, Budapest, Hungary;
Faculty of Social Sciences, Eötvös Loránd University, Budapest, Hungary

Miklós Zorkóczy Legalise Zorkoczy Law Office, Budapest, Hungary

The Challenges of Artificial Intelligence in the European Legal Space

Marton Varju and Judit Sándor

Abstract European policy and regulation on artificial intelligence are torn between the priorities of industrial and technology policy, as well as the imperatives of protecting individuals and safeguarding values from the deployment of a technology that poses significant moral, social, legal and other harm. The dilemma faced by policy-makers is not novel; new technologies that promise collective and individual benefits, but present substantial risks have forced reactions from international, regional and national regulators. The different regulatory outputs have all offered some kind of a balance between technology development and technology control. With European and international rule-making on artificial intelligence in full swing, it is necessary to examine—from different perspectives, including those of users in concrete technological contexts—what balance has been struck between the needs of European industry and the public sector, and the needs and imperatives arising from society, and whether the dilemmas faced by regulators have now been addressed at least adequately, without seriously compromising the different key interests involved.

1 Artificial Intelligence and the European Legal and Policy Maze

In the European Union framework, policy on artificial intelligence (AI), which accepted the need for regulation quite quickly, has from the beginning recognised the industrial and economic relevance of the technology, as well as its societal harms and risk, especially its threat to common European values and fundamental human

---

M. Varju (✉)
Institute for Legal Studies, HUN-REN Centre for Social Sciences, Budapest, Hungary
e-mail: varju.marton@tk.hun-ren.hu

Faculty of Social Sciences, Eötvös Loránd University, Budapest, Hungary

J. Sándor
Central European University (CEU-PU), Vienna, Austria

M. Varju and K. Mezei (eds.), *The Challenges of Artificial Intelligence for Law in Europe*, Data Science, Machine Intelligence, and Law 6,
https://doi.org/10.1007/978-3-031-86813-9_1

rights.[1] The choice of this particular framing for the EU's engagement with the technology was entrenched politically in the incoming von der Leyen Commission's political guidelines, which emphasised that the introduction and the widespread use of the technology in Europe depend on a fundamental level on establishing a balance between its economic and social benefits and its social and ethical risks, in particular its risks for privacy and personal safety (von der Leyen 2019). The equal priority given to the human and ethical aspects of AI in the EU had its basis in the reports published by the European Commission's expert advisory groups. The 2018 statement of the European Group on Ethics (European Group on Ethics in Science and New Technologies) on Artificial Intelligence, Robotics and 'Autonomous' Systems (EGE 2018) was drafted on the basis of a mandate to examine specifically the ethical principles—as they follow from EU values and the Charter of Fundamental Rights—that can be used in the development of the detailed ethical and legal rules for these technologies. The central principle advocated by the statement was that human beings must be afforded the opportunity to decide which values should be served and respected by technologies, including autonomous technologies in particular.

The statement, which was not expected to identify concrete regulatory principles, drew up a comprehensive list of relevant ethical principles and thus mapped a broad range of potential ethical risks that may be addressed by future value- and rights-focussed policy and regulation. It listed the principles in nine larger groups: human dignity, autonomy of the person, responsibility, justice, equity and solidarity, democracy, the rule of law and accountability, security, secure operation and the protection of the integrity of users, the protection of privacy and personal data, and sustainability. The ethical principles that were intended to influence policy and regulation more directly were compiled by the High-Level Expert Group on AI in its Ethics Guidelines for Trustworthy Artificial Intelligence (HLEG 2019a).[2] The guidelines offered a clear general direction for EU action by adopting 'trustworthy AI'—a human-centred notion of the technology that is based on fundamental rights and the ethical principles therein—as its central concept. It explained the idea of human-centred AI as meaning that AI is merely a tool for humankind, the use of which should serve the public interest and the interests of humankind, as well as the objective of increasing human welfare and freedom. The document contrasted the value-based expectation of trustworthiness with the utility- and efficiency-based objectives of EU industrial and economic policy, and maintained that they should and can be achieved in parallel.[3]

Adopting the notion of trustworthy AI meant a complex policy agenda for the EU that required addressing purely technological issues, as well as issues relating to the social, economic and legal environment of the technology. The guidelines expressed that AI will be regarded as trustworthy and ready for roll-out when it is lawful, ethical,

---

[1] See, in this regard, European Commission (2016, 2017, 2018a), and Joint Research Centre (2018).

[2] See, further, HLEG (2019b, 2020).

[3] See, in this regard, the idea advocated by the Expert Group (HLEG 2020) that the ethical oversight of AI and the control of its trustworthiness can guarantee a competitiveness of the European AI sector that is based on responsibility.

and technologically and socially stable at the same time. The regulatory concept defined in this way rested heavily and directly on the protection of the EU's fundamental rights, as well as other significant rights protected in EU law, in particular in EU data and consumer protection law. The protection of fundamental rights was recognised as both a limitation of and a distinct future objective for AI. Enhancing the autonomy and other fundamental qualities of human beings was acknowledged as a central expected benefit of the technology. The fundamental rights requirements of the guidelines largely overlap with the ethical principles identified in the 2018 statement. The ethics principles of the document included a number of concrete requirements with evident relevance for future regulation. The explainability of AI was defined as a requirement of technological transparency and openness, and an obligation to explain to users how decisions were made. The prevention of harm and damage represents a requirement for the safe and secure operation of AI systems, and the prohibition that AI systems cause or aggravate harm and damage for human beings. The guidelines also made it clear that equity, fairness and the autonomy of the person (and his or her ability to supervise and control the operation of AI) constitute fundamental barriers to the deployment of AI systems, and that AI systems should also enhance these human capacities and common social values.

The European Commission developed the details of the EU's own AI policy within the same ideological and conceptual framework. In its 2018 AI communication (European Commission, 2018b),[4] it established as general premises of the EU policy framework, and as a distinct task for prospective EU regulation on AI, that technological development must be based on the protection of (EU) values and (EU) fundamental rights, as well as on trust among the technology partners. Having recognised the multifaceted character of the desired policy and regulatory framework, the communication proposed a correspondingly multifaceted approach to regulation. Accordingly, the EU's regulatory framework would consist of existing EU regulation or regulation in the pipeline on data protection and information technology security (network and information security), the EU legislation on product safety and product liability, and prospective regulation for the protection of fundamental rights and freedoms. As topics for future regulation, it mentioned the explainability and transparency of AI systems, the protection of intellectual property rights, and certain risks associated with AI, such as public and national security risks, the security of operation and liability for secure operation, discrimination by AI systems and the discriminatory and other negative social impacts of AI technology roll-out, and decisional bias and prejudice in the use of AI systems. These topics indicate an intention to regulate a comprehensive framework to ensure the accountability of AI systems.

The Commission's 2019 communication (European Commission 2019) (on increasing trust in human-centred AI), which repeated the previously mentioned fundamentals, set out a distinct strategy for EU policy and regulation. It asserted that a value- and rights-focussed regulation, which enabled the development and introduction of human-centred and ethical AI systems, was an important guarantee of European leadership and competitiveness—on a global level—in the technology.

[4] See, further, European Commission (2018a).

The strategy implied that the EU will be able to establish and maintain a leading position in the technological race by way of regulation, even without extensive technological capabilities. The core objective of EU policy and regulation was defined as guaranteeing a technology that humans (users) can trust, especially because it corresponds with the fundamental values of European societies. The 2020 White Paper on AI (European Commission 2020) specified further the EU's policy and regulatory strategy, having regard to both the risks, especially the fundamental rights risks, and the social and economic benefits, also including the benefits for the protection of fundamental rights, of the technology. In the document, the Commission made an explicit commitment to deliver the policy and the regulation that guarantees both technological development and the safeguarding of the fundamental values and rights that threatened by the technology in question. In particular, it anchored the seemingly self-contradictory promise that Europe's competitiveness—and possibly its competitive advantage in AI—will be secured by subjecting the technology to regulatory controls that enable the protection of values and fundamental rights.

Thus, the AI White Paper prepared the ground for EU regulatory intervention that claims to strive to satisfy both market and non-market oriented regulatory needs and create an acceptable balance between them. The document, just as the previously published policy documents, did not consider explicitly whether and how the parallel, arguably competing, and possibly contradictory objectives of regulation can be reconciled. Nor did they address what influence these aspirations and their evident complexity might have on the effectiveness of regulating the technology, and whether effective regulation is in fact possible considering evident uncertainties, for example the uncertain relationship between the current and the future social risks and benefits of AI deployment, which EU policy has not explored in depth. The EU documents sought to respond to the problem essentially by claiming that the paradox inherent in the EU's regulatory strategy will be resolved by the ability of value- and rights-based AI regulation to meet every regulatory need. The White Paper clarified that the concept of trustworthiness was introduced for this purpose. AI systems that are regulated to meet standards of trustworthiness will satisfy expectations of a social, moral and economic nature concurrently. It emphasised that trustworthy AI not only meet ethical and fundamental rights requirements, but they also represent the technology that markets and market participants (will) want.[5] With the basic paradox of prospective AI regulation in the EU thus settled, as claimed by the Commission, the White Paper went on to launch a rather reduced agenda for regulation: the distinguishing of trustworthy and risky AI systems, and the exclusion of high-risk AI systems from the market.

The White Paper's detailed regulatory agenda, which turned out to be less ambitious than what should have followed from the general objectives and strategic aims of EU policy, is characterised by the same kind of ambiguity. The agenda did not commit to the enactment of restrictive regulation that would establish and enforce the promised high standard of fundamental rights protection. In fact, it repeated the

[5] Regulation that ensures the protection of values and fundamental rights will enable the introduction and the roll-out of the regulated technology, on both supply and demand sides.

already mentioned compromise position that the EU is interested in developing a regulatory framework which, besides protecting European citizens, guarantees the industrial development of the EU and furthers market integration that will enable the development and the deployment of AI systems in the European economy. In the first place, the agenda noted that the EU already regulates the fundamental rights issues affected by AI systems, such as privacy protection, data protection and non-discrimination. Reviewing and updating existing EU regulatory frameworks, as well as addressing the possible problems in regulatory implementation and enforcement can provide an appropriate solution. The possibility of comprehensive regulatory reform or the adoption of radically new regulation were not mentioned explicitly. The White Paper merely hinted at these possibilities when it suggested that existing regulatory frameworks need to treat possible future developments with sufficient flexibility. Finally, the document proposed a restrictive approach to any future regulation. It held that regulatory change or new regulation may only address problems that are clearly defined and have a practical regulatory solution.

The 2021 communication (European Commission 2021a) (on fostering a European approach to AI) reaffirmed the previously established general framework for EU policy and regulation. It confirmed that EU action follows two objectives and has two distinct pillars: fostering technological development and deployment, and protecting European values and fundamental rights. Since the communication accompanied the launching of the EU's AI regulatory package by the Commission, which had been explicitly promised in the von der Leyen Commission's political guidelines, it presented a detailed account of the (existing and proposed) EU regulatory landscape. It distinguished between measures that enable European economies and societies to gain access to the opportunities presented by AI and measures that address the social, moral and other risks of the technology. The regulatory and other measures listed in the document make it clear—as had already been implied in the White Paper—that EU policy on AI and its implementation are constrained rather fundamentally by the limited competences and the limited political opportunities available at EU level. The measures already enacted, or those in the pipeline, rely on the EU's internal market harmonisation and/or data protection competences, which then determine the focus of regulatory intervention. Product safety and security, and other consumer (user) protection tools form a large part of the regulatory toolbox. The communication also introduced the proposed measure that would later become the AI Act. It set out its basic objective of regulating certain high-risk AI and restricting or prohibiting certain uses of AI systems, while keeping the general regulatory burden minimal and the governance structure light. In the Commission's assessment, regulatory intervention calibrated in this manner will ensure the desired balance between the protective and the enabling aspects of EU policy.

The concrete regulatory action pursued following this policy framework includes distinct proposals of new or amended regulation. The Artificial Intelligence Liability Directive (European Commission 2022a) proposed by the Commission aims to harmonise national rules on certain aspects of non-contractual fault-based civil liability for damages caused by the involvement of AI systems. It lays down common rules in two areas: the disclosure of evidence on high-risk AI systems to enable civil litigation for non-contractual fault-based damages and the burden of proof to facilitate such actions for damages. The New Product Liability Directive (European Commission 2022b)[6] proposed by the Commission extends product liability rules to new technologies, including AI systems and AI-enabled goods. It aims to ensure in particular that victims are compensated for damages (physical harm, property damage or data loss) caused by unsafe AI, without the injured person having to prove the manufacturer's fault, just as is the case with any other products in the market. Manufacturer's liability is extended to both hardware manufacturers and software providers and providers of digital services, and to changes made to products already placed on the market, for example changes brought about by software updates or machine learning. The proposal also lessens the burden of proof when under national law the injured person has to prove fault for the damage caused by an AI system. The EU's AI Act (European Commission 2021b) addresses and categorises risks caused by AI systems, prohibits AI systems causing unacceptable risks, defines high-risk AI systems, lays down safety requirements for such AI applications, and sets out specific obligations for users and providers of high-risk AI. The AI Act also introduces an administrative and governance framework for the EU AI market.

2 Artificial Intelligence and Human Rights

Innovative technologies always impact human rights and their protection and may even lead to the formulation of new rights. This is the case with AI as well, and while we do not yet know how much it will influence the future of our everyday lives, we need to prepare for its implications for our most basic values. It seems clear that AI and its applications will affect our fundamental liberties and privacy rights, as well as the so-called second generation of human rights, such as economic and social rights. Thus, besides prompting the need to develop a framework of detailed legal regulation, AI technologies pose far-reaching human rights questions too. As Nowotny put it when reflecting on the effects of the technology, "[t]he question of what it means to be human arises repeatedly, triggered by our ever more intimate and intense interactions with our artificial digital creations and creatures" (Nowotny 2021).

The European Union and other national and international actors have been actively urging the adoption of concrete legal norms to regulate the technology.[7] However, without understanding the human rights implications of AI and its use in markets and societies, our understanding of what specific legal regulatory norms are necessary and what the desired aims and outcomes of regulation are will remain limited. Furthermore, without the necessary human rights knowledge and solutions, we may not be able to maintain the continuity between the various periods and forms of emerging regulation in this field. Whenever an innovative technology emerges, its impacts on

[6] See also the relevant updated product safety rules in European Parliament and Council (2023a, b).

[7] See, as a recent development, European Parliament (2023).

various human rights cannot merely be used as an empty reference: they should be assessed, interpreted and analysed, and, in turn, mechanisms need to be established to address them. There seems to be a consensus that human rights and their interpretation in the field of AI could foster further regulations and would serve as a key element in the application of the regulation. The human rights-centred approach to AI was already promulgated in the UNESCO's 2019 Beijing Consensus on Artificial Intelligence (UNESCO 2019).

The Draft Framework Convention of the Council of Europe on Artificial Intelligence, Human Rights, Democracy and the Rule of Law (CAI 2023) is an important example of addressing the broader human rights implications of AI and its use. The Draft Convention states in its Article 6 that its rules "shall apply to activities within the lifecycle of artificial intelligence systems that have the potential to interfere with human rights, democracy and the rule of law." At the moment, however, it is not clear whether the Convention's rules will also apply to those entities that act on behalf of public authorities, since the draft includes still different alternative texts. In 2023, UNESCO adopted an important framework instrument for the ethical impact assessment of AI technologies (Ethical impact assessment: a tool of the Recommendation on the Ethics of Artificial Intelligence) (UNESCO 2023a). It proposes ethical assessment in two main pillars: first to assess whether specific algorithms are aligned with the values, principles and guidance set up by the Recommendation; second, "to ensure transparency by calling for information about AI systems and the way they were developed to be available to the public." The related 2023 Readiness Assessment Methodology Tool is available to assess and promote the resilience of legal, policy and institutional frameworks in the context of introducing AI into a national economy and society (UNESCO 2023b).

The UNESCO ethical impact assessment framework—similar to general human rights instruments—placed the principle of proportionality at the centre of the impact assessment of AI-systems and their use. It proposes that "[t]he choice to use AI systems and which AI method to use should be justified in the following ways: (a) the AI method chosen should be appropriate and proportional to achieve a given legitimate aim; (b) the AI method chosen should not infringe upon the foundational values captured in this document, in particular, its use must not violate or abuse human rights; and (c) the AI method should be appropriate to the context and should be based on rigorous foundations."

In many sectors, such as in governance, education and health care services, AI may have a revolutionary influence on the use and analysis of data. The more important question, however, is how we can preserve humanness, empathy and care in medical treatment, and make sure that diagnostic applications of AI do not amplify human errors and biases. For example, if our world is biased and it discriminates against women, then the future AI-dominated world would be even more discriminatory. Whenever an innovative technology emerges, its accessibility raises important ethical and legal questions. The availability of a new, cutting-edge technology may widen the gap between rich and poor patients. Patients deprived of the technology may face death and suffering, or may be treated with outdated therapies, while the privileged receive new and effective AI-enhanced treatment.

AI could be applied to enhance human rights and maintain dignity. For instance, in cases of a physical or mental disability, by using biotechnological or technical enhancement or assistance, AI may help individuals to live a good life. Robots may help the elderly to live independently by providing assistance to them in lifting heavy items or helping in navigation. AI could offer personalised treatment and may tackle individual biases in medical decision-making. However, adopting a techno-centric approach when using the technology, without access to humans, may lead to the isolation of the individual. Emerging technologies can make already-existing inequalities worse or, conversely, less severe. Since access to innovative technologies is usually only available to the well-off, their social and economic power may be further increased by technological power and control. However, when radical new technologies are applied to the benefit of the poor and the disabled, inequalities could be radically diminished.

2.1 Dignity

The concept of human dignity provides the basis of other human rights. No technology, no scientific curiosity, political or social interest may undermine, ignore, or violate human dignity. Put differently, no one shall be instrumentalised for the sake of any goals. In the human rights language of the Council of Europe's Oviedo Convention (Council of Europe 1997), the "primacy of the human being" is to be respected. Article 2 of the Oviedo Convention clearly states that "[t]he interests, and welfare of the human being shall prevail over the sole interest of society or science."

While human dignity is a core concept when we conceptualise human rights, it is regarded as vague and in need of clarification and elaboration whenever an innovative technology affects the human condition and requires a policy or legal response. In the case of AI and robotics, one fear is that humans will become expendable or commodified by some means beyond their control. If a robot can do the work of a human, but without sick leave or without rest, then the replaceability of humans in important aspects of life is a rational fear.

UNESCO developed the first-ever global standard on AI ethics in November 2021 in its Recommendation on the Ethics of Artificial Intelligence (UNESCO 2021). This framework was adopted by all 193 Member States. The Recommendation makes the protection of human rights and dignity its cornerstone. The Recommendation holds further that the use of AI should serve the development of human capabilities for inclusive, just and sustainable futures. The Council of Europe's Draft Framework Convention also grants a key role to human dignity when it stipulates in its Article 6 that "Each Party shall adopt or maintain measures to respect human dignity and individual autonomy related to activities within the lifecycle of artificial intelligence systems."

2.2 Privacy

AI interferes most evidently with the fundamental right to privacy. Privacy, as it has developed in jurisprudence, includes, *inter alia*, the right to control personal information, private decisions, private relationships, a private home, personal health, and private correspondence. AI can generate profiles, recognise faces (Introna and Nissenbaum 2010) and facial expressions, send nudges to users, and crosslink diverse types of data and information (Council of Europe 2021). It thus creates an evolving 'artificial panopticon' that inevitably shrinks and transforms our perceptions of privacy. While we are familiar with street cameras and the basic data protection implications of mass-surveillance, the impacts of using AI on privacy in many other fields are still unknown.

The right to privacy also involves the free development of identity and personality. The everyday challenge of distinguishing the fake from the authentic leads to the constant monitoring of the potential misuses of the self. If there are new technological possibilities to invade the zones of privacy, legal instruments also need to be strengthened to enhance legal protection in these new zones. The EU's draft AI Act (European Commission 2021b) addresses some of these issues by specifying some of the illegal uses of the AI, such as the use of "real-time" remote biometric identification systems in publicly accessible spaces, the use of "ex-post" remote biometric identification systems, with the exception of their use in law enforcement for the prosecution of serious crimes following judicial authorisation, the use of biometric categorisation systems using sensitive characteristics (e.g., gender, race, ethnicity, citizenship status, religion, or political orientation), the use of predictive policing systems (based on profiling, location or past criminal behaviour), the use of emotion recognition systems in law enforcement, border management, the workplace and educational institutions, and the indiscriminate scraping of biometric data from social media or CCTV footage to create facial recognition databases.

2.3 Equality and Non-discrimination

The use of AI-systems poses evident risks for equality and non-discrimination, which represent—respectively—positive and negative articulations of one unique principle. Indeed, equality requires the treatment of all cases equally, and non-discrimination serves to prohibit biased treatment for all motivated cases. All international treaties on human rights affirm the principle of equality. Human rights conventions also prohibit direct discrimination. Traditional forms of discrimination, such as different forms of gender-based discrimination, may be further amplified via the use AI (Lau 2024). The risks of discrimination posed by AI have been addressed in a number of policy tools, such as the Council of Europe's 2020 Policy Brief on 'Preventing the potential discriminatory effects of the use of artificial intelligence in local services' (Council of Europe 2020). AI tools, such as OpenAI's GPT-4 and Google's Gemini will introduce new categories of social relationships and change old ones. We still need to explore how to use them to enhance social relationships and to avoid the amplification of discrimination and bias.

2.4 Freedom of Expression and Freedom of Science

The use of AI in creative work or in the expression of ideas brings with it the threat that the ideas and original work by authors and artists will lose their essence, originality and authenticity. Some ninety years after Walter Benjamin published his essay on the effects of mechanical reproduction on works of art, AI may complete the process of eliminating human creativity and imagination. AI may be helpful in assisting scientists in their innovation and knowledge production, but it may also distort the knowledge system, just as ChatGPT has already transformed academia.

In politics, AI presents a new, effective and dangerous tool to generate and spread fake news, helping manipulation to become the new norm. After winning an election, the new government might capture the state and establish complete control over communications and the media to extend and prolong its power and rule. As a result, political change or the competition of political ideas and visions will be almost impossible. Another possible impact of the use of AI is the simplification of human expression. If humans know that their papers, ideas and thoughts will be researched and assessed using AI, they must adjust the form of their expression to make it as transparent, easy to access and searchable as possible. Researchers may adopt this strategy when drafting their academic papers. This could lead to a rigid and simplistic structure of writing and to the avoidance of metaphors and sophisticated language in order to enhance AI comprehension.

2.5 The Right to Health and Social Welfare Rights

Can we talk about human rights in the context of AI in health care? Certainly. Here, one of the main questions is to what extent the doctor–patient interaction could be substituted with AI-systems without doing harm to medical care (Wang et al. 2023). Human rights need a more nuanced and explicative analysis to be helpful in designing the normative framework for the use of AI in the context of health care. While the use of AI promises the enhancement of accuracy in medical therapies, one could assume that the right to healthcare and the right to personal care might be interpreted differently in the future. For example, effective healthcare could be provided with the assistance of technology; however, personal care will require human contact (Abràmoff et al. 2023).

The of use AI in healthcare has lagged in comparison with other sectors. Since the seventeenth century, technology and science have been based on the concept of an open future, which suggests that life is not a predetermined destiny and humans can shape it. Emerging technologies are often regarded as transformative technologies, confirming the earlier mentioned prediction. However, the way advanced technologies may transform our lives is not predetermined by the invention itself, but by careful and sensitive implementation, which is a multidisciplinary work and requires the engagement of society.

While robots can work without requesting holidays and sick leave, they may greatly increase unemployment. It has been suggested that the use of robots in production should be taxed, as a way of slowing the spread of automation, at least temporarily, and to compensate for the shift in the labour market and to fund other types of employment (Mazur 2019). Low-skill physical jobs are especially threatened. There is also a general prediction that automation will accelerate income transfer from workers to capital owners. The right to education could play a crucial role here, as high-skill jobs would be more difficult to replace and would guarantee higher job security. However, education itself will be directly and fundamentally impacted by the use of AI. UNESCO's guidance (UNESCO 2023c) on the use of generative AI in education and research—among others—sets an age limit of 13 for the use of AI tools in the classroom and calls for teacher training on this subject, for instance on the ability of AI-systems to create offensive and unethical materials. The UNESCO document specifically warns about the long-term consequences on the reliability of knowledge when future generative AI models use the texts that previously used generative AI models have generated.

3 Old and New Dilemmas in Technology Regulation

AI is among the most consequential technologies of our time.[8] It is predicted to have a decisive, potentially disruptive impact on how we live our lives and how we organise our societies and economies. The use of AI systems promises unprecedented individual and collective benefits, while it also poses significant harms and risks for both individuals and societies. AI deployment by private and public actors is regarded as posing a threat to fundamental human values and moral principles, expressed foremost in fundamental human rights. On the other hand, the availability of AI is expected to augment human capacities and enable better, more dignified lives and more just and equal societies. There are thus fundamental dilemmas that AI governance and regulation need to deal with, possibly by finding a balance, which may prove to be extremely precarious, between the different factors and interests involved.[9] Considering the potential uses of the technology and its impacts,

---

[8] See the description of consequences—both the potential benefits and the acknowledged risks—in Executive Order on the Safe, Secure, and Trustworthy Development and Use of Artificial Intelligence, Executive Order 14110 of October 30, 2023.

[9] See, in this regard, European Commission (2020), Executive Order 14110, and UK Secretary of State for Science (2023).

the balancing will need to integrate and reconcile a multitude of competing, sometimes conflicting objectives and priorities from fields as complex as security policy and geopolitics, national and transnational industrial and technology policy, and the protection of rights and values in changing and diverse societies. Governance and regulation also have to address the fundamental problem that the consequences of AI development and use are largely uncertain and unforeseeable (Reed 2018). Uncertainty and unforeseeability not only raise questions of about the timing of regulation (i.e., whether to progress incrementally to avoid obstructing technological development, or intervene robustly in the interest of precaution), but they also make it difficult to decide what to regulate and how.[10]

Beyond these issues specific to the technology, the regulation of AI will have to address the general dilemmas of technology regulation. The regulation of technologies is expected to secure both the legitimacy and the effectiveness of the regulatory intervention, and it needs to be based on appropriate connection with the technologies regulated (Brownsword 2008). In addition, technology regulation must demonstrate prudence and precaution in addressing the risk and harms of the technology (Brownsword and Goodwin 2012). Starting with the latter requirements, regulatory prudence is ensured when regulators take into account and address the different perceptions of risk and harm that may emerge in society (Brownsword and Goodwin 2012). Accommodating diverse societal perceptions in the context of a regulatory response is already a challenging task. However, prudential judgements by regulators also involve assessments of probability and seriousness, as well as comparisons of different levels of the seriousness of probable harm, and of probable harm and probable benefits, which leave regulators with practically impossible choices (Brownsword and Goodwin 2012). The requirement of precaution entails making decisions that are largely similar in character and present similar challenges. Fundamentally, it requires regulators to take protective steps, even when the case for regulatory intervention is unclear or uncertain, even though the regulatory approach may deprive society and the individual of benefits that can emerge from technological development (Brownsword and Goodwin 2012). Although both requirements are connected to the principle of responsible regulation, they provide different reasons for regulatory intervention which, however, are not interchangeable (Brownsword 2011).

The requirement of legitimacy essentially refers to the broader normative underpinnings of the rules and limitations introduced in regulation in the particular, complex and fundamentally contradictory social, political and moral environment.[11] Achieving legitimacy assumes that regulators make complex choices, in particular regarding the focus of regulation, which can fall on responsibility, the protection of rights, or the harm-benefit balance, or the specific means selected to operationalise the chosen focus of regulatory intervention (Brownsword 2008). These choices should reflect the preferences of their social environment and should evolve together with

[10] See Wheeler (2023). Analyse from this perspective the industry recommendations for AI regulation, Google (2023) and Microsoft (2023).

[11] See Brownsword (2008).

the changes occurring therein, provided that these are possible (Brownsword 2008). The effectiveness of regulation concerns whether regulation is able to achieve its objectives (Brownsword 2008). As with legitimacy, achieving regulatory effectiveness assumes the making of difficult, often extremely complex choices, for instance regarding the appropriate standard or timing of regulatory control, or appropriate regulatory design (Brownsword 2008). The relevant choices need to be made in a dynamic, often volatile environment, where public attitudes and demands regarding basic regulatory issues, such as legitimacy, the focus of regulation, or compliance, may change rapidly and/or fundamentally (Brownsword and Yeung 2008). As a final requirement, regulation must be able to establish and maintain adequate connection with the technology, and keep up with technological change (Brownsword 2008). It also involves difficult choices, such as the choice between concrete and detailed, and flexible and adaptable regulation, both of which have advantages and disadvantages (Brownsword 2008).[12]

As already indicated, technology regulation, which takes place in a broader regulatory environment or space, must be able to integrate and address the plurality of expectations, interests, norms etc. that emerge from its social, economic and political context. The challenge of plurality is particularly difficult for technology regulation in the international or transnational arena where intra-national differences become combined with cross-national multiplicity. The choice of introducing common regulatory standards based on assumed common moral requirements or other social demands presents a challenge primarily to the legitimacy of regulation (Brownsword 2008). It can also undermine the prudence of regulation by ignoring divergence in the social perception of risk and harm relating to a particular technology (Brownsword 2008). Regulatory legitimacy is compromised when the common regulatory standards lead to an "under-interpretation of fundamental values"; in other words, the expression of an assumed moral unity in regulation comes at the cost of diluting moral standards (Brownsword 2008). The operationalisation of common standards through uniform common rules will eventually jeopardise the local variation of those standards and prevent legitimate disagreement on fundamental issues in technology governance. Accordingly, even when the economic, other policy or the legal case for common regulation is clear, regulators must recognise that finding moral agreement may not always be possible and moral diversity should be allowed to stand in the way of regulation or the introduction of a particular regulatory solution or approach (Brownsword 2008).[13] It is a question of choice in terms of regulatory effectiveness when regulators continue to push for regulation and leave significant gaps in the regulatory framework to recognise these areas of disagreement.

---

[12] The first choice satisfies expectations of regulatory predictability, but risks persistent regulatory crisis as a result of technological developments overtaking legal rules. The second choice may not be affected by technological change, but falls short of the expectations of calculability and consistency. See Brownsword (2008).

[13] Regulators may decide to devise a procedural solution to address such moral disagreements. Instead of introducing common standards, they regulate a procedure for resolving moral disagreements when they arise. Procedural frameworks lend legitimacy to the outcome, even though complete societal agreement has not been achieved. See Brownsword and Yeung (2008).

The ultimate dilemma for the regulation of AI and for technology regulation in general is whether legal regulation can maintain its position as a central, almost exclusive instrument of social control and will not have to give up that function to technology itself.[14] Technology—in particular AI—can become the dominant agent controlling and governing human activities in both social and private life, replacing control and governance by legal rules (Koops 2008; Brownsword 2019).[15] Brownsword defined this possibility as "the use of technologies [...] with a view to managing certain kinds of risk by excluding (i) the possibility of certain actions, which in the absence of this strategy, might be subject only to rule regulation, or (ii) human agents who otherwise might be implicated [...] in the regulated activities" (Brownsword 2019). In other words, this particular use of technologies "seeks to design out harmful options or to design in protections against harmful acts" (Brownsword 2019). In this light, the expectation that legal regulation should draw up the relevant limits and establish the necessary balances may be misplaced, and the pressure on legal regulation to present a response to the challenges of AI that is legitimate, effective and prudent, and is adequately connected to the technology and its rapid changes can be relieved by combining legal and technology-based regulatory solutions. However, the using of technologies to set the relevant norms—for instance, to use technological design to regulate the use of AI systems—raises fundamental questions of legitimacy and democratic and social acceptability, in light of the currently accepted framework of enacting and applying norms, especially legal norms (Koops 2008). In addition, the control and the governance of the technologies used as regulatory instruments must also be guaranteed, potentially in legal regulation (Brownsword 2008).

4 The Structure of the Book

With the previously explained challenges and dilemmas in mind, the present volume analyses the challenges arising from AI and the related technologies for law and regulation in Europe—both at the national and the European level—in three larger parts. The chapters in the first part examine the broader, international context of European law and regulation, focusing on the achievements, the shortcomings and the potential problems arising from the development of international AI standards and principles. The second part contains chapters that focus on policy and regulation in the European Union, and examine—from different perspectives—the provisions of the regulation commonly known as the AI Act and other legislation prepared in

[14] See, Brownsword (2008, 2019), Koops (2008) and Hildebrandt (2018).

[15] Brownsword does not speak about complete replacement, but about co-existing and co-evolution (Brownsword 2019). He argues that legal rules "need to be updated and revised so that they are fit to serve their intended purposes or policies", and their supervision and enforcement need to be upgraded too; however, technological solutions should also be invited to "supplement or supplant" legal rules in achieving their objectives (Brownsword 2021). New technologies are "both regulatory targets as well as regulatory tools" (Brownsword 2008).

the framework of EU AI policy. The chapters in the third part examine the legal and regulatory challenges of using AI and related technologies in specific contexts, such as policing, criminal justice, copyright or health care.

International rule-making on AI is almost in full swing. It aims to provide guidance and/or blueprints for policy and regulation at the national level, as well as to prevent discordant developments in different sites of technology production and in different technology markets. However, despite their good intentions and the expertise behind the different international initiatives, it is not guaranteed that states, and possibly individual AI actors, facing intensive technological competition, will receive the new norms favourably and without discontent. The chapter by Hárs considers this possibility. It argues that although the timing and the direction of regional and international AI regulation is generally appropriate, and there is a certain benefit in the parallel development of international standards, their implementation, which ultimately falls on states and their administrations, may reveal that the regulatory optimism of the current time is unwarranted. The European Union has become one of the main forums of transnational rule-making in the field of AI and digital technologies. However, its ability to regulate the technology has been affected by its limitation as a polity, as well as by its capacity to meet effectively and adequately the diverse regulatory demands.

Turbék examines developments that his chapter assesses as the first steps taken towards the emergence of international AI law. There are significant differences between the measures that constitute the current international framework for AI regulation. However, they also share similar concepts and similar approaches when imposing requirements on states, as well as on technological actors in the AI field. As demonstrated by the short history of AI-related rule-making at the international level, the prospect of a comprehensive global framework regulation of AI is currently rather slim. In fact, achieving harmonious regulatory developments and avoiding the pitfalls of regulatory competition in the current regulatory setting requires concerted efforts from all participants. Also, the fault lines that may prevent agreement on common technological standards, for example in determining the details of how the supposedly common values should be protected from the threats of technology, are already visible.

The chapter by Varju analyses the EU's regulatory efforts from the perspective of its broader regulatory strategy, in particular its central notion and target: technology sovereignty. The EU's understanding of technology sovereignty suggests that a balanced response is possible to the challenges faced in the development, production and supply of crucial technologies in the current geoeconomic and geopolitical environment, and that the EU can impose its value- and rights-driven standards without undermining the interests of technological development and economic growth. Varju argues that such a regulatory response may be an illusion, and the resultant regulatory outputs, for instance the EU's own AI Act, may leave stakeholders disappointed.

According to Grozdanovski's analysis, the AI Act and the related EU measures regulating digital and data processing technologies are the products of the same regulatory paradigm that influenced the design of the GDPR. They do not simply complement the EU's data protection regulatory framework, but also carry forward its central paradigm of human-centredness and its various manifestations in legal principles and requirements. This means that technological development, economic progress and market opportunities could not serve as the only objectives of EU AI regulation. It also had to integrate the protection of values and the securing of trust into its framework in order to satisfy social expectations regarding the technology. However, it remains a question for the future whether the EU has managed to transform its values into effective, legally binding requirements for AI technologies placed on the European market.

Whether the EU legal rules adopted are able to protect the individual is the central question raised in the chapter by Schütte which examines the EU's efforts to regulate liability for damage caused by AI systems. She argues that the legal measures prepared may have a limited impact not only because they were designed to interfere only minimally with national tort laws, but also because they were unable to regulate future scenarios of AI-related damages. The current law is likely to leave humans defenceless, forcing them to absorb responsibility even when the responsibility is not theirs or should be shared with others. The solution may come from national judicial practice, provided that judicial interpretation can overcome the limitations of national laws on damages.

The AI Act will have a direct impact on national and EU policies and the use of AI systems in their implementation. Policing and criminal justice are policy areas where the deployment of AI holds great promise, for instance by increasing effectiveness and accuracy, but may also augment the risks and the harms that are associated with the exercise of public powers in these domains. The chapter by Mezei examines the risk framework and the prohibitions and restrictions of the AI Act from the perspective of the usage of AI systems in the criminal justice system. On the one hand, it recognises the safeguards introduced by the EU measure and highlights why they are necessary in light of current law enforcement practices. However, Mezei also indicates provisions which, in light of the complications that may arise for the use of AI-systems in the field, will require clarifications. As the previous chapters, Mezei's chapter suggests that the balance struck in the AI Act between the needs of technology development and the needs of technology control may be more precarious than that suggested by the EU legislature.

Migration and security policies represent other crucial areas of EU and state action where the deployment of AI, as it appears, would offer significant benefits. However, the concerns are also significant as already demonstrated by the legal turmoil surrounding key European regulatory frameworks adopted in the policy area. The chapter by Molnár introduces the central instruments of the EU's policy conglomerate entitled the "area of freedom, security and justice", and identifies in parallel the gaps in the protection of fundamental rights, in particular the right to effective legal protection and to an effective legal remedy as applied in the context of the automated processing of personal data. The chapter makes it clear that the regulation of the use of AI systems in the administration of European migration and security policies is an unavoidable necessity; however, it also maintains that the AI Act will not create a legal panacea.

The chapter by Harkens introduces important examples from the United Kingdom of the use of algorithmic tools for the prevention, detection and the investigation of crime, and surveys—with the intention of informing EU Member States of what may be forthcoming—the legal controversies, in particular those affecting fundamental rights, that have emerged in this context. Harkens warns that the stakes are already high; as indicated by the court rulings delivered in the national jurisdiction finding clear incompatibilities between the applicable legal principles and rules and the technical and institutional practices in the design and/or the use of algorithmic policing technologies. With the introduction of the AI Act, which addresses the fundamental rights implications of the design and the use of AI systems, the EU will be in a somewhat better position than the UK; however, the institutional and operation complexities of using algorithmic tools in public administration and law enforcement, which pose a direct challenge to the adequate protection of fundamental rights as shown by the British examples, will need to be addressed if the effectiveness of the AI Act is taken seriously.

Burdziak's chapter considers the use of algorithmic tools in criminal sentencing, in particular whether they are likely to improve human decision-making in this aspect of criminal trials. He argues that algorithms can help judges by increasing the objectivity of sentencing decisions and decisions on conditional early release, and avoiding cognitive bias and heuristics. However, the chapter also identifies the serious legal risks of involving algorithms, especially those affecting the protection of fundamental rights that are central to ensuring the legality of the criminal process. In order to address and mitigate these risks, Burdziak proposes concrete regulatory solutions by putting forward draft legislative provisions that national legislators could introduce into national criminal laws.

The other area in which the deployment of AI systems is expected to cause controversies in society and for the individual, besides the promised beneficial outcomes and other advantages, is health care. Based on the risks of algorithmic bias and discrimination, the chapter by Lau argues that the use of AI in health care will anchor more deeply and possibly augment the discriminatory treatment of women in medicine, unless the technological area and its governance can internalise the considerations of the FemTech movement. Lau endorses the human rights-focussed regulation of AI in the European legal space, but also warns that the biases and discrimination present in medicine are ingrained more deeply than can be remedied by these early attempts at AI regulation.

The use of AI has started to cause some disturbance in the creative world, and therefore its impacts should be considered from the perspective of intellectual property law. The mainstream position in copyright law is that the results created by AI do not warrant legal protection; however, this does not mean that certain aspects of copyright law do not have to be reassessed in light of technology-related developments in creative fields. The chapter by Grad-Gyenge considers what questions and areas in copyright law may need a fresh look, having regard to social expectations as well as pressures from the markets for music, art and other creative disciplines. It argues in particular that copyright law may fulfil a role of keeping a distinction between human and non-human creative products, and act as a gatekeeper regarding AI use that threatens to reduce or eliminate human creation.

The chapter by Eszteri focuses on currently available automated technologies, namely smart contracts embedded into blockchain technology, and analyses their legal implications for the already operational legal framework available in the EU, the GDPR. Eszteri makes it clear that compliance with the GDPR, in particular its specific provisions on automated data processing operations is a fundamental legal hurdle for any automated contract, including those which rely on AI-based machine learning. Even though the GDPR was developed with other technologies in mind, the drafters ensured that its application can be extended to cover complex automated systems based on AI that use personal data. However, Eszteri warns that the GDPR's framework needs to be regularly evaluated and also developed in administrative and legal practice so that technological developments cannot evade its guarantees protecting privacy.

Although the regulation of algorithmic tools is generally considered a necessity, it remains questionable whether the current compartmentalised framework of regulation, which treats consumer protection, competition, data protection etc. issues separately, is able to achieve what is expected from it. The chapter by Pünkösty argues that data and digitalisation create complex problems and challenges in markets and societies, which require a similarly complex regulatory response that is able to combine the tools of the presently separate regulatory areas. Moreover, effective and appropriate regulation—in its present and future forms—requires the clarification of the ethical foundations of legal intervention, as well as its integration into our regulatory frameworks. Pünkösty warns, however, that algorithmic and data ethics is as complex as the problems posed by big data and algorithms, and we should think in terms of an ethical matrix rather than simplistic principles. The challenge is therefore twofold: we need to construct the desired ethical matrix and then we should reconstruct regulation in a similar manner to match the complexity of the matrix of ethics and the matrix of challenges in algorithmic governance.

Regulation must also consider the needs and expectations of actors in the technology development and deployment process. This is particularly important when these processes involve overlapping contributions from multiple actors and thus responsibility for the technology and its uses is dispersed and overlapping, as is the case with the development of AI systems. As a further issue, regulation must not only impose restrictions to address technology risks, but must also enable technological development, especially when its conditions in the particular socio-economic setting are less favourable than in competing economies. The chapter by Zorkóczy examines EU regulation and policy from this perspective, focusing in particular on the hurdles in the technology development process. What from a regulatory perspective seems like a compliance issue, from the perspective of developers is a question of process design and organisation, and of allocating tasks and responsibilities among the multiple participants. Ethical-legal requirements such as the explainability of the algorithm, or the de-biasing of the AI-product need to be integrated into the earliest phases of the development process, and followed through in the entire life-cycle, long after the compilation of the data set used to train the system.

References

Abràmoff MD, Tarver M, Loyo-Berrios N et al (2023) Considerations for addressing bias in artificial intelligence for health equity. NPJ Digit Med. 6: 170. https://doi.org/10.1038/s41746-023-00913-9
Brownsword R (2008) Rights, regulation and the technological revolution. Oxford University Press
Brownsword R (2011) Responsible regulation: prudence, precaution and stewardship. North Irel Law Q 62(5):573–597
Brownsword R (2019) Law, technology and society. Routledge
Brownsword R (2021) Law 3.0. Routledge
Brownsword R, Goodwin M (2012) Law and the technologies of the twenty-first century. Cambridge University Press
Brownsword R, Yeung K (2008) Tools, targets and thematics. In: Brownsword R, Yeung K (eds) Regulating technologies: legal futures, regulatory frames and technological fixes. Hart
CAI: Council of Europe Committee on Artificial Intelligence (2023) Draft framework convention of the council of Europe on artificial intelligence, human rights, democracy and the rule of law. CAI(2023)28. https://rm.coe.int/cai-2023-28-draft-framework-convention/1680ade043
Council of Europe (1997) Convention on Human Rights and Biomedicine. ETS No 164. https://rm.coe.int/168007cf98
Council of Europe (2020) Preventing the potential discriminatory effects of the use of artificial intelligence in local services. https://rm.coe.int/icc-brief-preventing-the-potential-discriminatory-effects-of-the-use-o/1680a03272
Council of Europe (2021) Consultative Committee of the Convention for the protection of individuals with regard to automatic processing of personal data. Guidelines on facial recognition. https://edoc.coe.int/en/artificial-intelligence/9753-guidelines-on-facial-recognition.html
EGE: European Commission, Directorate-General for Research and Innovation, European Group on Ethics in Science and New Technologies (2018) Statement on artificial intelligence, robotics and 'autonomous' systems. https://doi.org/10.2777/531856
European Commission (2016) Digitising European industry—reaping the full benefits of a Digital Single Market. COM(2016) 180 final
European Commission (2017) A renewed EU industrial policy strategy. COM(2017) 479 final
European Commission (2018a) Coordinated plan for artificial intelligence. COM(2018) 795 final
European Commission (2018b) Artificial intelligence for Europe. COM(2018) 237 final
European Commission (2019) Building trust in human-centric artificial intelligence. COM(2019) 168 final
European Commission (2020) White Paper in artificial intelligence—a European approach to excellence and trust, COM(2020) 65 final
European Commission (2021a) Fostering a European approach to artificial intelligence. COM(2021) 205 final
European Commission (2021b) Proposal for a regulation laying down harmonised rules on artificial intelligence. COM(2021) 206 final
European Commission (2022a) Proposal for a directive on adapting non contractual civil liability rules to artificial intelligence. COM(2022) 496 final
European Commission (2022b) Proposal for a directive on liability for defective products. COM(2022) 495 final
European Parliament (2023) Amendments adopted by the European Parliament on 14 June 2023 on the proposal for a regulation of the European Parliament and of the Council on laying down harmonised rules on artificial intelligence. OJ C, C/2024/506, 23 Jan 2024

European Parliament and Council (2023a) Regulation (EU) 2023/1230 on machinery. OJ L 165, 29.6.2023, pp 1–102
European Parliament and Council (2023b) Regulation (EU) 2023/988 on general product safety. OJ L 135, 23.5.2023, pp 1–51
Google (2023) Recommendations for regulating AI. https://ai.google/static/documents/recommendations-for-regulating-ai.pdf
Hildebrandt M (2018) Algorithmic regulation and the rule of law. Phil Trans R Soc A 376:20170355. https://doi.org/10.1098/rsta.2017.0355
HLEG: High-Level Expert Group on Artificial Intelligence (2019a) Ethics guidelines for trustworthy AI. https://digital-strategy.ec.europa.eu/en/library/ethics-guidelines-trustworthy-ai
HLEG: High-Level Expert Group on Artificial Intelligence (2019b) Policy and investment recommendations for trustworthy AI. https://digital-strategy.ec.europa.eu/en/library/policy-and-investment-recommendations-trustworthy-artificial-intelligence
HLEG: High-Level Expert Group on Artificial Intelligence (2020) Assessment list for trustworthy AI. https://futurium.ec.europa.eu/en/european-ai-alliance/pages/welcome-altai-portal
Introna LD, Nissenbaum H (2010). Facial recognition technology: a survey of policy and implementation issues. Lancaster University Management School Working Paper 2010/030. https://www.researchgate.net/publication/228275071_Facial_Recognition_Technology_A_Survey_of_Policy_and_Implementation_Issues
Joint Research Centre of the European Commission (2018) Artificial intelligence: a European perspective. https://publications.jrc.ec.europa.eu/repository/bitstream/JRC113826/ai-flagship-report-online.pdf
Koops B-J (2008) Criteria for normative technology. In: Brownsword, R, Yeung K (eds) Regulating technologies: legal futures, regulatory frames and technological fixes. Hart
Lau PL (2024) AI gender biases in women's healthcare: perspectives from the United Kingdom and the European legal space. In: Moberg A, Gill-Pedro E (eds) Yearbook of socio-economic constitutions. Law and the governance of artificial intelligence. Springer
Mazur O (2019) Taxing the robots. Pepperdine Law Rev 46(2):277–330
Microsoft (2023) Developing and deploying AI responsibly: elements of an effective legislative framework to regulate AI. Written testimony of Brad Smith Cice Chair and President, Microsoft Corporation. https://blogs.microsoft.com/on-the-issues/2023/09/12/developing-and-deploying-ai-responsibly-elements-of-an-effective-legislative-framework-to-regulate-ai/
Nowotny H (2021) In AI we trust. Power, illusion and control of predictive algorithms. Polity
Reed C (2018) How should we regulate artificial intelligence? Phil Trans R Soc A 376:20170360. https://doi.org/10.1098/rsta.2017.0360
UK Secretary of State for Science (2023) UK white paper: a pro-innovation approach to AI regulation. https://www.gov.uk/government/publications/ai-regulation-a-pro-innovation-approach/white-paper
UNESCO (2019) International conference on artificial intelligence and education, planning education in the AI era: lead the leap, Beijing. ED/PLS/ICT/2019/13. https://unesdoc.unesco.org/ark:/48223/pf0000370967
UNESCO (2021) UNESCO recommendation on the ethics of artificial intelligence, No. 61910. https://unesdoc.unesco.org/ark:/48223/pf0000380455
UNESCO (2023a) Ethical impact assessment: a tool of the recommendation on the ethics of artificial intelligence. SHS/REI/BIO/REC-AIETHICS-TOOL-EIA/2023. https://unesdoc.unesco.org/ark:/48223/pf0000386276
UNESCO (2023b) Readiness assessment methodology: a tool of the recommendation on the ethics of artificial intelligence. SHS/REI/BIO/REC-AIETHICS-TOOL/2023. https://unesdoc.unesco.org/ark:/48223/pf0000385198
UNESCO (2023c) Guidance for generative AI in education and research. https://unesdoc.unesco.org/ark:/48223/pf0000386693

von der Leyen U (2019) Political guidelines for the next European Commission 2019–2024. https://ec.europa.eu/info/sites/info/files/political-guidelines-next-commission_en_0.pdf
Wang Y, Li N, Chen L, Wu M, Meng S, Dai Z, Zhang Y, Clarke M (2023) Guidelines, consensus statements, and standards for the use of artificial intelligence in medicine: systematic review. J Med Internet Res 25:e46089
Wheeler T (2023) The three challenges of AI regulation. https://www.brookings.edu/articles/the-three-challenges-of-ai-regulation

Navigating Uncharted Waters: Human Rights and Artificial Intelligence in Emerging International Regulation

András Hárs

Abstract The speed of development of artificial intelligence has been extraordinary over the last decade and, as usual, the various fields of law have been struggling to keep up. However, new challenges bring with them new possibilities and several international organisations have emerged to vie for a leadership role in the possible regulation of the field. Since 2019, United Nations Educational Scientific and Cultural Organization (UNESCO), the Organization for Economic Co-operation and Development (OECD), the European Union and the Council of Europe have been engaged in different stages of norm-creation. From vying to become the primary platform of negotiations on AI to aiming the harmonisation of state policy and conduct to racing to adopt the first binding set of rules, these international organisations took divergent approaches to regulating AI. Four different international organisations with different agendas, members, possibilities and tools. How different is their understanding of the challenges brought by the advancement of AI technologies? Which path appears to be the most favoured by members of the international community and can we talk about competition or cooperation when it comes to international regulation? How do they regard human rights and what steps do they propose to take in order to ensure human rights protection? The chapter aims to analyse the abovementioned issues.

> We cannot afford to continue playing catch-up regarding AI. Action is needed now to put human rights guardrails on the use of AI, for the good of us all. [...] Artificial intelligence can be a force for good, helping societies overcome some of the great challenges of our times. But AI technologies can have negative, even catastrophic effects if they are used without sufficient regard to how they affect people's human rights—Michelle Bachelet, former United Nations High Commissioner for Human Rights. (United Nations 2021)

A. Hárs (✉)
Department of International Law, Faculty of Public Governance and International Studies, Ludovika University of Public Service, Budapest, Hungary
e-mail: hars.andras@uni-nke.hu

M. Varju and K. Mezei (eds.), *The Challenges of Artificial Intelligence for Law in Europe*, Data Science, Machine Intelligence, and Law 6,
https://doi.org/10.1007/978-3-031-86813-9_2

1 Introduction and the Status Quo in Terms of Domestic Policies

As a disclaimer, it needs to be stated that the present study examines artificial intelligence (AI) regulation from the point of view of human rights within the framework of public international law. The approach and methodology are based on international law and not on other fields. This chapter is not about ethics and what that approach can bring to the table. That discussion reaches beyond international law, and law in general, and has been widely discussed elsewhere.[1]

Regulation can take place on different levels. It is worth noting that in the current international environment, states remain the principal regulators and the primary level for regulations can be found at the domestic stage. International norms at this moment—and presumably for the next few years to come—are likely to remain the exception, with a much more limited capacity to influence developers and users of AI-based technologies. Nonetheless, as will be seen in the latter parts of the chapter, international regulation can play a pivotal role in harmonising the myriad of state policies and showing the benefits of inter-state cooperation when it respects human rights norms. With that said, it can be established that the three torchbearers in the field of AI research, development and application are the United States, China and the European Union (EU).

In the United States, a white paper was issued in October 2022 entitled: Blueprint for an AI Bill of Human Rights (The White House 2022). It addresses "automated systems", notes the possible adverse effects of AI on human rights and attempts to protect individuals and communities while exercising "civil rights, civil liberties, and privacy, including freedom of speech, voting, and protections from discrimination, excessive punishment, unlawful surveillance, and violations of privacy and other freedoms in both public and private sector contexts." It does not contain a reference to international human rights norms but at least it takes note of human rights implications and attempts to create uniquely domestic mechanisms to protect them. Earlier movement can be seen in Executive Order 13960 of December 2020: Promoting the Use of Trustworthy Artificial Intelligence in the Federal Government, which does allude to civil rights and civil liberties without explicitly mentioning existing human rights norms.[2] Overall, the 2022 Blueprint is a major steppingstone which outlines governmental expectations and protection avenues. Nonetheless,—as the name suggests—it is a blueprint for a regulation in its current form, the first steps in the creation of a major policy. The Blueprint initiative was discontinued however, as the Trump administration has rolled back virtually all federal regulation in terms of AI upon the idea that any regulation will result in limiting the development capacity of tech companies, thereby resulting in losing their competitive edge against emerging players such as China (White House 2025).[3]

[1] See Floridi et al. (2018) and Opderbeck (2021).

[2] See Executive Order 13960, Sections 2-3.

[3] https://www.whitehouse.gov/presidential-actions/2025/01/removing-barriers-to-american-leadership-in-artificial-intelligence/.

The Chinese AI policy is one of the earliest, dating back to 2017. Its declared objective is for China to be the leader of AI development globally 'in some applications' by 2025, with major regulation arriving in the same year. By 2030, China aspires to be the global centre in all manner of AI technologies and especially regarding the application of AI-based technologies in the economy (DIC & MOST 2017). It does not contain human rights provisions, which can be explained by two factors. Firstly, as it was adopted in 2017, the focus of AI was not directed on human rights but on the rather more general notions of understanding and explaining the phenomenon. In contrast, by 2022 several think-tanks in China had emphasised the human rights ramifications of automated decision making, especially regarding its employment effect (White Paper 2022). Secondly, the Chinese approach is very much business-oriented, with a strong goal of competitiveness and achieving a global leadership position. An underlying tone is that they view stricter regulation as capable of stymying research and development and a possible threat to achieving national ambitions (Roberts et al. 2021). With the creation of Deepseek and proving that a cost-effective model based on real-time information-gathering can be just as—if not more—competitve than the American models that are built on large, pre-existing databases, China has risen to the forefront as the main challenger to the US-dominated market (Nature)[4].

There are a few points to note when comparing the AI policies of the US, China and Europe. Firstly, the research potential of the US (e.g., Google, Amazon, Apple, Facebook) and China (e.g., Baidu, Alibaba, Tencent) is much greater than that of Europe. In the US, highly competitive prices and the prestige of working for a tech-leader are driving AI researchers to these countries, whereas in China, strong support by the state, supplemented by an educational system that emphasises computer science and mathematics are key elements in their dominant position. Europe appears to lag behind with much of its human capital having drained away to the US. Further aggravating the situation is the fragmented nature of markets along with stringent rules on data protection limiting accessibility to teaching databases and generally, the collection of data (Franke 2019). The European Union has realized its highly unfavourable position and during the February 2025 AI Summit, principle heads of state such as Emmanuel Macron of France have issued calls for strengthened multilateralism (Elysee).[5] Naturally, building on already available technologies is a major boon for the EU as not having to research fundamental, underlying tech can catapult it to a veritable challenger, albeit this is not likely to happen in the immediate future. With that said, long-term planning is one of the strengths of the EU and as such, at the end of February's AI Summit, Ursula von der Leyen of the European Commission has announced a 200 billion Euro investment in AI which would also include 'gigafactories' (European Commission).[6]

It can be argued that major policy documents, recommendations and (draft) treaties can provide the framework based on which domestic AI regulation can be developed to fill in the gaps, i.e., to provide meaningful content for the seemingly fuzzy international norm. However, solely referencing a human right without alluding to its

---

[4] https://www.nature.com/articles/d41586-025-00259-0

[5] https://www.elysee.fr/en/sommet-pour-l-action-sur-l-ia.

[6] https://ec.europa.eu/commission/presscorner/detail/en/ip_25_467.

meaning will render it an empty political slogan; lip service without a valid purpose. Indeed, the earlier the policy document was created, the less reference is made to human rights (Fukuda-Parr and Gibbons 2021). In his 2019 comparative study, Asaro (2019) did not find human rights to be in the centre of attention of AI policies. A year later, the Berkman Klein Center for Internet and Society (Fjeld et al. 2020) found that 54% of guidelines and policies contained human rights provisions or were at least "conscious" of AI's implications for human rights. In 2021, Fukuda-Parr and Gibbons (2021) highlighted a shift towards human rights. However, it can be argued that some of the documents that have been analysed either pay lip-service to the idea of human rights or confuse ethics and human rights altogether.[7]

On the level of universal international organisations, the United Nations and its specialised agencies, such as the United Nations Educational, Scientific and Cultural Organization (UNESCO), formulated a global agreement on the ethical aspects of AI in November 2021 (UNESCO 2021). A non-binding document by nature, it aims to create a common denominator for UNESCO member states when it comes to shared guiding values and principles regarding AI development. The Organization for Economic Co-operation and Development (OECD) took a similar approach when its Council adopted a recommendation in May 2019 (OECD 2019). The OECD document emphasises the need for the trustworthy and responsible nature of development. It has also been promoting the idea of states harmonising their domestic policies on the matter. Its recommendations do not go beyond the establishment of overarching principles and providing a forum at which OECD member states can cooperate and share information and good practices.

Among the major regional organisations, the EU has been the most prolific regulator, being involved in the creation of an array of norms. The European Parliament, for instance, adopted three different norms in October 2020 on civil liability regimes, intellectual property rights, and the ethical aspects of AI (European Parliament 2020a, b, c). Earlier in 2021, in the Commission's proposal to the Parliament for an Artificial Intelligence Act (European Commission 2021) emphasis was put on ensuring transparent processes, safety, and security, as well as meeting existing human-rights obligations. As enshrined in these documents, the approach of the EU is to look for and explicitly name the natural and legal person behind the AI system or technology and to categorise various AI-based systems based on the threat they pose as it is set out in the EU's AI Act which was adopted in August 2024 (AI Act).[8] Last but not least, the Council of Europe (CoE), the principal organisation for the protection of human rights in the wider European context has come to the forefront with its framework convention which was opened for signature in September 2024 (CoE Framework Convention).[9] CoE member states aspire for the organisation to have the first binding international treaty on AI which would also put safeguards or guardrails on AI when it comes to its human rights effects.

[7] As can be seen, the development of AI policies and recommendations have multiplied in recent years and studies dating back 2–3 years are no longer up-to-date.

[8] https://eur-lex.europa.eu/legal-content/EN/TXT/?uri=CELEX:32024R1689.

[9] https://www.coe.int/en/web/artificial-intelligence/the-framework-convention-on-artificial-intelligence.

On this basis, the following sections of the article aim to analyse how the select international organisations regulate AI from a human rights standpoint, with the goal of understanding how they perceive human rights in their key documents. Examining these developments from a comparative and analytical perspective will enable the formulation of recommendations regarding how decision-makers on the international level can better regulate in the near future.

2 Causes and Consequences of International Regulation

The question is immediately raised: if states are reluctant to recognise AI as anything else but 'things' (or *res* in Roman law-based continental systems) then what could the role of international organisations be? What sort of danger—and whose protection—is warranted by regulation? In order to solve this conundrum, we have to understand that just as states have realised the potential economic benefit as well as risks to their citizens, so have international organisations grasped the economic and human rights issues AI brings. Going back two thousand years to ancient Greece, it was Aristotle who envisioned automation bringing an end to slavery (Dawes 2020). Contemporary economists have emphasised that via the creation of a new framework that supports democracy and inclusion in decision-making a fairer society could be developed (Stiglitz 2018). In 2017, NGOs have called for the redefinition of workers' rights in an effort to prepare for the age of AI (McKay et al. 2017). In the meantime, other authors have iterated their conviction that building public trust and avoiding slipping into authoritarian regimes is paramount when it comes to the application of AI-based technologies (Donahoe and MacDuffee Metzger 2019).

A major benefit in moving towards a more human rights centred approach lies in the universal recognition of these norms. In the twenty-first century, human rights have become the cornerstone of the international community, as is demonstrated by the several hundred multilateral international treaties in the field, by human rights related universal institutions (e.g., the High Commissioner, the Human Rights Council), by the regional organisations promoting them (e.g., the CoE, the EU, the African Union, the Organization of American States among others) and by the regional human rights courts which have emerged over the last few decades (e.g., the European Court of Human Rights, the Inter-American Court of Human Rights and the African Court of Human and People's Rights), with two international treaties supporting more than 170 state parties.[10] Human rights also serve as the basis of a well-rounded education for a generation that is aware of its rights and possibilities and not afraid to act on that basis (Aust 2010). Therefore, firstly, this universal knowledge and appreciation can serve as an anchor for bringing AI closer to the individual,

---

[10] The International Covenant on Civil and Political Rights with 173, and the International Covenant on Economic Social and Cultural Rights with 171 state parties according to the United Nations Treaty database. New York, 16 December 1966, UNTC 14531, 14668.

alleviating some of the fears and uncertainties that accompany previously unknown technologies.

Secondly, the aforementioned institutions, coupled with a plethora of NGOs and domestic human rights advocacy groups are constantly monitoring and protecting human rights, which can provide a security net for individuals and deterrence for would-be offenders in the case of violations. Thirdly, a human rights-based approach creates a rule of law environment, where governmental decisions have to be in conformity with international obligations and their domestic equivalents, thereby stemming unlawful and exploitative attitudes. Last but not least, human rights are a value-based system which provides an orientation not just in the form of concrete obligations, but also principles which can be relied upon when in doubt about whether an AI-based technology will be beneficial or detrimental to those using it.

As a brief summary, it can be established that a human rights-based approach can serve multiple goals, such as centring regulation on and around the human when it comes to decision-making, covering the material and procedural issues faced by emerging AI technologies, and highlighting the tasks of both the private sector and states. It also has the added benefit of building on a structure that is accepted by the majority of the international community (Donahoe and MacDuffee Metzger 2019). Donahoe and MacDuffee Metzger issued a call for states and members of the international community in general to rally to the flag of human rights so that the application of human rights to the realm of AI can bring about benefits for mankind (Donahoe and MacDuffee Metzger 2019). An issue pertaining to this line of thought is how to convince states to incorporate human rights requirements in the development and application of AI? There are states who already only pay lip service to human rights even though the most important documents have been binding on them for decades (Fukuda-Parr and Gibbons 2021). As of this moment, any further extension seems like a utopia. Nonetheless, it explains why international organisations are regulating AI in such a 'soft' manner—binding and enforceable regulation is likely to meet with outright hostility from states. Whereas a compromise solution, and—broadly speaking 'respecting' human rights in general terms without actually looking into their enforcement in the respective countries suits states better—even though it does not achieve the aims these organisations set for themselves.

3 Principal International Organisations in the Field of Regulating AI

When it comes to the work of international organisations, an apparent race can be observed setting trajectories for AI regulation. From the point of view of the legal status of these organisations and their capacity to engage in AI-related norm creation, we can safely assume that they are relying on the implied powers principle.[11] This means that no international organisation has a foundational document

[11] On the implied powers or (*pouvoirs implicite*) tenet see, Klabbers (2002) and Shaw (2003).

which would explicitly enable them to delve into this domain and promote related international treaties; AI regulation generally falls into the broad category of the functions they were tasked with during their establishment. With the exception of the EU as explained in some detail below. For instance, the UNESCO promotes scientific advancement for the betterment of mankind. Upon its creation in 1945, even the so-called Turing Test[12] was 5 years away. As a result, nothing in its constitution could have envisioned such a scope of interest for the organisation. Nonetheless, it can be easily understood that the development and application of AI, not only in science, but also in our everyday lives, brings it into direct contact with the goals of the organisation which specifies the enhancement of collaboration between nations in the field of science while promoting human rights as a primary aim.[13]

Similarly, the OECD is poised to harmonise the approaches and agendas of its member states while also providing expertise and disseminating best practices to others.[14] Since unified state practice and similar AI policies could have a direct effect on economic growth and development, it is no wonder that the OECD will be active in the field of AI regulation. Thirdly, the EU approaches the issue from a slightly different perspective. Being the organisation with the broadest range of competencies it highlights the effects AI can have on the consumer and emphasises the ways AI can influence everyday life, while also creating a web of assurances concerning transparency, limitations in application and responsibility.[15] Last but not least, the CoE can has promoted unification of state policies during the work of the CAHAI, the Ad Hoc Committee on Artificial Intelligence and its successor, the CAI (Committee on Artificial Intelligence). The finalized version of the text—as it was opened for signatures by future State parties—focuses not only on principles but incorporating safeguards and remedies while taking the same approach as the EU by calling or a ban on certain systems: the so-called 'red lines' that cannot and should not be crossed (CoE Explanatory Report).[16]

Another aspect regarding the motives and goals of the abovementioned four international organisations is worth mentioning at this point. It is somewhat unclear—and is dependent on our attitude toward these organisations—whether we presume that they possess altruistic motives insofar as they are selflessly working toward the improvement of human living standards, and sacrificing their time and resources to work towards a common goal, or are trying to prove that they are still significant more than half a century after their establishment and are trying to demonstrate their usefulness and their capacity to meet the demands of the twenty-first century. Naturally, the latter is a somewhat cynical approach (or realistic, depending on the preferences of the observer) which comes up time and time again in academic discussion. The

---

[12] The Turing Test was the first notable thought experiment which postulates that in order for an entity to be labelled intelligent, it needs to be able to deceive or convince the other side during communication into believing that they are actually talking or writing with a human partner.

[13] UNESCO (1945, Article 1).

[14] OECD (1960, Article 1(3)).

[15] European Commission (2021, Articles 1(1) and 3(5)).

[16] https://rm.coe.int/1680afae67.

truth lies in the eye of the beholder and most likely in between the two extremes. It is worth noting that besides the four main regulators described here, there are other international organizations with state-of-the-art regulatory tools such as the World Bank Group, WIPO, the WTO, ILO, UNDP, etc (Lee, 2022).[17] However, there are not human rights focused and due to limitations in length, analyzing their norm-creation had to be omitted.

3.1 The European Union

Among the major regional organisations, the EU has been the most prolific regulator (at least soft law-wise) of AI technologies. An early iteration was the RoboLaw Project (2024), which explored 5 fields where regulation is desirable "… *in order to promote innovation in the internal market and foster competitiveness making robotics a strategic sector while adhering to European values*": (i) health, safety, consumer, and environmental regulation; (ii) liability (including product liability and liability in certain sectors); (iii) intellectual property rights (both to the robot itself and to works created by the robot); (iv) privacy and data protection; and (v) capacity to perform legal transactions (e.g., whether intelligent agents can enter into contracts). Since the conclusion of the project, the EU has been involved in the creation of a flurry of measures. The European Parliament for instance adopted three different measures in October 2020 on civil liability regimes (European Parliament 2020a), intellectual property rights (European Parliament 2020b), and on the ethical aspects of AI (European Parliament 2020c). Earlier in 2021, the Commission put forward a legislative proposal for an Artificial Intelligence Act which placed a distinct emphasis on transparent processes, safety and security as well as meeting existing human rights obligations (European Commission 2021). As enshrined in these documents, the approach of the EU is to look for and explicitly name the natural and legal person behind the AI system or technology.

The question thus arises: why should the rest of the world be interested in how the EU assesses the regulatory tasks arising from AI and the related technologies? One possible explanation is that, as one of the largest markets in the world, Europe is an economic target too large to ignore (Franke 2019). Leveraging this economic power in order to ensure compliance with legal standards has been a key tool in the arsenal of the EU.

The key *raison d'être* behind the emergence of regulatory norms on the EU level—as articulated by the EU's AI Act draft of 2021—can be traced back to concern about 'fragmented fundamental rights protection', and individual national regulatory measures compromising the common European protection of rights and values, if regulation is left in the hand of states alone. As a result, in order to ensure safety, as well as the maintenance of fundamental rights and to avoid a 'patchwork' of

[17] Lee J (2022) Artificial Intelligence and International Law. Springer

legislation, the EU's AI Act was proposed.[18] The aim of the heightened protection should benefit all sides according to the proposed document. Some of the positive effects the EU is counting on include the benefits of enhanced transparency for consumers, of legal certainty for operators and of an increase in competitiveness on a unified market for states.[19]

The EU takes a unique approach by labelling AI systems based on the risks they pose: prohibited technologies that pose an unacceptable risk such as mass surveillence, social scoring and manipulation of behaviour causing harm. High-risk systems are necessitating conformity assessment—this is especially true in case of AI use by law enforcement, in self-driving vehicles or if the technology in question affects access to education or employment. Herein lies a major risk in terms of how certain expressions or categories are defined. For instance an example for a prohibited technology according to the AI Act is 'real-time' biometric identification (or RBI) in publicly accessable places for law enforcement. Some exceptions apply where RBI can be used such as—inter alia—imminent threat to life, foreseeable terrorist attacks and organized crime. However, there is very little in terms of boundaries for governments labeling anti-goverment protests as 'posing an imminent threat to life', thereby enabling the use RBI tools and applying either criminal charges or fines on protesters. Needless to say, if RBI is used on such a manner, the right to assembly could be violated even by virtue of discouraging citiziens from taking part in rallies or protests for fear of repercussions via RBI. Limited-risk applications where clarity and transparency is needed and minimal risk instances which can be regulated by a code of conduct include chatbots and emotion recognition systems that can be used in hospitals for instance (Narimisaei et al. 2024).[20] A unique regulatory method of the AI Act lies in its tiered or layered implementation and effect, which means that the higher risk an AI system poses, the sooner the AI Act will be applicable. For systems posing an unacceptable risk, this timeframe is 6 months (essentially February 2025), whereas for general purpose AI this would be 12 months from adoption (August 2025) and for other high-risk systems 24–36 months depending on which Annex of the AI Act they fall into (AI Act 2024).[21] Due to the rapid adoption of the final version of the AI Act, it is safe to say, that most EU member states are ill-equipped not only to enforce the ban on systems posing unacceptable risks but to establish a domestic authority which will have competence to evaluate and categorize various AI systems.[22]

[18] European Commission (2021, Article 2(2)).

[19] European Commission (2021, Article 2(4)).

[20] Narimisaei J et al (2024) Exploring emotional intelligence in Artificial Intelligence systems: a comprehensive analysis of emotion recognition and response mechanisms. Ann Med Surg 86(8):4657–4663

[21] EU AI Act 2024/1689, https://eur-lex.europa.eu/legal-content/EN/TXT/?uri=CELEX:32024R1689.

[22] European Commission (2021, Article 3(3)).

3.2 The UNESCO

The United Nations has its own research centre in The Hague (UNICRI—Centre for Artificial Intelligence and Robotics)[23] with the organisation itself focusing on the advantages and possibilities of emerging technologies, as it regards it as a valuable tool used to reform not only the internal processes of the organisation, but also in realising the Sustainable Development Goals as well (United Nations 2018). The UNESCO took a somewhat different route. In November 2021, it formulated a global agreement on the ethical aspects of AI (UNESCO 2021). A non-binding document by nature, it aims to bring UNESCO member States to a common denominator when it comes to the shared guiding values and principles regarding development. The declared goal of the recommendation is to "protect, promote and respect human rights", noting the importance of an approach that is built on ethics which—in turn—are built on human rights. The document does not define AI, but notes the rapidly changing and evolving nature of the underlying technology. It mentions however that AI capable of prediction and decision-making should come under regulation.

As stated by the recommendation, the goal of the regulation is to protect, promote and respect human rights and fundamental freedoms, human dignity and equality, including gender equality; to safeguard the interests of present and future generations; to preserve the environment, biodiversity and ecosystems; and to respect cultural diversity in all stages of the AI system life cycle.[24] The document directly mentions the UN Charter as well as several international treaties[25] along with the work of universal institutions, such as the Human Rights Council, as well as the Sustainable Development Goals of the United Nations. The importance of human dignity and the freedom from harm and subjugation (Article 13 and 14) are strongly emphasised as core values guiding all regulatory attempts. An important element of the recommendation can be found in the 'areas of policy action' which propose how states could regulate AI if they are mindful of the goals and principles enshrined in the recommendation. These range from impact assessment to governance and stewardship to data policy to environment and ecosystems, gender and culture among others, essentially encompassing the majority of issues a state can face—all through the lens of ethics.[26]

---

[23] http://www.unicri.it/in_focus/on/UNICRI_Centre_Artificial_Robotics.

[24] UNESCO (2021, Article 8 para c).

[25] Including, in particular the Universal Declaration of Human Rights (1948), the Convention Relating to the Status of Refugees (1951), the Discrimination (Employment and Occupation) Convention (1958), the International Convention on the Elimination of All Forms of Racial Discrimination (1965), the International Covenant on Civil and Political Rights (1966), the International Covenant on Economic, Social and Cultural Rights (1966), the Convention on the Elimination of All Forms of Discrimination against Women (1979), the Convention on the Rights of the Child (1989), and the Convention on the Rights of Persons with Disabilities (2006), the Convention against Discrimination in Education (1960), the Convention on the Protection and Promotion of the Diversity of Cultural Expressions (2005) as international treaties along with a plethora of declarations and General Assembly resolutions.

[26] UNESCO (2021, Articles 50–52).

Overall, it can be said that UNESCO's recommendation is bolstered by the widest array of the human rights framework. It has to be noted, nonetheless, that while it repeats and emphasises previous commitments, at certain points even explaining the contents of individual rights, it also operates with the vaguest expressions and does not attach any enforceable obligations on states. However, we have to bear in mind that the role of UNESCO is cooperative in nature and with close to 200 member states and a vastly different legal status to that of the EU, it does not have the same possibilities. As a result, the recommendation is also much more limited in its concrete regulatory goals.

3.3 The OECD

In a similar fashion, the OECD has also tried to grasp the reins of leadership when it comes to global norms on AI. Its Council adopted a recommendation in May 2019 (OECD 2019). The OECD emphasises the trustworthy and responsible nature of development. It has also been promoting the idea of States harmonising their domestic policies when it comes to AI development. In that context, it approached the task from the opposite perspective to UNESCO. The OECD aims to track the domestic AI policy of states in an attempt to improve and harmonise them, providing them with a toolkit to do so. Its 2021 policy toolkit (OECD 2021) notes, for instance, that there are four possibilities where AI oversight can be allocated. Either existing ministries' tasks can be furthered (Estonia, France, US), or a new governmental or even independent body can be established for the task (e.g., UK, US, Singapore). Another possibility is to have experts on an advisory group or panel (e.g., Austria, Canada, Spain, US) or to establish oversight and advisory bodies for AI and data ethics (e.g., Germany, New Zealand, UK, Singapore). As can be seen, some states—such as the US, the UK and Singapore—apply additional safeguards by using multiple tools and agencies to check how AI is developed and applied in their respective countries. Whether this can lead to reinforced scrutiny benefiting citizens or to a competition between the various agencies and offices remains to be seen and will largely depend on the foundational document separating competencies or on the work of the highest echelons of government keeping order in their backyard. The OECD, following its mandate, is not actively promoting any of the abovementioned avenues. It only takes note of the benefits such an institution can provide and leaves it to the states to decide which direction would be most suitable for their needs.

In regards he protection of human rights, the OECD recommendation stipulates that the development of AI technologies should "respect human rights" with the possibility of human oversight maintained at all times. It notes: "AI actors should respect the rule of law, human rights and democratic values, throughout the AI system lifecycle. These include freedom, dignity and autonomy, privacy and data protection, non-discrimination and equality, diversity, fairness, social justice, and internationally recognised labour rights" (OECD 2019). The document does not go beyond the establishment of overarching principles and the provision of a forum where OECD member States can cooperate and share information and good practices.

3.4 The Council of Europe

The CoE—as one of the main promoters of human rights in the wider European Continent—has been closely following the effects of emerging technologies on European values and fundamental rights. In 2017, the CoE sponsored studies on data protection and the implications of big data on human rights (Council of Europe 2017). In 2019, the work of its CAHAI began which—according to its mandate—focused on the "legal framework for the development, design and application of artificial intelligence" according to the standards of the CoE.[27] The outcome document, issued by CAHAI in December 2021 notes that besides a binding multilateral (or transversal) norm, sectorial regulation might also be warranted.[28] It also aims to rely on norms that are enshrined in human rights treaties signed and ratified under the auspices of the CoE in such a way as to enable accession to those treaties by non-party states.[29] Specifically, it bases its regulation around the concept of human dignity and refers to the Universal Declaration of Human Rights as the foundational point from which regulation can be derived,[30] resulting in a highly anthropomorphic point of view.

Similarly to the EU, the CAHAI has also adopted a risk-based approach, although the ceiling here is somewhat different. The 2021 outcome document appears to mimic the principles and methodology used by the EU while at the same time the outcome document warns against the duplication of regulation.[31] The reason it is still somewhat different is that it highlights the importance of impact assessment in terms of human rights, democracy and the rule of law (HUDERIA). As another similarity with the EU approach, the outcome document recommends that a later international treaty should designate 'low-risk', 'high-risk' and 'unacceptable risk' categories based on an impact assessment.[32] Should the application of AI overstep this 'red line', a moratorium is proposed in case the technology leads to an infringement of human rights, especially if it leads to the characterisation of individuals, mass surveillance, or access to services.[33]

The CAHAI ended its term in 2021 and since 2022 CAI took over its role with the mandate to draft an international treaty in the field of AI and HUDERIA. CAI has released its Draft Convention on 18 December 2023 (CAI 2023). The Draft Convention relies more heavily on existing human rights provisions. Besides the

---

[27] https://rm.coe.int/cahai-2020-2021-rev-en-pdf/16809fc157 (last accessed 15 March 2024).

[28] CAHAI (2021, Article 4).

[29] CAHAI (2021, Article 7).

[30] CAHAI (2021, Article 16).

[31] CAHAI (2021, Article 15).

[32] CAHAI (2021, Article 19).

[33] CAHAI (2021, Article 21).

Universal Declaration of Human Rights, the two international covenants of 1966: the ICCPR and the ICESCR along with the 1989 New York Convention on the Rights of the Child are called upon. From a regional standpoint, the 1950 European Convention on Human Rights along with its additional protocols, the 1961 European Social Charter and the 1996 Revised European Charter are referenced directly in the current version of the text.[34] The EU's division of AI systems based on risks does not apparently manifest itself in the 2023 iteration of the text although it does envision a substantial—albeit vaguely formulated—risk and impact assessment framework.[35] Key human-rights related notions in the draft are responsibility, transparency and safeguards. However, states are essentially given free rein on how they wish to implement these provisions. The ultimately lax nature of the text can be attributed to the need to reach a political compromise with the underlying thought that based on the framework states will find the best domestic solution in their own jurisdictions. Furthermore, the final text proudly states that it is 'tech-neutral' i.e. it does not provide a definition of AI. This seemingly elegant solution enables the Framework Agreement to also be applicable to emerging, currently unforeseen types of AI, which might fall outside of the scope of a much more rigorous definition and understanding such as the one applied by the EU (CoE Explanatory Report).

As can be seen, the development of the legal framework is currently set firmly by the CoE with a framework convention that contains the finalized text and which was opened to signature in September 2024. Hopes are high the framework convention is going to come into effect in the following years with the Conference of State Parties serving as guardian regarding its implementation and enforcement. It should be noted however, that even though the US was a main sponsor of the agreement, it is highly unlikely that the Trump adminsitration is going to take steps towards the full ratification of the international legal instrument. Overall, the outcome document takes a significant first step towards the creation of a binding international treaty and it derives some of its ideas and rules from the work of other international organisations such as UNESCO, the EU and the OECD. Besides serving as a basis for the first ever AI-human rights treaty, it is somewhat unclear how it can be differentiated from a more robust legislation such as that of the EU.

4 Comparison and Analysis

The following section and the comparative chart serve to identify some of the shared points as well as fundamental differences regarding the regulation of AI by the various international organisations.

[34] CAI (2023, Article 13).

[35] CAI (2023, Article 16).

Aspect	UNESCO	OECD	EU	CoE
Name and date	Recommendation on the ethics of artificial intelligence, November 2021	Recommendation of the Council on artificial intelligence, May 2019	AI Act, August 2024	Framework Convention,September 2024
Legal nature	Recommendation	Recommendation	Binding—tiered/delayed effect	2021—non-binding[36]; 2023—binding after adoption
Number of Supporting States	193	37	27	2021 version: 47; 2023 version: 46; 2024 final version: EU+14
Buzzwords	Ethics and principles	Trustworthy and responsible	Human centric, safe, transparent, human oversight, risk mitigation	Human rights, democracy, rule of law
Human rights attitude	"Protect, promote and respect human rights"	"Respect human rights and democratic values"	"According to EU values, fundamental rights and principles"; framework for "high-risk" systems only	Preventing and/or mitigating risks; principle-based risk assessment
Referenced norms	UN Charter; select int. treaties; universal institutions (Human Rights Council)	UDHR; Sustainable Development Goals	EU Charter of Fundamental Rights	UDHR; ICCPR; ICESCR; CRC; ECHR+ protocols; 1961 European Social Charter; 1996 Revised European Charter
Emphasis	Human dignity; freedom from harm and subjugation (Article 13.)	Human-centred technology development (Chapter IV, Article 1(2))	Building trust and confidence (citizens), and supporting competition in development and market (companies, states, academia)	Human dignity

(continued)

[36] But forms the basis of a regulatory attempt which can lead to an international treaty.

(continued)

Aspect	UNESCO	OECD	EU	CoE
Uniqueness	Widest support for international human rights law, but vaguest formulation; policy actions for states	Provides a reference material for future negotiations; toolkit for states	Legal nature, comprehensiveness, tiered effect and layered risk-system	First binding human rights treaty on AI—pending sufficient number of ratifications

Source Author's own compilation

It is apparent from the timeframe that there has been a flurry of regulatory activity from 2019 to 2021 with all four international organisations adopting some kind of a legal-regulatory framework (or the first preparatory attempt at one) in that roughly three-year timeframe. When we contrast this to domestic policies by states, it is obvious that these attempts closely follow the initiative of states (2017–2021) in adopting national legislation. The role of these organisations—and how they have seemingly found their calling on the subject of AI—is enhancing cooperation, which is true for all four, settling on common principles which can later on be built upon, and which are also shared by all four of them. At this point, a divergence can be observed, as different organisations have different possibilities, with UNESCO and the OECD not moving beyond this point, whereas the EU and the CoE—having the broadest capabilities in regulation—are moving towards binding regulations. It is in the nature of international norms that non-binding recommendations are much easier to agree upon, setting principles such as human dignity which no state calls into question, rather than adopting a binding norm with a possible observing and enforcement mechanism (Risse 2019). The latter, of course, takes much longer and at the present time we are at a pivotal moment in history in which we can see new international norms taking shape. This also means that there is no guarantee that the EU or the CoE regulatory attempts will actually become final and binding, although the chances of this are quite high.

It is worth mentioning that the regulatory attempts of international organisations do not only mention but also respect one another, as can be seen by the reference in the CoE Framework Agreement regarding the work of the UNESCO, the OECD and the EU.[37] The other side of the coin is the presence of some degree of competition, in that international organisations have to define themselves and the uniqueness of their regulation compared to other, earlier regulators and convince states why their initiative deserves their attention. In order to solve this conundrum, it can be safely stated that these regulations are not exclusive in nature and can co-exist side-by-side peacefully. Several European States for instance, are supporting and taking an active role in the creation and development of all four regulatory attempts.[38] So far it remains to be seen whether China can be integrated or whether it would accept invitation to this regulatory framework that is primarily promoted by western states. It is a supporter of the non-binding UNESCO document but compliance with the EU's AI Act will depend on the limiting effect of the EU's regulation on Chinese access to European markets. China has also indicated a commitment towards multilateralism during the February 2025 Summit, altough some countries—such as the US—have cast doubt on the sincerity of the Chinese declaration (DW 2025).[39] For other regions such as Latin-America or India, the AI Act can be seen as a good practice resulting in voluntary compliance with local peculiarities taken into account as well. On a side note, India is coming into the forefront as a possible fourth contender as indicated

[37] CAHAI (2021, Article 8).

[38] Such as Hungary, Finland and France.

[39] Deutsche Welle (2025) https://www.dw.com/en/us-uk-decline-to-sign-paris-ai-summit-declaration/a-71575536

by its likely hosting of the next AI Summit but also via its emerging tech sector, recent domestic regulation and a young, well-trained workforce (HT 2025).[40] As for the CoE treaty, the likeliest scenario is that it will have nominal effect on the Chinese mainland, even though Chinese companies operating in CoE member states will need to abide by these norms if and when they are incorporated to the domestic legal systems in the wider European (CoE) context.

Another shared characteristic is that all of the norms above are highly anthropomorphic, not considering the later developmental stages of AI such as AGI or ASI but human needs and interests in the forefront of regulation. This is the rationale behind a human rights-based approach. It also explains why these documents focus so heavily on assurances, safeguards, and basic principles, since on the one hand, the manifestation of collective societal fear from AI-based technologies can result in panic or paranoia if not assuaged sufficiently, and on the other hand, AI-based technologies can lead to mass human rights violations by either companies or states employing or benefiting from them.

It can be established that states are the primary target of these regulations, as international organisations rely on their support, whereas the secondary targets and stakeholders consist of other international organisations, NGOs, developers, and companies along with the academic community. The role of the latter is to provide feedback and evaluation aiding the next wave of regulation (as can be specifically seen in the case of the EU and the CoE).

A major flaw of all four regulatory frameworks is that they treat human rights as a homogenous background concept, as if the content, extent and application of these rights were settled, while only a few human rights are explicitly mentioned or explained in the context of AI. Of course this is a false presumption based on political compromise, the reasons for and consequences of which are explained in the next chapter. A prime example is the concept of human dignity from which human rights can be derived. On the level of the UNESCO, this serves as a basis for promoting, protecting and respecting human rights without explaining any of these terms. The recommendation merely alludes to these goals taking it for granted that there is a universal understanding of human dignity which will roughly be similar in all—nearly 200—supporting states. Such a „watered-down" human rights concept can be regarded as a natural consequence of multilateralism, especially when it comes to reaching consensus with close to 200 states whose support needs to be obtained in short notice. It nonetheless creates a vastly different view of human dignity than the interpretation of the CoE, which—in great part through the evolving practice of the ECtHR—has shaped a firm and concrete interpretation of the concept, separating the understanding of human dignity for the individual human rights obligation in question. Treating the human dignity concept of these two documents the same way can be a tempting oversimplification.

[40] Hindustan Times (2025) https://www.hindustantimes.com/india-news/india-looks-to-host-4th-ai-meet-between-nov-and-jan-officials-101739211719729.html

5 Mapping Out Challenges

The next question to consider is, if the international community aspires to regulate AI and joins forces under the umbrella of international organisations to go beyond highlighting principles and coordinating the effort of states, how would these organisations carry out this monumental task? The first conundrum to solve is which norms and in which form—which source of international human rights law—will and could be transferred? Human rights can be found in myriads of international treaties covering either a specific human right or a geographical region, or which provide a catalogue of protected rights without analysing their contents. Another non-negligible source is international customary law which will prove to be extremely hard to define regarding its contents and the subjects of international law to be applied. Secondly, it is unclear how it is possible to transfer human rights into the AI domain when the exact boundary of human rights norms is uncertain and these rights are sometimes enshrined through decades of jurisprudence. Furthermore, political statements, such as "ensuring respect" for human rights can prove to be an insurmountable barrier when one tries to convert their meaning into binary—on the language of an AI-based system.

Thirdly, as alluded to above, international law does have a semblance of hierarchy since *ius cogens*, treaties and customary international law are supported by an incredibly diverse (and sometimes splintered) framework of academic analyses and jurisprudence. This could make it an impossible challenge to find what norms would be applicable. Also complicating the issue is the fact that between the domestic and universal levels lie three regional human rights regimes in Europe, Africa and America, each with their own distinct practice. It would cause considerable hardship if we had to create layers of regional human rights norms, as potential conflicts with the domestic and universal levels cannot be resolved through a hierarchy of norms as human rights do not operate that way. Finally, it can be safely stated that human rights do not operate in a closed and finalised world. Norms are being created, changed and thrown out. This process is sometimes rapid and in other cases slow or can even result in changing the *status quo*.[41] How can we code development and change? Would this mean giving the power to alter the contents of these norms to AI? The latter suggestion would probably raise some eyebrows in the academic community and meet with outright hostility from the public but the question remains valid. As can be seen from the few questions raised here, human rights are not only one of the most important fields of international law but also among the most controversial and difficult to grasp.

[41] A prime example can be seen with the debate on abortion in the United States.

6 Concluding Remarks

The race to regulate AI is palpable and is not likely to decrease in intensity in the coming years. International organisations are ideally suited to guiding a state's regulatory approach and action regarding AI, as on the one hand they possess the knowledge and drive to support and coordinate decision-making and on the other hand they cannot force their views onto states which might lead to the primary decision-makers becoming resentful and malcontent. Most of the current challenges can be overcome through political will. International organisations seem to possess it, but whether states will also move towards firm, human rights-based regulation remains to be seen. Overall, it can be established that the diversity of forums and initiatives can be beneficial under special circumstances. In the case of AI, the divergent approaches of UNESCO, the OECD and the EU can serve the overarching goal of creating a human rights framework which could then serve, provided that it is also embraced by non-Western powers, as a genuine global benchmark for regulation. Their regulation is primarily not competitive in nature but complementary (albeit sometimes redundant for states that are members of all of these organisations). Nonetheless, a substantial change in regulatory attitude is required: a more proactive approach, for which the four organisations appear to be ready. The greater question is whether states will follow their lead and implement regulation domestically based on international guidelines.

References

Asaro, P (2019) A review of private sector AI principles. A report prepared for UNIDIR. Unpublished report prepared for UN, Geneva. Institute for Disarmament Research

Aust A (2010) Handbook of international law. Cambridge University Press

CAHAI: Council of Europe Ad Hoc Committee on Artificial Intelligence (2021) Outcome document: possible elements of a legal framework on artificial intelligence, based on the Council of Europe's standards on human rights, democracy and the rule of law. https://rm.coe.int/possible-elements-of-a-legal-framework-on-artificial-intelligence/1680a5ae6b

CAI: Council of Europe Committee on Artificial Intelligence (2023) Draft framework convention on artificial intelligence, human rights, democracy and the rule of law. CAI(2023)28. https://rm.coe.int/cai-2023-28-draft-framework-convention/1680ade043

Council of Europe (2017) Study on the human rights dimensions of automated data processing techniques (in particular algorithms) and possible regulatory implications. DGI(2017)12. https://rm.coe.int/algorithms-and-human-rights-study-on-the-human-rights-dimension-of-aut/1680796d10

Dawes J (2020) Speculative human rights: artificial intelligence and the future of the human. Hum Rights Q 42(3):573–593

DIC: Department of International Cooperation & MOST: Ministry of Science and Technology P. R. China (2017). Next generation artificial intelligence development plan. China Science & Technology Newsletter. http://fi.china-embassy.gov.cn/eng/kxjs/201710/P020210628714286134479.pdf

Donahoe E, MacDufee Metzger M (2019) Artificial intelligence and human rights. J Democr 30(2):115–126

European Commission (2021) Proposal for a regulation of the European Parliament and of the Council laying down harmonized rules on artificial intelligence (Artificial Intelligence Act), COM(2021) 206 final

European Parliament (2020a) European Parliament resolution of 20 October 2020 with recommendations to the Commission on a civil liability regime for artificial intelligence. OJ C 404, 6.10.2021, pp 107–128

European Parliament (2020b) European Parliament resolution of 20 October 2020 on intellectual property rights for the development of artificial intelligence technologies. OJ C 404, 6.10.2021, pp 129–135

European Parliament (2020c) European Parliament resolution of 20 October 2020 with recommendations to the Commission on a framework of ethical aspects of artificial intelligence, robotics and related technologies. OJ C 404, 6.10.2021, pp 63–85

Fjeld J, Achten N, Hilligoss H, Nagy A, Srikumar M (2020) Principled artificial intelligence: mapping consensus in ethical and rights-based approaches to principles for AI. Berkman Klein Center for Internet & Society. https://dash.harvard.edu/handle/1/42160420

Floridi L, Cowls J, Beltrametti M, Chatila R, Chazerand P, Dignum V, Luetge C, Madelin R, Pagallo U, Rossi F, Schäfer B, Valcke P, Vayena E (2018) AI4People—an ethical framework for a good AI society: opportunities, risks, principles, and recommendations. Minds Mach. 28(4):689–707

Franke U (2019) Harnessing artificial intelligence. https://ecfr.eu/publication/harnessing_artificial_intelligence/

Fukuda-Parr S, Gibbons E (2021) Emerging consensus on 'ethical AI': human rights critique of stakeholder guidelines. Global Policy. https://doi.org/10.1111/1758-5899.12965

Klabbers J (2002) An introduction to international institutional law. Cambridge University Press

McKay C, Pollak E, Fitzpayne A (2017) Automation and a changing economy: policies for shared prosperity. Aspen Institute. https://www.aspeninstitute.org/publications/automation-and-a-changing-economypolicies-for-shared-prosperity/

OECD: Organisation for Economic Co-operation and Development (1960) Convention on the Organisation for Economic Co-operation and Development (OECD), Paris, 14 December 1960, UNTC 12736

OECD: Organisation for Economic Co-operation and Development (2019) Recommendation of the Council on Artificial Intelligence. https://legalinstruments.oecd.org/en/instruments/OECD-LEGAL-0449

OECD: Organisation for Economic Co-operation and Development, Galindo L, Perset K, Sheeka F (2021) An overview of national AI strategies and policies. OECD Going Digital Toolkit Notes, No. 14, OECD Publishing, Paris. https://doi.org/10.1787/c05140d9-en

Opderbeck DW (2021) Artificial Intelligence, rights and virtues. Washburn Law J 60(3):445–474

Risse M (2019) Human rights and artificial intelligence: an urgently needed agenda. Hum Rights Q 41(1):1–16

Roberts H, Cowls J, Morley J, Taddeo M, Wang V, Floridi L (2021) The Chinese approach to artificial intelligence: an analysis of policy, ethics, and regulation. AI & Soc 36:59–77

RoboLaw Project (2024) Regulating emerging robotic technologies in Europe: robotics facing law and ethics. Final report. http://www.robolaw.eu/deliverables.htm

Shaw M (2003) International law. Cambridge University Press

Stiglitz J (2018) We're going towards a more divided society. *The Guardian*. https://www.theguardian.com/technology/2018/sep/08/joseph-stiglitz-on-artificial-intelligence-were-going-towards-a-more-dividedsociety

The White House (2022) Blueprint for an AI bill of human rights—making automated systems work for the American people. https://www.whitehouse.gov/wp-content/uploads/2022/10/Blueprint-for-an-AI-Bill-of-Rights.pdf

UNESCO (1945) Constitution of the United Nations Educational Scientific and Cultural Organization (UNESCO), London, 16 November 1945, UNTC No. 52

UNESCO (2021) UNESCO Recommendation on the ethics of Artificial Intelligence, No. 61910. https://unesdoc.unesco.org/ark:/48223/pf0000380455

United Nations (2018) UN Secretary General's Strategy on New Technologies. https://www.un.org/en/newtechnologies/

United Nations (2021) United Nations High Commissioner's Office Press Release on 15 September 2021. https://news.un.org/en/story/2021/09/1099972

White Paper (2022) Artificial intelligence white paper, China Academy of Information and Communications Technology (CAICT) (translation editor: Ben Murphy) https://cset.georgetown.edu/publication/artificial-intelligence-white-paper-2022/

The Principle of Fairness in International AI Law in the Making

Zoltán Turbék

Abstract As the potential and the risks of artificial intelligence are becoming increasingly evident, the number of international organisations that aim to regulate the use of this technology is also growing. The question arises of what the parallel preparation and adoption of the instruments mean for legal and regulatory development. Will these instruments contradict each other and result in conflicting rights and obligations, or can they serve as complementary pieces of a larger normative framework? Would this process lead to a fragmented international legal landscape, or is there still room to harmonise the developing legal frameworks and determine common norms and principles? This chapter contains a comparative analysis of the normative frameworks developed by the OECD, UNESCO, the EU and the Council of Europe, focusing in particular on how they address the principle of fairness and non-discrimination in the context of regulating the use of AI systems. Our aim is to identify the risks and the challenges that may arise from these parallel processes. At the end of the chapter, we will also offer a set of recommendations and practical steps that could facilitate harmonious developments in this new field of law that we may call an emerging 'international AI law.'

1 Introduction

As the potential and the risks of artificial intelligence (AI) are becoming increasingly evident, the number of international organisations that aim to address the use of this technology is also growing. Organisations such as the Organisation for Economic Co-operation and Development (OECD), the United Nations Educational, Scientific and Cultural Organization (UNESCO), the European Union (EU) and the Council

The views expressed in this chapter are solely those of the author and they do not represent the views, policy or official position of the Ministry of Foreign Affairs and Trade of Hungary.

Z. Turbék (✉)
Permanent Mission of Hungary to the UN in Geneva, Geneva, Switzerland
e-mail: ZTurbek@mfa.gov.hu

M. Varju and K. Mezei (eds.), *The Challenges of Artificial Intelligence for Law in Europe*, Data Science, Machine Intelligence, and Law 6,
https://doi.org/10.1007/978-3-031-86813-9_3

of Europe (CoE) and some others, have launched and engaged in processes in recent years that intend to develop general principles governing, and sometimes detailed norms regulating, the use of AI systems. Seeing all these parallel processes and the mushrooming of regulatory initiatives, the question arises of what the preparation and the eventual adoption of the different instruments mean for legal and regulatory development in this specific technology area. It is unclear whether these instruments, many of which will have concrete normative implications, will contradict each other and result in conflicting rights and obligations, or whether it is possible to ensure that the different international documents will serve as complementary, mutually supportive pieces of a larger normative framework. It is also uncertain whether, if direct legal collusions are avoided, the different international frameworks would lead to a fragmented international legal landscape, which is characterised by a duplication of norms and regulatory competition, or whether there will still be room to harmonise the developing legal frameworks and determine common generally accepted basic norms and principles.

In this chapter, given the limitation of its length, we will carry out a comparative analysis of the regulatory and other normative frameworks developed by the OECD, UNESCO, the EU and CoE. We will focus in particular on how they address the specific issues of fairness[1] and non-discrimination in the context of regulating the use of AI systems. Our aim is to identify the risks and the challenges that may arise from the parallel development of legal and regulatory instruments which also contribute to the birth of international AI law. We will also offer a set of recommendations and practical steps that could facilitate harmonious developments in this field of law.

2 The 'Four Musketeers' of International AI Law: The OECD, the UNESCO, the EU and the Council of Europe

In the past years, four major international instruments have been developed for regulating the use of AI systems.[2] These are the OECD Recommendation on Artificial Intelligence (OECD 2019), the UNESCO's Recommendation on the Ethics of Artificial Intelligence (UNESCO 2021), the EU's Artificial Intelligence Act (AI Act) (European Commission 2021), and the Council of Europe's Framework Convention on Artificial Intelligence, Human Rights, Democracy and the Rule of Law (CoE Framework Convention) (CAI 2024a). The OECD recommendation is the first intergovernmental standard on AI. It was adopted by the OECD Council at Ministerial level on 22 May 2019, following an inclusive preparatory process that ensured the

[1] On fairness, see, for example, Wachter et al. (2021).

[2] For the purpose of this chapter, an AI system is a machine-based system that for explicit or implicit objectives, infers, from the input it receives, how to generate outputs such as predictions, content, recommendations, or decisions that may influence physical or virtual environments. Different AI systems vary in their levels of autonomy and adaptiveness after deployment. See CAI (2024a, Article 2).

participation of a broad range of stakeholders. In addition to the 38 OECD member states, a significant number of non-OECD members (e.g., Argentina, Brazil, Egypt, Malta, Peru, Romania, Singapore, Ukraine) also adhered to this instrument. The UNESCO's recommendation, which is the first-ever truly global standard on AI ethics, was adopted by all 193 member states[3] in November 2021, as a result of a very intensive multi-stakeholder negotiation process that took place mainly online during the COVID-19 pandemic.

The AI Act of the EU, which will be adopted in the form of a legally binding regulation, is the first-ever comprehensive legal regulation of the use of AI systems. It establishes regulatory obligations for both providers and users depending on the level of risk posed. Originally proposed by the European Commission in April 2021, the general approach on policy was adopted by the Council in 2022 (Council 2022), and the European Parliament adopted its position in June 2023 (European Parliament 2023a). Following a complex and lengthy three-way negotiation process, the so-called trialogues, the three EU institutions reached a political agreement on 8 December 2023 (European Parliament 2023b), which was approved by the European Parliament on 13 March 2024 (European Parliament 2024) and is waiting for final endorsement by the Council in the coming months.

The CoE Framework Convention was prepared by the CoE's Committee on Artificial Intelligence (CAI). The CAI, following 2 years of intensive negotiations and, before that, 2 years of preparation in the CAI's predecessor committee, in the Ad-hoc Committee on AI (CAHAI),[4] adopted provisionally on 14 March 2024 the final version of the first-ever AI treaty aiming to ensure that activities within the lifecycle of AI systems are fully consistent with human rights, democracy and the rule of law. The draft text will be referred to the CoE Committee of Ministers for adoption and opened for signature at a later stage. The treaty will also be open for ratification to non-members of the CoE. The Framework Convention was negotiated by 46 CoE member states, with many observer states (e.g., Argentina, Australia, Canada, Costa Rica, the Holy See, Israel, Japan, Mexico, Peru, the USA, Uruguay), and with the continuous involvement of civil society organisations, industry representatives and relevant international organisations.

Both the OECD and the UNESCO recommendations are soft law instruments. In the case of the OECD, recommendations are adopted by the Council and are not legally binding. They represent a political commitment to the principles they contain and entail an expectation that Adherents will do their best to implement them.[5] Emanating from the organisation's supreme governing body and hence possessing

---

[3] The UNESCO recommendation was adopted before the US returned to the organisation as its 194th member state.

[4] The CAI's work builds on the work carried out between 2019 and 2021 by the CAHAI. The CAHAI was tasked to prepare a feasibility study and to propose potential elements—on the basis of broad multi-stakeholder consultations—for a legal framework for the development, design and application of AI. Before the suspension of its CoE membership rights as a consequence of the Russian aggression against Ukraine, the Russian Federation also actively participated in the work of this committee.

[5] https://www.oecd.org/legal/legal-instruments.htm.

great authority, UNESCO recommendations are intended to influence the development of national laws and practices. These are norms that are not subject to ratification, but the member states are invited to apply them.[6] In contrast, both the EU AI Act and the CoE Framework Convention are legally binding. The EU AI Act was adopted as an EU regulation, which is defined in Article 288 TFEU as a legal act that has general application, is binding in its entirety and is directly applicable in all EU Member States. The CoE Framework Convention is a treaty under the 1969 Vienna Convention on the Law of Treaties (United Nations 1969). While its provisions will bind only its future Parties, it aims to become a global standard for value- and human rights-focused AI regulation. The AI Act has similar ambitions, aiming to rely on the so-called 'Brussels effect' to influence future AI regulation beyond the boundaries of the EU.

The provisions of the OECD recommendation are addressed to OECD members and non-members adhering to it, as well as to so-called AI actors, namely those who play an active role in the AI system's lifecycle, including organisations and individuals that deploy or operate AI. The UNESCO recommendation is addressed to the member states, which can serve as both AI actors and authorities responsible for developing legal and regulatory frameworks throughout the entire AI system life cycle, and for promoting business responsibility. It also provides ethical guidance to all AI actors, including the public and private sectors, especially as a basis for the ethical impact assessment of AI systems.

The AI Act binds the Member States, as well as public and private actors in the field. The latter are covered by the AI Act, following the AI Act's terminology, as a "provider", a "user/deployer", an "authorized representative", an "importer", a "distributor", an "operator", or an "affected person". The CoE Framework Convention is addressed to the ratifying CoE member states and other states, as well as the EU, should the latter decide to become a party. Earlier versions of the treaty[7] also contained provisions addressed specifically to AI providers and users. The final version, although it refers to and hopes to influence the activities of both public and private actors, contains obligations only for the parties to the treaty.

3 Fairness as a Central Regulatory Concept

Fairness is one of the central concepts used by the instruments in developing their regulatory approach. The relatively short OECD recommendation (OECD 2019) mentions the term fair, fairly and fairness 5 times. The much longer UNESCO recommendation (UNESCO 2021) uses the terms fair or fairness 13 times. The final version of the EU AI Act contains (European Parliament 2024) the term fair/fairness 15 times and the term trustworthy/trustworthiness 19 times. The expression

[6] https://www.unesco.org/en/legal-affairs/standard-setting/recommendations.

[7] See the Zero Draft Framework Convention on Artificial Intelligence, Human Rights, Democracy and the Rule of Law (CAI 2023a).

"to ensure a fair sharing of responsibilities along the AI value chain" also appears in the document,[8] as does the principle of "diversity, non-discrimination and fairness".[9] One of its background policy documents, the Ethics Guidelines for Trustworthy Artificial Intelligence (HLEG 2019), which was prepared by the EU High-Level Expert Group on AI (HLEG) and was published on 8 April 2019, used the terms un/fair/ness 54 times. The European Commission's proposal for the regulation published in April 2021 mentioned fairness in more traditional legal contexts only, such as the right to a fair trial and fair and just working conditions.

The CAI zero draft of the CoE Framework Convention (CAI 2023a) published in January 2023 used the term fair only once in the context of "equal and fair access to public debate and inclusive democratic processes". It mentioned non-/discrimination 6 times and equal/ity 5 times. The final version of the treaty (CAI 2024a) refers to fairness twice: in the context of "individuals' fair access to and participation in public debate"[10] and when it mentioned the need "to adopt or maintain measures aimed at overcoming inequalities to achieve fair, just and equitable outcomes".[11] The terms discrimination/non-discrimination appear 5 times and un/equal/ity are used 7 times in the text.

The OECD recommendation (OECD 2019) calls on AI actors to respect—amongst others—fairness throughout the AI system lifecycle, to develop AI systems that are consistent with the principle of fairness (and commercial fairness), as well as to include appropriate safeguards to ensure a fair and just society as affected by the deployment of the technology. Governments are also encouraged to consider promoting mechanisms that support the safe, fair, legal and ethical sharing of data, and—in the context of building human capacity and preparing for labour market transformation—that ensure a fair transition for workers affected by AI deployment. They may also introduce mechanisms to ensure that the benefits of AI are broadly and fairly shared.

The UNESCO recommendation (UNESCO 2021) also refers to the term fairness in various contexts. It states that fairness must be upheld, so that no country or no person is left behind, either by having fair access to AI technologies and their benefits, or by providing sufficient protection against their negative implications. It also refers to the demands of global fairness when it calls for addressing the positive and negative impacts of AI technologies. Furthermore, it calls on AI actors to promote social justice and safeguard fairness and non-discrimination of any kind in compliance with international law.[12] This provision implies an inclusive approach to ensuring that the benefits of AI technologies are available and accessible to all. According to the document at the international level, the most technologically advanced countries have a responsibility of solidarity with the least advanced to ensure that the benefits of AI technologies are shared in such a way that access to and participation in the

[8] European Parliament (2024), Preamble, Recital (85).

[9] European Parliament (2024), Preamble, Recital (27).

[10] CAI (2024a, Article 5.2).

[11] CAI (2024a, Article 10.2).

[12] UNESCO (2021, para 28).

AI system's life cycle for the latter contributes to a fairer world order. AI actors should make all reasonable efforts to minimise and avoid reinforcing or perpetuating discriminatory or biased applications and outcomes throughout the life cycle of the AI system to ensure the fairness of such systems. The other manifestations of fairness in the recommendation include the right to a fair trial, the fair sharing of data, providing current workers and new generations a fair chance of finding jobs in a rapidly changing market, and ensuring a fair transition for at-risk employees.

In the EU context, fairness continues to be addressed within the framework of the broader principle of trustworthiness. The ethics guidelines of the HLEG (2019) made it clear that fairness is one of four key ethical principles/imperatives that need to be respected to ensure that AI systems are developed, deployed and used in a trustworthy manner. The European Commission's proposal for the AI Act (European Commission 2021) mentioned the right to a fair trial and the right to fair and just working conditions, and it incorporated the concept of trustworthiness and other related concepts (e.g., non-discrimination). The proposal also referred to the Charter of Fundamental Rights of the European Union (EUCFR) several times.[13] The final version of the AI Act (European Parliament 2024) recalls seven non-binding ethical principles for AI developed by the HLEG, which are intended to help ensure that AI is trustworthy and ethically sound. It specified that one of those principles is "diversity, non-discrimination and fairness", which "means that AI systems are developed and used in a way that includes diverse actors and promotes equal access, gender equality and cultural diversity, while avoiding discriminatory impacts and unfair biases that are prohibited by Union or national law".[14] It provides that the principles should be implemented, when possible, in the design and use of AI systems, and they should serve as the basis of codes of conduct to be drafted in accordance with the AI Act.

The CoE Framework Convention (CAI 2024a) relies on the concept of fairness in the context of addressing the access of individuals to public debates concerning the technology, and when demanding fair, just and equitable outcomes of the use of AI systems, which shall be achieved through measures aimed at overcoming inequalities.

Based on this overview, when the instruments mention fairness explicitly, they use it either as a generally framed, rather unclear concept, or they raise it in certain, rather specific legal or other contexts. Some of the instruments, in particular the EU's AI Act, dilute further the meaning of fairness when they rely on it as a component of much broader regulatory or policy concepts, such as trustworthy AI or responsible AI.[15] The OECD recommendation (OECD 2019) refers to the "principles for responsible stewardship of trustworthy AI", which OECD members and other interested parties agreed to promote and implement, and which consist of five complementary principles relevant to all stakeholders, including the principle of "human-centred

---

[13] The EUCFR also deals with fairness in the context of the protection of personal data (Article 8), the right to property (Article 17), fair and just working conditions (Article 31), the right to good administration (Article 41), the right to an effective remedy and to a fair trial (Article 47), as well as with equality and non-discrimination (Chapter III).

[14] European Parliament (2024), Preamble, Recital (27).

[15] For the term 'responsible AI', see, for example, Microsoft (2022). For the notion 'trustworthy AI', see OECD (2019) and HLEG (2019).

values and fairness". The concept of trustworthiness also appears in the UNESCO recommendation (UNESCO 2021) alongside the concept of fairness, which is used in both international and national contexts. The final version of the CoE Framework Convention uses the expression "fair, just and equitable outcomes" in the context of overcoming inequalities.[16]

The OECD recommendation (OECD 2019) does not specify whether its requirement of fairness should be applied at the international level as a principle applicable among countries, or at the national level covering issues of fairness within societies and among individuals. The instrument calls for actions by national government at the national level; however, it also deals with international cooperation, more specifically including cooperation with developing countries and promoting the development of global technical standards for interoperable and trustworthy AI.[17]

In contrast, the UNESCO recommendation (UNESCO 2021) explicitly mentions the demands of global fairness, a fairer world order, as well as the need for an inclusive approach and cooperation among international, regional and national communities, and it formulates the goal of not leaving any country or anyone behind in the technological race. It also underlines that strengthening global cooperation and solidarity is needed. Regarding the latter objective, it highlights that the most technologically advanced countries have a responsibility of solidarity with the least advanced. The instrument also addresses fairness at the national/societal level when it calls on States to promote inclusive access for all, including local communities, to AI systems, and to promote equity between rural and urban areas, and among all persons regardless of any grounds. It also calls for the adoption of measures to allow meaningful participation in technology governance by marginalised groups, communities and individuals.

The EU AI Act (European Commission 2021) does not specify whether it aims to apply the principles of trustworthiness and fairness at the international level in inter-state relations. However, the relevant provisions allow the interpretation that trustworthiness and fairness will be applied only at the national level to individuals and groups of society. Similarly, the CoE Framework Convention's (CAI 2024a) focus is not on the promotion of solidarity at a global level. Nor does it oblige its Parties to adopt special measures to help less developed states. Rather, it calls upon its Parties to adopt or maintain measures that aim at overcoming inequalities at the national level in order to achieve fair, just and equitable outcomes, in line with their applicable domestic and international human rights obligations, in connection to activities within the lifecycle of AI systems. Nevertheless, it addresses the issue of international cooperation, and it encourages Parties to assist states that are not Party to the framework convention in acting consistently with the provisions laid out therein and becoming Party to the convention.

[16] See CAI (2024a, Article 10, para 2): "Each Party undertakes to adopt or maintain measures aimed at overcoming inequalities to achieve fair, just and equitable outcomes, in line with its applicable domestic and international human rights obligations, in relation to activities within the lifecycle of artificial intelligence systems."

[17] OECD (2019, para 2.5).

The concepts of equal treatment and non-discrimination have been internalised in the instruments in a divergent fashion. The OECD recommendation (OECD 2019) mentions non-discrimination and equality in general terms only, without defining in detail the protected grounds and values. In contrast, the UNESCO recommendation (UNESCO 2021) specifies the protected characteristics. It states that "[a]t the national level, Member States should promote equity between rural and urban areas, and among all persons regardless of race, colour, descent, gender, age, language, religion, political opinion, national origin, ethnic origin, social origin, economic or social condition of birth, or disability and any other grounds, in terms of access to and participation in the AI system life cycle."[18] It also notes that "[h]uman dignity relates to the recognition of the intrinsic and equal worth of each individual human being",[19] and it calls for "promoting active participation of all individuals or groups regardless of" the already listed grounds.[20]

The EU's AI act observes in its preamble that AI systems may lead to discrimination between persons or groups and may perpetuate historical patterns of discrimination, such as that based on racial or ethnic origins, gender, disabilities, age or sexual orientation, or may create new forms of discriminatory impacts.[21] The early versions of the draft CoE Framework Convention contained a long list of protected characteristics.[22] However, due to the political sensitivities of certain elements of the listed grounds for some negotiating states, the list was excluded from the final version. The Framework Convention now establishes merely that "implementation of the provisions of this Convention by the Parties shall be secured without discrimination on any ground, in accordance with their international human rights obligations".[23] Nevertheless, the treaty makes an explicit reference to "inequalities including those experienced by women and individuals in vulnerable situations".[24]

4 Implementation

The OECD recommendation calls on AI actors to "implement mechanisms and safeguards, such as capacity for human determination, that are appropriate to the context and consistent with the state of [the] art".[25] The UNESCO recommendation urges AI

---

[18] UNESCO (2021, para 28).

[19] UNESCO (2021, para 13).

[20] UNESCO (2021, para 19).

[21] European Commission (2021), Preamble, Recital (58).

[22] CAI (2023a, Article 3). CAI (2023b, Article 17) states that "implementation of the provisions of this Convention by the Parties shall be secured without discrimination on any ground such as sex, gender, sexual orientation, (gender identity), race, colour, language, age, religion, political or any other opinion, national or social origin, association with a national minority, property, birth, state of health, disability or other status, or based on a combination of one or more of these grounds."

[23] CAI (2024a, Article 17).

[24] CAI (2024a, Article 17).

[25] OECD (2019, para 1.2. b).

actors "to make all reasonable efforts to minimize and avoid reinforcing or perpetuating discriminatory or biased applications and outcomes throughout the life cycle of the AI system to ensure fairness of such systems".[26]

The EU AI Act (European Commission 2021) calls for the application of the seven non-binding ethical principles for AI identified by AI HLEG, including the principle of "diversity, non-discrimination and fairness" to be translated, when possible, in the design and use of AI models. The principles should serve as a basis for the drafting of codes of conduct under the EU AI Act, which also encourages all stakeholders, including industry, academia, civil society and standardisation organisations to take into account, as appropriate, the ethical principles for the development of voluntary best practices and standards.

The CoE Framework Convention requires each Party to "adopt or maintain measures with a view to ensuring that activities related to the lifecycle of artificial intelligence systems respect equality, including gender equality, and the prohibition of discrimination, as provided under applicable international and domestic law."[27] The same provision also holds that "each Party undertakes to adopt or maintain measures aimed at overcoming inequalities to achieve fair, just and equitable outcomes, in line with its applicable domestic and international human rights obligations, in relation to activities within the lifecycle of artificial intelligence systems."[28]

In its preamble, the OECD recommendation (OECD 2019) recognises that certain existing national and international legal, regulatory and policy frameworks already have relevance to AI. It also notes that the appropriateness of some of these frameworks may need to be assessed and new approaches may need to be developed, and it recognises that new laws/policies possibly need to be adopted.

The UNESCO recommendation requires compliance with international law (but does not mention domestic law) when it calls on AI actors to promote social justice and safeguard fairness and non-discrimination of any kind.[29] However, it also states that "AI actors and Member States should respect, protect and promote human rights and fundamental freedoms [...] in accordance with national and international law, in particular Member States' human rights obligations, and ethical guidance throughout the life cycle of AI systems, including with respect to AI actors within their effective territory and control".[30]

The UNESCO recommendation also talks about the possible need to amend existing national legislation or prepare new legislation addressing AI systems, while ensuring that these also comply with member states' human rights law obligations.[31] It adds that "Member States should implement policies to ensure that the actions of AI actors are consistent with international human rights law, standards and principles

[26] UNESCO (2021, para 29).
[27] CAI (2024a, Article 10).
[28] CAI (2024a, Article 10).
[29] UNESCO (2021, para 28).
[30] UNESCO (2021, para 42).
[31] UNESCO (2021, para 65).

throughout the life cycle of AI systems, while taking into full consideration the current cultural and social diversities, including local customs and religious traditions, with due regard to the precedence and universality of human rights."[32]

The EU AI Act in its preamble states that its provisions should be applied in accordance with the values of the EU as enshrined in the EUCFR.[33] It also notes that it is vital for AI and its regulatory framework to be developed in accordance with EU values as enshrined in Article 2 of the Treaty on European Union (TEU), the fundamental rights and freedoms enshrined in the EU Treaties and, pursuant to Article 6 TEU, the EUCFR.[34] In the specific context of the principle of "diversity, non-discrimination and fairness", it also refers to the relevant rules of EU or national law prohibiting discrimination.[35]

The CoE Framework Convention provides that the measures that need to be adopted or maintained by a Party to overcome inequalities and thus achieve fair, just and equal outcomes, shall also be in line with the Party's applicable domestic and international human rights obligations.[36] The earlier mentioned provision of the framework convention that obliges each Party to adopt or maintain measures with a view to ensuring that activities related to the lifecycle of AI systems respect equality, including gender equality, and the prohibition of discrimination, also makes a reference to the applicable international and domestic law.[37]

In addition, the CoE Framework Convention requires each Party to adopt or maintain measures to ensure that the activities within the lifecycle of AI systems are consistent with obligations to protect human rights, as enshrined in applicable international law, and in its domestic law.[38] Its Article 6 states that each Party shall implement the general common principles set forth in Chapter III in regard to AI systems in a manner appropriate to its domestic legal system and the other obligations of the framework convention.[39] Thus, the CoE Framework Convention uses existing domestic and international legal obligations already applicable to the given Party as a framework within which the provisions need to be implemented. However, it does not require the Parties to go any further and accept new, additional obligations.[40]

As relevant background instruments, the OECD recommendation refers to internal OECD documents (e.g., the OECD Guidelines for Multinational Enterprises [OECD 2011]), as well as the 2030 Agenda for Sustainable Development adopted by the United Nations General Assembly (United Nations 2015) and the 1948 Universal Declaration of Human Rights (United Nations 1948), which in its Article 7 deals

[32] UNESCO (2021, para 65).

[33] European Commission (2021), Preamble, Recital (2).

[34] European Commission (2021), Preamble, Recital (6).

[35] European Commission (2021), Preamble, Recital (6).

[36] CAI (2024a, Article 10.2).

[37] CAI (2024a, Article 10).

[38] CAI (2024a, Article 4).

[39] CAI (2024a, Article 6).

[40] This provision is aimed at satisfying potential future parties which find it difficult to ratify treaties in areas where they lack legislation at the domestic level.

with discrimination and equality. The UNESCO recommendation refers to a long list of relevant human rights instruments (e.g., the 1948 Universal Declaration of Human Rights [United Nations 1948]), several human rights conventions and UN declarations, the 2030 Agenda for Sustainable Development (United Nations 2015), relevant UNESCO documents, as well as the Human Rights Council resolutions on 'The right to privacy in the digital age' (HRC 2015) and on 'New and emerging digital technologies and human rights' (HRC 2019).

The EU AI Act (European Commission 2021) also relies on a number of background instruments. It mentions instruments from EU primary law (the Treaties of the European Union and the EUCFR), EU secondary law (e.g., the General Data Protection Regulation [European Parliament and Council 2016]), and from international law, in particular the UN human rights conventions (e.g., the Convention on the Rights of Persons with Disabilities [United Nations 2006], the Convention on the Rights of the Child [United Nations 1989], the Convention on the Status of Refugees [United Nations, 1951]).

In its preamble, the CoE Framework Convention (CAI 2024a) lists a number of applicable international (UN and European) human rights instruments. It also refers to the obligation "to protect human rights, as enshrined in applicable international law".[41] As clarified by the Explanatory Report attached to the CoE Framework Convention (CAI 2024b), no provision of the framework convention is intended to create new human rights or human rights obligations, or to undermine the scope and content of the existing applicable protections. Rather, by setting out various legally binding obligations contained in its Chapters II to VI, the framework convention aims to facilitate the effective implementation of the applicable human rights obligations of each Party in the context of the new challenges raised by AI. At the same time, the framework convention reinforces the role of international human rights law and the relevant aspects of domestic legal frameworks in relation to activities within the lifecycle of AI systems that have the potential to interfere with human rights, democracy and rule of law.

In the course of the implementation of the OECD and UNESCO recommendations, there is no court operating under the auspices of these organisations that would be able to interpret and further elaborate the meaning of the provisions of these instruments. Therefore, this remains to be the task of the relevant bodies, e.g., policy-making organs, secretariats of the respective international organisations. In contrast, both the EU and the CoE can rely on their own internal courts, namely the Court of Justice of the EU and the European Court of Human Rights, to interpret, within their respective mandates, the provisions of the EU and the CoE instrument in the case of a legal dispute. The AI Act may also be interpreted by the relevant EU organs in the course of their operation. The CoE Framework Convention's interpretation may also be a task of the Conference of the Parties and any peaceful means chosen by the Parties for the settlement of disputes.

[41] CAI (2024a, Article 4).

Regarding the question of remedies, the OECD recommendation (OECD 2019) does not mention any remedies for the violation of its provisions. However, it highlights that those adversely affected by an AI system should be able to challenge its outcome and the logic that served as the basis for its prediction, recommendation or decision. In contrast, the UNESCO recommendation provides that an "effective remedy should be available against discrimination and biased algorithmic determination."[42] It also adds that the "Member States should ensure that harms caused through AI systems are investigated and redressed, by enacting strong enforcement mechanisms and remedial actions, to make certain that human rights and fundamental freedoms and the rule of law are respected in the digital world and in the physical world."[43]

As it follows from its role as an instrument of market regulation, the EU AI Act dedicates a specific part—Section 4—to remedies. Its provides specifically the right of any natural or legal person having grounds to consider that there has been an infringement of the provisions of the AI Act to submit reasoned complaints to the relevant market surveillance authority.[44] The exercise by the market surveillance authority of its powers must be subject to appropriate procedural safeguards in accordance with Union and national law, including effective judicial remedies and due process.[45] The CoE Framework Convention also contains a specific provision—Article 14—on remedies. It requires each Party—to the extent remedies are required by its international obligations and consistent with its domestic legal system—to adopt or maintain measures to ensure the availability of accessible and effective remedies for violations of human rights resulting from the activities within the lifecycle of AI systems.[46]

As part of their implementation framework, the instruments address cooperation with other international organisations and/or frameworks for AI regulation. The OECD recommendation dedicates a separate title[47] to "International co-operation for trustworthy AI", in which it urges governments to work together in the OECD and other global and regional fora to foster the sharing of AI knowledge and encourage international, cross-sectoral and open multi-stakeholder initiatives to garner long-term expertise on AI. It also provides that governments should promote the development of multi-stakeholder, consensus-driven global technical standards for interoperable and trustworthy AI, and encourage the development, and their own use, of internationally comparable metrics to measure AI research, development and deployment, and, finally, gather the evidence base to assess progress in the implementation of these principles. The recommendation instructs the OECD's Committee on Digital Economy Policy to continue its important work on AI building on the recommendation and taking into account work in other international fora.

---

[42] UNESCO (2021, para 29).

[43] UNESCO (2021, para 55).

[44] European Commission (2021, Article 85).

[45] European Commission (2021, Article 99).

[46] CAI (2024a, Article 14).

[47] OECD (2019, Title 2.5).

The UNESCO recommendation explicitly recognises that the General Conference—when adopting the instrument—was "conscious of the many existing national policies, other frameworks and initiatives elaborated by relevant United Nations entities, [and] intergovernmental organizations, including regional organizations [...] related to the ethics and regulation of AI technologies".[48] It also states that UNESCO "will work in collaboration with other relevant United Nations entities, while respecting their mandate and avoiding duplication of work" and "will also work with other international, regional and sub-regional governmental and non-governmental organization".[49]

In its preamble, the EU AI Act provides that the notion of AI systems, as applied in the novel regulatory framework, should be clearly defined and should be closely aligned with the work of international organisations working on AI.[50] In this way the EU legal framework can ensure legal certainty, facilitate international convergence and a wide acceptance, while providing the flexibility to accommodate the rapid technological developments in the field. As a manifestation of this commitment, the AI Act uses the definition for AI systems as elaborated by the OECD.

The preamble of the CoE Framework Convention notes the relevant efforts to advance international understanding and cooperation on AI by other international and supranational organisations and fora. Similarly to the EU AI Act, the drafters of the framework convention also decided to use the OECD definition for AI systems. This choice is supported not only by the high quality of the work carried out by the OECD and its experts, but also by the need to enhance international co-operation on AI and facilitate efforts aimed at harmonising AI governance at a global level, including the harmonisation of the relevant terminology.[51] Such an approach also allows for the coherent implementation of different instruments relating to AI within the domestic legal systems of the Parties.

5 Analysis

As has been made apparent by the earlier short overview of the four AI instruments, elaborating and adopting non-binding soft law instruments on AI is a somewhat faster and politically easier process than developing legally binding instruments. This appears to hold true even when the membership of the given organisation is much broader than of other organisations.[52] The processes in both the EU and the CoE had started already in 2019, if we take into consideration the work of the HLEG

[48] UNESCO (2021), preamble.

[49] UNESCO (2021, paras 137 and 138).

[50] European Commission (2021), Preamble, Recital (12).

[51] CAI (2024b, para 23).

[52] See UNESCO's almost universal membership compared to the EU, which only has 27 Member States.

and the CAHAI, which shows that the elaboration of hard law instruments takes longer.

The four instruments address their provisions predominantly to states, either the member states of the international organisation in question, or states that wish to become adherents or Parties to the instrument. With the exception of the CoE Framework Convention, the instruments also contain provisions that are directly addressed to AI actors or actors playing a specific role in the lifecycle of AI systems.

Fairness (or certain aspects of fairness) is one of the central notions of the instruments, irrespective of the legal nature of the given instrument or the mandate or membership of the international organisation adopting it. However, they do not use a common, generally accepted definition or understanding of the concept of fairness. The instruments use the term in different contexts and apply different meanings. Although they recognise common elements of fairness (e.g., non-discrimination of individuals), they also introduce specific aspects/interpretations that are not commonly shared (e.g., fairness at the global level). The instruments often use terms related to the concept of fairness, such as non-discrimination, or use broader, more comprehensive concepts, such as trustworthiness or responsible AI, which include fairness as one of the components.

The legally binding instruments tend to use the concept of fairness less often or in a much narrower/more legalistic/restrictive sense, for example in the context of the right to a fair trial. In contrast, the non-binding recommendations are more inclined to refer to the concept frequently and they do not shy away from using various, often more political interpretations, such as a fairer world order.

If the international organisation adopting the instrument includes less developed countries or they are invited to participate in the negotiations, fairness is likely to attract a meaning that reaches beyond the national level and/or societal relations or the status of the individual. In the relevant instruments, fairness also gained an international/inter-state dimension demanding global/international solidarity. As demonstrated by the example of the UNESCO document, the expectation that developed countries support less advanced countries in the context of AI development and deployment may also be part of the notion.

All instruments highlight the importance of equality and non-discrimination in the context of the use of AI systems. In formulating their provisions, they followed different approaches. The OECD recommendation does not list any grounds and the final version of the CoE Framework Convention refers to the grounds of discrimination only indirectly. In contrast, both the UNESCO and the EU instruments contain an indicative list that is kept open for other possible grounds for discrimination. As these lists are not exhaustive, it can be interpreted that discrimination on any other, not explicitly mentioned grounds[53] is also prohibited (in line with the applicable national law or international obligations). Negotiating the lists specifying the

[53] See for example the list mentioned in UNESCO (2021, para 13): "Human dignity relates to the recognition of the intrinsic and equal worth of each individual human being, regardless of race, colour, descent, gender, age, language, religion, political opinion, national origin, ethnic origin, social origin, economic or social condition of birth, or disability and *any other grounds*."

grounds of discrimination can be very difficult and politically challenging, because certain terms (e.g., gender, especially when it is used/interpreted as a concept different than sex) can be considered as influenced by specific ideologies not shared by all governments.[54] Each instrument calls for actions to be taken to ensure respect for the principle of equality and non-discrimination. These provisions are rather generic and do not specify the concrete actions. They leave it to the AI actor or the Party to concretise the action taken, while often also leaving some flexibility for implementation. For example, the UNESCO document (UNESCO 2021) calls for making "all reasonable efforts".

The provisions of the four international instruments that deal with fairness and other related issues are rather short or leave room for interpretation and further elaboration. The policy-making organs, the conference of the parties, the secretariats, and—in the case of the EU and the CoE—the internal courts, will likely play a role in interpreting and further elaborating the requirements arising from the respective documents. National courts may also have an important role in interpreting the relevant requirements.

The international instruments also recognise the role of existing domestic and/international law in regulating AI technologies that already deal with certain aspects of fairness and non-discrimination. The OECD and UNESCO recommendations conclude that new laws/policies might need to be adopted. In contrast, the CoE Framework Convention only provides that the parties' actions should comply with the existing domestic law or international legal obligations already applicable to the given Party. It does not require the Party to go any further and fill legal gaps, if any exist. As a related development, all four instruments refer to and thus recognise the existence of relevant conventions and other documents dealing with specific aspects of fairness.

As a further common characteristic, the four instruments we studied acknowledge the efforts taken by other organisations/fora in this field and encourage cooperation/coordination among the relevant initiatives with the intention to ensure legal certainty, harmonisation and compatibility among the international initiatives. Furthermore, each instrument recognises explicitly or indirectly the importance of the availability of effective remedies against AI use and problematic decisions/outcomes rising from the use of AI.

---

[54] See in this regard, the case of the CoE convention on preventing and combating violence against women and domestic violence (Council of Europe 2011), also known as the Istanbul Convention, which was not ratified by several CoE member states because they did not agree with some of the concepts used in the convention.

6 Concluding Remarks

Generally speaking, there are several significant differences among the four international instruments we studied. They were adopted by different organisations acting under different mandates, their legal nature and their legal format are different, and they put forward different requirements for the technology area. However, there are also numerous similarities among them, and they even share common elements. For example, they all anchor equality and non-discrimination as core principles, they support multi-stakeholder approaches in technology governance, they regard the availability of legal remedies against technology usage as crucial, and they encourage coordination among the different initiatives for AI regulation to ensure a harmonious development of rules. The differences seem justified as the complex challenges posed by AI technologies cannot be solved by a single best solution. It is also unrealistic to expect that a binding comprehensive instrument could be developed in the short-term that would be acceptable to the whole UN membership. A universal UN treaty on AI is not yet within our reach.

The four instruments were adopted only 2 years ago or were very recently negotiated. Therefore, their effectiveness in regulating AI systems remains to be seen. It is also unclear what level of regulatory competition they may engender and what would be the acceptable level of regulatory competition between different international and regional instruments. As provided by the instruments themselves, regulatory coordination among the organisations is of paramount importance, as is minimising the potential negative effects of parallel regulation, such as the unnecessary duplication of efforts, the fragmentation of the regulatory framework, and the burdening of AI actors with overregulation or conflicting/contradictory regulatory requirements. Coordination and the elimination of unnecessary conflicts are also necessary in the implementation phase. The instruments should complement each other, build on each other's respective strengths, and should make sure that implementation takes place in a harmonised framework characterised by a similarity of language and concepts, similar impact assessment frameworks, and by similar obligations imposed on public and private actors.

To ensure harmonious development in international AI regulation, we can learn from the lessons learned in other fields. Some of the solutions are already implemented, while others still need to be borrowed based on experiences in fields such as nuclear law or counterterrorism measures. The practices already in place—wholly or in part—include the attending of each other's meetings when it concerns AI policy or regulation, encouraging the organisation of joint events, supporting participation in *globalpolicy.AI* and similar initiatives, sharing of information and best practices, as well as possibly regulatory concepts and solutions, effective coordination at national level, in particular within government and public administration (so that national positions represented in different international fora are harmonised), setting up dedicated AI offices at national level and appointing technology ambassadors and special envoys, and coordinating participation in multi-stakeholder processes so that the same participants (NGOs, companies, international organisations, etc.) attend these processes and a duplication of efforts is avoided.

In the future, harmonious developments in international AI law and regulation can be ensured by adopting innovative and ambitious measures, such as setting up a Group of Friends of like-minded states and other actors to help raise awareness and facilitate the sharing of information and the implementation of coordination efforts, creating a new, carefully assembled, ambitious platform for digital cooperation or the strengthening of already existing fora, such as the Internet Governance Forum to facilitate multi-stakeholder coordination, or the launching of joint legislative assistance projects to help states currently lacking the expertise needed for implementing the relevant international instruments. Alternatively, the relevant international organisations could conclude a memorandum of understanding (or a 'compact' as happened in the field of counterterrorism) to facilitate inter-agency coordination beyond the already ongoing work carried out by the Inter-Agency Working Group on AI.[55] An AI fund or facility could also be established to finance implementation efforts and joint projects (similar to the Global Environment Facility/GEF[56]). The fund or facility should work on the basis of conditionality, which means that access to funds would be subject to compliance with certain pre-determined rules.

The four instruments analysed in this paper, as well as the other parallel attempts to regulate AI technologies or certain aspects of the technology, could be seen as different "pieces of the same normative puzzle". Ideally, these parallel regulatory experiments and the experiences of their implementation in the coming years will likely lead to the crystallisation of common fundamental principles and the identification of uniform requirements. For this, we should look for and identify the emerging 'unity within diversity',[57] which could also serve as the pillars/building blocks of a future global AI treaty. These developments could also result in the birth of a new branch of international law. As this chapter has demonstrated, we can already identify some similarities and common elements at this relatively early stage of the process. As technological change is very rapid, this new branch of law cannot be static or too rigid. It will need to be able to react/adapt to the changing technological needs, and in order to be able to do that it will have to apply innovative legal and institutional solutions.

References

CAI: Council of Europe Committee on Artificial Intelligence (2023a) Zero draft framework convention on artificial intelligence, human rights, democracy, and the rule of law. https://rm.coe.int/cai-2023-01-revised-zero-draft-framework-convention-public/1680aa193f

CAI: Council of Europe Committee on Artificial Intelligence (2023b) Consolidated working draft of the framework convention on artificial intelligence, human rights, democracy, and the rule of

[55] https://unsceb.org/inter-agency-working-group-artificial-intelligence.

[56] https://www.thegef.org/who-we-are.

[57] See, in this regard, Schermers and Blokker (2011).

law. https://rm.coe.int/cai-2023-18-consolidated-working-draft-framework-convention/1680abde66

CAI: Council of Europe Committee on Artificial Intelligence (2024a) Draft framework convention on artificial intelligence, human rights, democracy, and the rule of law. https://search.coe.int/cm/Pages/result_details.aspx?ObjectId=0900001680af0734

CAI: Council of Europe Committee on Artificial Intelligence (2024b) Draft explanatory report to framework convention on artificial intelligence, human rights, democracy, and the rule of law. https://www.coe.int/en/web/artificial-intelligence/cai

Council: Council of the European Union (2022) General approach—proposal for a regulation of the European Parliament and of the Council laying down harmonized rules on artificial intelligence. https://data.consilium.europa.eu/doc/document/ST-14954-2022-INIT/en/pdf

Council of Europe (2011) Convention on preventing and combating violence against women and domestic violence. https://www.coe.int/en/web/gender-matters/council-of-europe-convention-on-preventing-and-combating-violence-against-women-and-domestic-violence

European Commission (2021) Proposal for a regulation of the European Parliament and of the Council laying down harmonized rules on artificial intelligence (Artificial Intelligence Act), COM(2021) 206 final

European Parliament (2023a) Compromise Amendments on the Draft Report Proposal for a regulation of the European Parliament and of the Council on harmonised rules on Artificial Intelligence (Artificial Intelligence Act). https://www.europarl.europa.eu/meetdocs/2014_2019/plmrep/COMMITTEES/CJ40/DV/2023/05-11/ConsolidatedCA_IMCOLIBE_AI_ACT_EN.pdf

European Parliament (2023b) Artificial Intelligence Act: deal on comprehensive rules for trustworthy AI. https://www.europarl.europa.eu/news/en/press-room/20231206IPR15699/artificial-intelligence-act-deal-on-comprehensive-rules-for-trustworthy-ai

European Parliament (2024) European Parliament legislative resolution of 13 March 2024 on the proposal for a regulation of the European Parliament and of the Council on laying down harmonised rules on Artificial Intelligence (Artificial Intelligence Act). https://www.europarl.europa.eu/doceo/document/TA-9-2024-0138_EN.pdf

European Parliament and Council (2016) Regulation (EU) 2016/679 of the European Parliament and of the Council of 27 April 2016 on the protection of natural persons with regard to the processing of personal data and on the free movement of such data, and repealing Directive 95/46/EC (General Data Protection Regulation). OJ L 119, 4.5.2016, pp 1–88

HLEG: High-Level Expert Group on Artificial Intelligence (2019) Ethics guidelines for trustworthy AI. https://digital-strategy.ec.europa.eu/en/library/ethics-guidelines-trustworthy-ai

HRC: UN Human Rights Council (2015) The right to privacy in the digital age. https://ap.ohchr.org/documents/dpage_e.aspx?si=A%2FHRC%2FRES%2F28%2F16

HRC: UN Human Rights Council (2019) New and emerging digital technologies and human rights. https://ap.ohchr.org/documents/dpage_e.aspx?si=A/HRC/41/L.14

Microsoft (2022) Microsoft Responsible AI Standard, v2. https://query.prod.cms.rt.microsoft.com/cms/api/am/binary/RE5cmFl?culture=en-us&country=us

OECD: Organisation for Economic Co-operation and Development (2011) OECD guidelines for multinational enterprises on responsible business conduct, 2011 edition. https://www.oecd-ilibrary.org/finance-and-investment/oecd-guidelines-for-multinational-enterprises-on-responsible-business-conduct_81f92357-en

OECD: Organisation for Economic Co-operation and Development (2019) Recommendation of the council on artificial intelligence. https://legalinstruments.oecd.org/en/instruments/OECD-LEGAL-0449

Schermers HG, Blokker NM (2011) International institutional law—unity within diversity. Brill

UNESCO (2021) UNESCO recommendation on the ethics of artificial intelligence, No. 61910. https://unesdoc.unesco.org/ark:/48223/pf0000380455

United Nations (1948) Universal Declaration of Human Rights. https://www.un.org/sites/un2.un.org/files/2021/03/udhr.pdf

United Nations (1951) Convention relating to the status of refugees. https://www.ohchr.org/en/instruments-mechanisms/instruments/convention-relating-status-refugees

United Nations (1969) Vienna convention on the law of treaties 1969. https://legal.un.org/ilc/texts/instruments/english/conventions/1_1_1969.pdf

United Nations (1989) Convention on the Rights of the Child. https://www.ohchr.org/en/instruments-mechanisms/instruments/convention-rights-child

United Nations (2006) Convention on the Rights of Persons with disabilities. https://social.desa.un.org/issues/disability/crpd/convention-on-the-rights-of-persons-with-disabilities-crpd

United Nations (2015) Resolution adopted by the General Assembly on 25 September 2015. Transforming our world: the 2030 Agenda for Sustainable Development. https://documents.un.org/doc/undoc/gen/n15/291/89/pdf/n1529189.pdf?token=Ml8zRYTOy79e2aVhw9&fe=true

Wachter S, Mittelstadt B, Russell C (2021) Why fairness cannot be automated: bridging the gap between EU non-discrimination and AI. Comput Law Secur Rev 41:105567. https://doi.org/10.1016/j.clsr.2021.105567

Technology Sovereignty and AI Regulation in the EU: Regulatory Strategy and the Paradox of Choice

Marton Varju

Abstract Technology sovereignty has become a central EU policy objective, as well as a core idea behind a particular regulatory strategy devised for EU technology policies, including the policy on artificial intelligence. However, technology sovereignty raises complex problems that burdens policy-makers with dilemmas rather than clear-cut solutions. The EU's policy approach and its chosen regulatory strategy seem to ignore the complexities inherent in technology sovereignty and maintain that the EU, unaffected by the dilemmas, can adopt an appropriate response. The EU's strategic choice of introducing a high-standard, value-driven regulation of technology markets, including the European market for AI systems, faces another, partly related problem. EU regulatory measures, which interfere directly and in divergent ways with national industrial and economic policy, need to be adopted using the competences and the decision-making framework available, which put their own restraints on the regulatory outputs. The AI Act is a measure of EU technology regulation that bears the mark of these origins. Although it pursues ambitious general objectives, including those derived from technology sovereignty, it reads as a conventional internal market product safety measure. It is a product of practical compromises rather than of grand strategic choices, which may disappoint the expectations originally linked to it.

The chapter was supported by the European Union project RRF-2.3.1-21-2022-00004 within the framework of the Artificial Intelligence National Laboratory and by the Ministry of Innovation and Technology NRDI Office within the framework of the FK_21 Young Researcher Excellence Program (138965).

M. Varju (✉)
Institute for Legal Studies, HUN-REN Centre for Social Sciences, Budapest, Hungary
e-mail: varju.marton@tk.hun-ren.hu

Faculty of Social Sciences, Eötvös Loránd University, Budapest, Hungary

M. Varju and K. Mezei (eds.), *The Challenges of Artificial Intelligence for Law in Europe*, Data Science, Machine Intelligence, and Law 6,
https://doi.org/10.1007/978-3-031-86813-9_4

1 Introduction

As a specific manifestation of the European Union's current broader, geopolitically focussed political agenda, technology sovereignty has become a central notion and a supposed objective of EU technology policy and regulation. It has provided an important frame also for the impending regulation of technologies associated with the domain of artificial intelligence (AI). In the EU policy context, technology sovereignty is construed as a multifaceted target that involves the offering of a balanced response to the challenges of the production and the supply of crucial technologies in the current geoeconomic and geopolitical environment. It also incorporates a distinct strategy for the EU to realise its ambitions: the adoption of declaredly value- and rights-driven, high-standard technology regulation that determines the conditions of access to the European market. However, the EU's policy target seems to overlook the fact that the achieving of technology sovereignty involves dilemmas rather than straightforward choices, and that the choices made are likely to lead to paradoxical outcomes. Furthermore, as a result of this limitation, the technology sovereignty tools or strategies developed may not be able to deliver on their promised aims and may fall short of the relevant actors' expectations. This is a particular risk in the EU context where, despite the centralised determination of general policy directions, in concrete decision-making situations the divergent interests, economic positions, and industrial and technological visions of individual Member States unavoidably impact and may even undermine the implementation of the proposed common policy response. When placed in the 'blender' of EU decision-making, proposals for detailed and concrete technology regulation can be reoriented and distanced from their original, ambitious objectives.

In this chapter, we aim to analyse the EU's developing policy and regulatory framework for AI from the perspective of the notion and policy target of technology sovereignty. Our starting point is that technology sovereignty, despite its accessibility as a political or policy label, makes policy design and the delivery of policies, in particular through the regulation of technology and its narrower and broader risks, a complex, and from the perspective of the actual outputs realised, a controversial exercise. We will explore how technology sovereignty may aim for the realisation of competing and/or contradictory goals, and how the dilemmas inherent in the concept—in the particular socio-economic situation of a given polity—may lead to inadequate trade-offs, or to compromise solutions that fail to satisfy the expectations of stakeholders. This then leads to our analysis of EU policy developments and of how the dilemmas and paradoxes of technology sovereignty may impact the already complex dynamics of EU decision-making. The adoption of regulatory measures in the EU is usually affected by the internal diversity of preferences, interests and visions regarding markets, societies and technologies, as well as by the functionally limited competences to adopt regulation applicable in the entire, internally diverse European market. There is already evidence of how these factors have influenced EU technology regulation in domains where the protection of values and rights was part of the regulatory package, and how, as a result, these measures settled for a more narrowly framed, sometimes disappointing solution than their original regulatory agendas. We will close the chapter by scrutinising the EU's new AI Act and examine whether the predictions previously laid out in the chapter bore relevance for the structure and the regulatory content of the measure.

2 Technology Sovereignty as a Regulatory Concept

Despite its simplicity as a political and policy buzzword, technology sovereignty—especially when its implementation is considered—presents decision-makers with difficult dilemmas that make policy design and regulation a complex exercise without a guarantee that the desired objectives can and will be realised. The dilemmas inherent in the notion of technology sovereignty require the making of difficult choices which may then lead to controversial, (therefore) unstable and/or unsustainable trade-offs between competing political, economic and social priorities and objectives, and also between the actors and social groups representing them. The definitions that have emerged for the notion reveal a multifaceted target mixing explicitly political and more objective policy objectives with the aim of creating a readjusted framework for technology supply and governance in a changing geopolitical and geoeconomic environment.[1] In short, technology sovereignty stands for the parallel goals of reducing dependencies on foreign-sourced technologies and achieving autonomy in technology production and supply (and with that securing abilities and capacities to deliver public and also private goods), which goals may be driven by strategic considerations, often with an evident geopolitical edge, and which may relate to broader, territorially defined political and policy objectives, such as the protection of perceived local/regional values, the protection of technology security as well as security in a traditional sense, ensuring local/regional socio-economic resilience, maintaining political and other influence globally, or securing or furthering industrial and/or socio-economic competitiveness (VDE 2013; Bauer and Erixon 2020; Csernatoni 2021; Chrétien and Drouard 2022). When examined more closely, although its internal complexity makes the concept rather attractive, many of these objectives are evidently in competition and/or may be impossible to reconcile with each other.

The core dilemma involved in technology sovereignty, which the one dimensional, "prescriptive" policy responses and technology sovereignty tools tend to overlook, concerns the conflict between its inherently protectionist intentions in technology

[1] Mainstream positions advocate a concept and policy of technology sovereignty which, having regard to the realities of the current geopolitical context, is not framed exclusively in inward-looking patriotic terms, such as complete technological and industrial autonomy, independence and self-determination. Instead, acknowledging that individual states and national economies have limited capacities, technology sovereignty should entail both the developing and preserving of local technological and industrial capacities, and the maintaining of prudently constructed, selective structural dependencies on other states and economies based on reliable partnerships. See Bauer and Erixon (2020), Edler et al. (2020), Crespi et al. (2021), Chrétien and Drouard (2022), and Tolstukhina (2022).

supply and governance, and its broader promise of securing and increasing socio-economic resilience and competitiveness (Bauer and Erixon 2020; Calderaro and Blumfelde 2022). The aim of reducing technological dependencies, in particular by territorial decoupling or by promoting inferior home-made technologies and technology applications, has the paradoxical effect of weakening the economy and society by reducing access to globally available, foreign-sourced innovative technologies, as well as products and services based on such technologies (Bauer and Erixon 2020; Edler et al. 2020).[2] In fact, the genuine, sustainable technology sovereignty of local/regional economies and societies can be directly undermined by aggressive policies of technology protectionism and ill-considered decisions to decouple from global technological supply- and value-chains (Bauer and Erixon 2020). When national administrations, public services, undertakings and users need access to the necessary technologies and technology-based products and services, restricting their availability in national/regional markets, either by restrictive regulation or by hostile foreign trade and investment policy, will inevitably lead to counterproductive outcomes (Bauer and Erixon 2020; Calderaro and Blumfelde 2022). In such a context, policies will be driven towards establishing a compromise solution trying to balance between the different factors[3]; however, these solutions, assuming that they are in fact possible, may fall short of the expectations and leave actors dissatisfied as to the outcomes achieved. They may also undermine cooperation with closer allies and partner economies—even among the Member States of the EU competing from very different positions in the technological race[4]—seeing their (sovereign) interests threatened by the compromise established.

Others have analysed this dilemma inherent in technology sovereignty as there being a "structural tension" between the integrated nature of the global technology economy and the efforts of states to develop and maintain effective localised responses to the hazards and harms of technologies (Ilves and Osula 2020). States are compelled to address the local risks and other negative impacts of technologies; however, because of this "structural tension", they introduce regulation and other

---

[2] The conflict is between technology sovereignty and the current growth model in European economies based on global specialisation and division of labour combined with free trade. The paradox may run even deeper as decoupling national economies and industries from foreign dependencies may in fact be necessary to secure productivity and competitiveness, while recognising that decoupling may undermine national economies in those two areas. See Edler et al. (2020).

[3] See, for instance, proposals for a better differentiated policy as regards specific technological domains depending on trade needs and integration into global value chains, or the policy that only one-sided technological dependencies need to be eliminated and other stable partnerships can and should be maintained (VDE 2013; ASD 2020; Bauer and Erixon 2020; Edler et al. 2020; Chrétien and Drouard 2022). The holistically framed, multitiered systemic solutions advocated represent a perhaps more stable and sustainable balanced response/compromise (VDE 2013; Edler et al. 2020; Chrétien and Drouard 2022); however, these have a long, uncertain time horizon and may in fact fuel competition between partners who should instead cooperate and provide mutual advantages (Calderaro and Blumfelde 2022).

[4] There are considerable and "widening technological capability gaps between the EU Member States", in particular in the field of AI, which have been responsible for divergent/inconsistent approaches in national policy-making (Calderaro and Blumfelde 2022).

tools that make a "difficult and costly trade-off" between maintaining access to technologies available in the global market and surrendering control and capacity over the relevant hazards and harms (Ilves and Osula 2020). When making this trade-off, which is unavoidable as a result of the persistent local demand for both technology access and technology control, states also need to face the problems arising from the costs—both direct and indirect—of their intervention (Ilves and Osula 2020). The choices made by states in the context of technology sovereignty policy will therefore have to assess whether undertakings in their territory can or want to meet the cost of compliance with the technology regulation introduced, or whether the national economy can meet the costs of general technology choices (Ilves and Osula 2020). The latter costs, the costs of adopting a new technology or adapting existing technologies to new technological requirements, in particular when states follow a strategic decision to restrict the access of foreign-sourced technologies, shed a new light on the technology sovereignty dilemma.[5] Specifically, although reducing the dependency on foreign technologies can increase local technological autonomy, that autonomy may only be illusory when the costs of technology change are prohibitive, or when the state and its economy—by excluding itself from global technological supply-chains—deprives itself of the best, or the only available technology (Ilves and Osula 2020).

As a related problem, considering the rapidly evolving nature of technologies, it is difficult to foresee which technology sovereignty policies will succeed and which will fail, if not in the short- then in the long-term. For instance, restrictive, protectionist regulatory solutions may be able to secure control in the short run. However, without actual domestic capabilities to develop and supply technologies, international competitors with access to the necessary capabilities and capacities will be able to sidestep such territorial policies (Csernatoni 2021; Calderaro and Blumfelde 2022; Chrétien and Drouard 2022). They may not only maintain their position in the technological race, but eventually they may also take control of the regulatory agenda regionally and even globally (Csernatoni 2021; Calderaro and Blumfelde 2022; Chrétien and Drouard 2022). In this light, the expectation of states or other polities that they can achieve technology sovereignty exclusively by adopting their own technology regulation seems unrealistic. As a further issue, causing another difficult dilemma for technology policies, the priorities of technology sovereignty in the narrower domain of technology production may not correspond to, or may in fact contradict those pursued on the application side of crucial technologies (ASD 2020; Calderaro and Blumfelde 2022).[6] For instance, actors on the application end of technologies that are necessary for maintaining national sovereignty, such as those

[5] The calls for differentiated, instead of monolithic technology sovereignty policies aim to make sure that these costs are adequately determined, and that restrictions or the programmes for capacity building are realistic and necessary (ASD 2020).

[6] The notion of strategic autonomy as a core aspect of technology sovereignty had emerged originally in the context of EU defence and security policy giving the broader frame of this particular technology policy direction (Csernatoni 2021; Calderaro and Blumfelde 2022). See also, in this connection, the systemic notion of technology sovereignty that also covers the ability to fulfil sovereign tasks in public services, policing, defence, energy, transport etc. (Edler et al. 2020), and

in defence and security policy, public infrastructures, health care, or energy and transport, will assess access to critical foreign technologies differently from those with stakes in developing domestic technology capacities, and will push for different technology sovereignty tools (VDE 2013; Calderaro and Blumfelde 2022).[7] It seems therefore that even though technology sovereignty implies a general possibility of choice, its choices may in fact lead to paradoxical outcomes and/or outcomes that satisfy the expectations of none of the affected.

3 Technology Sovereignty in European Union Policy

The orientation of the EU's own technology sovereignty policy was first revealed in the public political messages formulated by the European Commission around 2019. The Commission's position could build on the broader political objective of European sovereignty launched in the 2018 State of the Union address (Juncker 2018). This objective was defined as the securing of the strategic autonomy and capacity of Europe in the world, through both maintaining multi- and bilateral relationships with other countries and developing European capacities in a number of strategic areas, including technological development and technology regulation (Juncker 2018). In 2019, the incoming Commission made it clear that technology sovereignty was central to its economic and industrial policy agenda. The notion used by the Commission (Breton 2019; von der Leyen 2019a, b) projected a multifaceted policy framework, which basically pursues a balanced approach, and which (therefore) includes a broad spectrum of priorities, such as the "mastery and ownership" of key technologies in Europe, global leadership in (digital) technology standardisation, reinforcing the ethical and the human aspects of EU technology governance, and the development of European capacities in "critical technology areas", as well as achieving technological self-determination and avoiding external dependencies that pose geopolitical, geostrategic and other risks.

The Commission's 2020 digital transformation framework document (European Commission 2020a) put forward a similarly ambitious, although rather loosely defined agenda. Similar to the earlier mentioned general policy framework, the document with its all-encompassing approach seems to suggest that a balanced response is possible to the dilemmas of technology sovereignty. It understood technology sovereignty, which was associated primarily with technological integrity and resilience, as demanding both the development of autonomous technological and industrial capacities that are capable of producing globally competitive products and services, and the reduction of technological dependencies—although in the most

the position that technology sovereignty is a key determinant of traditional areas of state sovereignty, such as security and defence (ASD 2020).

[7] For example, industrial policy needs may favour open markets and undisrupted value chains; security policy needs, however, may favour protectionist regulation and autonomous technology production (Calderaro and Blumfelde 2022).

crucial areas only—on other countries and economies (European. The clearly stated ambition that Europe will regulate itself to an autonomous, strategically leading position in the world and in global markets by introducing its own technological standards and by pioneering the regulation of certain values for technology development and use also formed part of the package. The document envisioned the implementation of this latter plan by indicating that Europe, as a globally relevant arena for the development and the introduction of novel technologies, should be able to impose its preferences in technological standards and value-based requirements towards technologies on technology actors and other entities around the world.[8]

In the narrower technological domain of AI, EU policy associated technology sovereignty with technological self-determination and self-reliance (European Commission 2018), in particular with developing hard and soft technological capacities in Europe necessary for assuming global technology leadership and ensuring Europe's global competitiveness (European Commission 2020b). The policy framework also explicitly embraced regulation as a tool for Europe—based on its perceived influence as a major global market—to regulate its way to global technological leadership and technology autonomy. The 2020 AI White Paper declared that the introduction of advanced, risk-based AI-regulation in Europe and ensuring that technology actors comply with European AI standards should give the European economy and the technologies developed there a distinct advantage in global technology and economic competition (European Commission 2020b). These strategic advantages were expected to arise specifically from the EU's complex approach to regulating AI that combines both the laying down of technological standards and the legal regulation of the values, rights and moral principles that can make AI technologies trustworthy and ready to be introduced responsibly in the market and in society at large (European Commission 2020b).[9] The White Paper did not clarify whether it had considered the dilemmas and risks inherent in such a regulatory strategy. Nor did it discuss whether the approach has political feasibility considering how differently individual Member States may react the proposed course of action.

The geopolitical dimension of technology sovereignty gained a renewed emphasis in the 2022 Versailles Declaration (European Council 2022). The document, which identified threats of historical proportion to European values and "our European model", declared the need to take "further decisive steps" towards constructing "European sovereignty" and take "more responsibility for our security". It referred specifically to the reduction of Europe's dependencies and proposed designing a novel growth and investment model for the European economy. The three key areas

[8] Basically, access to the European market comes at the price of complying with European requirements designed to serve the interests and the needs of Europe and Europeans.

[9] The protection of European values and fundamental rights, and generally a human-focussed approach to data governance, also appeared in the European strategy on data (European Commission 2020c) published in parallel with the AI White Paper. The data strategy also introduced and defined the concept of data sovereignty, which referred to the objective of creating a self-reliant, but internationally open single European data space where access to data and their exploitation are subject to compliance—for both European and non-European actors—with the applicable EU legislative measures and with European fundamental rights and values.

of action included the increasing of European defence capabilities, the reduction of Europe's energy dependencies, and building a "a more robust economic base". The capacity for autonomous action was identified as the core objective within the first area of action. In this regard, the declaration emphasised—among others—the need for technological development and the integration of innovative technologies in security and defence frameworks. It also prioritised actions in technology-intensive or technology-based dimensions of European security, such as cyber-resilience and the protection of critical infrastructure. The reduction of strategic dependencies, in particular on foreign-sourced technologies was addressed in the context of the third area of action relating to Europe's economic resilience. In this regard, the declaration specified the sensitive technologies or technology-relevant resources[10] where more European autonomy was needed.[11] Like previous policy documents, the declaration put forward a sweeping plan for enhancing Europe's techno-economic sovereignty, without giving much detail to its internal contradictions and its feasibility.

The Versailles Declaration identified a variety of approaches as to how dependencies may be reduced in the individual technology areas addressed. The supply of the EU with critical raw materials is expected to be ensured by means of "strategic partnerships, exploring strategic stockpiling and promoting a circular economy and resource efficiency". To secure access to semi-conductors, Europe will aim to "diversify supply value-chains, maintain technological leadership and further develop EU production capacity". Access to crucial health technologies is supposed to be ensured by "supporting innovation and sustainable European production", financing research and development, developing production capacities for critical products, and "making Europe a leader in biomedicines". In the digital technologies, covering in particular AI, Cloud and 5G, the declaration mentioned investment in these technologies, examining "the feasibility of creating digital partnerships", strengthening the EU legal framework by adopting the legislative measures that are in preparation, and weighing in "on the standardisation of some key technologies". Matching its all-encompassing scope, the declaration also put forward a generously framed toolkit for the EU that included the fostering of "industrial initiatives", the strengthening of "research and innovation capabilities", pursuing an "ambitious and robust trade policy", promoting EU "standards, market access, sustainable value chains and connectivity", and completing and strengthening the EU's unilateral "trade and competition policy toolbox" towards third countries.

With the 2022 declaration, the general policy framework seems to have reached a high point both in commitment and in detail. However, its generous formulation makes it difficult to determine whether it has considered the dilemmas that are involved in the EU's chosen policy strategy, as well as those that may arise in the context of EU decision-making and its particular internal dynamics. Contradicting the EU policy's general preference for a balanced response, policy analyses,

[10] The declaration addressed specific sectors and not technologies; however, its focus fell on the technologies applied in these sectors.

[11] These were critical raw materials, semi-conductors, health technologies, digital technologies, and food technologies.

as already mentioned earlier, have observed that the EU's plan to secure its technology sovereignty both internally and abroad by high-standard, restrictive technology regulation for the European market, without having sufficient hard capacities in world-leading technology production, holds considerable risks, as it may reduce Europe's access to the necessary technologies and may prevent the development of a European technology base as an alternative source of supply (Bauer and Erixon 2020; Calderaro and Blumfelde 2022).[12] It was also pointed out that the high regulatory standards may also damage nascent European industry and may provoke retaliatory measures from economies that have robust capacities for innovation and technology production (Bauer and Erixon 2020). In addition, without global partners sharing the same approach towards technology regulation, that see their competitiveness secured for instance by value-based, human rights focussed technology regulation, there is a distinct possibility that the EU's assumed international clout in technology regulation and standard-setting may not actually materialise (Bauer and Erixon 2020). The expectation that high-standard common technology regulation will ensure that Europe's interests prevail in global technology markets may in fact be overly optimistic and not particularly realistic (Bauer and Erixon 2020).[13]

Furthermore, the EU's technology sovereignty policy is also hindered by disagreement among the Member States and by the related possibility that the Member States may in fact prefer and be able to agree on a low-intensity and -impact common policy only. First, the Member States may disagree with restrictive EU technology sovereignty measures as they may undermine current national models for socio-economic growth (Edler et al. 2020). Also, individual Member States, which have different capacities for home-grown innovation and technology production and have different resources at their disposal, have different capabilities to achieve technological decoupling and shift to a new, less internationally open growth model (Edler et al. 2020). Similarly, the different Member States hold different positions in global and European competition, which means their ability to tolerate a restriction of access to the foreign-sourced technologies that they need, as well as their willingness to accept such restrictions are divergent. Second, the Member States are likely to react differently to a common technology sovereignty policy depending on whether their economies have national champions in the technology sector, or economic operators in the national economy have a higher level of technology uptake compared to other national economies (Ilves and Osula 2020). The specialisation of the national

[12] Arguably, the choice of high-standard, value-driven technology regulation was not made freely, but was instead enforced by the circumstance that Europe lacks competitive innovation and production capabilities in digital technologies, and generally the EU lacks the competences and the tools to stay in technology competition apart from the tools of regulation and technological standard-setting. Practically, the EU had no other choice in responding to the dilemma of technology sovereignty but to introduce value-focussed, exclusionary (protectionist) market/technology regulation. See Calderaro and Blumfelde (2022).

[13] The EU was also said to have a "sovereignty gap", which refers fundamentally to its functional limitation as a technology policy actor. In contrast, states have a genuine ability in the technology economy to address unilaterally the threats arising from technologies to their autonomy and to safeguard their interests and preferences (Ilves and Osula 2020).

economy within the larger European market, differentiation in regards the contribution of domestic enterprises to the European value chain, and the differences in interests relating to the resilience and competitiveness of European-scale industries may also determine national agreement with a common technology sovereignty policy.[14]

The potential for disagreement among the Member States, which may in particular be fuelled by the earlier mentioned dilemmas inherent in implementing technology sovereignty, provides an unfavourable political environment for putting in place the EU's envisioned high-impact technology sovereignty policy, including the desired value-driven, high-standard technology regulation. In such an environment, policy output is likely to be determined by what the Member States can agree on, rather than by what was deemed desirable during policy design and development. This possibility was highlighted in the European technology sovereignty discourse in the context of assessing the risks and costs of EU policy and the related rationale for the Member States to push for fragmented, lower standard common policy solutions. First, the Member States may oppose European regulatory centralisation in technology policy as it has the potential for increasing interdependencies among them and could involve the shifting of competences from the national to the European level in areas with evident security implications, such as investment, ownership and market access (ASD 2020). Furthermore, there is no guarantee that the benefits of a European technology sovereignty policy will be distributed evenly among the Member States, and some states may even be excluded from the advantages and opportunities of the resulting technological change (ASD 2020). The policy may also enable the emergence of dominant national economies in the technological domain, leaving other national economies increasingly dependent on them (ASD 2020). The introduction of high EU regulatory standards may also interfere with national strategic visions and ambitions emerging from conditions such as the existing and the planned future technological capacities of a national economy (ASD 2020).[15]

4 Technology Sovereignty and Technology Regulation in the EU Decision-Making Blender

As discussed in the previous section, the EU's technology policy, in particular its regulatory strategy, when placed in the context of the inter-State politics of EU decision-making, faces certain challenges. In this complex and challenging setting, the dilemmas inherent in technology sovereignty are likely to cause a further disruption of policy-making and regulation. The broad premises of this possibility were

---

[14] There is evidence of political conflict among the Member States, each aiming to protect its own economic model, that impacted EU technology policy output concerning the preferred industrial and economic policy direction (Bauer and Erixon 2020).

[15] Or they may in fact interfere with more traditional economic policy aims, such as recovery from an economic crisis or securing economic convergence with the other Member States (Bauer and Erixon 2020).

indicated already by Bauer and Erixon in their comprehensive criticism of EU technology sovereignty policy. They explained in particular that the restrictive technology sovereignty tools proposed in the EU policy framework are likely to favour certain national economies and thus prioritise the interests of certain Member States (Bauer and Erixon 2020). There is a particular possibility that the economies of the Western core Member States will be favoured, and the smaller, more open, less autonomous and more dependent economies of the other Member States will be harmed, especially when their access to technologies is restricted as a result of EU policy (Bauer and Erixon 2020). The EU's regulatory strategy pursued under the framework of technology sovereignty may in fact be unsupported and may potentially be challenged by the Member States which see their competitiveness and chances for socio-economic development and convergence threatened by the value-focussed high-standard regulation planned by the EU, and which need access to foreign-sourced, cutting-edge technologies to close the historical gap in their development (Bauer and Erixon 2020).

In the context of EU regulatory policies, such complications and conflicts are not without precedent. In the EU internal market framework, where the regulatory harmonisation competences have been regularly used to adopt technology regulation, the Member States have clashed over regulation that by levelling out regulatory differences interfered with their national policy or other preferences. The Member States, which compete with each other for resources and markets, usually make every effort possible to safeguard specific national competitive advantages, as well as local considerations in the public interest, and fight off centralised EU regulatory burdens that threaten to undermine the competitiveness of the national economy, or of particular national industries.[16] National governments are prepared to agree only to those common European rules that are essential for the operation of the internal market, seeing the realisation of that particular economic objective and its perceived advantages as an acceptable trade-off for altering the regulatory environment of economic activities in the national economy.[17] This was evidently the case in the old internal market framework where decision-making was based on the unanimity rule. There, the necessity of satisfying the demands of every national government led to the drafting of EU measures of high regulatory detail (Pelkmans 1977),[18] which then

[16] This is not to assume that the Member States would have uniform, monolithic preferences, and that they do not have to choose between the interests of their export-oriented and their more inward-looking industries, for example. See, in this regard, Dehousse (1992).

[17] Different Member States have different bargaining positions and advantages in the process of internal market regulation; for instance, those opposing high standard common regulation can delay the legislative process or secure concessions in exchange for their acceptance of the new European regulatory burden on their industries. In contrast, Member States with high standards of regulatory protection—seeing that their regulatory standards and the socio-economic model manifested in them may be threatened by lower standard EU harmonisation measure—would push for high standard internal market regulation and actively build majority coalitions in the Council, so that the interests of their producers and their advantages in economic competition are not harmed. See Dehousse (1992).

[18] Decision-making was sluggish and cumbersome, and the rules adopted were unsuitable for rapidly changing (technological) markets, or for guaranteeing effective monitoring and compliance at national level (McGee and Weatherill 1990; Craig 2002).

made those measures politically undesirable as they threatened to impose excessive uniformity, contrary to national economic and industrial priorities (Pelkmans 1987). The new approach to internal market harmonisation, which was supported by the replacement of the unanimity rule with qualified majority voting in the Council, was introduced to streamline decision-making (McGee and Weatherill 1990; Craig 2002). This change, however, did not liberate EU policy-making from the strategic calculations made by individual Member States, and it left—as before—EU regulation exposed to the pressures of inter-State socio-economic rivalries (McGee and Weatherill 1990; Dehousse 1992).

According to Garrett's (1992) classic analysis of inter-State cooperation in the context of the EU internal market, the Member States define their participation in market integration on the basis of its benefits, which are supposed to be mutually available for each participant, as well as its domestic, predominantly shorter-term political costs that may arise from the negative impacts of open markets and cross-border competition on national industries and on particular segments of society. Their commitment depends fundamentally on whether—having regard to the state, the performance and the needs of the national economy and society—the benefits of progressing with market integration surpass the costs of participation, and, in parallel, on whether the social, economic and political costs of limiting market integration, or of keeping market integration limited, remain tolerable and manageable for national governments. The benefits expected by national governments are usually confined to the national territory, such as maintaining the competitive advantage of a key national industry, or attracting incoming foreign investment; however, the European internal market may also offer cross-border advantages, such as providing a springboard for national goods and services to achieve global competitiveness, or elevating national champions to global relevance. The plural nature of potential benefits, which may arise from the furthering of market integration for a national economy, entails that the preferences of national governments may oscillate—depending on what industrial interests they can afford to ignore—between common high-standard regulation and much lower intensity interventions in national policy (Garrett 1995).

These conditions are hardly ideal for the implementation of the EU's ambitiously framed technology sovereignty policy. Considering that the Member States are characterised by divergent levels and trajectories of economic and technological development, it does not seem likely that they will abandon their usual strategies and will act united in introducing, as proposed by the EU technology sovereignty framework, a homogenous cross-border regulation of technologies that are capable of changing the economic and social fortunes of individual countries.[19] It is similarly unlikely that they will be able to agree on the required level of European level centralisation

[19] In the 1980s, the Member States had powerful incentives for cooperation and common action towards liberalising trade among themselves. Their national economies had grown interdependent, strategies of protectionism and neo-protectionism had been exhausted, and they had to increase their competitiveness at the global level. Nevertheless, they disagreed significantly on the desirable model, and without the institutional changes introduced in the Single European Act, which enabled the large Member States to dominate the agenda, common policy-making would have stalled. See Garrett and Weingast (1993).

by means of common technology regulation, and that they will not be aiming to keep the relevant regulatory and administrative competences at national level. Also, if the internal market's legal harmonisation competence is used to adopt the high-standard regulatory measures desired in technology sovereignty policy, which in practice is the only available legislative competence in the EU, there are significant practical obstacles to regulation. The most general impediment is that the logic of protecting the EU's technological sovereignty as a collective virtue and a common objective is arguably incompatible with the logic of regulatory harmonisation in the internal market, which is supposed to be restricted to the more confined task of levelling out regulatory differences among the Member States.[20] Furthermore, although the competence regulated in Article 114 TFEU has some functional flexibility (Weatherill 2006, 2012), its use to adopt regulatory measures remains limited to the regulation of the risks and risk impacts of technologies that are relevant for the placing of products and services in the European market. The strategic aim of promoting a particular techno-social order for European countries and their economies—as put forward by the objective of technology sovereignty—may in fact be beyond the scope of that limited regulatory competence.

The distortion of the regulatory strategy pursued in EU policy, when measures are enacted in internal market harmonisation competences under Article 114 TFEU subject to the particular dynamics of decision-making in this policy area among the Member States, has been extensively explored in the context on EU biomedical technology regulation. The central issue examined in this regard was that the EU—as made sure by its Member States—does not have a general competence to regulate the market, including the specific harms and hazards of technologies. Rather, it needs to rely on the functionally limited and therefore less versatile competences under Article 114 TFEU, which then leads to regulation that is limited in its scope, nature and substance. As analysed by Flear (2017),[21] technology regulation using internal market competences, which entails a centralisation of the "notion of risk" at the European level, tends to prioritise certain social, economic, moral etc. harms or hazards, and marginalise and obscure others, depending on the risk concept embraced by the EU measure in question. The EU measure adopted may (therefore) also ignore alternative understandings of risks, as well as alternative framings of technology regulation. As a core criticism, Flear (2017) argued that measures adopted in internal market harmonisation competences rely on the trade- and consumer-focussed concept of product safety to regulate technological risks, which not only limits the scope

[20] The basic aims of the internal market are creating a level-playing field and maintaining equal conditions of competition among national economies, which are contradicted by technology sovereignty aims, such as the promotion of certain technology champions or the favouring of technology choices that benefit certain Member States and disadvantage others.

[21] He accepted that the EU acting in the framework of the internal market has genuine "regulatory capacity and efficacy" both *ex ante* and *ex post* to "centralise" "the harms or hazards relating to product safety" as a particular risk posed by new technologies (Flear 2017).

of (risk) regulation, but also excludes debates on and contestations of the relevant "norms, values, and ends".[22]

Flear (2017) also pointed out that the earlier mentioned focus on product safety, as an evident limitation of EU technology regulation, narrows down the "meaning and framing of technological risk" in EU measures, covering basically risks in product development and marketing that are relevant for the freedom of movement and fair competition in the internal market. This is an evident consequence of the use of Article 114 TFEU competences that are available to address the uncoordinated and therefore divergent regulation of technological risks based on particular national risk profiles that fragment the EU internal market. Therefore, technology regulation adopted under Article 114 TFEU is generally prevented from addressing the broadest range of harms and hazards of a given technology, and is generally shaped and directed to enable attaining the EU's socio-economic "pragmatic priorities and aims" expressed in the internal market (and not a different or broader set of aims). Flear (2017), nevertheless, also made the important point that the actual measures adopted in internal market competences provide evidence of a less limited approach to technology regulation. The relevant EU measures address a broad range of risks (risk impacts, risk levels, risk types, as well as harms and hazards pertaining to risk) suggesting the implementation of a broader regulatory objective than just the integration of the European markets. If the Member States are able to reach an agreement in decision-making based on their respective interests and visions, internal market harmonisation measures may in fact be put to the service of realising the broader objective of creating an internal market that sustains a competitive economy and society based on innovation and technological progress.

5 The EU's AI Act

The EU's proposal (European Commission 2021) for an 'Artificial Intelligence Act' (AI Act) —as made apparent in its explanatory memorandum and by the legislative text itself—pursues a busy, multi-tiered agenda for regulation. The AI Act makes it explicit that its provisions aim to regulate the technology (the cohort of relevant technologies) and its (their) applications on the basis of at least two distinct frames of regulation. The most evident frame is the market, in particular the integrated European market for AI systems, as manifested in the central objective of the measure to regulate by introducing the necessary common European product safety rules in the development of AI systems for the market, as well as their placing on and use in the market. The other, intimately related regulatory frame of the AI Act is the

22 Flear (2017) also claimed that EU technology regulation in internal market competences is aligned to the "market-oriented norms, values, and rationalities" of EU market integration. See further the assessment that the narrow framing of risk in EU health technologies regulation is the result of the functional limitation of the available EU competences, which then leads to "lop-sided" regulation addressing risks in certain domains and ignoring others (Farrell 2017).

protection of European values and fundamental rights, which is considered an indispensable condition for the availability of AI systems in Europe's integrated market. As a further objective latched onto the regulation of the safety and the fundamental rights risks of the technology and its applications, the measure—by implementing its particular agenda of risk regulation—is supposed to secure Europe's politically highly valued sovereignty in the technological domain. The AI Act interprets technology sovereignty in harmony with the earlier explained general definition in EU policy. As part of this interpretation, which also influences its general regulatory approach, it proposes in particular that a balance is established between the parallel priorities of making sure that the technology is available in Europe and of subjecting the technology to adequate controls. Believing that such a balance is attainable, the legislative proposal expresses that the AI Act follows a balanced regulatory approach. In other words, the measure, having regard to their precisely identified "risks and problems", introduces only the minimum necessary and proportionate regulatory burdens on the technology and its applications.[23]

Following the market as its frame of regulation, the AI Act defines as its central objective the regulation of the risks of AI systems as products or product components (the risks of products and services making use of AI technologies and of stand-alone AI systems) by introducing common rules applicable throughout the EU. It also internalises the traditional rationale of internal market harmonisation measures that the introduction of these common regulatory standards benefits market operators in the internal market and enable cross-border trade for the products and services in question. The explanatory memorandum of the AI Act specifies further its market-focussed objectives. According to it, the measure aims specifically to ensure that the technology placed on the EU market is safe, the applicable EU product safety measures are effectively applied and enforced, the regulatory environment is sufficiently certain to facilitate investment and innovation, and the EU market for AI systems achieves sufficient integration, and the fragmentation of the market, in particular by means of unilateral national restrictions and controls on the technology, is prevented. As declared by the legislative proposal, the AI Act's product safety objective, in harmony with its general approach of balanced and proportionate regulation, has been tailored to address specific risks that are associated with certain uses of the technology. It therefore introduces a differentiated regulation of AI systems that distinguishes between prohibited AI technologies (prohibited AI practices), high-risk AI systems subject to horizontal mandatory requirements, and (non-high risk) AI technologies subject to minimum regulatory (transparency) obligations.

This is the regulatory framework, as shaped by the earlier mentioned aim of creating a balance between technology availability and necessary technology controls, that is supposed to respond also to the regulatory frame of protecting EU values and fundamental rights. The AI Act makes it clear that its provisions

[23] The minimum regulation of the AI Act includes a "proportionate and effective" set of standards that are based on "a clearly defined risk-based approach", which is used to "tailor the type and content" of the standards "to the intensity and scope of the risks that AI systems can generate".

address both safety risks and risks affecting EU values and fundamental rights.[24] Its explanatory memorandum mentions specifically that AI systems are expected to comply with the applicable legal rules, which are the rules regulating product safety as well as Union rights and values, and allow their effective enforcement. As in the case of safety risks, the regulation of risks on Union values and rights is subjected to the promise of proportionate, minimum necessary and precisely targeted regulation, "which does not create "unnecessary restrictions to trade". The proposal defines such regulation as "legal intervention [...] tailored to those concrete situations where there is a justified cause for concern or where such concern can be reasonably anticipated in the near future".[25] The measure therefore does not treat the protection of values and rights as an absolute and automatic priority, but considers it instead in the context of its general policy proposition of balancing between the interests of technology availability and control. The technology area where values and rights are given evident priority is the category of prohibited AI (practices) as their prohibition stems—according to the AI Act—from such technologies (practices) contradicting "Union values of respect for human dignity, freedom, equality, democracy and the rule of law and Union fundamental rights, including the right to non-discrimination, data protection and privacy and the rights of the child."

In the case of high-risk AI systems, which stand in the focus of the AI Act's regulatory efforts, it is much less visible—compared to prohibited AI—how the protection of values and fundamental rights has been integrated into the regulatory framework. The relevant provisions of the AI Act are dominated by considerations of product safety, as manifested in particular in the reliance on existing non-AI specific EU product safety legislation as essential components of the measure's multi-layered regulatory structure. Further, it is not readily apparent what risks to values and fundamental rights are addressed and where the balance is struck between the interests of legal controls based on values and rights and ensuring that the technology is available in Europe. Articles 6 and 7, which establish the framework for the classification of AI systems as a high-risk, refer to both "risk of harm to the health and safety" and the "risk of adverse impact on fundamental rights". However, while the assessment of safety risks can fall back on a detailed, objective and arguably precise regulatory and institutional framework, no similar arrangement has been provided for the assessment of risks to Union values and fundamental rights.[26] Moreover, the horizontal

[24] The preamble of the AI Act clarifies that harms to values and rights can be both material and immaterial. It also claims that the core regulatory provisions of the AI Act determining the "common normative standards" (the mandatory requirements) for the category of high-risk AI systems, which are essentially technical requirements, should also be "consistent with the Charter of fundamental rights of the European Union". They should also be non-discriminatory and in line with the EU's international trade commitments.

[25] It is explained that the introduction for both types of risks of minimum necessary regulation makes sure that regulation does not unduly constrain or hinder technological development or otherwise disproportionately increase the cost of placing AI solutions on the market.

[26] See the Chapter by Grozdanovski in this volume criticising the fundamental rights frame of the AI Act as failing to quantify what exactly will merit protection.

mandatory requirements prescribed[27] for high-risk AI systems seem to cover objective technological risks only, and not risks of adverse impact on European values and fundamental rights. The addressing of the latter type of risks is not excluded; however, without a transparent and readily available risk assessment framework, it is difficult to see how their "unacceptability" in regard "to important Union public interests" and their "significant harmful impact" will be determined.[28]

The AI Act therefore faces a number of unresolved issues, the most relevant being the apparent imbalance between its detailed rules regarding risks in product development and marketing and its much less developed regulation of risks relating to European values and rights. It is as though the measure's regulatory content does not match its ambitious agenda of establishing an adequate balance between ensuring the access of European industry and society to the technology and making sure that the technology is developed and functions "according to Union values, fundamental rights and principles". Essentially, the AI Act is a rather orthodox measure of internal market product safety regulation determining minimal requirements for market access in the EU. For the same reason, the measure also seems to contradict its other ambition that the global leadership of Europe in AI will be secured by fostering the development of AI that is "secure, trustworthy and ethical".[29] Its current rather limited regime for the protection of values and rights, which involves the prohibition of certain AI applications and an unstructured framework for the adverse impacts of high-risk AI on values and rights, may be diluted further when it is brought before the Member States in the Council. Arguably, the limitations of the AI Act and how its rules have been distanced from its ambitious regulatory agenda are both consequences of the particular circumstances of EU internal market decision-making. The Member States are likely to agree on traditional issues of product safety that are necessary for the operation of the internal market. A more robust common regulatory framework may be too costly or risky from the perspective of their particular interests and regulatory needs. They also need to be convinced that the AI Act can be adopted lawfully under the functionally limited competences available in Article 114 TFEU. From the perspective of technology sovereignty, which is the final objective of the measure, this in an unsatisfactory situation. The AI Act seems unprepared to internalise the complex dilemmas arising from technology sovereignty and its regulatory limitations prevent it from providing correspondingly complex responses to them.

[27] These are regulatory compliance, a risk and a quality management system, quality of data and data governance, technical documentation and record-keeping, transparency and the provision of information to users, human oversight, robustness, accuracy and cybersecurity.

[28] The preamble of the AI Act tries to qualify the assessment by stating that "the extent of the adverse impact" on fundamental rights "is of particular relevance".

[29] The explanatory memorandum of the AI Act states that the laying down of the harmonised legal requirements of trustworthy AI will strengthen "Europe's competitiveness and industrial basis in AI", enable the protection of the "Union's digital sovereignty", and will empower the EU to use its "tools and regulatory powers to shape global riles and standards".

6 Conclusions

Achieving European sovereignty is a central target for EU technology and other related policies. The EU's active policy on AI and its gradually developing regulatory framework have also internalised the notion and have made the particular regulatory strategy devised in the context of the EU's understanding of technology sovereignty part of its toolkit. However, the EU's approach, which insists on a balanced response addressing the components of a generously framed policy framework, seems rather schematic, as if aiming to reduce the complexity of the dilemmas inherent in technology sovereignty. The EU's chosen regulatory strategy of introducing high-standard, value-driven regulation of technology markets appears to overlook these dilemmas and also how these dilemmas may impact decision-making among the Member States in the Council over common technology regulation that interferes directly with national industrial and economic policy. The EU's novel AI Act is representative of this regulatory strategy. It was assigned a multifaceted regulatory agenda, and it is supposed to deliver its different objectives while maintaining a balance between them, in particular by introducing the minimum necessary and proportionate regulatory standards. However, despite its ambitions, the AI Act reads as a fairly conventional internal market product safety harmonisation measure. Although it makes recognisable steps towards the protection of EU values and fundamental rights, its handling of risks related to this area has remained limited and low-impact. The AI Act's formulation raises doubts about its ability to deliver on its technology sovereignty objective, not only because the EU's ambition to regulate itself an autonomous position in the global technological race is itself problematic. As an internal market harmonisation measure, it is prevented by both the legislative competences available and the politics of internal market regulation from adequately realising more generic strategic priorities.

References

ASD: Aerospace and Defence Industries Association of Europe (2020) Industry considerations on technological sovereignty. ASD Concept Paper. https://www.asd-europe.org/index.php/industry-considerations-on-technological-sovereignty-concept-paper/

Bauer M, Erixon F (2020) Europe's quest for technology sovereignty: opportunities and pitfalls. ECIPE Occasional Paper. https://ecipe.org/publications/europes-technology-sovereignty/

Breton T (2019) Questionnaire to the commissioner-designate for the Internal Market, Thierry Breton. https://www.europarl.europa.eu/resources/library/media/20191113RES66410/20191113RES66410.pdf

Calderaro A, Blumfelde S (2022) Artificial intelligence and EU security: the false promise of digital sovereignty. Eur Secur 31(3):415–434

Chrétien J, Drouard E (2022) European technological sovereignty. Renaissance Numérique. https://www.renaissancenumerique.org/en/publications/european-technological-sovereignty/

Crespi F, Caravella S, Menghini M, Salvatori C (2021) European technology sovereignty: an emerging framework for policy strategy. Intereconomics 56(6):348–354

Craig P (2002) The evolution of the single market. In: Barnard C, Scott J (eds) The law of the Single European Market. Hart

Csernatoni R (2021) The EU's rise as a defense technological power: from strategic autonomy to technological sovereignty. Carnegie Europe Paper. https://carnegieeurope.eu/2021/08/12/eu-s-rise-as-defense-technological-power-from-strategic-autonomy-to-technological-sovereignty-pub-85134

Dehousse R (1992) Integration v. regulation? On the dynamics of regulation in the European Community. Journal of Common Market Studies 30(4):383–402

Edler J, Blind K, Frietsch R, Kimpeler S, Kroll H, Lerch C, Reiss T, Roth F, Schubert T, Schuler J, Walz R (2020) Technology sovereignty: from demand to concept. Fraunhofer ISI. https://www.isi.fraunhofer.de/content/dam/isi/dokumente/publikationen/technology_sovereignty.pdf

European Commission (2018) Artificial intelligence for Europe. COM(2018) 237 final

European Commission (2020a) Shaping Europe's digital future. COM(2020) 67 final

European Commission (2020b) White Paper on Artificial intelligence—a European approach to excellence and trust. COM(2020) 65 final

European Commission (2020c) A European strategy for data. COM(2020)66 final

European Commission (2021) Proposal for a regulation of the European Parliament and of the Council laying down harmonised rules of artificial intelligence (Artificial Intelligence Act). COM(2021) 206 final

European Council (2022) Versailles Declaration, 11 March 2022. https://www.consilium.europa.eu/media/54773/20220311-versailles-declaration-en.pdf

Farrell A-M (2017) Risk, legitimacy, and EU regulation of health technologies. In: Cremona M (ed) New technologies and EU law. Oxford University Press

Flear M (2017) Regulating new technologies: EU internal market law, risk, and socio-technical order. In: Cremona M (ed) New technologies and EU law. Oxford University Press

Garrett G (1992) International cooperation and institutional choice: the European Community's internal market. Int Organ 46(2):533–560

Garrett G (1995) The politics of legal integration in the European Union. Int Organ 49(1):171–181

Garrett G, Weingast B (1993) Ideas, interests, and institutions: constructing the European Community's internal market. In Goldstein J, Keohane RO (eds) Ideas and foreign policy: beliefs, institutions, and political change. Cornell University Press

Ilves L, Osula A-M (2020) The technological sovereignty dilemma—and how new technology can offer a way out. Eur Cybersecur J 6(1):24–35

Juncker J-C (2018) State of the Union 2018: the hour of European sovereignty. https://ec.europa.eu/info/sites/info/files/soteu2018-speech_en_0.pdf

McGee A, Weatherill S (1990) The evolution of the Single Market—harmonisation or liberalisation. Mod Law Rev 53(5):578–596

Pelkmans J (1977) European integration, methods and economic analysis. Longman

Pelkmans J (1987) The new approach to technical harmonization and standardization. J Common Market Stud 25(3):249–269

Tolstukhina A (2022) EU technological sovereignty and its limits. https://valdaiclub.com/a/valdai-papers/eu-technological-sovereignty-and-its-limits/

VDE: Association for Electrical, Electronic and Information Technologies (2013) Technology sovereignty: methodology and recommendations. VDE Position Paper. https://www.vde.com/resource/blob/2013656/66f71138ba34b7b3ad0e2aa248b71abd/vde-position-paper-technological-sovereignty-data.pdf

von der Leyen U (2019a) Speech by president-elect von der Leyen in the European Parliament plenary when presenting her College of Commissioners and their programme. https://ec.europa.eu/commission/presscorner/detail/en/speech_19_6408

von der Leyen U (2019b) Political guidelines for the next European Commission 2019–2024. https://ec.europa.eu/info/sites/info/files/political-guidelines-next-commission_en_0.pdf
Weatherill S (2006) Supply of and demand for Internal Market regulation: strategies, preferences and interpretation. In: Nic Shuibhne N (ed) Regulating the Internal Market. Elgar
Weatherill S (2012) Maximum versus minimum harmonization: choosing between unity and diversity in the search for the soul of the Internal Market. In: Nic Shuibhne N, Gormley L (eds) From Single Market to Economic Union: essays in memory of John A. Usher. Oxford University Press

The Ontological Congruency in the EU's Data Protection and Data Processing Legislation: The (Formally) Risk-Based and (Actually) Value/Rights-Oriented Method of Regulation in the AI Act

Ljupcho Grozdanovski

Abstract This Chapter explores the idea of *axiological congruency* between (ethical) values and the EU law on new technologies, with a focus on the 'normative kinship' between the GDPR and the AI Act. Such a comparative analysis is appropriate considering that the GDPR provided the 'normative template' for the design of the AI Act, as the recently enacted, ambitious, horizontal regulation, seeking to foster progress by 'engineering' trust in AI, while at the same time upholding a high standard of fundamental rights protection. Tracing the inception of the AI Act to the HLEG's Guidelines, this Chapter argues that the four principles of ethics (respect of human autonomy, avoidance of harm, fairness and explicability) are axiologically rooted in the principle of human dignity, given that the fundamental threat of AI systems is that of 'moral opacity'—a feature of highly complex automated processes which are often hidden from view for the average user. By seeking to safeguard human autonomy and agency (as key expressions of human dignity), the AI Act is 'axiologically congruent' with the GDPR, which also pursues the same goal through safeguards meant to shield off threats coming from various forms of personal data processing. Based on values similar to those underlying the GDPR, the AI Act nevertheless departs from the latter, in the way in which it translates values into law. As an admittedly risk-regulating instrument, it follows a logic of product safety, and is designed on the assumption that a high standard of fundamental rights protection can be achieved through technical safety standards, in particular those applied to the so-called high-risk systems. In assuming this, the AI Act is open to criticism, because it places the burden of fundamental rights protection primarily—though not exclusively—on market operators who are presumed to understand those standards and apply them correctly. For example, transparency, combined with human oversight, is, without question, an important principle (and standard) to apply, but its technical feasibility (i.e., actually programming AI systems where human oversight is possible *throughout their life cycles*) might not be as feasible as the AI Act assumes

L. Grozdanovski (✉)
FNRS/University of Liège, Liège, Belgium
e-mail: lgrozdanovski@uliege.be

M. Varju and K. Mezei (eds.), *The Challenges of Artificial Intelligence for Law in Europe*, Data Science, Machine Intelligence, and Law 6,
https://doi.org/10.1007/978-3-031-86813-9_5

it will be. The Chapter concludes that the implementation of the AI Act and the case law that will emerge in connection to it will bring important insight on whether the approach of 'standardizing values' for the purpose of protecting fundamental rights was, indeed, the adequate regulatory route to take, in lieu of that—showcased by the GDPR—of protecting fundamental rights by creating individual entitlements.

1 Introduction

Artificial intelligence (AI)[1] has become a prominent topic in recent savant and regulatory discourse, namely in the European Union. Curiously, the 'Pavlovian reflex' of national, European and international regulators was to engage in a quest for principles of ethics that would shape subsequent, binding instruments.

This 'ethics first' approach is, in many ways, not surprising: industrial revolutions have often been associated with ethical challenges, as each generation of new technologies posed (or was seen as posing) various kinds of threat to human welfare and wellbeing.[2] But AI is thought to be different from its predecessors, since it impacts the world in new, unprecedented ways. This impact is largely due to the fact that AI constitutes a class of intelligent rather than automated devices, 'intelligence' here being understood as the capacity to predict and problem-solve in a context with fully or partially unknown variables.[3] The growing human-AI co-existence/co-dependence/co-acting has incited scholarship to pinpoint the various ways in which AI is likely to change the world and its existing paradigms. Though much can be said in this regard, our ambition in this introductory section is to explain why AI gave the incentive to revisit abstract (yet cardinal) concepts like the 'right' and 'good', in view of tailoring adequate normative responses to the AI phenomenon.

An insightful glimpse into the nature and scope of AI's real-life impact(s) can be detected in a relatively recent strand of social sciences scholarship which upholds the so-called *Anthropocene* thesis. Following the Holocene (the evolutionary epoch in

[1] For the purpose of this Chapter, we will use the definition of AI included in the EU HLEG's (High-Level Expert Group on AI) Ethics Guidelines (HLEG 2019): "software (and possible also hardware) systems designed by humans that, given a complex goal, act in the physical and digital dimension by perceiving their environment through data acquisition, interpreting the collected structured or unstructured data, reasoning on the knowledge, or processing the information, derived from this data and deciding the best action(s) to take to achieve the given goal. AI systems can either use symbolic rules or learn a numerical model, and they can also adapt their behaviour by analysing how the environment is affected by their previous actions." This definition is, *mutatis mutandis*, taken over in the content of Article 3(1) in the EU's AI Act (European Parliament 2024).

[2] One of the topical examples of the threats that new technologies raise is the replacement of human labour, often triggering strong human resistance to the use of those technologies. The so-called Luddite movement can be cited as an example here, concerning an organisation of English textile workers who, fearing their replacement by the advances of industrialisation, destroyed textile machinery. For a comment on this movement, as an illustration of perceptions of, and reactions to threats caused by new technologies, see McGowan and Geobey (2020).

[3] See Mahmoud Zadeh et al. (2019).

which it was humans who adjusted to their shifting environments), 'Anthropocene' is the epoch where the adjustment effort is reversed: it is the environment that makes the adjustment to individual and collective human action (or 'impairment'). Biber (2017) for example highlighted three key essential features of the Anthropocene: 1. humans are a substantial, if not a dominant driver of a wide range of global systems such as the atmosphere, oceans, global biodiversity, and cycling of important elements; 2. human impairments are often the product of the aggregation of large numbers of relatively small activities (even individual actions); 3. there is a substantial increase in the speed with which new human impairments of natural systems arise and expand, in large part because of the rapid increase in global technological change. For Biber (2017), these 'human impairments' have affected and will continue to affect the ways in which our societies function, gradually reshaping the role of law which—Biber predicts—will be called to strike a careful balance between "protecting individual liberties and managing impacts that individual actions have on society."[4]

This 'fine-tuned' balance between individual liberties and the (potentially negative) actions on society, would be achieved through several strategies namely, mitigation, adaptation, restoration, substitution and doing nothing (Biber 2017). It is useful to keep these in mind—namely (risk) mitigation and adaptation[5]—because they are *mutatis mutandis* echoed in the strategies that regulators (in particular the European Commission) considered in selecting the approach best suited toward the regulation of AI.

Against the backdrop of the Anthropocene scholarship,[6] AI gives a telling example of a specific kind of human intervention that the world should now adjust to. The 'impairment' here comes from the fact that the portion of nature that the human genius has found a way to artificially mimic (and reshape?) is... *human* nature (rather, aspects of human rationality and agency). This has incited part of scholarship to qualify AI technologies as *actants*: agency-apt entities, capable of making decisions with concrete consequences, much like their 'natural' counterparts i.e., human actors.[7] In this context, Floridi suggested that AI—more so than previous technologies—has the ability to affect the world *ontologically*. In a comment of his

---

[4] This has been the stance in connection to AI technologies which quickly became "overwhelming for governments" because law, as it currently stands, does not allow us to fully anticipate, and protect against AI's negative or undesired effects, Weaver (2019).

[5] For Biber (2017), 'risk mitigation' involves "efforts to reduce human impairments of global resources" whereas 'adaptation' involves "societal efforts to reduce or eliminate the negative impacts caused by human impairments of global resources without reducing the activities or impairments that cause those impacts." These trends of reducing a risk and adaptation to risks (by essentially defining a level of acceptability of risks) is one of the features of the EU's AI regulation which we will discuss further in this Chapter.

[6] As put by Biber (2017), "there are causal connections between some of the most trivial everyday activities and the harms that occur across the planet. It is hard to see how most individuals would have foreseen the wide range of harms that would result from everyday actions in the Anthropocene or the wide range of people around the world harmed by those actions."

[7] The postulate here is that there is no absolute qualitative distinction between humans and nonhumans, both being understood to be actors ('actants') i.e., "any entity (defined) by an association profile of other entities called actors", Watkin (2016).

work, he reasserted two of his pivotal concepts that capture the tech-induced shifts of reality: the so-called *infosphere* and *re-ontologising*. *Infosphere*—a *pendant* of the biosphere—denotes "the whole informational environment constituted by all informational entities" (Floridi 2012). It is an environment comparable to, but different from, cyberspace "since it also includes offline and analogue spaces of information" (Floridi 2012).

Re-ontologising refers to a "very radical form of (re)engineering (…) that not only designs, constructs or structures a system (e.g., a company, a machine or some artefacts) anew, but one that also fundamentally transforms its intrinsic nature, that is, its ontology or essence (…) nano-technologies and biotechnologies are not merely re-engineering but actually re-ontologizing our world" (Floridi 2012). This 're-ontologising' of the world (and of humans as a prominent part thereof) is not necessarily negative: in some of his more recent work, Floridi et al. (2018) suggested that AI can, in fact, be a contributor to, and a catalyser for the social good.[8] As is often the case with new technologies, they are never 'all good' and 'all bad' as their advantages (e.g., an increase in GDP, overall increase of people's levels of education[9]) often come accompanied by threats (e.g., replacement of human labour by AI systems, data/privacy-violations etc.).

In sum, if history has taught us anything, it is that technological progress yields generally positive results, but comes at a price of *accepting* a series of unwanted consequences.[10] Biber's (2017) intuition is confirmed here: technologies push us to redefine the ethical concepts of 'the good' and 'the right,' placing on the law the (heavy) burden of striking the careful balance between individual liberties and the undesired effects that AI technologies are likely to have.

The incentive to push toward more AI innovation and use (as a key feature of what the European Commission labelled as the *ecosystem of excellence* (European Commission, 2020)[11] needed to be balanced against the guarantees of individual rights protection, thus warranting an increased level of *trust* in AI technologies, as

[8] They posited that ethics enables organisations to take advantage of "the social value that AI enables" (Floridi et al. 2018).

[9] On the 'upskilling' potential of new technologies, see Acemoglu (2002) and Autor and Salomons (2018).

[10] We allude here to a level of acceptability of risks, which we will discuss in Sub-Sect. 3.2.

[11] The EU White Paper on AI (European Commission 2020) proposed "to build an ecosystem of excellence that can support the development and uptake of AI across the EU economy and public administration, there is a need to step up action at multiple levels." These 'levels' translate to several actions which include: working with the Members (through a revised version of their Coordinated plan published in 2018); facilitating the creation of excellence and testing centres that combine European, national and private investments; establish and support through the advanced skills pillar of the Digital Europe Programme networks of leading universities and higher education institutes to attract the best professors and scientists and offer world-leading masters programmes in AI; focus on SMEs (through at least one digital innovation hub per Member State and launching a pilot scheme to provide equity financing for innovative developments in AI); partnership with the private sector (through private partnership in AI, data and robotics to combine efforts, ensure coordination of research and innovation in AI, collaborate with other public–private partnerships in Horizon Europe); promoting the adoption of AI by the public sector (through open and transparent sector dialogues giving priority to healthcare, rural administration and public service operators in order to

well as in the legal instruments designed to regulate them (naturally, this was the main feature of what the European Commission qualified as the *ecosystem of trust* (European Commission 2020).[12] To be operative, this excellence/trust diptych needed solid axiological anchoring so that the excellence in technological development would not be pursued to the detriment of trust that the law would—ideally—provide the guarantees against subtly intrusive (e.g., manipulative[13]), privacy-disregarding AI systems. In this landscape, the turn toward ethics becomes clearer because ethics (as the conceptual realm of 'the good') enables organisations to both take advantage of the social value that AI enables and anticipate, avoid or minimise costly mistakes (Floridi et al. 2018).

This ethics-first-law-second trend has certainly been the hallmark of the EU's regulatory trajectory in the field of AI. In 2015, the European Commission published its Digital Single Market Strategy (European Commission 2015) which contains a number of key normative actions integrated in three key pillars: better access for consumers and business to online goods and services; creating the right conditions for digital networks and services to flourish and maximising the growth potential of the European Digital Economy. Already in the Strategy, data, and by extension data processing technologies, were seen as "a catalyst for economic growth, innovation and digitalisation across all economic sectors." The Strategy also cautioned that "businesses and consumers still do not feel confident enough to adopt cross-border cloud services for storing or processing data, because of concerns relating to security, compliance with fundamental rights and data protection more generally." The GDPR (European Parliament and Council 2016) was meant to resolve many of the rights-related issues in connection to personal data processing. However, it soon became apparent that many of the 'new,' AI-related issues (agency, liability and fault, opacity etc.) fell beyond that instrument's scope.

The EU institutions, like the European Parliament and the European Council began to highlight the need for a European reflection on ethical standards that would apply to high-level data processing as well as to robotics and AI (European Parliament 2015; European Council 2017). In 2018, the European Commission published the AI for Europe Communication (European Commission 2018), which includes a number of actions meant to ensure Europe's 'lead' in the so-called AI race[14] but also lay

---

present an action plan to facilitate development, experimentation and adoption); securing access to data and computing infrastructures and international cooperation."

[12] In connection to the ecosystem of trust, the White Paper (European Commission 2020) referred to the seven requirements (discussed further in this Chapter) identified in the HLEG's Ethics Guidelines (HLEG 2019): human agency and oversight; technical robustness and safety; privacy and data governance; transparency; diversity, non-discrimination and fairness; societal and environmental well-being and accountability.

[13] We allude to Article 5(a) AI Act (European Parliament 2024) which creates an *ex officio* ban to place on the market AI systems that deploy subliminal techniques beyond a person's consciousness "in order to materially distort a person's behaviour in a manner that causes or is likely to cause that person or another person physical or psychological harm."

[14] The Communication stresses the possibility to 'capitalize' on world-class researchers, labs and startups, common rules in the Digital Single Market, wealth of industrial, research and public sector data.

down appropriate ethical and legal frameworks, "based on the Union's values and in line with the Charter of Fundamental Rights."[15] The drafting of ethics guidelines was foretold in the Communication for the purpose of addressing a variety of issues ranging from the future of work, fairness, safety and security to social inclusion and algorithmic transparency. In 2018, the European Commission did indeed constitute an independent high-level expert group on AI (the HLEG), which included experts from the most relevant fields related to AI (law, philosophy and computer science). In 2019, the HLEG famously published its Ethics Guidelines (HLEG 2019), followed, in 2020, by the Assessment List for Trustworthy AI (ALTAI) (HLEG 2020), which laid out seven basic requirements, discussed further in this Chapter.

In 2020, the European Parliament issued a Resolution (European Parliament 2020), recommending the European Commission to submit a legislative proposal on a framework of ethical aspects of AI. Following this Resolution, the Commission made public a proposal for a regulation laying down harmonised rules on AI (the AI Act) (European Commission 2021), which—in the Commission's own words—follows a "proportionate risk-based approach" by proposing "a single future-proof definition of AI" and by suggesting a four-level taxonomy (minimal, non-high, high, unacceptable), with corresponding standards and obligations.

The shift from ethics to law in the EU's regulatory trajectory seems to be characterised by a general-to-specific transition: the initial normative quest was focused on values and principles of ethics (by definition, general in content) which the AI Act 'converted' into binding, *specific* (and ideally practicable) legal standards and duties. The cursory overview of the stages of that 'shift' allows us to raise two questions: first, which (logical, axiological, historical, legislative…) referents were used to select the ethical values that would subsequently shape the EU's regulation of AI? This question will be addressed in Sect. 2. Second, there is the issue of their normative translation: did the AI Act give an adequate legal translation of the content and objectives of the selected values? This issue will be raised in Sect. 3.

2 The Selection of Values as Cornerstones of the EU's Data-Processing and AI Regulation

In mainstream regulatory discourse, *algorithmic opacity* is often mentioned as the root cause of the many and varied harms AI systems are capable of causing. That human beings require protection from those harms is beyond doubt, but an open question still remains: which aspects of the human *persona* deserved reinforced safeguards against autonomous, opaque and potentially harmful decisions and predictions? In the EU, the principle selected to act as primary 'axiological shield' against AI opacity was

[15] The features of these frameworks include high standards in terms of product safety and liability, rules on network and information systems security and stronger rules on the protection of personal data, enhanced trust and explainability of AI systems.

human dignity (Sub-Sect. 2.1) which—as the HLEG's Ethics Guidelines show—was particularised into four principles of ethics, which defined the normative benchmark against which the AI Act was subsequently designed (Sub-Sect. 2.2).

2.1 Human Dignity as Axiological 'Anchor' of the EU's Regulation on Data Processing and AI...

Defining values is no small feat, given their inherent importance but also indeterminacy. For the purpose of this Chapter, the concept of value will be defined in reference to Brey (2012) who noted that "values depend on valuation. Valuation is the act of valuing something, or finding it valuable, and to find something valuable is to find it good in some way. (...) Those things that people find valuable that are both ideal and general, like justice and generosity, are called values, with disvalues being those general qualities considered to be bad or evil, like injustice and avarice." Values thus correspond to "*idealized qualities or conditions in the world that people find good*. For example, the value of justice corresponds to some idealized, general condition of the world in which all persons are treated fairly and rewarded rightly." In addition, Brey (2012) distinguished values from norms, which he defined as "rules that prescribe which kinds of actions or state of affairs are forbidden, obligatory or allowed."

Brey (2012) highlights a *consequentialist (outcome-focused) approach* to the selection of the values that eventually find their way into positive law. These 'embedded-value norms' are characterised by "a special kind of *built-in consequence*. They are tendencies to effectuate norms by bringing it about that the environment behaves or is organized according to the norm." The author gives the example of the non-acceptance of online cookies: a web-browser can be set *not to accept* cookies from websites, thus enforcing the norm that websites should not collect information about their users. Digital artefacts (like AI) "thereby also promote the corresponding value, if any (e.g., privacy)."

The consequentialist perspective suggested by Brey (2012) provides a vantage point for our analysis of the so-called AI ethics, which essentially seeks to posit a normative understanding of 'the good' under the effect of sophisticated, data-processing technologies.[16] This allows us to raise two important questions. First, which *existing* principles of ethics can be referred to in view of tailoring an 'updated' conception of 'the good'? Second, how can that conception be particularised through a set of specific values?

[16] The HLEG Ethics Guidelines (HLEG 2019) provide: "AI Ethics is a sub-field of applied ethics, focusing on the ethical issues raised by the development, deployment and use of AI. Its central concern is to identify how AI can advance or raise concerns to the good life of individuals whether in terms of quality of life, or human autonomy and freedom necessary for a democratic society."

The first question essentially deals with conceptualising the *desired* effects AI can (or even should) generate.[17] To map those out, Floridi et al. (2018) raised four key questions: by whom, how, where and when the positive and/or negative impact will be felt? These questions correspond to four components of a generic understanding of 'the good' which—arguably—includes (1) autonomous self-realisation; (2) the preservation of human agency; (3) the development of individual and societal capabilities and the fostering; and (4) enhancement of social cohesion. The realisation of each of these aspects—Floridi et al. argue—is largely conditioned by the *types of use* of intelligent systems which the authors placed in four categories: 'proper' use (directed at enhancing human potentialities), under-use (creating so-called opportunity costs); over-use and misuse (both of which generate risks for some type of harm). Though Floridi et al. espouse an optimistic view of AI[18] (as being more a catalyst of than a hindrance to 'the good'), they make an important point, shared by countless other studies, reports and regulatory strategies: AI per se is not the problem; *its use* however might be.

Although Floridi et al. (2018) suggested the key inquiries (by whom/how/when/where) that allow to methodologically frame the exploration of 'the good' in connection to AI, the problem is that, due to its continued innovation and development, AI is a somewhat unpredictable class of technologies, making it difficult to map out—in a set-in-stone kind of way—the totality of their unwanted or negative effects. In this context, we could—in a *reductionist* attempt—seek to define 'the good,' not positively (i.e., through its essential features) but negatively (i.e., through what may be viewed as the 'ultimate bad'). We posit here that a *negative effect* usually associated with AI is the *restriction of people's ability for self-determination.*[19] In the jargon of computer ethics, this threat is qualified as *moral opacity* that is, the attribute of operations of technological systems "that are very complex and difficult to understand for laypersons and that are often hidden from view for the average user" (Brey 2012).[20] These practices are 'morally opaque' because "they involve distant actions

[17] The issue of referents in ethics is relevant because, as stressed by Rességuier and Rodrigues (2020), principles of ethics are not ethics, but where ethics ultimately leads.

[18] "AI may enable self-realisation, by which we mean the ability for people to flourish in terms of their own characteristics, interests, potential abilities and skills, aspirations and life projects" (Floridi et al. 2018).

[19] The HLEG Ethics Guidelines (HLEG 2019) provide: "human beings should remain free to make decisions for themselves. This entails freedom from sovereign intrusion, but also requires intervention from government and non-governmental organisations to ensure that individuals or people at risk of exclusion have equal access to AI's benefits and opportunities, and "Human interacting with AI systems must be able to keep full and effective self-determination over themselves, and be able to partake in the democratic process. AI systems should not unjustifiably subordinate, coerce, deceive, manipulate, condition or herd humans. Instead, they should be designed to augment, complement and empower human cognitive, social and cultural skills."

[20] The EU General Data Protection Regulation (GDPR) (European Parliament and Council 2016) in its preamble (Recital (39)) alludes to the 'moral opacity' threat by stating that "natural persons *should be made aware of risks*, rules, safeguards and rights in relation to the processing of personal data and how to exercise their rights in relation to such processing."

over computer networks by system operators, providers, website owners and hackers and remain hidden from view from users and from the public at large" (Brey 2012).

To assert that new technologies can be morally opaque goes counter the long-standing idea that technology is per se ethically neutral (Brey 2012). However, practice reveals instances where AI *can be* morally opaque, by virtue of their ability to autonomously exert force or behaviour (Brey 2012). But ethics offers numerous values—justice, freedom, privacy, honesty...—that can be used to 'shield off' the threat of moral opacity (Brey, 2012). However, both the GDPR and the AI Act show us that the apex axiological referent in the quest for those values is the *principle of human dignity* because—as already mentioned—that which is most threatened by morally opaque, automated processes is, indeed, humans' ability to self-define (human autonomy) and capability to pursue personal and common goals (human flourishing). The human autonomy/dignity interrelationship can be explained by the fact that dignity is an *essentialist notion*, relating to the "the intrinsic and equal worth of each individual human being" (UNESCO 2021). Autonomy is the *instrumental pendant* of human dignity, implying freedom from constraint in the way in which a person asserts their individuality. The regulatory approach that developed based on the human dignity principle is the so-called *human-centrism* the goal of which is to precisely preserve *individual autonomy* as the "quintessence of human rights" and "a protection against State—or any other public or private—interference" (Mishra 2019).[21]

The problem here is that though cardinally important, human dignity remains conceptually unfathomable. Floridi (2021) noted this. Commenting on the axiological kinship between the GDPR and the AI Act,[22] he stressed that the latter "uses and anachronistic terminology to define this approach as 'human-centric' that is, as an approach that places humanity at the centre of technological development. Yet this is both trivially true and dangerously ambiguous." For Floridi (2021), the 'ambiguity' and 'triviality' of human-centrism stems from the fact "any technology, AI included, must be at the service of humanity, its values, and needs." In other words, human dignity *does* provide the ultimate referent for the pursuit of the common good in the age of AI and gives the *necessary orientation and impulse* regarding the guarantees and safeguards that AI regulatory frameworks should provide. But for human dignity to be a *workable benchmark* for the design of ethical and legal frameworks on AI, it needed to be 'broken down' into specific values that targeted the points on which

[21] In the HLEG's Ethics Guidelines (HLEG 2019), human-centrism is understood as a commitment to the use of AI in the service of humanity and the common good, with the goal of improving human welfare and freedom. In the GDPR (European Parliament and Council 2016), human centrism is understood as a 'mission' that the processing of personal data be designed "to serve mankind," operationalised through the protection of the right to data protection, but also through the other rights enshrined in the EU Charter of Fundamental Rights, such as the respect of private and family life, freedom of thought, conscience and religion, freedom of expression and information, freedom to conduct a business, the right to an effective remedy and to a fair trial, and cultural, religious and linguistic diversity (Preamble, Recital (4)).

[22] "from an ethical perspective the AI Act inherits the same foundational approach seen in the GDPR: it is based on protecting human dignity and fundamental rights", Floridi (2021).

protection from AI's moral opacity was to be established. This process of particularisation is the object of the second question, mentioned above. In the EU, it was the HLEG who seminally made the general-to-particular axiological leap.

2.2 … *Particularised in Principles of Ethics Meant to Shield Off 'Morally Opaque' Data-Processing Operations*

As proceduralists tell us,[23] the address of any ethical inquiry (like: what is justice?) does not require scientific discovery but a discursive context i.e., a forum where selected representatives can express their views in conditions of equal participation and deliberation.[24] Using deliberation to give answers to ethical questions is not a new idea in—what can be qualified as—the epistemology of ethics (Anderson 2020). Think of Habermasian discursive model (Habermas 1984)[25] or even Rawls' 'veil of ignorance' thought experiment (Rawls 1999). The EU debates on ethics in connection to AI were no exception to this trend.

In 2017, the 'discursive procedure' (rather, forum) created by the European Commission took shape in the HLEG. Much like Rawls's representatives were charged with deliberating on, and selecting the principles of justice,[26] the members

[23] The so-called proceduralist scholarship developed following Rawls' *Theory of justice* (1999) where the author conceptualised a specific type of deliberative procedure in which representatives discussed and deliberated on justice behind the so-called 'veil of ignorance' (i.e., ignorance of the actual 'injustices' plaguing the real world). For Rawls, this state of ignorance guaranteed participatory and deliberative parity of his representatives, as well as their reliance on their own moral sensibility in reaching consensus when deciding on the basic principles of justice. Fundamentally, proceduralists are interested in testing the moral acceptability of the procedures through which society is organised, which in turn affects the legitimacy of the outcomes of those procedures. For an overview of proceduralism (in particular, in connection to legitimacy and justice), see Ceva (2012).

[24] Anderson (2020) refers to a 'collective willing' because the address of ethical inquiries usually requires some type of shared empirical and normative conditions of—what the author called—'conditional' compliance'.

[25] Habermas (1984) conceptualised a so-called ideal speech situation characterised by three rules: (1) *rule of (equal) participation*; (2) *rule of equal communicative opportunity* and 3) *rule against compulsion*. The application of these rules is meant to uphold a level of baseline participatory and deliberative equality which proceduralists consider as prerequisite for the design (as well as the outcomes) of a given procedure to be considered as morally acceptable. For a comment on Habermas, see Solum (2004).

[26] For Rawls (1999), 'ignorance' was an epistemic precondition (which he called 'original position') meant to create the context in which his representatives could select the two fundamental principles of justice, namely *liberty* (i.e., a basic liberty can be limited or denied only for the sake of one or more other basic liberties, and never for a greater public good understood as a greater net sum of social and economic advantages for society as a whole) and *difference* (starting from equal division, the more advantaged are not to be better off at any point to the detriment of the less well off (…) a deeper idea of reciprocity implicit in it is that social institutions are not to take advantage of contingencies of native endowment, or of initial social position, or of good or bad luck over the course of life, except in ways that benefit everyone, including the least favoured).

of the HLEG also discussed and deliberated on the principles of ethics in the field of AI (presumably, in conditions of participatory and deliberative parity). Unlike Rawls's representatives however, the HLEG's deliberation did not unfold behind a veil of ignorance, but against the backdrop of an already existing EU regulation on data processing and protection (i.e., the GDPR) and knowledge of some already materialised risks of AI-related harm, the most prominent one being, no doubt, the risk of unfair biases. The HLEG even listed examples of 'key concerns' raised by AI which include identification methods of individuals (say, biometric identification), citizen scoring and lethal autonomous weapons (HLEG 2019).

In this context, and echoing Floridi et al.'s (2018) view of AI as being a source of social value, the HLEG kept its sight on the ultimate 'good' that AI is meant to bring, namely human flourishing, enhanced individual and societal well-being as well as progress and innovation (HLEG 2019).[27] For this conception of 'the good' to be achieved, the Guidelines (HLEG 2019) highlight a psychological prerequisite and an axiological postulate. The prerequisite is trust: trustworthy AI—the Guidelines state—is warranted when three factors are present: *lawfulness* (i.e., AI should comply with all applicable laws and regulations); *ethics* (i.e., AI should adhere to ethical principles and values) and *robustness* (both from a technical and a social perspective, considering that AI can cause 'unintentional harm'). The axiological postulate is the above-mentioned principle of human dignity as the "common foundation" of fundamental rights and conducive to—the Guidelines confirm—a *human-centric approach* by virtue of which "the human being enjoys a unique and inalienable moral status of primacy in the civil, political, economic and social fields" (HLEG 2019).

Against this backdrop, the HLEG (2019) famously suggested its four principles of ethics namely, *respect of human autonomy*, *avoidance of harm*, *fairness* and *explicability*. It can be argued that these principles express the basic quadrants of human dignity. For instance, the *respect of human autonomy* seeks to ensure people's full and effective self-determination over themselves, namely by not subordinating, coercing, deceiving, manipulating and by augmenting, complementing and empowering their cognitive, social and cultural skills (HLEG 2019). The *prevention of harm* principle entails 'due protection' to vulnerable groups and in situations where AI systems can "cause or exacerbate adverse impacts due to asymmetries of power or information" such as between employers and employees, businesses and consumers or governments and citizens (HLEG 2019). *Fairness* is defined in its two versants: substantive and procedural. Substantive fairness implies a commitment to "ensuring equal and just distribution of both benefits and costs and ensuring that individuals and groups are free from unfair bias, discrimination and stigmatisation" (HLEG 2019). Procedural fairness is defined as "the ability to contest and seek effective redress against decisions

[27] In the HLEG's Ethics Guidelines (HLEG 2019), human flourishing has, in particular, been associated with so-called virtue ethics. From the vantage point of virtues, human flourishing is "an inclusive term that is open to figures of thought from other philosophical traditions, such as utility, duty and care. At the same time this openness can be problematic because it is difficult to determine when and how exactly flourishing has been achieved." See further Stahl (2021).

made by AI systems and by the humans operating them" (HLEG 2019). Finally, explicability "means that processes need to be transparent, the capabilities and purpose of AI systems openly communicated, and decisions—to the extent possible—explainable to those directly and indirectly affected" (HLEG 2019). On the basis of this 'tetrarchy of principles,' the Guidelines went on to define seven key requirements for a Trustworthy AI namely, human agency and oversight, technical robustness and safety, privacy and governance, transparency, diversity, non-discrimination and fairness, societal and environmental well-being and accountability (HLEG 2019).

Placed in the broader context of the debates on ethics in connection to AI—canvassed in the previous sub-section—the HLEG's principles and the corresponding requirements do not depart from what eventually became *conventional* AI regulatory discourse. Most of the national, regional and international instruments on ethics and AI share much of the content of the HLEG's Guidelines. For example, the principles highlighted in UNESCO's Recommendation (UNESCO 2021) on the ethics of AI include proportionality and 'do no harm,' safety and security, fairness and non-discrimination, sustainability, right to privacy and data protection, human oversight and determination, transparency and explainability, responsibility and accountability, awareness and literacy, multi-stakeholder and adaptive governance collaboration. Similarly, the Recommendation of the OECD's Council for AI (OECD 2019) includes, in a first section addressed to stakeholders, the principles of inclusive growth, sustainable development and well-being; human-centred values and fairness; transparency and explainability; robustness, security and safety and accountability.[28] Among the national instruments, the American Blueprint for an AI Bill of Rights (The White House 2022) outlines five principles that ought to guide the design, use and deployment of automated systems. These include safe and effective systems, algorithmic discrimination protections, data privacy, notice and explanation (equivalent to the HLEG's explicability principle), human alternatives, consideration and fall-back (equivalent *mutatis mutandis* to the right to a human explanation in the context of the GDPR/AI Act). In Germany, the Opinion of the Data Ethics Commission highlighted human dignity, self-determination, privacy, security, democracy, justice and solidarity, sustainability (German Data Ethics Commission 2022).

If these instruments are a testament to anything, it is that the global collective has succeeded in arriving at a *fairly universal model* of AI ethics. This is commendable, given that—as Carsten Stahl (2021) points out—we live in an ethically pluralist world, which does not *prima facie* warrant global consensus on *any* ethical issue.[29] To illustrate this, Stahl (2021) cited the so-called Delphi study—involving 93 experts on

[28] The second section of the Recommendation (OECD 2019) includes recommendations for national policies and international cooperation for trustworthy AI. These recommendations include (i) investing in AI research and development; (ii) fostering a digital ecosystem for AI; (iii) shaping an enabling policy environment for AI; (iv) building human capacity and preparing for labour market transformation; (v) international cooperation for trustworthy AI.

[29] We allude here to Lauer (2021) who correctly observes that "even in a field that has been grappling with ethical questions and issues for thousands of years, the attempt to define an ethical approach specific to the field, and divorced from broader ethical philosophy and questions, remains a moving target."

ethics—which showcased the difficulty of transcending the multitude of (economic, political, social...) factors that impact the 'extracting' of the essence of global AI ethics. These factors included *inter alia* the cost of innovation, the risk of harm to physical integrity, lack of access to public services, lack of trust, security problems, disappearance of jobs, power asymmetries, negative impact on health, etc. And yet, as the cited instruments show, human dignity and the corresponding values (expressed as principles) seem to be largely shared by regulators worldwide.[30]

The practical issue of implementing those values remains open. Notions like transparency, explainability, fairness, robustness etc. intuitively ring true and seem appropriate for the purpose of safeguarding the principle of human dignity. But how should they be represented and translated into legal language? The difficulty with value representation is, of course, the risk of *mis*representation. On this point, Brey (2012) writes: "expressive embedded values in artefacts represent the values of designers or users of the artefact. This does not imply, however, that they also *function to realize these values*. It is conceivable that the values expressed in artefacts cause people to adopt these values and thereby contribute to their own realization." In other words, prescribing values for AI does not guarantee that AI will always operate in conformity with those values. Hence, the level of caution advised regarding the *types of legal expression* given to the values the HLEG—so thoughtfully—selected. Enter the AI Act.

3 The Expression of Values in Binding Obligations Enshrined in the EU's Data Processing and AI Regulation

Based on the HLEG's Ethics Guidelines (HLEG 2019), the European Commission chose a risk-based regulatory approach and technical standardisation as a regulatory model for the AI Act. Intuitively, this might seem surprising since a human-centric instrument ought to aim at safeguarding—by conferring—individual rights. Yet, we find in the AI Act (European Parliament 2024) the regulatory schema shared by most instruments on health and environmental risks, product safety and product liability: the compliance with technical standardisation generates a presumption of lawfulness. Within the meaning of this legislation, the direct function of technical standards is not to safeguard fundamental rights but to regulate market operators (Sub-Sect. 3.1). However—as will be discussed—the AI Act is an 'unusual' instrument because said safeguard is, in fact, *achieved through* the standards that market operators are required to observe (Sub-Sect. 3.2).

[30] Stahl (2021) observed that "a key to understanding ethics (...) is that humans recognise that we all, despite many and far-reaching differences, have much in common. We could call this state 'the shared features of the human condition.'"

3.1 *Of Technical Standards and Safeguard of Rights*

Given their common axiological rooting in human-centrism, it is not surprising that the GDPR and the AI Act converge *functionally* as they share many of the principles that shape the safeguards they seek to afford. In the GDPR (European Parliament and Council 2016), those principles—listed in Article 5—are lawfulness, fairness and transparency, purpose limitation, data minimisation, accuracy, storage limitation and integrity and confidentiality. The provisions of the AI Act largely express (through technical standards, discussed further in this sub-section) the above-mentioned requirements for trustworthy AI (human agency and oversight; technical robustness and safety; privacy and data governance etc.).

A combined reading of both instruments also confirms that they mirror each other in the ways in which they integrate their (largely shared) foundational principles into binding provisions. For example, Article 13 (transparency and provision of information to users), Article 14 (human oversight) and Article 86 (right to explanation) in the AI Act (European Parliament 2024) echo the obligation of information, enshrined in Article 15 GDPR, as well as the right to a human explanation (in the context of automated data processing) pursuant to Article 22 GDPR. Similarly, the requirements of accuracy, robustness and cybersecurity as per Article 15 AI Act complement, in many ways, the right to rectification enshrined in Article 16 GDPR.[31]

This 'mirroring' can also be detected in the fact that both the GDPR and the AI Act include cases of fundamental rights violations considered as intolerable. For example, in Article 9(1) the GDPR sets out a (quasi) absolute prohibition[32] of discrimination based on racial or ethnic origin, political opinions, religious or philosophical beliefs, or trade union membership, and the processing of genetic data, biometric data for the purpose of uniquely identifying a natural person, health or data concerning a natural person's sex life or sexual orientation. Similarly, the AI Act prohibits (through an *ex officio* ban under Article 5) the use of AI systems that pose a so-called unacceptable risk (i.e., an inadmissible violation of a fundamental right). Article 5 lists the AI

[31] A comprehensive table and a comment on how the AI Act's provisions mirror the GDPR's is provided in Grozdanovski & De Cooman (2023).

[32] This prohibition is (quasi)absolute because there are cases where the processing of the personal data listed in Article 9(1) can be exceptionally permitted. As per Article 9(2), these exceptions include cases where the data subject has given explicit consent (a); where the processing is necessary for the purposes of carrying out the obligations and exercising specific rights of the controller/data subject in the field of employment, social security and social protection(b); where the processing is necessary to protect the vital interests of the data subject or of another natural person where the data subject is physically or legally incapable of giving consent (c); where the processing is carried out in the course of its legitimate activities with appropriate safeguards by a foundation, association or any other not-for-profit body with a political, philosophical, religious or trade union aim (d); where the processing relates to personal data which are manifestly made public by the data subject (e); where the processing is necessary for the establishment, exercise or defence of legal claims (f); where the processing is necessary for reasons of substantial public interest, on the basis of Union or Member State law (g); where the processing is necessary for reasons of public health (i); where the processing is necessary for archiving purposes in the public interest, scientific or historical research purposes or statistical purposes (j).

'practices' that fall in the scope of the ban. These include, namely, AI systems that deploy subliminal techniques beyond a person's consciousness in order to materially distort that person's behaviour in a manner that causes, or is likely to cause them physical or psychological harm (Article 5a); the placing on the market, putting into service or use of an AI system that exploits any of the vulnerabilities of a specific group of persons due to their age, physical or mental disability, in order to materially distort the behaviour of a person pertaining to that group (Article 5b).

Because of their common axiological foundation (i.e., human dignity) and functional convergence (on the level of their basic principles), one would assume that the GDPR and the AI Act would also mirror each other *instrumentally* i.e., in terms of the 'normative means' through which they achieve their regulatory objectives. Surprisingly—or perhaps, not—this is not the case.

Indeed, if one looks at the ways in which the principles-to-law leap is performed in each instrument, a particularity can quickly be discerned: the GDPR's principles take the shape of *subjective rights*. For instance, the principle of transparency is translated in the *right of access* by the data subject to relevant information about the data processing (purposes, categories of personal data, period of data storage etc. (Article 15)); the principle of accuracy is expressed in the *right to rectification* (Article 16), the principles of purpose limitation and data minimisation are expressed in the *right to be forgotten* (Article 17), the *right to restriction of processing* (Article 18)[33]; the principles of lawfulness and fairness can be considered as expressed in the *right to object* to a specific data processing (Article 21), and the right to human explanation in the context of automated data processing (Article 22).

Alternatively, in the AI Act, the EU legislature translated the selected foundational principles (lawfulness, fairness and transparency etc.) into *technical standards* creating obligations for compliance, in particular as far as high-risk AI systems are concerned. For these systems, the AI Act sets out obligations for data and data governance (Article 10),[34] record keeping (Article 12),[35] transparency and provision of information to users (Article 13), human oversight (Article 14),[36] accuracy,

[33] Article 19 is relative to the obligation regarding rectification or erasure of personal data or restriction of processing.

[34] Data governance' translates to appropriate data governance and management practices which concern, in particular, relevant design choices, data collection, relevant data preparation processing operations etc. (see Article 10(2)(a-g)). It also includes the obligation for the training, validation and testing data to be relevant, representative, free of errors and complete (Article 10(3)) and that biases be monitored, detected and corrected (Article 10(5)).

[35] Record keeping is ensured through logging meant to ensure a level of traceability of the AI system's functioning throughout its lifecycle.

[36] By virtue of this provision, human oversight shall be ensured through identified and built into the high-risk AI system by the provider; identified by the provided before placing the high-risk AI system on the market or putting it into service (Article 14(3)). These measures are meant to enable the individuals to whom human oversight is assigned to fully understand the capacities and limitations of a given high-risk system (Article 14(4-a)); they remain aware of the possible tendency of automatically relying or over-relying on the output produced by a high-risk AI system (Article 14(4-b)); be able to correctly interpret the high-risk AI system's output (Article 14(4-d)); be able to decide, in any particular situation, not to use the high-risk AI system or otherwise disregard,

robustness and cybersecurity (Article 15). In light of this, the 'big' question is of course: why do the GDPR and AI Act give different normative expressions to their ground-principles which, for the most part, they share?

If we look at the designs of the instruments considered from a market perspective, it becomes apparent that the GDPR follows a right-first-market-second approach: it aims to create a system of protection of fundamental rights and freedoms, *in particular* the right to the protection of personal data, while at the same time, ensuring the unrestricted free movement of personal data within the Union (Article 1). By contrast, the AI Act explicitly states that its purpose is to "*improve the functioning of the internal market* by laying down a uniform legal framework in particular for the development, marketing and use of artificial intelligence *in conformity with Union values*" (Preamble, Recital (1)).[37] This suggests that the GDPR seeks to *create a standard of protection* for the right to data protection, whereas in the AI Act, human rights appear as an almost external *conformity standard* ("...in conformity with Union values") that AI systems must comply with.[38] In other words, unlike the GDPR, the AI Act neither gives expression to fundamental rights, nor does it aim to define a standard of protection for those rights.

Against the backdrop of the EU's regulatory methods and strategies, the 'instrumental' divergence between the GDPR and the AI Act becomes clearer. Because the former defines a standard of protection of the right to data protection, the *effectiveness*[39] of that standard depends on the beneficiaires'capabilities to claim the level of protection afforded to them. The EU's usual legislative trend has been to achieve this through the conferal of subjective rights or entitlements. Telling examples can be derived from the EU's Secondary law in the fields of non-discrimination and the EU citizenship.[40] Alternatively, the AI Act's normative philosophy seems to be more

override or reverse the output of the high-risk Ai system (Article 14(4-d)); be able to intervene on, or interrupt the system through a 'stop' button or a similar procedure (Article 14(4-e)).

[37] This is also supported by the fact that the legal basis for the AI Act is Article 114 TFEU, which, in essence, gives the habilitation to enact harmonising measures 'completing' the internal market (save in the fields of fiscal measures, free movement of persons or the rights and interests of employed persons).

[38] Commenting on fundamental rights protection in connection to AI, the European Commission (2021) stressed that "the obligations for *ex ante* testing, risk management and human oversight will also facilitate the respect of other fundamental rights by minimising the risk of erroneous or biased AI-assisted decisions in critical areas such as education and training, employment, important services, law enforcement and the judiciary. In case infringements of fundamental rights still happen, effective redress for affected persons will be made possible by ensuring transparency and traceability of the AI systems coupled with strong ex post controls."

[39] With regard to subjective rights, we will define effectiveness in reference to the CJEU's citizenship case law in which the CJEU stressed that the effectiveness of the rights associated with the Union citizen status is defined in reference to the genuine enjoyment of the substance of the rights which the Member States' nationals derive from their status as Union citizens. See *inter alia* Case C-82/16 K.A. et al. EU:C:2018:308, para 70.

[40] In the field of EU citizenship, see European Parliament and Council (2004). In the field of non-discrimination, see Council (2000a, 2000b, 2006).

akin to that of risk-regulating instruments in, say, the field of product safety, health and environment.

It follows that, though axiologically and functinoally akin, the GDPR and the AI Act ultimately belong to different families of normative instruments. The former is *prima facie* a rights-based (and rights-conferring) instrument whereas the latter, a risk-based (and risk-regulating) one. However, scholarship has astutely noted that this classification is not as black-or-white: though predominantly rights-based, the GDPR integrates a 'risk rationale'. Similarly, the risk-based nature of the AI Act notwithstanding, this instrument integrates a strong 'rights rationale.' It can even be argued that the EU's risk-regulation model under the effect of new technologies has inaugurated a novel, risk-*and*-rights-based normative approach, under which technical standards are no longer 'mere' instructions addressed to market operators but means through which human rights protection is supposed to be practically achieved. The standards in the AI Act tailored for the so-called high-risk systems give a telling example of this 'new' trend.

3.2 Of Safeguard of Rights Through Technical Standards

The AI Act defines the notion of 'high risk' by using typical 'technical standardisation' jargon. As per Article 6, a system is considered high-risk if two cumulative conditions are met: first, the system is intended to be used as a safety component of a product or is itself a product, covered by the relevant EU legislation[41]; second, the product which integreates AI as a component, or the AI system itself, is required to undergo a third-party conformity assessment with a view to placing that product on the parket or putting it into service.[42] The eight high-risk types of systems are listed in Annex III of the AI Act and include biometric identification and categorisation of natural persons; management and operation of critical infrastructure; education and vocational training; employment, workers management and access to self-employment; access to and enjoyment of essential private services and public services and benefits; law enforcement; migration, asylum and border control management and administration of justice and democratic processes.

This technical standardisation jargon receives a human rights flavour in the provision on the Commission's power to add—through delegaed acts—AI systems to Annex III, when two conditions are fulfilled: 1. the AI systems are intended to be used in an area listed in that Annex,[43] 2. the AI systems pose a risk of harm to health and safety "or *a risk of adverse impact on fundamental rights*, that is, in respect of its severity and probability of occurrence, equivalent to, or greater than the risk of harm or of adverse impact posed by the high-risk systems" already mentioned in Annex

[41] European Parliament (2024), Article 6(1)(a). The EU legislation referred to in this provision is listed in Annex II of the AI Act.

[42] European Parliament (2024), Article 6(1)(b).

[43] European Parliament (2024), Article 7(1)(a).

III.[44] The reference to 'adverse impact on fundamental rights' echoes the definition of risks suggested in the European Parliament's Resolution on a framework of ethical aspects of AI, robotics and related technologies (European Parliament 2020). As per this Resolution, a high risk is a "*significant risk* entailed by the development, deployment and use of artificial intelligence, robotics and related technologies to cause injury or harm to individuals or *society in breach of fundamental rights and safety rules as laid down in Union law*, considering their specific use or purpose, the sector where they are developed, deployed or used and the severity of injury or harm that can be expected to occur."[45]

In the landscape of the EU's existing risk regulation, the AI Act is atypical because its definition of risk seems to relate to the probability of human rights violations which… are not measurable. Indeed, in standard risk scholarship, we may refer to the definition given by Möller (2012) who defined risks as unwanted events which may or may not occur; the causes of unwanted events which may or may not occur; the probability of unwanted events which may or may not occur; the fact that a decision is made under conditions of known probabilities; the statistical expectation value of unwanted events which may or may not occur. However, it is Knight who authored the seminal distinction between risks proper and (mere) uncertainties. For him, risks are *measurable or quantifiable uncertainties* as opposed to unmeasurable ones.[46] As we argued elsewhere (Grozdanovski and De Cooman 2023), knowledge about risks is usually derived from sound, verifiable data which ought to convincingly (though not conclusively) showcase the existence and likelihood of a specific type of threat. The probability of human rights violations cannot be supported by evidence comparable to that of risks in the fields of, say, environment and health (Quelle 2018). The GDPR confirms this in its Article 35 relative to the Data Protection Impact Assessment (DPIA).

The DPIA is a procedure that allows controllers (and, when applicable, processors) to determine if a specific type of data processing "is likely to result in a *high risk* to the rights and freedoms of natural persons." In the presence of such a risk, the controller carries out an assessment of the impact of the envisaged processing.[47] The DPIA is performed in the following cases: systematic and extensive evaluations of personal aspects relating to natural persons through automated processing, including profiling, based on which decisions are made with legal effects concerning the natural person[48]; in the case of processing on a large scale of special categories of data referred to in Article 9(1) GDPR or of personal data relating to criminal convictions and offences referred to in Article 10 GDPR,[49] and in the case of a systemic monitoring of a publicly accessible area on a large scale.[50] For the sake of comparison, the risk

[44] European Parliament (2024), Article 7(1)(b).

[45] European Parliament (2020), Article 4(e).

[46] See Riesch (2011).

[47] European Parliament and Council (2016), Article 35(1).

[48] European Parliament and Council (2016), Article 35(2)(a).

[49] European Parliament and Council (2016), Article 35(2)(b).

[50] European Parliament and Council (2016), Article 35(2)(c).

assessment procedure in Article 44 of the REACH Regulation (European Parliament and Council 2006a) (relative to the criteria for substance evaluation) lists *specific criteria* that the European Chemical Agency should consider when making those assessments. These criteria include, *inter alia*, hazard information (e.g., structural similarity of a given substance with known substances of concern or with substances that are persistently bio-accumulate), exposure information and tonnage.[51]

The combined reading of the REACH Regulation and the GDPR unveils a fundamental difference between 'old school' and—as it were— 'new age' understanding of the concept of risk. The REACH Regulation is clearly 'old school' as it seems to require *evidence proper* (measurable and verifiable data) on the properties and effects of chemical substances. The GDPR—and by extension the AI Act—are 'new age' since the assessments of risks contained in their provisions do not seem to require the gathering of hard evidence, but a roughly plausible assessment of likelihood, as opposed to probabilities *sricto* sensu. This is understandable, considering that the risk of fundamental rights violations cannot be numerically represented: there is seldom, if ever evidence showing a 40% chance that a specific data processing might e.g., take into account a person's ethnic background.

Bearing in mind this 'new age' way of defining risks, are the GDPR and the AI Act rights-based, risk-based...or both? The answer here may come from the way in which each instrument *represents risks*.

By suggesting the four-level risk scale (minimal, non-high, high and unacceptable), the AI Act in fact defines *thresholds of acceptability of threats of fundamental rights violations*. To do so, it seems to borrow from pre-existing risk-regulating instruments the approach of defining *levels of gravity* which (if empirically verified) provide the basis for technical standards as a means of regulation of the practical effects of grave events. Glasson (2008) eloquently explains the difference and complementarity between thresholds and standards: "'*thresholds*' refer to discrete points that must be exceeded to begin producing a given effect or result to elicit a response (...) '*Standards*' provide guidance that regulates the effect of an activity (normally human activity) on a receptor." Against the backdrop of Glasson's distinction, the four risk levels in the AI Act can be understood as relating to four different thresholds of gravity that the European Commission *presumes*, since there is no way of actually measuring the probability of harm associated with each level of risk. In reference to these thresholds, the AI Act defines technical standards (namely for high-risk systems) addressed to five categories of addressees, at least four of which are market operators i.e., providers,[52] importers,[53] distributors,[54] and deployers.[55]

Alternatively, the GDPR neither canvasses a threshold of gravity, nor does it define technical standards to be observed by data controllers and processors. In the context of the above-mentioned DPIA, the controller is required to consult the supervisory

---

[51] European Parliament and Council (2006b), Article 44(1)(a-c).

[52] European Parliament (2024), Articles 17–23.

[53] European Parliament (2024), Article 99.

[54] European Parliament (2024), Article 24.

[55] European Parliament (2024), Article 26.

authority prior to processing, in instances where they might suspect a high risk.[56] If that authority is of the opinion that the intended processing would, indeed, infringe the GDPR, it is required to provide written advice to the controller and, if applicable, the processor.[57] The analysis of the AI Act and the GDPR through the prism of Glasson's threshold/standard definition warrants the conclusion that the former is a risk-regulating one after all: unconventional, different from the comparable EU legislation, but risk-regulating nonetheless. By contrast, the GDPR is a rights-conferring instrument because—again—its primary purpose is not to define a baseline security level for the right to data protection.

Scholars have tackled the seemingly hybrid risk/rights-based nature of the GDPR and the AI Act. De Gregorio and Dunn (2022) seminally characterised the GDPR as bottom-up meaning that the evaluation of risk and the mitigation thereof is left to the discretion of data controllers and processors. The AI Act establishes a more rigid top-down structure, because it "imposes differentiated duties depending on the risk scores of regulated AI systems (and) does not leave the task of evaluating such risk scores to the targets of regulation: in fact, it is the AI Act itself that, on a top-down basis, identifies the various categories of risk" (De Gregorio and Dunn 2022). The distinguishing factor between the two would then be the *discretion* left to their addresses to monitor human rights violation (De Gregorio and Dunn 2022). De Gregorio's and Dunn's observations are, of course, pertinent. It remains however that the distinction between the acts considered is due to the fact that both are—as mentioned earlier—*instrumentally* opposed that is, the normative means (subjective rights/risks) through which they particularise their foundational values are drawn from different families of regulation.

The final open question is a rather delicate one: *who is the AI Act really for?* The answer—Anderson (2022) argues—may be, directly or indirectly, business interests, which may not be a serious issue if it remains within the legal realm. It becomes a 'serious' issue from the perspective of the ethics/law interrelationship because it seems to suggest a "false sense of ethical responsibility in terms of the public good." Market efficiency requires that a certain level of risk be tolerated: for there to be a viable market of any product labelled as risky, economic operators and users need to *accept* that the risk associated with that product might materialise. The problem with the so-called high-risk AI systems is that their deployment and use presuppose a level of acceptance of human rights violations which is unorthodox, to say the least. Hence, the need for a stronger trust-building market narrative, especially targeted at AI users.

The ethical market narrative has been in vogue for some time now and can be correlated with what Laux et al. (2023) have called the *conflating of trust and trustworthiness,* especially when it comes to the acceptability of risks. However, 'conflating of trust' runs the risk of blurring the distinction between "acceptability judgments made by domain experts and the trustworthiness of AI systems implemented in society"

[56] European Parliament and Council (2016), Article 36(1).

[57] European Parliament and Council (2016), Article 36(2). The period referred to in this Article is up to eight weeks of receipt of the request for consultation.

(Laux et al. 2023). Others have criticised that the AI Act outsources decisions about which risks are 'acceptable' to AI providers with an economic interest to market the AI system (Laux et al. 2023). But the performance/excellence-driven AI race provides a context in which policymakers have a strong incentive to—as Laux et al. (2023) put it—"engineer trust."

Ultimately, is the AI Act a market-oriented, risk-regulating instrument coated with a seducing discourse on values and rights? If so, does the AI Act truly succeed in achieving the level of fundamental rights protection it pledges to achieve? The answer seems to be a (relatively thin) 'yes.' While they do seem to be primarily turned toward markets, the technical requirements in the AI Act (transparency, human oversight etc.) are precisely meant to infuse values into the design of AI systems released in the market. The ambition is that the design, especially of high-risk AI, be value-sensitive throughout a system's life cycle. But scholars like Flanagan et al. (2009) rightly point out that achieving a design "that soundly incorporates values requires not only competence in the technical arts and sciences, but also a reflective understanding of the relevant values and how these values function in the lives of people and possibly groups affected by the systems in question." Brey (2012) made a similar observation. For him, technical value-sensitivity is not an issue of slavish, to-the-letter compliance with the AI Act's provisions, but a multi-layered process of investigation. For this author, there is, first, a *conceptual investigation* aimed at conceptualising and describing the values implicated in a design, as well as the stakeholders affected by it, "and consider the appropriate trade-off between implicated values, including both moral and non-moral values." There is, second, an *empirical investigation*, which focuses on the human context in which "the technological artefact is to be situated, so as to better anticipate on this context and to evaluate the success of particular designs." These include empirical studies of human behaviour, physiology, attitudes, values and needs of users and other stakeholders, and may also consider the organisational context in which the technology is used. Finally, there are the so-called *technical investigations* which "study how properties of technological artefacts support or hinder human values and how computer systems and software may be designed proactively in order to support specific values that have been found important in the conceptual investigation."

It is too early to tell how the values-turned-to-standards in the AI Act will be practically understood and applied in this instrument's implementation. At this stage, may it suffice stressing that the AI Act is a *typical* risk-regulating instrument because it seeks to regulate specific conducts in the market; it is an *atypical* such instrument because, in its normative design, fundamental rights safeguards are 'standardised' taking the form of "side-constraints that bound the moral space in which corporations may legitimately pursue economic ends" (Arnold 2016).

4 Concluding Remarks

It follows from the above that the GDPR arguably provided the template for subsequent legislation on data-protection and data processing (and data processing technologies). This is not to say that this legislation is populated by normative clones of the GDPR that is, instruments that particularise the right to data protection and are invariably rights-based (and rights-conferring). On the contrary, they differ in their normative designs, though they do seem to subscribe to the human-centric approach discussed in this Chapter. Indeed, said instruments are *consistent* with the GDPR in two important ways. First, they *complement* its provisions by establishing additional, specific frameworks on, say, the re-use of data by public authorities and, more generally, the principles governing the processing of both personal and non-personal data. Second, those instruments carry the imprint of human-centrism, insofar as they are rooted in the *human dignity postulate* and particularise the foundational principles (fairness, transparency, accuracy, autonomy etc.) associated with it.

For instance, the Digital Markets Act (DMA) (European Parliament and Council 2022a) sets out a series of obligations for platforms labelled as gatekeepers[58] (the aim of which is clearly to prevent abuse of dominance by creating entry barriers) with the purpose of contributing to the proper functioning of the internal market. To do so, the DMA seeks to ensure for all businesses, "*contestable and fair markets* in the digital sector across the Union where gatekeepers are present, to the benefit of business users and end users."[59] The DMA's wording is illustrative of—what may be viewed as—a 'woke' approach to regulating markets, since profit-driven and monopoly-aspiring big-tech companies are now constrained in their conduct by human-centric values such as fairness (which, seems to be omnipresent, weaving through the GDPR and the AI Act). The Data Act (European Parliament and Council 2023) follows the rights-giving approach of the GDPR as it seeks to ensure a high level of consumer protection through the "*new right* to access user data in situations previously not covered by Union law." In a similar vein, the Data Governance Act (DGA) (European Parliament and Council 2022b), regulating the re-use of personal data by public authorities, draws inspiration from many of the GDPR's principles in defining commercial and statistical confidentiality,[60] the protection of intellectual property rights of third parties,[61] and the protection of personal data.[62] The conditions for re-use of data are framed by the (standard) principles of non-discrimination,

[58] Article 3(1) defines gatekeepers as undertakings that have a significant impact on the internal market, provide a core platform service which is an important gateway for business users to reach end users and enjoy, or are likely to enjoy, an entrenched and durable position in their operations. The remainder of Article 3 particularises these conditions into more specific requirements.

[59] European Parliament and Council (2022a), Preamble, Recital (7).

[60] European Parliament and Council (2022b), Article 3(1)(a-b).

[61] European Parliament and Council (2022b), Article 3(1)(c).

[62] European Parliament and Council (2022b), Article 3(1)(d).

proportionality, objectivity,[63] and (the GDPR-inspired) principles of anonymisation or pseudonymisation of personal data.[64]

Our comparative study of the AI Act and the GDPR (as basis for possible subsequent studies of the recent legislation mentioned above) reveals a level of what we have called (Grozdanovski and De Cooman 2023), *axiological congruence* understood as the fit between "the preferences of the citizens and the committed policy positions of their representatives" (Bingham Powell 2013). Human-centrism seems to be the *locus* where the 'fit' is found between the EU's ambition for economic gains and excellence (namely through increased innovation) and the citizens' need for increased trust in the various types of data processing and data processing technologies (like AI). This concomitant pursuit of the excellence/trust objectives showcases the EU's regulatory strive toward 'having the cake and eating it too,' since the regulation of digital markets and market operators is meant to deliver technological and economic progress while at the same time engineering trust through normative means that uphold a high standard of fundamental rights protection. In the USA, the 2019 Executive Order on AI[65] is in a way much simpler in that, it very clearly commits to the American win in the AI race, human rights protection being mentioned but certainly not in the forefront of the policy priorities for AI regulation.

In the EU, what Brey (2012) called *value-sensitive design* does not seem to only apply to the technical standardisation which frames the 'manufacturing,' use and deployment of new technologies (like AI), but it also seems to apply to the *normative design* of the instruments that regulate various aspects of data processing and protection. The assumption seems to be the following: values-prescribing regulation yields value-conform technology. It remains to be seen if and how this assumption will be challenged in practice. We can reasonably anticipate disputes stemming from differences between the ways in which the AI Act prescribes values and the ways in which market operators understand and apply them. For example, transparency (combined with human oversight) is, without question, an important principle (and standard) to apply, but its technical feasibility (i.e., actually programming AI systems where human oversight is possible *throughout their life cycles*) might not be as feasible as the AI Act assumes it will be. Hopefully, future case law in connection with the AI Act will reveal if, through the that instrument, the EU legislature translated the foundational, ethical AI-related values into appropriate binding (and practically enforceable) legal obligations.

[63] European Parliament and Council (2022b), Article 5(2).

[64] European Parliament and Council (2022b), Article 5(3).

[65] Executive Order 13,859, 11 February 2019, Federal Register, vol. 84, n° 31, 3967–3972.

References

Acemoglu D (2002) Technical change, inequality and the labour market. J Econ Lit XL:7–72
Anderson E (2020) The epistemology of justice. South J Philos 58(1):6–29
Anderson MM (2022) Some ethical reflections on the EU AI Act. IALL 2022: 1st International Workshop on Imagining the AI Landscape after the AI Act (2022), Amsterdam. http://iail2022.isti.cnr.it
Arnold DG (2016) Corporations and human rights obligations. Bus & Hum Rights J 1(2):255–275
Autor D, Salomons A (2018) Is automation labor-share-displacing? Productivity growth, employment, and the labor share. Brooklyn Papers on Economic Activity. https://www.brookings.edu/wp-content/uploads/2018/03/1_autorsalomons.pdf
Biber E (2017) Law in the anthropocene epoch. Georg Law J 106(1):1–68
Binhgam Powell Jr G (2013) Representation in context: election laws and ideological congruence between citizens and governments. Perspect Polit 11(1):9–21
Brey P (2012) Values in technology and disclosive computer ethics. In: Floridi L (ed) The Cambridge handbook of information and computer ethics. Cambridge University Press
Ceva E (2012) Beyond legitimacy. Can proceduralism say anything relevant about justice? Critical Rev Int Soc & Polit Philos 15(2):183–200
Council: Council of the European Union (2000a) Council Directive 2000/43, of 29 June 2000, implementing the principle of equal treatment between persons irrespective of racial or ethnic origin, OJ L 180, 19.7.2000, pp 22–26
Council: Council of the European Union (2000b) Council Directive 2000/78, of 27 November 2000, establishing a general framework for equal treatment in employment and occupation, OJ L 303, 2.12.2000, pp 16–22
De Gregorio G, Dunn P (2022) The European risk-based approaches: connecting constitutional dots in the Digital Age. Common Mark Law Rev 59(2):473–500
European Commission (2015) A Digital Single Market Strategy for Europe, COM(2015)192 final
European Commission (2018) Artificial intelligence for Europe. COM(2018) 237 final
European Commission (2020) White Paper in artificial intelligence – a European approach to excellence and trust, COM(2020) 65 final
European Commission (2021) Proposal for a regulation of the European Parliament and of the Council laying down harmonized rules on artificial intelligence (Artificial Intelligence Act), COM(2021) 206 final
European Commission (2022) Proposal for a directive of the European Parliament and of the Council on adapting non-contractual civil liability rules to artificial intelligence (AI Liability Directive). COM(2022) 496 final
European Council (2017) Conclusions of the European Council meeting of 19 October 2017. CO EUR 17/CONCL 5
European Parliament (2015) Report with recommendations to the Commission on civil law rules on robotics. 2015/2103(INL)
European Parliament (2020) Resolution of 20 October 2020 with recommendations to the Commission on a framework of ethical aspects of artificial intelligence, robotics and related technologies. 2020/2012(INL)
European Parliament (2024) European Parliament's Corrigendum (19 April 2024) to the position of the European Parliament adopted at first reading on 13 March 2024 with a view to the adoption of Regulation (EU) 2024/… of the European Parliament and of the Council laying down harmonized rules on Artificial Intelligence (Artificial Intelligence Act). https://www.europarl.europa.eu/doceo/document/TA-9-2024-0138-FNL-COR01_EN.pdf
European Parliament and Council (2004) Directive 2004/38 of the European Parliament and of the Council, of 29 April 2004, on the right of citizens of the Union and their family members to move and reside freely within the territory of the Member States. OJ L 158, 30.4.2004, pp 77–123

European Parliament and Council (2006a) Regulation No. 1907/2006, of the European Parliament and of the Council, of 18 December 2006, concerning the Registration, Evaluation, Authorization and Restriction of Chemicals (REACH), establishing a European Chemicals Agency. OJ L 396, 30.12.2006, pp 1–849

European Parliament and Council (2006b) Directive 2006/54, of the European Parliament and of the Council, of 5 July 2006, on the implementation of the principle of equal opportunities and equal treatment of men and women in matters of employment and occupation, OJ L 204, 26.7.2006, pp 23–36

European Parliament and Council (2016) Regulation (EU) 2016/679 of the European Parliament and of the Council of 27 April 2016 on the protection of natural persons with regard to the processing of personal data and on the free movement of such data, and repealing Directive 95/46/EC (General Data Protection Regulation). OJ L 119, 4.5.2016, pp 1–88

European Parliament and Council (2022a) Regulation (EU) 2022/1925, of the European Parliament and of the Council, of 14 September 2022 on contestable and fair markets in the digital sector. OJ L 265, 12.10.2022, pp 1–66

European Parliament and Council (2022b) Regulation (EU) 2022/868 of the European Parliament and of the Council, of 30 May 2022 on European data governance (Data Governance Act). OJ L 152, 3.6.2022, pp 1–44

European Parliament and Council (2023) Regulation (EU) 2023/2854 of the European Parliament and of the Council of 13 December 2023 on harmonised rules on fair access to and use of data. OJ L, 2023/2854, 22.12.2023, ELI: http://data.europa.eu/eli/reg/2023/2854/oj

Flanagan M, Howe DC, Nissenbaum H (2009) Embodying values in technology. Theory and practice. In: Van Den Hoven J, Weckert J (eds) Information technology and moral philosophy. Cambridge University Press.

Floridi L (2012) Ethics after the information revolution. In: Floridi L (ed) The Cambridge handbook of information and computer ethics. Cambridge University Press.

Floridi L (2021) The European legislation on AI: a brief analysis of its philosophical approach. Philos & Technol 34:215–222

Floridi L, Crowls J, Beltrametti M, Chatila R, Chazerand P, Dignum V, Luetge C, Madelin R, Pagallo U, Rossi F, Schafer B, Valcke P, Vayena E (2018) AI4People – an ethical framework for a good AI society: opportunities, risks, principles and recommendations. Mind Mach 28:689–707

German Data Ethics Commission (2022) Opinion of the Data Ethics Commission. https://www.bmi.bund.de/SharedDocs/downloads/EN/themen/it-digital-policy/datenethikkommission-abschlussgutachten-lang.pdf;jsessionid=45F818C7780A67FF1F90C0F02E04165B.live882?__blob=publicationFile&v=6

Glasson J (2008) Thresholds and standards – definitions and dimensions. In: Schmidt M, Glasson J, Emmelin L, Helbord H (eds) Standards and thresholds for impact assessment, vol 3. Springer

Grozdanovski L, De Cooman J (2023) Forget the facts, aim for the rights! On the obsolescence of empirical knowledge in defining the risk/rights-based approach to AI Regulation in the European Union. Rutgers Comput & Technol Law J 49(2):207–330

Habermas J (1984) The theory of communicative action: reason and rationalization of society. Beacon Press.

HLEG: High-Level Expert Group on Artificial Intelligence (2019) Ethics guidelines for trustworthy AI. https://digital-strategy.ec.europa.eu/en/library/ethics-guidelines-trustworthy-ai

HLEG: High-Level Expert Group on Artificial Intelligence (2020) Assessment list for trustworthy AI. https://futurium.ec.europa.eu/en/european-ai-alliance/pages/welcome-altai-portal

Lauer D (2021) You cannot have AI ethics without ethics. AI & Ethics 1:21–25

Laux J, Wachter S, Mittelstadt B (2023) Trustworthy artificial intelligence and the European Union AI Act: on the conflation of trustworthiness and acceptability of risk. Regul & Governance 18(1):1–30

Mahmoud Zadeh SM, Power DMW, Zadeh RB (2019) Autonomy and unmanned vehicles. Springer, Augmented Reactive mission and motion planning architecture

McGowan K, Geobey S (2020) 'Harmful to the commonality': the Luddites, the distributional effects of systems change and the challenge of building a just society. Soc Enterp J 18(2):306–320
Mishra A (2019) State-centric approach to human rights: exploring human obligations. Rev Québecoise Droit Int, pp 49–66
Möller N (2012) The concepts of risk and safety. In: Roeser S, Hillerbrand R, Sandin P, Peterson M (eds) Handbook of risk theory: epistemology, decision theory, ethics, and social implications of risk. Springer
OECD: Organisation for Economic Co-operation and Development (2019) Recommendation of the Council on Artificial Intelligence. https://legalinstruments.oecd.org/en/instruments/OECD-LEGAL-0449
Quelle C (2018) Enhancing compliance under the General Data Protection Regulation: the risky upshot of the accountability- and risk-based approach. Eur J Risk Regul 9(3):502–526
Rawls J (1999) A theory of justice (revised ed.). Harvard University Press
Rességuier A, Rodrigues R (2020) AI ethics should not remain toothless! Acall to bring back the teeth of ethics. Big Data Soc 7(2):1–5
Riesch H (2011) Levels of uncertainty. Phil Trans Roy Soc A 369:4730–4750
Solum L (2004) Procedural justice. South Calif Law Rev 78(1):181–321
Stahl BC (2021) Artificial intelligence for a better future. An ecosystem perspective on the ethics of AI and emerging digital technologies. Springer
The White House (2022) Blueprint for an AI Bill of Rights. Making automated systems work for the American people (October 2022), White House Office of Science and Technology Policy. https://www.whitehouse.gov/ostp/ai-bill-of-rights/
UNESCO (2021) UNESCO Recommendation on the Ethics of Artificial Intelligence, No. 61910. https://unesdoc.unesco.org/ark:/48223/pf0000380455
Watkin C (2016) French philosophy today: new figures of the human in Badiou, Meillassaux, Malabou. Cambridge University Press, Serres and Latour
Weaver JF (2019) Value-based regulation of artificial intelligence. RAIL: J Robot, AI & Law 2(3):219–226

Liability for Damage Caused by AI—The AILD and Existing Liability Concepts

Béatrice Schütte

Abstract While the EU's AI Act has entered into force in 2024, this is not (yet) the case for any binding legislation on liability for AI-related damage at the EU level. The EU institutions issued a proposal for a Directive on AI liability (AILD) in September 2022, but withdrew it in February 2025. As opposed to what the name of the Directive suggested, it did not harmonise the substance of liability. These issues were and still are left to be regulated by the Member States. As the regulatory landscape on AI in general is still evolving and discussion on AI liability will continue, this contribution presents some takeaways from the failed Directive. In addition, this chapter delves into traditional concepts of civil liability and their compatibility with liability for damage caused by artificial intelligence and shows examples of national laws of Member States. It will further explore selected national civil liability laws and approaches as to their suitability to tackle damage caused by artificial intelligence. The AI Liability Directive strived to mitigate the information asymmetry between a wrongdoer and an injured party where AI is involved to a certain extent. It did not present any solutions to the often difficult question of how to attribute the behaviour of AI systems to a human based on the prevailing human-centric approach to AI.

1 Introduction

Discussions about the question of how to regulate liability for damage caused by artificial intelligence (AI) have been ongoing at the EU level and also among academics for several years: are existing civil liability rules sufficient? Should liability be harmonised at the EU level? In September 2022, the European Commission issued

This research has been conducted with the help of project funding granted by the Academy of Finland, decision number 330884 (2020).

B. Schütte (✉)
University of Lapland, Rovaniemi, Finland
e-mail: beatrice.schutte@ulapland.fi

Information Society Law Center (ISLC), University of Milan, Milan, Italy

M. Varju and K. Mezei (eds.), *The Challenges of Artificial Intelligence for Law in Europe*, Data Science, Machine Intelligence, and Law 6,
https://doi.org/10.1007/978-3-031-86813-9_6

a proposal for a directive on AI liability (the AILD) (European Commission 2022). However, the regulatory process stalled and Member States and EU legislators seemed unable to reach an agreement. In February 2025, the proposal was withdrawn. The proposed directive was a liability framework in name only: as per its Article 1(1), it laid down common rules on "the disclosure of evidence on high-risk artificial intelligence (AI) systems to enable a claimant to substantiate a non-contractual fault-based civil law claim for damages and on the burden of proof in the case of non-contractual fault-based civil law claims brought before national courts for damages caused by an AI system". That means that any questions relating to the substance of liability such as causation, fault or recoverable damage are left to the Member States.[1] The AILD would have been applied in combination with the respective applicable national law.

Questions related to liability for technological aids are not new. Already in the 1970s there were discussions concerning liability for computer transactions.[2] This was also taken up in Germany in the 1980's, with the argument that the interdependency and complexity of software made it impossible to grant failure-free results, as it was human (referring to the programmer) to make mistakes. Yet, in the 1980's, the monotony of the programming process was mentioned as the reason for the risk of mistake (Grützmacher 2016). In the 2005 United Nations Convention on the Use of Electronic Communications in International Contracts (United Nations 2005) it is stated that a person (whether a natural person or a legal entity) on whose behalf a computer was programmed should ultimately be responsible for any message generated by the machine. As a first reflex, one might be tempted to argue that AI is a different story. However, electronic data processing is based on algorithms, and so is AI, even though algorithms and technology in general have become far more sophisticated over the years.

Clear liability rules can be considered a driver of the adoption of AI technologies, as in a survey carried out by the Commission, one third of companies considered liability concerns as one of the main obstacles to the uptake of AI (European Commission 2020).[3]

The purpose of this contribution is to explore what lessons we can learn from the failed AILD proposal. After the withdrawal of the proposal, traditional liability concepts used in national laws deserve attention. One of these is certainly that of *respondeat superior*, i.e., liability for others. So far, *respondeat superior* relates mainly to the liability for damage caused by employees. However, it is also worth considering liability for damage caused by children or animals. Further, one should delve into the French landmark framework of liability for damage caused by things (*responsabilité du fait des choses*) as well as into traditional negligence liability in selected national laws.

This contribution is structured as follows: Sect. 2 provides a brief overview of the proposed AILD and its main points and takeaways. After that, I will show what

---

[1] European Commission (2022), Explanatory Memorandum, Point 11.

[2] See, for example, Chandler (1977).

[3] See also Novelli et al. (2024).

tort liability could look like in national laws when they are applied together with the AILD. Afterwards, I will introduce the *respondeat superior* rules in terms of liability for damage caused by employers, but also liability for damage caused by animals, and examine if and to what extent they can be applied directly or analogously to damage caused by AI systems. Sections 6 and 7 will present other selected national approaches that could serve as a basis of liability for AI-related damage.

2 The AILD in a Nutshell

The scope of application of the proposed directive was described precisely in Recital (15) in its Preamble, and Article 1: it applied to non-contractual fault-based claims for damage caused by the output of an AI system, or its failure to produce output due to wrongdoing on the part of a human actor. The directive would not apply when damage is caused by a human assessment that is followed by a human act or omission, if the AI system only provides information or advice that the human actor takes into account. For example, no liability would arise if an AI-enabled software provides a physician with several diagnostic options on the basis of test results, and the physician decides which of the options to examine more closely.[4] The same likely would apply if a company's HR department uses an AI-enabled program during a recruitment process, which merely marks the candidates best suited for the position, while the actual choice of candidates is made by HR employees.

The AILD focused chiefly on damage caused by high-risk AI in the course of professional activities. This can, in addition to Article 1(1) be drawn from Article 4 (5) AILD, which establishes an exception for AI systems that are not high-risk.[5] Thus, the AILD is aligned (Hacker 2023) with the European Union's proposed Artificial Intelligence Act (AI Act) (European Commission, 2021).

The most important provisions of the AILD were Article 3 and Article 4. While the former sets out rules on the disclosure of evidence and a rebuttable presumption of non-compliance, the latter regulates a rebuttable presumption of a causal link in the case of fault. Both provisions are meant to alleviate the burden of proof on the injured party, which could otherwise be a significant obstacle to even filing a damages claim due to characteristics of AI such as opacity or autonomy and the related information asymmetry.

Pursuant to Article 3, Member State courts may order—upon the request of the claimant or, before a claim is lodged, the potential claimant—that providers and persons subject to the obligations of a provider pursuant to Article 24 or Article 28(1) of the AI Act, or users, disclose relevant evidence at their disposal, which pertains to the specific high-risk AI system suspected of having caused the damage that is in dispute. The courts cannot order such disclosure on their own initiative.

---

[4] See also Schütte (2024).

[5] See also, for example, Hacker (2023).

If the defendant or the potential defendant fail to comply with such an order, their non-compliance will be rebuttably presumed.

The definitions of providers and users are the same as in the AI Act; however, the AI Act uses the term 'deployer' instead of user.

Article 3 has been criticized for being unclear regarding its scope, referring to providers and persons subject to the obligations of a provider in Article 3(1), and to 'defendants' in Article 3(5). The notion of the latter could include stakeholders beyond providers and persons subject to their obligations.[6]

Article 4 of the AILD sets out that, under certain conditions, national courts shall rebuttably presume the causal link between the fault of the defendant and the output produced by the AI system or the failure of the AI system to produce an output. The conditions must be cumulatively met. Firstly, the claimant must have demonstrated, or the court must have presumed pursuant to Article 3(5), the fault of the defendant, or of a person for whose behaviour the defendant is responsible, consisting in the non-compliance with a duty of care laid down in Union or national law directly intended to protect against the damage that occurred.

Secondly, it must be considered reasonably likely, based on the circumstances of the case, that the fault has influenced the output produced by the AI system or the failure of the AI system to produce an output. And thirdly, the claimant must have demonstrated that the output produced by the AI system or the failure of the AI system to produce an output gave rise to the damage.

Article 4 AILD further distinguishes among claims filed against a provider, a user or a non-professional user, and between claims concerning high-risk and low-risk AI systems. If a claim is filed against the provider of a high-risk system, the presumption applies in relation to the provider's failure to comply with specific obligations set out in the AI Act, such as designing the system so as to ensure transparency and human oversight.[7]

In claims filed against the user of a high-risk AI system, the causal link can be presumed if the claimant proves that the user did not comply with its obligations to use or monitor the AI system in accordance with the accompanying instructions of use or, where appropriate, suspend or interrupt its use pursuant to Article 29 AI Act, or exposed the AI system to input data irrelevant for the system's intended purpose pursuant to Article 29(3) of the AI Act.

For claims concerning AI systems that are not classified as high-risk, the presumption only applies if the national court considers it excessively difficult for the claimant to prove the causal link.[8] In relation to non-professional users, causation is only presumed if the defendant materially interfered with the conditions of the operation of the AI system or if the defendant was required and able to determine the conditions of operation of the AI system and failed to do so.[9] This classification reflects the risk-based approach enshrined in the AI Act.

---

[6] See, for example, de Bruyne et al. (2023).

[7] See European Commission (2022), Article 4(2).

[8] European Commission (2022), Article 4(5).

[9] European Commission (2022), Article 4(6).

In Article 4, the use of the terms 'non-compliance' and 'fault' gives rise to confusion. While Article 1(3) states that the AILD shall not affect, among others, national rules on how fault is defined, Article 4 mentions in this context "the fault of the defendant, or of a person for whose behaviour the defendant is responsible, consisting in the non-compliance with a duty of care laid down in Union or national law directly intended to protect against the damage that occurred". Thus, it was unclear whether this was a definition limited to Article 4, or whether the EU legislator aimed to introduce an objectivized standard of fault for the purpose of AI liability. If there will be another attempt at harmonising liability for AI-related damage, such confusion should be avoided. The EU legislator should decide whether they want to harmonise the substance of liability with regard to AI to a certain extent, for instance by introducing an objectivized standard of fault, or whether this will be left to the Member States.

With its focus on procedural aspects, the AILD proposal significantly deviated from a previous proposal issued by the European Parliament, which introduced the concept of the liability of the 'operator' of an AI system, including strict liability for high-risk AI and fault-based liability for AI systems not classified as high-risk.[10]

Due to its focus on high-risk AI, the AILD still left room for the application of other liability concepts for damage caused by low-risk AI or by prohibited AI systems, which are not mentioned at all in the AILD. Strangely, it seems that people suffering damage due to a prohibited AI system would not have been able to benefit from the alleviations enshrined in the directive. To fully reflect the risk-based approach taken by the AI Act, any future framework harmonising AI liability should address damage caused by prohibited AI systems. A prohibition in the AI Act does not guarantee that such AI systems will never be used. Injured parties should be able to rely on alleviations when they try to obtain compensation. The alleviations enshrined in the proposal were certainly the most important part, as the complexity and opacity of AI systems make it complicated or impossible to obtain compensation without having advanced knowledge about the system in question. This should be considered if another attempt at regulating AI liability is made.

3 Fault-Based Tort Liability Rules

As the AILD must be applied together with national substantial liability rules, this section will shed light on what this could look like in practice, once the directive is in force. This will be illustrated using German and Danish law as examples, representing two different legal families. The focus will be on negligent behaviour, as with the intentional use of an AI system to inflict damage on another person, the characteristics of AI will be less decisive.

---

[10] European Parliament (2020), Annex B, Articles 4 and 8.

3.1 Germany

Under German law, one may consider applying the basic liability rule of § 823 I of the German Civil Code. Pursuant to § 823 I BGB, "A person who, intentionally or negligently, unlawfully injures the life, body, health, freedom, property or another right of another person is liable to make compensation to the other party for the damage arising from this". German tort law relates to the violation of a standard of conduct and not to the question whether the wrongdoing behaviour is personally reproachable (Münchener Kommentar 2024a). Yet, if a person possesses special knowledge and skills, these must be used in order to prevent damage (Münchener Kommentar 2024a). Negligence liability for AI-related harm could be based on the failure to act with due care in terms of monitoring a dangerous item and not complying with the duty to protect others from the inherent dangers of the item, a requirement that applies with or without the use of any kind of tools.[11] It may, however, be difficult to determine when an item such as an AI system is sufficiently dangerous to generate corresponding monitoring duties.[12]

Under the scope of § 823 I BGB, so-called organisational duties, or duties to ensure public safety are generally acknowledged. A person who creates or maintains a source of danger in their sphere of responsibility must take all required and reasonable measures to prevent the danger from turning into actual harm (Jauernig Kommentar 2023). That means that, for instance, the operator of a technology is obliged to install measures that a reasonable and prudent person would consider necessary to prevent others from suffering harm. In this regard, it is required to sufficiently consider the specific failure risks when employing new (not yet understood) technologies and to implement appropriate prevention. If the AI system undergoes changes during its life-cycle, the operator may not rely on continuous quality without further tests (Bilski and Schmid 2019). The exact shape of these duties depends on the state of the art and the general expectations in terms of safety when a system is placed on the market (Bilski and Schmid 2019). The higher the risk of damage and the higher the potential profit related to the operation of an autonomous system, the stricter are the duties of care for the operator (Grützmacher 2016). Therefore, one cannot generally say whether § 823 I BGB can or cannot be applied to damage caused by AI systems, but instead one must decide on a case-by-case basis. In the future, it is likely that certain duties in regard to AI technologies will be determined and failure to comply with these duties will result in negligence liability. However, it should be noted that the technology develops at a much faster pace than the law does so that the latter will most probably always be at least one step behind the technological state of the art. Evaluating whether or not the person interacting with an AI system observed the standard of care will be easier the less autonomous and opaque such a system is.

---

[11] See, for example, Selbst (2020).

[12] See, for example, Janal (2016).

3.2 Denmark

Further, application or applicability of negligence liability is also being discussed under Danish law. General negligence liability is regulated by the so-called judge-made *culpa* rule. Under the scope of the culpa rule, one is liable for damages caused intentionally or negligently, culpa being the generic term for both (Eyben and Isager 2013). It is often also claimed that the tortious act has to be unlawful, although in practice this is hardly ever relevant (Eyben and Isager 2013). A coherent formulation of the rule would be: One is liable for adequate damage caused through an unlawful act that can be attributed to one as intentional or negligent, provided that a matter protected by the means of tort law has been infringed and that there are no particular subjective reasons to be free from liability (Vinding Kruse 1989).

So, the general requirements are that there has to be (1) a basis of a claim, (2) a causal link between the behaviour and the damage and (3) a legally relevant damage. Furthermore, there must be no objective reasons to be free from liability.[13] In general, basis of a claim means either culpa, i.e., faulty behaviour or stricter liability. Originally, culpa means negligence but within the scope of the culpa rule it is used as a general term for both intentional and negligent behaviour. No distinction is made at this point as to contractual or non-contractual liability (Iversen and Lindencrone Petersen 2013).

A person can be liable under the scope of the culpa rule, if they fail to meet a general duty to act, for instance a duty to uphold a certain level of safety. In this regard, it is deemed possible to hold an operator or owner liable, even if they do not immediately control the AI system (Petersen and Hebsgaard Muff 2019). The burden of proof rests also under Danish law primarily with the harm-sufferer, which means that it can be—depending on the complexity of a system—extremely difficult to prove the wrongdoer's fault, if anyone actually acted faultily. It is considered probable that the courts will stretch the culpa responsibility as far as possible, for instance by imposing a general duty of care on the owner (Petersen and Hebsgaard Muff 2019).

4 (Analogous) Applicability of *Respondeat Superior* Rules

Particularly in Germany and Austria, but also on the international level, discussion is ongoing regarding possible (analogous) applicability of *respondeat superior* rules to damages liability for AI-related harm.

The idea of applying the framework of liability for others in relation to cases where technical aids are involved is not new. It was already discussed in the 1980's regarding automation-supported data-processing (where there was no faulty human conduct)

---

[13] In older literature, the way in which the noxious act had to be unlawful was formulated—*retsstridig*. See, for example, Ussing (1962).

(Karner 2019). This is also similarly enshrined in Article 12 United Nations Convention of the Use of Electronic Communications in International Contracts (United Nations 2005), according to which automated message systems are attributed to the person on whose behalf the computer was programmed. This evaluation corresponds to the general principle that the employer of a tool should be responsible for the results of its use, seeing as the tool has no will of its own.[14] Even analogies to liability for damage caused by slaves in Roman law have been discussed in this context.[15]

In this section, I will first give a general overview of the *respondeat superior* concept and then delve into the discussion regarding its analogous applicability to AI-related harm. I will mainly look at the principal's liability for damage caused by their agents, but also briefly refer to the animal keeper's liability.

4.1 Concept of Respondeat Superior Liability in General

Within the framework of liability for others, the defendant is not held liable for their own wrongful actions, but because of their relationship with the actual wrongdoer (Giliker 2010). It covers situations where the wrongdoer is under the defendant's supervision, control or directions or must follow their directions (Martín-Casals and Solé Feliu 2008). The best-known field of application is the relationship between employer and employee, but also that of parents and children. Most, if not all national laws of the EU Member States have corresponding rules in place.[16]

The concept of liability for others is known in all Member States and mainly applied in regard to the liability of the employer for torts committed by their employees. Most prerequisites are shared across the Member States, namely an employer-employee relationship, and a tort committed by the employee in the course of the employment (Martín-Casals and Solé Feliu 2008).

However, the concrete approach taken differs across the Member States. In most countries, in addition to the requirements mentioned above, the employee must act faultily, i.e., intentionally or negligently. It should be noted here that the approach taken by German law differs from that of other Member States in the sense that German law does not require faulty behaviour by the employee.[17]

---

[14] See, for example, Pagallo (2013), Cerka et al. (2015), and Opitz (2019).

[15] See, for example, Lior (2020).

[16] See, for example, § 831 BGB for German law, DL 3-19-2 for Danish law, and Article 1242 French Civil Code.

[17] See in detail below, Sect. 4.2.2.

4.2 *Discussion on (Analogous) Applicability*

Considerations regarding the analogous application of the rules on liability for damage caused by employees or animals are based on the idea that the human behind them has duties of supervision.

The idea seems justified as in many sectors AI systems are increasingly replacing humans. This allows entrepreneurs to earn more money and to save money at the same time. But that means they should also bear the cost of accidents. This approach is in line with the general idea that the person who retains control over a potential source of danger/damage shall bear the cost of accidents if eventually harm is caused by the source of danger.[18]

In this section, I will first look at the discussion related to analogous applicability of the rules on liability for others, more exactly those on liability for employees. For this purpose, I selected the current German and Austrian rules as well as the Austrian draft for new civil liability rules. In these two countries, the discussion regarding analogous applicability to AI-related harm has been most prominent. I will further refer to the suggestion of applying the rules on liability for damage caused by animals to AI-related harm.

4.2.1 Austria

Austria is one of the countries where they discuss an analogous application of the rules on liability for others, i.e., rules of liability for employees where technical means are replacing the human workforce.

For non-contractual liability § 1315 ABGB states in this regard that in general a person employing an unfit or knowingly dangerous agent is liable for any damage that the agent causes to third parties in the performance of their duties. Liability under the scope of § 1315 ABGB is thus less comprehensive than in contractual liability where the principal is liable for any fault of the agent.[19]

The argument for an analogous application of § 1313 a or §1315 ABGB is that by employing technical means of support, the principal increases the radius of their business transactions and saves money. Thus, the principle shall also bear the possible additional costs of deciding not to perform the tasks themselves (Kronthaler 2019). In addition, the principal holds, at least to a certain extent, the power over an activity or thing that can be of certain danger to third parties (Ondrasova 2015). Critics reject the equal treatment of humans and machines. § 1315 ABGB is based on human misconduct. Just as in relation to the above-mentioned draft of new civil liability rules, the main question is which acts or omissions of technical means are to be attributed to the principal (Kronthaler 2019). Pursuant to § 1315 ABGB, liability is established based on two defects within the sphere of the principal, namely the unfit and the dangerous agent. For an analogous application, one must therefore find a

[18] See, for example, European Parliament (2020, para 7).

[19] See, for example, Barta (2004).

comparable situation, which would be an unfit or dangerous technical aid. An unfit technical aid would be a device that lacks a necessary function. A dangerous aid would be a device that is uncontrollable due to a defect or failure (Ondrasova 2015). Critics say that the legislator had only human auxiliaries in mind and that therefore an analogy is not possible without further indications within the law (Ondrasova 2015).

4.2.2 Germany

Academic discussion on a possible analogy to *respondeat superior* liability is also ongoing in Germany. In German law, pursuant to § 831 BGB, a person who employs another to perform duties for him, is liable to make good any damage the employed person causes to a third party in the performance of their duties. The principal is exempt from liability if they can prove that they observed the standard of care in the selection and supervision of the employee. As opposed to other national laws, the fault of the employee is not attributed to the principal, but instead the principal is liable for a presumption of their own fault in selecting and supervising the employee. German law does not require a faulty act of the employee. Those in favour of this approach deem the case where another person has actual control over the situation very well comparable to the case where an autonomous AI system is operating (Denga 2018). An AI system is a tool that is used according to the will of the operator. German private law acknowledges liability for the conduct of another—be it a person or a thing. Liability pursuant to § 831 BGB is not only based on the presumption of the principal's fault; there is also the presumption that the principal's failure to appropriately select and to supervise the agent has actually caused the damage. Both presumptions can be refuted (Denga 2018).

It has also been suggested that AI systems must have legal personality before the rules on liability for others can be analogously applied (Münchener Kommentar 2024b). This is supported by the argument that when autonomous agents have their own margin of discretion, there is a legal void regarding their 'autonomous misconduct'. The person who employs the autonomous agent and instructs it by means of digital commands qualifies as the principle under the scope of § 831 BGB. The provision further requires that the digital assistant breach its duty of care (Münchener Kommentar 2024b). In this regard, one must ask how one can establish duties of care for a digital agent. It is also assumed that the digital agent acts in the course of employment also in cases where it gets out of control, as this is a risk the principal has to bear also in relation to human agents (Münchener Kommentar 2024b). Just as in relation to human agents, the principal is not liable under § 831 BGB if they prove that they acted with due care in selecting, instructing and supervising the agent.

For the purpose of its analogous application, it might become necessary to supplement § 831 BGB with so-called digital organisational duties (Münchener Kommentar 2024b). Against an analogous application it has been argued that autonomous systems do not perform actions willingly and consciously and that the purpose of these systems, as opposed to supervised persons, is to act independently. Constant supervision would neutralise the advantages of these systems. In addition, critics state that the possibility of exoneration provided by § 831 BGB will usually have the effect that the operator is not liable (Grützmacher 2016).

5 Applicability of Rules on Liability for Animals

In order to ensure sufficient protection of potential victims of AI-related harm, some academics suggest the application of the rules on liability for animals. In this context, it has been stated that if pursuant to the state of the art, machines are not capable of acting like a reasonable human (which is not the case just yet) and thus, should be deemed dangerous, "it is but a short step to draw an analogy with the liability at common [and civil] law of the owner or keeper of an animal that is either known or presumed to be dangerous to mankind" (Pagallo 2013). Several national tort laws of EU Member States recognize a strict liability of the keeper of the animal for damage caused by the same animal (Opitz 2019). This rule is also based on the assumption that the owners must take precautions to prevent others from being harmed by the animal. An analogous application of the corresponding liability rules to robots is supported by the argument that both animals and robots are "neither human nor totally without responsibility" (Opitz 2019). They attribute to both animals and robots the ability to think and act independently from their human owners and to learn based on the trial-and-error method (Opitz 2019). The analogy between animals and AI, or robots, has been suggested because both are not human, they are others (Johnson and Verdicchio 2018).

Further, academics suggest that users of non-defective low-risk robots be subject to negligence liability, comparably to domesticated animals in common law jurisdictions like the US. This type of robot has limited autonomy due to its programming and therefore the probability for these devices to show highly unpredictable 'behaviour' is relatively low. Users of high-risk robots should be subject to strict liability (Asaro 2016; Opitz 2019). The classification in terms of high-risk or low-risk should be based on various factors such as size, function and the environment in which a robot operates but also alteration or the risk of owners failing to perform necessary maintenance. Against an analogous application of the rules on liability for animals the argument has been brought forward that animals act based on their natural instincts while robots act based on algorithms that were programmed by humans. Animals are sentient beings, while robots are not. Another argument brought forward against an analogy is that animals, as opposed to robots can roam freely. This argument might no longer hold the more autonomous robots become (Johnson and Verdicchio 2018; Opitz 2019). And one must consider the fact that many animals cannot roam freely either but are instead restrained by fences, leashes and the like. In ongoing discussions in Denmark, it is mentioned that back in the days when the country was still an agricultural society, court practice established strict liability for damage caused by "the autonomous units nowadays called domestic animals" (Petersen and Hebsgaard Muff 2019).

However, all things considered, the situation of animals differs more significantly from that of a programmed algorithm or robot. Even though animals might be employed by a human for certain tasks, like horses drawing a carriage, dogs herding sheep or protecting a property, these tasks differ very much from the fields where modern AI systems are employed.

6 The Austrian Draft on New Civil Liability Rules

In a draft on a new law on civil liability published in Austria, corresponding rules for liability for damage caused by technical aids were already proposed in 2005. A working group of the Austrian Federal Ministry of Justice presented a draft of a new set of civil liability rules. This includes, among others, the—contractual and non-contractual—liability for technical support mechanisms that are being used instead of a human agent.[20]

Pursuant to § 1306 (4) of the draft the principal is liable for the failure of technical aids he employs comparably to an agent, provided that the injured party proves that the principal failed to meet the standard of care when selecting and monitoring the technical aid or that the technical aid was not fit for purpose. If the principal is an entrepreneur, the burden of proof is shifted. This approach is based in the increasing number of machines used instead of humans. A person shall not be able to circumvent liability by simply serving themselves of a machine instead of a human servant (Bundesministerium für Justiz 2008; Wagner 2008). The use of an unfit technical aid creates a risk comparable to the one resulting from employing an unfit human agent (Ondrasova 2015). The draft does clearly define the scope of a technical aid, which was criticised as it could mean that the wording of the draft exceeds the envisioned scope of liability.

It is, however, assumed that the draft provision, at least to a certain extent, targets computers and automated data processing tools. If the decisive criterion is autonomy, it remains to be clarified to what degree the technical aid must be autonomous in order to fall under the scope of the draft provision (Ondrasova 2015). Yet, the approach which treats human agents and machines alike has been criticised, arguing there is a fundamental difference between actions performed by a human and machine operations (Reischauer 2006). Liability for damage caused by an agent is not strict, but it requires a misconduct of the agent. Consequentially, one must ask how to determine the misconduct of a machine. The draft refers to a failure, which, again raises the question of whether in the case of an unavoidable breakdown of an otherwise reliable machine it would not be consequent to exonerate the principal from liability (Wagner 2008). However, the draft rules have not yet been implemented into law. Given that they were published in 2005, it is also very likely that they never will.

[20] See, for example, Bundesministerium für Justiz (2008).

7 Other National Liability Rules Relevant for AI-Related Damage

7.1 The French Rule on Liability for Damage Caused by Things

In this context, it also seems appropriate to consider the (analogous) application of the French '*responsabilité du fait des choses*', liability for damage caused by things. While many EU Member States enacted liability rules only for potentially hazardous items or installations such as nuclear power plants, French law includes general strict liability rules for all kinds of items. This principle was first introduced in two judgments handed down by the Cour de Cassation, namely *Teffaine* (1896) and *Jand'heur* (1930) (Dalloz 2024).[21] Article 1242 (1) of the French Civil Code (Cc) states that one is responsible not only for damage caused by one's own behaviour but also for damage caused by persons one is responsible for and by things under one's custody. Liability is strict. The '*gardien*', the keeper, of the item can only invoke an unforeseeable and unavoidable cause or the harm-sufferer's fault as defences.

There are no official definitions of the terms 'thing' and 'keeper'. Under the scope of article 1242 Cc, a 'thing' is any inanimate object, no matter whether it is defective, natural or artificial, dangerous or not dangerous, and movable or immovable. Only things governed by special regimes such as animals, defective products, buildings or motor vehicles do not fall under the scope of article 1242 Cc (Dalloz 2024). The custodian is the person who has the power to use, direct, and control the thing at the time of the accident. This is usually the owner, but also persons other than the owner can be the custodian, as it is a factual concept, not a legal one. The thing must have contributed to the realisation of the damage. This is easy to establish when there has been contact between the moving thing and the harm-sufferer or their property. The custodian need not participate actively. When a non-moving thing causes damage, the harm-sufferer must prove that the thing was instrumental in causing the damage and 'behaved' abnormally. This is particularly the case when the thing is defective or in an abnormal position. If there was no contact between the harm-sufferer and the custodian's thing, the former must prove that the thing was still the cause of the damage. This applies mainly in situations where the thing by its abnormal presence causes another person to commit a harmful act due to fear or lack of skill.[22]

The field of application of this concept is very flexible. In terms of applicability to AI, the prevailing approach in French law is that it can be applied to 'incorporated' AI, meaning movables that rely on AI technologies such as robot lawnmowers and similar devices. It is not applicable to AI that is not incorporated, which includes

---

[21] In '*Teffaine*', the Cour de Cassation held the owner of a machine liable when the explosion of the machine caused the death of another person, based on the rules on liability for damaged buildings. In '*Jand'heur*', this approach was confirmed, and the Cour de Cassation held that the owner of a 'non-live thing' (*chose inanimée*) is responsible for damage caused by the thing.

[22] See Van Dam (2013).

algorithms included in computer programmes and very autonomous AI systems.[23] The draft of the reformation of the French law on civil liability further mentions explicitly that the liability for damage caused by things only applies to corporal things (Dalloz Actu Etudiant 2016). This is supported by the argument that AI is to be considered an immaterial agent whereas the law so far only acknowledges material agents, such as other humans or animals, or immaterial objects, and thus there is a legal void. Other arguments relate to the requirement of direction and control and state that in the case of an autonomous AI system this requirement is not fulfilled.[24] However, most AI systems in use nowadays are not fully autonomous so that there is still a human in charge who at least decides if, when and for what purpose to use an AI system.[25]

In addition, it has been suggested there be a distinction between the custody of structure and custody of behaviour when damage is caused by a thing with own and dangerous dynamics. The custody of behaviour is attributed to the owner while custody of structure rests with the manufacturer. In the latter case, it will be difficult to draw the line in relation to liability for defective products (Courtois 2016). As the French responsibility for damage caused by things does not depend on the defectiveness of the thing, attributing responsibility for the structure of a non-defective AI system might in fact overburden the manufacturer and hinder innovation.

Yet, liability for damage caused by things based on the custody of behaviour, i.e., attributed to the owner or the operator, if different from the owner, seems a practicable solution. Because even though an owner or operator might not fully understand the decision-making process of an AI system, they are still the ones that ultimately decide whether or not to use such a system.

In relation to French law, one must always keep the 'non-cumule' principle in mind which means that tort law rules are not applicable as long as there is a contract based on which the harm-sufferer can obtain compensation.[26] This would in practice limit the scope of application of the rule on liability for damage caused by things to cases where the wrongdoer and the harm-sufferer have no previous—contractual—relationship.

7.2 Danish Liability with Reversed Burden of Proof

In addition, Danish law also recognizes a negligence liability with a reversed burden of proof, i.e., a presumption of the wrongdoer's fault. Courts apply this sharpened form of liability either based on specific legal provisions or based on policy considerations (Kure 2015). In the decision U 1995.550/2 Ø handed down by the Eastern Regional Court of Denmark, a hospital was held liable for damage caused to a person

[23] See, for example, Dalloz Actu Etudiant (2016).

[24] See, for example, Janal (2016).

[25] See also, for example, Courtois (2016).

[26] See, for example, Borghetti (2019).

resulting from a malfunction of an elevator. The hospital could not prove that the accident had not been avoidable by means of a more appropriate construction and installation of the elevator and its safety systems.

It is thus probable that in the future courts will shift the burden of proof in comparable case constellations, i.e., when harm-sufferers are unable to prove the wrongdoer's fault due to lack of (technical) knowledge. This can be relevant in cases outside the scope of the AILD, for instance in claims concerning AI systems that are not considered high-risk, or that are prohibited. Within this rule, it would not be necessary for the claimant to try to have the disclosure of evidence ordered. Providers or users/deployers of AI systems could then be held liable by the courts if they cannot prove that a harmful event would not have been avoided with better maintenance and/or monitoring of the system.

7.3 Danish Law—Non-Law-Based Strict Liability

French law is not the only national law in the EU that has an outstanding particular liability norm. Danish law also has a remarkable rule called non-law-based strict liability (*ulovbestemt objektivt ansvar*). As the name indicates, it is not enshrined in legislation but has evolved through academia and court practice. It emerged in the early twentieth century when the Danish scholar Henry Ussing formulated in his doctoral thesis the hypothesis that there should be a non-law-based strict liability for "extraordinary activities causing unusual danger" (Ussing 1914). Ussing (1962) argued that society should not bear the cost of accidents resulting from dangerous activities providing profit to the person carrying out these activities. A further requirement he set up was that the danger inherent in the activity is known so that it is possible to consider whether the profit outweighs possible expenses such as the payment of compensation to harm-sufferers (Ussing 1962). However, his approach was not backed up in legal practice. Only from the 1980's on did courts start to award compensation in cases, regardless of whether culpa could be attributed to the wrongdoer. These cases had in common that there had been a significant risk of causing damage, the wrongdoer was aware of the risk of damage and there was no faulty behaviour of the wrongdoer.

In this context, the borders between the rules on product liability developed in Danish court practice and non-law-based strict liability are blurry, so that the plaintiff can actually be liable, based on what is to be considered more of a risk assessment (Petersen and Hebsgaard Muff 2019).

It is considered likely that in the future the courts will apply this liability rule when a defect of the AI system cannot be proven, or when damage has been caused by the use of a prohibited AI system. This is also based on the assumption that the owner or operator of an AI system has the best overview of its potential to cause damage and that they will therefore be held liable (Petersen and Hebsgaard Muff 2019).

8 Concluding Remarks

The AILD with its alleviations did not cover all cases of liability for damage caused by AI. Most incidents involving either AI systems not classified as high-risk, or prohibited AI systems fell outside its scope. The situation is similar in relation to AI systems used in the course of a private, non-professional activity. At least in theory, existing liability concepts can well be applied to AI-related harm. However, in practice, we might soon see the limits, depending on the degree of autonomy an AI system has. For how can a human operator be deemed negligent if they are unable to understand the decision-making process of a system which is opaque—probably even to its programmer if it is based on unsupervised machine learning? Is it already negligent to utilize a system one does not understand? How much are human operators supposed to understand about the systems they use? For the time being, at least the AI Act provides a set of obligations for actors along the AI value chain that can help determine whether the standard of care has been observed or not.

The AILD could have helped to overcome information asymmetry between the provider or user/deployer of an AI system and the injured party to a certain extent. However, this is only of use as long as humans have a sufficient degree of control over the decision-making of an AI system. This is particularly relevant because the AILD would only have applied to cases where the harmful output of an AI system, or its failure to produce an output—which then leads to harm—is the consequence of the fault of a human (input). Yet, when the technological development proceeds, some AI systems may become opaque even to their programmers. Even alleviations such as those enshrined in the AILD might not be of use any longer, as providers probably will not have useful evidence at hand. This may even render the idea of an analogous application of the *respondeat superior* liability rules—which does not seem completely far-fetched – useless, as also in that regard a certain degree of oversight would be required.

In this context, Madeline Claire Elish states that responsibility may even be misattributed to a human actor who in fact has only limited control over the behaviour of a complex automated or autonomous system, calling the human a "moral crumple zone" in this regard.[27] Pursuant to Nissenbaum, computational technologies create systemic gaps in accountability which must be addressed. Human operators end up absorbing responsibility in ways that do not reflect distributed control and interactional aspects composing the socio-technical system.[28] Against that one may argue that the unforeseeability of actions performed by machine-learning systems is itself foreseeable. It has also been argued that it is foreseeable for software developers that third parties interact with the software in a way that could cause harm.[29] The determination to (mis-)attribute responsibility to a human actor regardless of whether they

[27] Elish MC (2019) 'Moral Crumple Zones: Cautionary Tales in Human–Robot Interaction' Engaging Science, Technology, and Society 5, 41.

[28] Ibid. 50.

[29] Kowert W (2017) 'The foreseeability of Human-Artificial Intelligence Interactions' Texas Law Review 96, 191.

had sufficient control over an automated system's behaviour may also be a result of the need to provide harm-sufferers with a plaintiff and thus with the possibility to obtain compensation.

If this is meant to be the primary goal in relation to AI liability, one may in the future consider pragmatic approaches such as the French liability for damage caused by things, or policy considerations, as occurs in Danish court practice with a reversed burden of proof or a non-law-based strict liability. In any event, in the long run it is doubtful that alleviations to the burden of proof are enough to remedy the attribution of AI 'behaviour' to humans.

References

Asaro P (2016) The liability problem for autonomous artificial agents. AAAI Spring symposium series, 4. https://peterasaro.org/writing/Asaro,%20Ethics%20Auto%20Agents,%20AAAI.pdf

Barta H (ed) (2004) Zivilrecht – Grundriss und Einführung in das Rechtsdenken. WUV-Univ.-Verl

Bilski N, Schmid T (2019) Verantwortungsfindung beim Einsatz maschinell lernender Systeme. Neue JuristE Online-Z 19:657–661

Borghetti J-S (2019) The borderlines of tort law in France. In: Martín-Casals M (ed) The borderlines of tort law. Intersentia

Bundesministerium für Justiz (2008) Diskussionsentwurf der beim Bundesministerium für Justiz eingerichteten Arbeitsgruppe für ein neues österreichisches Schadenersatzrecht. Juristische Blätter 130(6):365–372

Čerka P, Grigienė J, Sirbikytė G (2015) Liability for damages caused by artificial intelligence. Comput Law Secur Rev 31(3):376–389

Chandler JP (1977) Computer transactions: potential liability of computer users and vendors. Wash Univ Law Q 1977(3):405–443

Courtois G (2016) Robots intelligents et responsabilités : quels régimes, quelles perspectives ? Dalloz IP/IT 6:287–290

Dalloz (2024) Dalloz fiche d'orientation art 1242. https://www.dalloz.fr/documentation/Document?id=DZ%2FOASIS%2F000843

Dalloz Actu Etudiant (2016). Focus sur responsabilité et intelligence artificielle. https://actu.dalloz-etudiant.fr/focus-sur/article/responsabilite-et-intelligence-artificielle/h/5af2e139483cae307e3ba1120a2580a3.html

de Bruyne J, Dheu O, Ducuing C (2023) The European Commission's approach to extra-contractual liability and AI – an evaluation of the AI liability directive and the revised product liability directive. Comput Law Secur Rev 51:105894. https://doi.org/10.1016/j.clsr.2023.105894

Denga M (2018) Deliktische Haftung für Künstliche Intelligenz. Computer und Recht 34(2):69–78. https://doi.org/10.9785/cr-2018-0203

Elish MC (2019) Moral crumple zones: cautionary tales in human-robot interaction. Engag Sci, Technol, Soc 5. https://doi.org/10.17351/ests2019.260

European Commission (2020) European enterprise survey on the use of technologies based on artificial intelligence – Final report. https://doi.org/10.2759/759368

European Commission (2021) Proposal for a regulation of the European Parliament and of the Council laying down harmonised rules of artificial intelligence (Artificial Intelligence Act). COM(2021) 206 final

European Commission (2022) Proposal for a Directive of the European Parliament and of the Council on adapting non-contractual civil liability rules to artificial intelligence (AI Liability Directive). COM(2022) 496 final

European Parliament (2020) Resolution of 20 October 2020 with recommendations to the Commission on a civil liability regime for artificial intelligence. 2020/2014(INL)
Eyben B, Isager H (2013) Lærebog i erstatningsret. Djøf.
Giliker P (2010) Vicarious liability in tort. Cambridge University Press, A comparative perspective
Grützmacher M (2016) Die deliktische Haftung für autonome Systeme – Industrie 4.0 als Herausforderung für das bestehende Recht? Computer und Recht 10. https://doi.org/10.9785/cr-2016-1015
Hacker P (2023) The European AI liability directives – critique of a half-hearted approach and lessons for the future. Comput Law Secur Rev 51:105871. https://doi.org/10.1016/j.clsr.2023.105871
Iversen B, Lindencrone Petersen L (2013) Danish business law. Djøf
Janal R (2016) Die deliktische Haftung beim Einsatz von Robotern – Lehren aus der Haftung für Sachen und Gehilfen. In: Gless S, Seelmann K (eds) Intelligente Agenten und das Recht. Nomos
Jaunernig Kommentar (2023) Jauernig Kommentar zum Bürgerlichen Gesetzbuch § 823. C. H. Beck
Johnson DG, Verdicchio M (2018) Why robots should not be treated like animals. Ethics Inf Technol 292. https://doi.org/10.1007/s10676-018-9481-5
Karner E (2019) Liability for robotics: current rules, challenges, and the need for innovative concepts. In: Lohsse S, Schulze R, Staudenmayer D (eds) Liability for artificial intelligence and the internet of things. Nomos
Kowert W (2017) The foreseeability of human-artificial intelligence interactions. Tex Law Rev 96(1):181–204
Kronthaler C (2019) Analoge Anwendung von § 1313 a ABGB auf technische Hilfsmittel? Österreichische Juristen-Zeitung, pp 945–949
Kure H (2015) Kompendium i Formueret. Karnov
Lior A (2020) AI entities as AI agents: artificial intelligence liability and the AI *respondeat superior* analogy. Mitchell Hamline Law Rev 46(5):1043–1102
Martín-Casals M, Solé Feliu J (2008) Liability for others. In: Koziol H, Schulze R (eds) Tort law of the European Community. Springer
Münchener Kommentar (2024a) Münchener Kommentar zum Bürgerlichen Gesetzbuch: BGB § 823. C. H. Beck
Münchener Kommentar (2024b) Münchener Kommentar zum Bürgerlichen Gesetzbuch: BGB § 831. C. H. Beck
Novelli C, Casolari F, Hacker P, Spedicato G, Floridi (2024). Generative AI in EU law: liability, privacy, intellectual property, and cybersecurity. https://doi.org/10.2139/ssrn.4694565
Ondrasova E (2015). Haftung für technische Hilfsmittel de lege lata. Österreichische Juristen-Zeitung, pp 443–457
Opitz P (2019) Civil liability and autonomous robotic machines: approaches in the EU and US. TTLF Working Papers No. 43. https://law.stanford.edu/publications/no-43-civil-liability-and-autonomous-robotic-machines-approaches-in-the-eu-and-us/
Pagallo U (2013) The laws of robots: crimes, contracts, and torts. Springer
Petersen S, Hebsgaard Muff S (2019) Ansvaret for skader forvoldt af autonome robotter. Erhvervsjuridisk Tidsskrift, ET.2019.2.
Reischauer R (2006) Reform des Schadensersatzrechts?. Österreichische Juristen-Zeitung, pp 391–400
Schütte B (2024) AI regulation in the EU: the future interplay between frameworks. In: Gill-Pedro E, Moberg A (eds) YSEC Yearbook of socio-economic constitutions. Springer
Selbst A (2020) Negligence and AI's human users. Boston Law Rev 100(4):1315–1376
United Nations (2005) United Nations Convention on the Use of Electronic Communications in International Contracts. https://treaties.un.org/doc/Treaties/2005/11/20051128%2004-23%20PM/Ch_X_18p.pdf
Ussing H (1914) Skyld og skade: bør erstatningspligt uden-for kontraksforhold vaere betinget af culpa?

Ussing H (1962) Erstatningsret. Juristforbundets forlag
Van Dam C (2013) European tort law. Oxford University Press
Vinding Kruse A (1989) Erstatningsretten. Jurist-og Økonomforbundets Forlag
Wagner G (2008) Reform des Schadensersatzrechts. Juristische Blätter 130:2–22

Artificial Intelligence in the Criminal Justice System: Exploring Risks and Opportunities Through the Lens of the European Union's AI Act

Kitti Mezei

Abstract The integration of artificial intelligence (AI) into the criminal justice system offers transformative opportunities to enhance efficiency, accuracy, and fairness in law enforcement and legal processes. However, it also presents significant risks, including potential biases, lack of transparency, and privacy concerns. This chapter examines the dual-edged nature of AI applications in the criminal justice system through the regulatory framework of the European Union's AI Act. By analysing these regulatory measures, this chapter highlights how the AI Act seeks to mitigate the inherent risks of AI while fostering its potential to improve justice outcomes. This exploration underscores the necessity of continuous monitoring and adaptive regulation to balance innovation with the protection of fundamental rights, ensuring that AI contributes positively to the criminal justice system. Furthermore, it delves into case studies in which AI has both succeeded and failed within the legal framework, offering insights into best practices and areas requiring caution. The chapter also discusses the ethical implications of AI in policing and judicial decisions, emphasising the importance of developing AI systems that are not only technically robust but also ethically sound.

The chapter was supported by the European Union project RRF-2.3.1–21-2022–00,004 within the framework of the Artificial Intelligence National Laboratory and by the Ministry of Innovation and Technology NRDI Office within the framework of the FK_21 Young Researcher Excellence Program (138,965).

K. Mezei (✉)
Institute for Legal Studies, HUN-REN Centre for Social Sciences, Budapest, Hungary
e-mail: mezei.kitti@tk.hun-ren.hu

M. Varju and K. Mezei (eds.), *The Challenges of Artificial Intelligence for Law in Europe*, Data Science, Machine Intelligence, and Law 6,
https://doi.org/10.1007/978-3-031-86813-9_7

1 Introduction

Artificial intelligence (AI) use cases have the potential to streamline the operations of law enforcement and judicial bodies, thereby bolstering security and the efficacy of criminal justice systems. They offer opportunities to enhance suspect and victim identification and aid in crime prevention and risk assessment. However, their adoption in these contexts can lead to adverse consequences, potentially infringing upon fundamental rights such as non-discrimination, data protection, privacy, freedom of expression, and the right to a fair trial. Particular concerns surround AI-driven technologies such as facial recognition, predictive policing, and reoffender risk assessment tools, which may exacerbate biases and perpetuate discrimination in criminal justice. Additionally, AI applications are susceptible to security vulnerabilities, serving as both vectors and targets for cyber-attacks, and they may be exploited by malicious actors for illicit purposes. Therefore, while AI holds promise for improving security and justice systems, careful consideration and oversight are essential to mitigate risks and harms and safeguard individual rights and privacy (European Parliament 2021).

The purpose of this chapter is to review the risks and opportunities of using AI systems in policing and fighting crime from the perspective of the EU's AI Act. In April 2021, the European Commission presented a proposal for a Regulation on Artificial Intelligence that became known as the AI Act (European Commission 2021). Later that year, in October 2021, the European Parliament adopted a resolution on using AI by the police and judicial authorities in criminal matters specifically (European Parliament 2021). After long debates, the EP approved the final text of the AI Act on March 13, 2024, followed by the Council formally adopting it on May 21, 2024. The AI Act will be published in the Official Journal of the EU around June 2024, and it will enter into force 20 days after publication with a specific application timeline from 6 to 36 months.

Cases involving AI in law enforcement have presented the greatest number of ethical and legal controversies from the start. The AI Act will apply both to public and private actors that develop such systems as "providers", or that use them for professional purposes as "users" or "deployers".[1] Public authorities will usually be considered "users", but they will act as "providers" when they develop their own AI systems in-house or purchase tailor-made AI systems. The use of AI, with its specific characteristics, can adversely affect several fundamental rights and the security of users. To address this, the AI Act adopted a risk-based approach, as is already visible from the first version of the draft regulation, according to which AI applications are classified into risk classes and corresponding legal actions are tailored to the specific risk level.[2] Risk in this context means the combination of the probability that a particular harm will occur due to the use of a particular technology and the severity of that harm. To this end, the AI Act made a clear distinction between unacceptable risk (prohibited category), high-risk, limited-risk and minimal-risk AI systems.[3]

---

[1] European Commission (2021), Article 2.

[2] For more on this issue, see Mahler (2022).

[3] European Commission (2021), Preamble, Recital (14).

Cases involving law enforcement use have been mainly classified as high-risk AI systems. The AI Act defines law enforcement authority and law enforcement activities.[4] Importantly, the AI Act will exclude AI systems used for military, defence, or national security purposes from the scope of the AI Act, regardless of whether public or private entities utilise them.[5] This exclusion is justified by both international law and the specific competencies governing defence and security within the EU. The exclusion is supported by Article 4(2) of the Treaty on European Union (TEU), which designates defence and national security matters as the sole responsibility of Member States. Additionally, the specificities of the Member States' defence policies, covered by Chapter 2 of Title V of the TEU, are subject to public international law. However, if these systems are also used for non-excluded purposes, such as civilian or law enforcement activities, they must comply with the AI Act. Conversely, AI systems developed for civilian or law enforcement purposes that are subsequently used for military, defence, or national security purposes are not subject to the AI Act. This allows entities engaged in national security, defence, and military activities to use AI systems without being affected by the regulation.[6] Arguably, these rules create a loophole that allows Member States to exempt themselves from the rules for any activity they deem relevant for "national security" (Leufer et al. 2023).

2 Prohibited Law Enforcement AI Use Cases

Following its risk-based approach, the AI Act proposes a category of prohibited AI systems.[7] This entails a completely prohibited category, which includes the prohibition of real-time remote biometric identification for law enforcement purposes in publicly accessible spaces[8] with narrow exceptions where the use is strictly necessary to achieve the public interest, which outweighs associated risks. These situations include searching for victims of crime, addressing threats to life or physical safety, and locating or identifying perpetrators or suspects of serious criminal offences

[4] European Commission (2021), Article 3: law enforcement authority "means any public authority competent for the prevention, investigation, detection or prosecution of criminal offences or the execution of criminal penalties, including the safeguarding against and the prevention of threats to public security; or any other body or entity entrusted by Member State law to exercise public authority and public powers for the purposes of the prevention, investigation, detection or prosecution of criminal offences or the execution of criminal penalties, including the safeguarding against and the prevention of threats to public security"; law enforcement "means activities carried out by law enforcement authorities or on their behalf for the prevention, investigation, detection or prosecution of criminal offences or the execution of criminal penalties, including safeguarding against and preventing threats to public security."

[5] European Commission (2021), Article 2(3).

[6] European Commission (2021), Preamble, Recital (24).

[7] European Commission (2021), Title II.

[8] Publicly accessible space "means any publicly or privately owned physical place accessible to an undetermined number of natural persons, regardless of whether certain conditions for access may apply, and regardless of the potential capacity restrictions".

(such as human trafficking or sexual exploitation or for the prevention of terrorist attacks) punishable by a custodial sentence or detention order of at least four years. Thus, the prohibition does not apply where these systems are used for any of the listed specific purposes because the severity threshold for such offences ensures that real-time biometric identification systems are proportionate and justified. In principle, relying on such an exception will require thorough assessments, technical and organisational measures, notifications and a warrant.[9] However, the AI Act allows the use of real-time and post-event biometric identification for law enforcement and private purposes under certain conditions in general, so there is no ban in these cases (Raposo 2022).

Moreover, some argue that holding law enforcement to a higher standard than other public or private actors when using real-time biometric identification systems is unjustifiable. Public–private partnerships are common in the development of AI systems. This blurs the lines between their roles and domains, making it challenging to determine when public involvement starts or ends, and where private entities intervene (Georgieva et al. 2022). Similarly, assessing similar risks differently for fundamental rights and values in deploying such systems is unreasonable.[10] Regulatory decisions often prioritise the immediacy of identification, but the focus should be on the use and its implications rather than solely on the timeline. Issues such as scope, consent, and technical architecture are similar in both public and private use of real-time systems, affecting individuals with no reason to be monitored. However, the crucial distinction lies in the fact that private parties are not bound by considerations of the common good, public values, or the checks and balances present in democratic societies (Georgieva et al. 2022; Veale and Borgesius 2021). For example, there is a moratorium in force in Italy, until 31 December 2025, on the introduction of video surveillance systems based on facial recognition using biometric data, in public places or places open to the public, by private individuals and public bodies. The use of such systems is currently only allowed to judicial authorities in the exercise of their functions.

The AI Act provides that a judicial body or an independent administrative authority must explicitly authorise the use of AI systems in each Member State for these purposes.[11] Authorisation should typically precede the use of the system, except

[9] Real-time biometric identification is held permissible for law enforcement if the following prerequisites apply: (a) *ex-ante* permission by a judicial authority; (b) targeted search; and (c) link with the investigation of committed serious crimes listed in Article 83(1) Treaty on the Functioning of European Union (terrorism, trafficking in human beings and sexual exploitation of women and children, illicit drug trafficking, illicit arms trafficking, money laundering, corruption, counterfeiting of means of payment, computer crime, and organised crime).

[10] As reported by the Dutch Data Protection Authority (DPA) (DPA 2020), it issued a formal warning to a supermarket for using facial recognition technology, which the supermarket claimed was for protecting customers, staff, and preventing shoplifting. This technology, connected to entrance cameras, uses biometric data to identify individuals. Such use is prohibited unless explicit consent is given or it is necessary for substantial public interest in security. The supermarket did not obtain explicit consent, as merely informing customers does not suffice, and the DPA did not accept the supermarket's claim that its use met the substantial public interest criterion.

[11] European Commission (2021), Article 5.

in urgent situations where obtaining prior authorisation is objectively impossible. In emergencies, system use should be minimal and subject to strict safeguards specified in national law. In such cases, law enforcement must promptly request authorisation, providing reasons for the delay, within 24 h. If authorisation is denied, system usage must cease immediately, and all related data, except data acquired legally, must be discarded. Additionally, decisions with legal consequences cannot solely rely on system outputs.[12] Arguably, allowing an independent administrative authority, rather than a judicial authority, to authorise the use of real-time remote biometric identification is a controversial choice. While these administrative bodies may be formally independent, they could still be vulnerable to government influence. Without judicial involvement, relying solely on administrative oversight may be inadequate from a checks and balances perspective. The decentralisation of the authorisation framework at the level of the Member States raises concerns, and particularly outlined in the AI Act are situations in which authority is devolved to agencies within Member States, grounded in the legal frameworks of those respective states. This approach raises concerns, particularly in Member States with questionable adherence to the rule of law. The issue is compounded when pre-authorisation for real-time biometric identification use can be omitted, allowing retrospective authorisation within 24 h in urgent situations. Such flexibility may increase the risk of misuse, particularly in countries where democratic institutions are weak (Hacker 2024).

Another banned use case is databases based on bulk scraping of facial images,[13] since there are cases in which specific harms stem from the online deployment of AI biometric systems (Georgieva et al. 2022). An issue of considerable controversy revolves around the involvement of private companies in implementing these technologies. For example, in February 2020, media outlets revealed leaked documents indicating that Clearview AI had secured contracts with over 600 law enforcement agencies globally, including in Europe (Clarke 2023; Georgieva et al 2022; Sanz 2022). This technology equips users with the capability to potentially identify every individual they encounter in real time, significantly enhancing law enforcement's ability to swiftly and accurately match faces against extensive databases. The system enables an investigating officer, for example, to submit an image of a person of interest for analysis and conduct a search within a database compiled by Clearview AI. This database purportedly contains publicly accessible images sourced from online postings, which may not necessarily pertain to the individual under investigation, raising concerns about privacy and the ethical implications of such technology (González Fuster 2020).

The AI Act will ban the use of predictive policing software to assess an individual's risk of committing future crimes based on personal traits. The final version of the ban is considerably weaker than that proposed by the EP in June. Such uses of AI-based tools in policing and criminal justice risk discrimination and a violation of fundamental rights, including the right to a fair trial and the presumption of innocence. Predictive policing usually encompasses various approaches (only some of which

[12] See European Commission (2021), Preamble, Recital (35).

[13] See, in this regard, Sobel (2021).

are prohibited), which can be broadly categorised into four types: predicting crimes by forecasting high-risk locations and times, identifying potential offenders at risk of committing or repeating crimes, creating profiles resembling those of past offenders, and predicting potential victims of crimes to identify vulnerable individuals or groups (Egbert and Leese 2020).

Predictive policing systems have already been deployed in Europe, in Austria, Germany and Switzerland (EUFRA 2022). The system called Precobs predicts the likelihood of burglaries occurring in specific areas within a given time frame by using the theory of near-repeat phenomena, which identifies patterns indicating subsequent crimes in the vicinity of previous burglaries.[14] In the Netherlands, two predictive policing systems, SyRI and CAS, were deployed in 2019. SyRI is a person-based predictive policing system that identifies individuals at risk of engaging in social security and tax fraud. However, after facing legal challenges for violating privacy rights, its use was discontinued in 2020. CAS, a place-based predictive policing system, was adopted nationwide in the Netherlands. It categorises areas into squares based on the potential risk of crime occurrence, creating heat maps that assist police in investigating areas or distributing patrols.

3 High-Risk AI Use Cases in Criminal Justice

The AI Act imposes several obligations on providers (and, to a lesser extent, users) of the high-risk systems listed in Annex III.[15] Obligations apply along the AI value chain and the whole life cycle of the technology. The AI Act places stringent requirements on a high-risk AI system provider and its importer, distributor and deployer. Importers and distributors are primarily responsible for ensuring the compliance of the high-risk AI systems they handle. Importers are tasked with verifying the system's conformity by examining various documentation, while distributors must confirm CE (*Conformité Européenne*) conformity with EU product safety and quality requirements.

An AI system is considered high-risk either because it is a safety component of an already strictly regulated product group or because it is used in an area where it poses a significant risk of harm to the health, safety or fundamental rights of natural persons. However, the AI Act states that "any AI system referred to in Annex III shall not be considered as high-risk if they do not pose a significant risk of harm, to the health, safety or fundamental rights of natural persons, including by not materially influencing the outcome of decision making".[16] The cases exempt from the high-risk classification are narrow procedural tasks, improvements to the

[14] The algorithm integrates geographical data with police statistics to identify patterns associated with professional serial burglars and predict potential near-repeat burglaries. This approach predates the use of AI systems and draws on criminological studies from the 1980s on crime hotspots.

[15] European Commission (2021), Title III.

[16] European Commission (2021), Article 6(3).

results of previously completed human activities, decision or outlier detection without replacing human assessments, and those in which the AI system is designed to detect decision-making patterns or deviations, not to replace or influence previous human assessments without proper review.[17] AI systems will be considered not to pose a significant risk of harm if they meet at least one of four criteria. Nonetheless, the AI Act also makes it clear that any AI system will automatically be considered to be high-risk if the AI system performs the profiling of individuals. General purpose AI systems used as high-risk AI systems or integrated into them will require providers to take additional steps too.

High-risk AI systems that are deployed by public authorities or entities acting on their behalf will have to be registered in a public EU database unless those systems are used for law enforcement and migration. The latter will have to be registered in a non-public part of the database that will be only accessible to relevant supervisory authorities. Other deployers may decide on their registration on a voluntary basis.

The high-risk areas include biometrics, education, employment, critical infrastructure, essential private and public services, law enforcement, border control and administration of justice, but only if there is a significant risk to fundamental rights.

Annex III categorises post-biometric identification and emotional inference for law enforcement purposes as high-risk applications. As a result, law enforcement agencies must comply with stricter requirements if they plan to utilise these tools. Biometrics, as permitted by relevant EU or national law, encompasses remote biometric identification systems, excluding AI systems used solely for identity verification. It also includes AI systems for biometric categorisation based on sensitive attributes and those used for emotion recognition.

High-risk AI uses also include law enforcement use cases[18] since their actions involving certain AI systems can wield significant power imbalances, potentially leading to surveillance, arrest, or deprivation of individuals' liberty, impacting fundamental rights as guaranteed by the EU Charter of Fundamental Rights. If AI systems lack high-quality training data, fail to meet performance standards or lack transparency, they may discriminate or produce unjust outcomes. This can hinder the exercise of procedural rights, such as the right to an effective remedy, a fair trial and the presumption of innocence (Gless 2020; Palmiotto 2018). Since the use of AI tools by law enforcement and other authorities risks creating inequality or exclusion, it is crucial to consider how these tools impact the defence rights of suspects, especially regarding the challenges in understanding how these systems work and

[17] European Commission (2021), (Article 6(3) a)-d)).

[18] These are, according to Annex III, AI systems intended to be used by law enforcement authorities or on their behalf or by Union institutions, bodies, offices or agencies in support of law enforcement authorities for assessing the risk of individuals becoming victims of criminal offences, employing polygraphs and similar tools, evaluating the reliability of evidence in criminal investigations or prosecutions, assessing the risk of individuals offending or re-offending, not solely based on profiling or assessing personality traits, characteristics, or past criminal behaviour, and finally, profiling individuals during the detection, investigation, or prosecution of criminal offences within the constraints of Directive (EU) 2016/680.

the difficulties in contesting their results in court, particularly for individuals under investigation.

In the Commission's original proposal, deep fake detection systems were considered to be high-risk. In contrast, deep fakes were classified as low- or minimal risk, or as specific or limited risk subject to transparency obligations. The difference in classification was based on the not particularly convincing assumption that the private sector uses the former while the latter would be mainly in the hands of the public sector, and individuals will need protection from state surveillance. The Commission's proposal was not accepted by the EP. The EP's position rested on the common-sense explanation that technology must not be classified as lower risk when the potential harm is significant. However, the listing of high-risk AI systems in Annex III remains problematic. Experts argue that deep fake detection systems should be included as high-risk because of their importance in verifying evidence integrity and counteracting malicious fakes, strengthening law enforcement authorities' capacity, or protecting judicial proceedings (Łabuz 2023). These countermeasures will probably play an increasingly important role in the face of a growing number of crimes involving the malicious use of deep fakes (extortion, impersonation, financial fraud, forging evidence). (Europol 2022).

The AI Act highlights that AI systems designed for administrative tasks by tax and customs authorities, and financial intelligence units under anti-money laundering laws should not be classified as high-risk.[19] Hadwick (2023) argues that despite several amendments to the AI Act, it still raises more questions than answers. In particular, the distinction between administrative and criminal proceedings is arbitrary, impractical and reductionist. Also, AI tax enforcement systems, with their varied functions ranging from administrative to law enforcement, defy simple categorisation within existing legal frameworks. Such uses should be categorised separately. In this regard, Hadwick (2023) advocated a risk-based approach distinguishing between non-coercive and coercive AI tax systems. Non-coercive applications include chatbots, nudging systems, and jurisprudence analysis. AI systems employed for coercive tax enforcement tasks include web scraping, statistical risk detection, and risk scoring for taxpayer selection. They pose significant risks to fundamental rights and tax procedures. Coercive AI systems may also conflict with the principle of legality by disrupting procedures to the extent that they deviate from procedural norms. For example, in the eKasa case, the Slovak Constitutional Court required specific frameworks and safeguards due to machine-learning's extensive surveillance implications. Additionally, these systems may jeopardise the right to privacy and data protection, as evidenced in the earlier-mentioned cases involving SyRI.[20] Moreover, the AI Act makes an exception in the case of AI systems deployed

[19] European Commission (2021), Preamble, Recital (59).

[20] The Hague District Court ruled on 5 February 2020 (*NJCM* et al. *v The Dutch State* (2020) The Hague District Court ECLI:NL:RBDHA:2020:1878 (*SyRI*)) that the Dutch Government's use of the SyRI algorithm system for welfare fraud detection violated the right to respect for private and family life, home, and correspondence. SyRI (System Risk Indication) analysed data anonymously to generate risk reports for individuals suspected of fraud or non-compliance with legislation. The court found that the legislation governing SyRI lacked sufficient safeguards for privacy protection,

to detect fraud in the offering of financial services, which should not be considered as high-risk.

The AI Act designates the use of AI systems as high-risk when used by judicial authorities or on their behalf for assisting in researching and interpreting facts and law, and applying the law to specific cases, including in alternative dispute resolution scenarios. Such uses should not replace human judgement as decision-making in the judicial context must remain under human control. The deployment of AI systems designed for purely ancillary administrative functions, which do not impact adjudication in individual cases, is not classified as high-risk. Such functions include anonymising or pseudonymising judicial decisions, documents, or data, internal communication among staff, and administrative duties. Controversially, in contrast to its earlier formulation in the earlier draft of the AI Act, the restriction does not cover administrative authorities the decisions of which are binding and subject to judicial review. Administrative authorities are often involved in decision-making processes that directly affect individuals' rights and interests, such as coercive regulatory enforcement involving extensive investigatory powers. The exclusion of administrative decision-making seems to ignore the potential risks associated with the use of AI systems in these areas, including the risks of bias, discrimination, or administrative errors impacting individuals.

There is a growing use of AI systems in judicial proceedings, for example to assess the risk of misconduct in a probation context. While the use of predictive tools in criminal trials in Europe, often termed "algorithmic justice" or "automated justice", has remained limited, recidivism algorithms have garnered significant attention in the United States (González Fuster 2020). Concerns have been raised regarding the potential indirect racial bias involved in the use of these algorithms, with instances of black defendants being disproportionately labelled as high-risk compared to white defendants. For example, the COMPAS system in the United States was scrutinised in a 2016 ProPublica investigation, which found racial disparities in risk assessments; the system's developer challenged this analysis (Angwin et al. 2016; Dietrich et al. 2016; Larson et al. 2016). In Catalonia, the RisCanvi algorithm is used to assist the determining of parole eligibility for inmates (Bellio 2021).[21]

In the criminal justice context, the ethical and legal issues concerning the collection and processing of data for the development, training and utilisation of AI systems present particularly difficult dilemmas (Geslevich Packin and Lev Aretz

---

rendering its application invalid. It assessed the legislation and SyRI's usage based on principles outlined in the GDPR and EU Charter of Fundamental Rights, particularly transparency, purpose limitation, and data minimisation. It concluded that the legislation did not provide adequate information about SyRI's functioning, including its risk models and decision-making processes. The violation of the right to private life followed especially from the opacity and lack of transparency of the legislation. See, in this regard, Biber (2023).

[21] RisCanvi evaluates five potential outcomes related to inmate behaviour, including violent recidivism and self-harm. The final decision is made by justice professionals. In most cases, the professional's evaluation aligns with the algorithm's findings. Foreigners, who did not re-offend, were nearly twice as likely to be inaccurately classified as high-risk by the machine-learning models as Spanish nationals. They were less likely to be categorised as unlikely to re-offend. The Catalonian Department of Justice has never subjected the use of RisCanvi to an external audit.

2018). Due process safeguards have attracted attention in cases like *State v. Loomis*, where the Wisconsin Supreme Court ruled that using an algorithmic risk assessment in sentencing did not violate due process rights despite lacking disclosure of the methodology.[22] The judgment introduced several procedural safeguards to inform judges about the limitations of such assessment frameworks. In another US case, the use of the SAVRY risk assessment tool in a juvenile sentencing proceeding was challenged. Defence lawyers successfully argued against its use, questioning its scientific validity and persuading the judge to disallow it in the specific case (Richardson et al. 2019).

Integrating AI systems into sentencing and risk assessments in criminal trials has the potential to significantly advance the criminal justice system (Ryberg 2024; Taylor 2023). AI technologies can aid judges in determining suitable sentences and assessing the probability of recidivism. When generating sentencing recommendations, algorithms analyse a broad range of factors, including prior criminal history, offence severity, and demographic information. They can improve sentencing consistency, thereby reducing disparities stemming from human biases and subjective decision-making. By incorporating a wider array of data points, AI systems offer judges additional information and assistance in sentencing, promoting a more standardised approach. AI may also be employed to predict an individual's likelihood of future criminal behaviour, informing decisions regarding parole, probation, or release conditions. Machine learning systems can analyse historical data to identify patterns and risk factors linked to recidivism, with increased data resulting in greater report accuracy. However, there are also significant risks, such as those arising from the use of artificially created or falsified data, incorrect translations, erroneous expert opinions, or knowingly false testimonies. Therefore, it is essential that human decision-making and judgement, as well as other human factors, such as compassion and empathy remain at the centre of justice systems, particularly in complex or exceptional cases. Responsibility for judicial decisions and for the application of legal and moral standards burden the humans who work in justice systems.

The AI Act requires that providers of high-risk AI systems observe comprehensive mandatory compliance obligations for risk mitigation, data governance, detailed documentation, record-keeping, human oversight, transparency, robustness, accuracy, and cybersecurity.[23] Most of these requirements must be incorporated into the design of the high-risk AI system at the earliest stages of design and development. The model followed by the AI Act is commonly known as the "regulation by design" approach, which involves compelling developers to ensure that the AI system's design meets not only quality and safety standards, but also specific legal, regulatory, fundamental rights, and ethical requirements (Yeung et al. 2020). Practically, it requires

[22] *State v. Loomis*. 881 N.W.2d 749 (Wis. 2016).

[23] European Commission (2021), Title III, Chapter 2.

developers to translate legal-regulatory requirements into technical specifications or the coding of digital systems (Van Cleynenbreugel 2021).[24]

In the AI Act's regulatory framework, harmonised technical standards, providing detailed technical specifications, methodologies and best practices for the technology, play an important role. They impose requirements beyond the general legal-regulatory framework and its principle-based rules.[25] The AI Act introduces a pre-marketing conformity assessment for high-risk AI systems, subject to an emergency exception that allows "law enforcement agencies to deploy a high-risk AI tool that has not passed the conformity assessment procedure in case of urgency".[26] There will be post-marketing periodic auditing for AI systems used in law enforcement and by the judiciary. Post-marketing monitoring required for providers of high-risk AI systems will follow the same methodological approach as continuous auditing.[27]

4 Limited-Risk AI Systems

As provided by Article 50 of the AI Act, other, non-high-risk, limited AI systems are subject only to transparency obligations. They apply in specific cases, and include obligations, such as the obligation to inform individuals when interacting with a chatbot, the obligation to disclose and clearly label where visual or audio deep fake content has been manipulated by AI, or the obligation to inform and obtain the consent of people who are exposed to permitted emotion recognition and biometric categorisation systems. The transparency obligations prescribed for providers in the AI Act will be applicable to only a small portion of deep fakes. The AI Act will not protect against the malicious use of deep fakes. There are further issues with these rules. It is problematic that in certain situations they place the burden of risk onto users, allowing providers to avoid responsibility for their conduct (Helberger and Diakopoulos 2023; Veale and Borgesius 2021). The transparency obligations in Article 50 will not be applicable to the use of AI systems for law enforcement purposes, as it would undermine the interests of crime detection, prevention and investigation.[28]

---

[24] The approach had already appeared in the field of data protection where privacy requirements need to be designed into systems ('privacy by design'). We can also talk about 'ethics by design' and 'security by design' approaches.

[25] For example, the ISO/IEC 42,001:2023 Information technology—Artificial intelligence—Management system standard was published around the same time as the final adoption of the AI Act. The standard should help companies using high-risk AI systems to design their processes correctly and the audit process will help them perform appropriately.

[26] European Commission (2021), Preamble, Recital (146).

[27] See Mökander et al. (2022).

[28] When notified, individuals may attempt to evade justice or alter their behaviour, potentially undermining the effectiveness of the technology.

5 Transparency for AI Systems in Criminal Justice

Transparency serves as a critical mechanism for individuals seeking legal redress. It enables them to address the risks of bias and discrimination, which may arise from the use of biased or incomplete data to train and operate AI and automated decision-making (ADM systems). AI systems used in law enforcement and justice systems are highly dependent on complex data sets. In the area of law enforcement, data sources encompass data ranging from data on historical criminal activity (used to train predictive models) to social media data (used to detect behavioural indicators linked with suspicious conduct). Demographic information, such as age, gender and race, may influence decisions regarding resource allocation. Additionally, travel, communication, and financial data play pivotal roles in uncovering the details of past criminal behaviour (Kafteranis et al. 2023). In such an environment, the bias and discrimination arising from incomplete, inaccurate or biased data may have radical and direct consequences for the individual. In the criminal justice system, AI and ADM systems rely heavily on law enforcement data.[29]

Therefore, high-quality and accurate data are paramount for accurate, fair and unbiased predictions, decisions or actions by AI systems. Accuracy, fairness and the lack of bias can also be ensured by regularly testing and auditing AI systems. Therefore, proposals for legal regulation often focus on the quality of datasets used for training and testing AI systems. For example, the AI Act's Article 10 states that the training, validation and testing of data sets shall be relevant, sufficiently representative, and to the best extent possible, free of errors and complete in view of the intended purpose. They also cover audit as a practical means for upholding transparency, particularly by identifying instances of harm caused and providing evidential support for potential legal redress. Adequate regulatory requirements on transparency extend to both the data used and the AI system itself. As a result, they rest on two main pillars: the requirement to provide reasons for decisions, if applicable, and the right of individuals to be informed, in a procedural setting, of the proceedings against them to ensure a fair hearing. The requirement of transparency is connected to the general discourse concerning the explainability of AI, which differentiates between technical/technological transparency (also involving the disclosure of algorithm source code) and the ability to explain or justify decisions (clarifying why a decision made by an AI system is deemed appropriate). Technical/technological transparency relates to the technical infrastructure of AI systems, mandating that these systems operate transparently and enable users to comprehend the decision-making process and underlying logic. This involves explaining how decisions were made, disclosing details about the training data utilised, and verifying the system's accuracy (Wolswinkel 2022).

To ensure compliance with the transparency requirement, the AI Act provides for control and review by supervisory authorities and courts. However, the requirement of procedural fairness requires that the individuals affected are also informed, in

[29] See EUFRA (2022) and Sachoulidou (2023).

particular of the decisions taken and the processes leading to decision-making.[30] Informing the individual is insufficient; the individual must also be provided with an explanation concerning how and why the decision was made. In its provisions regulating high-risk AI systems, the AI Act makes clear that people need to be involved in decision-making and that users have the right to request an explanation (an explanation for the decision taken by the deployer with output from certain high-risk AI systems as its main basis).[31] This is not a general requirement; it will only be applicable when the decision produces legal effects or similarly significant effects affecting the individual's health, safety or fundamental rights adversely. The explanation provided must be clear and meaningful, and must enable the individual to exercise his or her rights, for example by enabling the individual to understand and review the decision. The explanation must clarify the role and impact of the AI system in the decision-making procedure, the main parameters of the decision taken and the related input data. The right to an explanation will not apply to the use of AI systems for which exceptions or restrictions follow from EU or national law, and will apply only to the extent to which this right is not already provided for under EU legislation. When the right to explanation is violated, or when any other provision of the AI Act is breached, affected individuals have a right to lodge a complaint with the national supervisory authority. This complaint is without prejudice to any other administrative or judicial remedy that may exist (Puigpelat, 2023).

As mentioned earlier, the transparency requirement must include granting access to the source code (the instructions that lead to or support the decision). Otherwise, it may be impossible to detect unlawful outcomes with the use of AI systems. However, access by private individuals, and possibly by national supervisory authorities, to the software code raises questions about the protection of business secrets and intellectual property rights. As general principles, the obligation to disclose the software code must rest on reasonable grounds and must be proportionate. According to the AI Act, national supervisory authorities must be granted access to the source code of high-risk AI systems when they put forward a reasoned request and the following cumulative conditions are fulfilled: access to source code is necessary to assess the conformity of a high-risk AI system with the requirements set out in Title III, Chapter 2, and testing/auditing procedures and verifications based on the data and documentation previously provided have been exhausted or proved insufficient.[32] Post-market monitoring and reporting of AI system performance and incidents are required to ensure ongoing compliance and address emerging risks.

As a related provision introduced by the EP into the draft measure, the AI Act will impose an obligation for users of high-risk AI systems to carry out a fundamental rights impact assessment before using such systems. The impact assessment exercise must consider the specific context of the use of the AI system, and it includes the duty to consult the national supervisory authority and relevant stakeholders. Still uncertain is whether deployers will correctly select the relevant fundamental rights.

---

[30] European Commission (2021, Preamble, Recital (171).

[31] The explanation must be provided only when requested by the user.

[32] European Commission (2021), Article 74(13).

At EU level, a multi-stakeholder project ALIGNER, has published a customised fundamental rights impact assessment template for deploying AI systems for law enforcement purposes.[33]

6 Concluding Remarks

AI presents both significant opportunities and substantial risks in the criminal justice system. The AI Act provides a robust framework to manage these risks, ensuring that AI applications contribute positively to the criminal justice system while safeguarding individual rights and societal values. However, the chapter highlights some drawbacks of the new regulation. Various use cases will pose unique challenges for the AI Act to address effectively. For example, the AI Act allows the use of real-time and post-event biometric identification for law enforcement and private purposes under certain conditions, leading to an inconsistency in standards applied to public versus private entities. Public–private partnerships in AI development further blur the lines of responsibility, complicating regulatory enforcement. Criticism arises from the perceived unreasonable differing treatment of similar risks depending on the actor involved, whether public or private, which impacts fundamental rights and values. Despite legislators emphasising human oversight as a key mechanism to mitigate the risks of harmful algorithms, the functional quality of these policies has not been thoroughly examined. Notably, there is no clear guidance on what constitutes meaningful human oversight under EU policy. In theory, combining algorithms with human oversight could help to achieve the benefits of an AI system's accuracy, objectivity, and consistency while retaining human discretion. Transparency for AI systems can be challenging for several reasons, too. AI systems often operate as black boxes, where the decision-making process is not transparent. This lack of transparency can hinder human overseers' ability to hold the system accountable and ensure its decisions are justifiable and fair. AI systems can be highly complex, making it difficult for human overseers to fully understand and monitor their operations. This complexity can lead to challenges in interpreting the system's decisions and actions. Identifying and mitigating biases in AI systems is a complex task. Bias can be inherent in the data, and ensuring fairness requires continuous monitoring, evaluation, and adjustment of both data and algorithms.

[33] https://aligner-h2020.eu/fundamental-rights-impact-assessment-fria/.

References

Angwin J, Larson J, Mattu S, Kirchner L (2016) Machine bias: There's software used across the country to predict future criminals. And it's biased against blacks. https://www.propublica.org/article/machine-bias-risk-assessments-in-criminal-sentencing

Bellio N (2021) In Catalonia, the RisCanvi algorithm helps decide whether inmates are paroled. https://algorithmwatch.org/en/riscanvi/

Biber SE (2023) Between humans and machines: judicial interpretation of the automated decision-making practices in the EU. University of Luxembourg Law Research Paper No. 2023–19. https://ssrn.com/abstract=4662152

Clarke L (2023) An AI firm harvested billions of photos without consent. Britain is powerless to act. https://www.politico.eu/article/ai-ruling-obstruct-british-efforts-protect-citizens-images-us-data-harvesting/

Dietrich W, Mendoza C, Brennan T (2016) COMPAS risk scales: Demonstrating accuracy equity and predictive parity. https://go.volarisgroup.com/rs/430-MBX-989/images/ProPublica_Commentary_Final_070616.pdf

DPA: Dutch Data Protection Authority (2020) Dutch DPA issues formal warning to supermarket for use of facial recognition technology. https://www.autoriteitpersoonsgegevens.nl/en/current/dutch-dpa-issues-formal-warning-to-supermarket-for-use-of-facial-recognition-technology

Egbert S, Leese M (2020) Predictive policing and its origins. Routledge

EUFRA: EU Agency for Fundamental Rights (2022) Bias in algorithms – Artificial Intelligence and discrimination. Publications Office of the European Union

European Commission (2021) Proposal for a Regulation laying down harmonised rules on artificial intelligence. COM(2021) 206 final

European Parliament (2021) European Parliament resolution of 6 October 2021 on artificial intelligence in criminal law and its use by the police and judicial authorities in criminal matters. 2020/2016(INI)

Europol (2022) Facing reality? Law enforcement and the challenge of deepfakes. An observatory report from the Europol Innovation Lab. Publications Office of the European Union

Georgieva I, Timan T, Hoekstra M (2022) Regulatory divergences in the draft AI Act – Differences in public and private sector obligations. https://www.europarl.europa.eu/RegData/etudes/STUD/2022/729507/EPRS_STU(2022)729507_EN.pdf

Geslevich Packin N, Lev-Aretz Y (2018) Learning algorithms and discrimination. In: Barfield W, Pagallo U (eds) Research handbook on the law of artificial intelligence. Elgar

Gless S (2020) AI in the courtroom: a comparative analysis of machine evidence in criminal trials. Georg J Int Law 51(2):195–253

González Fuster G (2020) Artificial intelligence and law enforcement. https://www.europarl.europa.eu/RegData/etudes/STUD/2020/656295/IPOL_STU(2020)656295_EN.pdf

Hacker P (2024). Comments on the Final Trilogue Version of the AI Act. https://doi.org/10.2139/ssrn.4757603

Hadwick D (2023) Error 404 – match not found. eucrim 1/2023, 55–60

Helberger N, Diakopoulos N (2023) ChatGPT and the AI Act. Internet Policy Rev 12(1). https://doi.org/10.14763/2023.1.1682

Larson J, Mattu S, Kirchner L, Angwin J (2016) How we analyzed the COMPAS recidivism algorithm. https://www.propublica.org/article/how-we-analyzed-the-compas-recidivism-algorithm

Kafteranis D, Sachoulidou A, Tursen U (2023) Artificial intelligence in law enforcement settings. eucrim 1/2023, 60–66

Łabuz M (2023) Regulating deep fakes in the Artificial Intelligence Act. Appl Cybersecur & Internet Governance 2(1):1–42. https://doi.org/10.60097/ACIG/162856

Leufer D, Rodelli C, Hídvégi F (2023) Human rights protection…with exceptions: what's (not) in the EU's AI Act deal. https://www.accessnow.org/whats-not-in-the-eu-ai-act-deal/

Mahler T (2022, March) Between risk management and proportionality: the risk-based approach in the EU's Artificial Intelligence Act proposal. Nord Yearb Law Inform, pp 247–270

Mökander J, Axente M, Casolari F, Floridi L (2022) Conformity assessments and post-market monitoring: a guide to the role of auditing in the proposed European AI regulation. Mind Mach 32:241–268

Palmiotto F (2018) The black box on trial: the impact of algorithmic opacity on fair trial rights in criminal proceedings. In: Ebers M, Cantero Gamito M (eds) Algorithmic governance and governance of algorithms. Springer

Puigpelat OM (2023) The impact of the AI Act on public authorities and on administrative procedures. CERIDAP 4/2023. https://doi.org/10.13130/2723-9195/2023-4-6

Raposo VL (2022) The use of facial recognition technology by law enforcement in Europe: a non-Orwellian draft proposal. Eur J Crim Policy 29:515–533

Richardson R, Schultz JM, Southerland VM (2019) Litigating algorithms 2019 US report: new challenges to government use of algorithmic decision systems. https://ainowinstitute.org/publication/litigating-algorithms-2019-u-s-report-2

Ryberg J (2024) Criminal justice and artificial intelligence: how should we assess the performance of sentencing algorithms? Philos Technol 37. https://doi.org/10.1007/s13347-024-00694-3

Sachoulidou A (2023) Going beyond the 'common suspects': to be presumed innocent in the era of algorithms, big data and artificial intelligence. Artif Intell Law. https://doi.org/10.1007/s10506-023-09347-w

Sanz MBL (2022) About ClearviewAI's mockery of human rights, those fighting it, and the need for EU to intervene. https://edri.org/our-work/we-need-to-talk-about-clearview-ai/

Sobel BLW (2021) A new common law of web scraping. Lewis & Clark Law Rev 25(1):147–207

Taylor I (2023) Justice by algorithm: the limits of AI in criminal sentencing. Crim Justice Ethics 42(3):193–213

Van Cleynenbreugel P (2021) EU by-design regulation in the algorithmic society. In: Micklitz H-W, Pollicino O, Reichman A, Simoncini A, Sartor G, De Gregorio G (eds) Constitutional challenges in the algorithmic society. Cambridge University Press

Veale M, Borgesius F (2021) Demystifying the draft EU Artificial Intelligence Act: analysing the good, the bad, and the unclear elements of the proposed approach. Comput Law Rev Int 22(4):97–112

Wolswinkel J (2022) Artificial intelligence and administrative law. https://coe.int/documents/22298481/0/CDCJ(2022)31E+-+FINAL+6.pdf/4cb20e4b-3da9-d4d4-2da0-65c11cd16116?t=1670943260563

Yeung K, Howes A, Pogrebna G (2020) AI governance by human rights-centered design, deliberation, and oversight: an end to ethics washing. In: Dubber M, Pasquale F, Das S (eds) The Oxford handbook of ethics of AI. Oxford University Press

Algorithmic Decision-Making in Migration and Security in the EU: Challenges in Ensuring Effective Legal Remedies

Tamás Molnár

Abstract Discussions have recently intensified at the European Union level on the potential use of AI-driven technology in the area of migration and security. Likewise, the new generation of large-scale EU IT systems will use algorithms to screen third-country nationals against risk profiles. If carefully conceived, implemented and monitored, AI could bring substantial opportunities to improve the efficiency of the EU area of 'freedom, security and justice', while safeguarding and eventually strengthening fundamental rights. Yet, there are also a wide range of fundamental rights risks which include questions about access to effective legal remedies in cases of AI supported decision-making. The right to an effective judicial remedy (Article 47 of the EU Charter of Fundamental Rights) equally applies to decisions taken with the support of AI. Decision-making driven by AI can challenge this right of primary importance in various ways (e.g., accessing remedies becomes more difficult against such decisions; rebutting the results of the algorithm is highly complicated; courts lack knowledge/expertise on how to provide effective remedy). After outlining the European legal framework applicable to the intersection of AI and access to justice, this chapter zooms in on three case studies to illuminate the specific challenges the right to an effective remedy faces in the context of AI used for migration and law enforcement: (1) the European Travel Information and Authorisation System screening rules; (2) real-time facial recognition technology used for law enforcement purposes; and (3) algorithmic decision-making under the EU Passenger Name

---

The views expressed in this chapter are solely those of the author and its content does not necessarily represent the views or position of the European Union Agency for Fundamental Rights.

T. Molnár
EU Agency for Fundamental Rights, Vienna, Austria

T. Molnár (✉)
Department of International Relations, Corvinus University of Budapest, Budapest, Hungary
e-mail: tamas.molnar@uni-corvinus.hu; tamas.molnar@wu.ac.at

Institute for Law and Governance, WU Vienna University of Economics and Business, Vienna, Austria

M. Varju and K. Mezei (eds.), *The Challenges of Artificial Intelligence for Law in Europe*, Data Science, Machine Intelligence, and Law 6,
https://doi.org/10.1007/978-3-031-86813-9_8

Records Directive, notably in light of the CJEU ruling in *Ligue des droits humains* (C-817/19).

1 Setting the Scene

In recent years, discussions have intensified at the European Union (EU) level on the potential use of *Artificial Intelligence (AI)-driven technology* by public authorities in the areas of *migration, border control* and *security* more broadly.[1] It is illustrative in this regard that the European Commission (2021a) expressed its commitment to make the best use of new technologies for Schengen governance and commissioned various studies on the matter,[2] while EU home affairs agencies have become active on this front, too. For instance, the European Border and Coast Guard Agency (Frontex) (2021) has been exploring how to further use biometric technology and AI in its border management activities; the European Agency for the operational management of large-scale IT systems in the area of 'freedom, security and justice' (eu-LISA) (2020; 2021) established a working group to enquire into opportunities for the implementation of AI solutions within the large-scale EU IT systems falling within its own mandate, backed up with an earlier report on potential uses of AI in the operational management of these EU databases[3]; and the European Union Agency for Law Enforcement Cooperation (Europol) has equally been running projects looking into various aspects of using trustworthy AI in the internal security domain.[4,5] Linked to this is the 'soon-to-be-operational' new generation of large-scale EU information technology (IT) systems and their interoperability, the founding legal instruments of which explicitly regulate the use of AI as an integral part of their functioning.[6] One of them is the forthcoming European Travel Information and Authorisation System (ETIAS) (European Parliament and Council 2018a) that will start using algorithms[7]—the so-called 'screening rules'—to screen third-country nationals against

[1] For a wider review, see, for example, European Parliamentary Research Service (2021a) and European Parliament (2020a).

[2] See European Commission (2020a), (2020b), and (2020c).

[3] The identified use cases by eu-LISA for future implementation of AI-based solutions include enabling automatic screening of visa-free travellers on the basis of predefined risk indicators and screening rules (under the European Travel Information and Authorisation System (ETIAS)).

[4] See, for example, the project entitled 'Accountability Principles for Artificial Intelligence in the field of Internal Security (AP4AI)' (see at https://www.ap4ai.eu/), coordinated by the EU Innovation Hub for Internal Security. The project purports to "develop solutions to assess, review and safeguard the accountability of AI usage by internal security practitioners in line with EU values and fundamental rights".

[5] For further examples, see Van Den Meerssche (2022).

[6] For a succinct and accessible overview of these EU databases and their interoperability, see EUFRA and ECtHR (2020). For a thorough monographic treatise, see Vavoula (2022).

[7] In computer science, an 'algorithm' is the computational process or set of rules (a sequence of commands) that the computer follows to calculate a result, i.e., to transform an input into an output. For more, see, for example, EUFRA (2022).

pre-set risk profiles. The above developments are now intrinsically connected with the flagship Union legislative initiative, the proposed *EU AI Act* (European Commission 2021b)[8] (on which political agreement was reached by the co-legislators at the end of 2023[9]), which carries great (future) implications in the aforementioned policy areas, too.

If carefully conceived, implemented and monitored, AI could bring substantial *opportunities* to improve the efficiency of migration/border management and contribute to better internal security within the Union, while safeguarding and eventually strengthening fundamental rights (EUFRA 2021). As this author has previously written elsewhere, these opportunities include speeding up the process for applying for and granting international protection while improving transparency and consistency in decision-making; protecting individuals from identity fraud; supporting authorities in quickly identifying missing/abducted children; improving authorities' ability to quickly identify vulnerabilities and protection needs; more efficiently preventing, detecting and investigating terrorist acts and other serious criminal offences; and progressively reducing the costs of (immigration) law enforcement (Reichel and Molnár 2023).[10] Yet, there are also a wide range of *risks* from the fundamental rights perspective,[11] which include the risk of replacing independent thought and judgment with non-transparent automated control (Jones 2023), hence disturbing questions arise related to *ensuring effective legal remedies* in the case of algorithmic/AI-supported decision-making.

The *right to an effective remedy*, as enshrined at the European level in Article 47 of the Charter of Fundamental Rights of the EU (EUCFR) and in Article 13 of the European Convention on Human Rights (ECHR), equally applies to decisions taken with the support of AI technologies. However, opaque and unexplainable algorithms or AI used for decision-making by public authorities can challenge the right to an effective remedy in different ways. This makes access to (judicial) remedy—still available in principle at national level, via the general system of remedies in domestic laws—more difficult against decisions of (immigration) law enforcement agencies supported by AI technology. This challenge is coupled with the difficulty for affected persons to rebut the results of the algorithm/AI tool and that remedial bodies, notably courts, might not be in the position to provide such (effective) remedy at present (due to the lack of knowledge and expertise by judges, and other factors).

---

[8] See, notably, European Commission (2021b), Preamble, Recital (39), Article 6(2) and Annexes III and VIII on large-scale EU IT systems in the area of freedom, security and justice; as well as Preamble, Recitals (18)-(24), (33) and Articles 3(36)-(38) and 5 on 'remote biometric identification' technologies, to which facial recognition also belongs.

[9] See the latest version as an official document of the Council of the EU (Council 2024).

[10] For a detailed account of the current and possible uses of AI-driven new technologies in the field of migration and asylum, see, for example, Ozkul (2023).

[11] For examples of other fundamental rights being implicated by the use of AI-driven technology (e.g., human dignity, the right to privacy, protection of personal data, equality and non-discrimination, rights of the child, freedom of expression, right to social security and social assistance, right to good administration, etc.), see EUFRA (2020).

As for the latter, it is questionable whether courts have access to all relevant information, including digital materials, and have the full power to remedy rights violations (ordering remedial action).[12]

Remarkably enough, relatively little scholarly attention has been paid thus far to the development of effective legal remedies in cases in which using AI leads to wrongful conduct and causes breaches of fundamental rights (Jones 2023). By the same token, while international AI governance principles commonly include the principle of accountability, this often refers to impact assessment, audit, or oversight, rather than a requirement of remedy in the event of harms.[13] The same holds true for the (politically agreed) AI Act in the EU which—in its initial version at least—remained silent on the question of effective judicial remedies. This hiatus directly stems from the different focus of the draft AI Act, which is dominantly market access and the placing of AI systems on the market (with product safety considerations[14]), together with addressing the various risk-levels such systems entail.[15] Set against this background, this contribution seeks to draw legal scholars', reflective practitioners' and other stakeholders' attention to the need to engage more deeply with the right to an effective remedy under EU law and its ramifications in AI-enabled decision-making by public authorities in general and in the EU policy area of 'freedom, security and justice' under Title V TFEU in particular.

After outlining the European legal framework applicable to the intersection of access to effective remedies and using AI technology, together with the key challenges emerging (Sect. 2), this chapter zooms in on three case studies to illuminate the specific challenges the right to an effective (judicial) remedy faces within the context of AI used for border management and law enforcement purposes. Section 3 examines more closely the three select case studies, commencing with the ETIAS algorithmic 'screening rules' and their implications for effective remedies (while also discussing the possible interferences with the right to good administration) (Sub-Sect. 3.1); followed by the use of real-time facial recognition technology by law enforcement and the issues with access to remedies against 'false positives'[16] and related police/immigration action (Sub-Sect. 3.2). Lastly, Sub-Sect. 3.3 looks in more detail at the use of algorithmic decision-making under the EU Passenger Name Records Directive (European Parliament and Council 2016c) and the right to an effective remedy against false matches based on algorithmic risk assessment/profiling, notably in light of the findings of the recent ruling by the Court of Justice of the EU (CJEU) in *Ligue des droits humains.*[17] Section 4 formulates some concluding remarks and presents an outlook for future legal and policy developments.

---

[12] See, similarly, Korff (2021).

[13] See, for example, UNESCO (2021); HLEG (2019).

[14] As pointed out, for example, by Veale and Borgesius (2021).

[15] See, in this regard, the Chapters by Grozdanovski and by Varju in this volume.

[16] A 'false positive' refers to the situation where an image is falsely matched to another image on a watchlist. In the law enforcement context, this would mean that a person is wrongly identified as being on the watchlist by the system (EUFRA 2019).

[17] Case C-817/19 *Ligue des droits humains ASBL v Conseil des ministres* EU:C:2022:491.

2 The Right to an Effective Remedy Meets AI: The EU Fundamental Rights Framework and Its Key Challenges

2.1 The Contours of the Right to an Effective Remedy in EU Law in Data-Driven Environments—Recapping the Basics

Under *primary EU law*, everyone whose rights and freedoms guaranteed by Union law are violated has the right to an effective remedy before a tribunal and to a fair trial (*Article 47 EUCFR*).[18] This is thus an enabling right that helps individuals enforce other substantive rights (EUFRA and Council of Europe 2016). As the ancient Romans already simply—but effectively—summarised it: '*ubi jus, ibi remedium*'—'where there is a right, there must be a remedy, too'.

The preliminary question of whether Article 47 applies in a particular issue area or an individual case is indissociable from the question of whether the EUCFR, which under Article 6(1) TEU is declared to have the same legal value as the EU founding Treaties, applies in the first place (Aalto et al. 2014). The EUCFR becomes applicable when Member States are implementing EU law (Article 51(1) EUCFR)—or in the CJEU's words, when they "act in the scope of Union law".[19] Once Member State action has a sufficient link with EU law for the EUCFR to apply at all, an effective (judicial) remedy must be thus ensured. These preconditions for the *ratione materiae* applicability of Article 47 are certainly met in the area of migration and security owing to the mushrooming EU legislation in these (sensitive) policy fields that oftentimes interferes with people's fundamental rights.

This right of a horizontal character empowers individuals to challenge a measure affecting any right conferred to them by EU law, not only in respect of those guaranteed in the EUCFR (EU Network 2006; EUFRA and Council of Europe 2016). The CJEU underlined that Article 47 of the EUCFR constitutes a reaffirmation of the EU law's general principle of effective judicial protection—also flowing from Article 19 TEU[20]—and that the characteristics of a remedy must be determined in a manner that is consistent with this principle.[21] As a legal concept with two facets,

---

[18] Among the abundant literature on this EUCFR right of a cross-cutting character, see, for example, the following leading academic commentaries: Aalto et al. (2014); Krenc (2020).

[19] Case C-617/10 *Åklagaren v Hans Åkerberg Fransson* EU:C:2013:105, paras 19–20. For more on the applicability of the EUCFR at national level, see, for example, EUFRA (2018b); CJEU (2021).

[20] Article 19 TEU: "Member States shall provide remedies sufficient to ensure effective legal protection in the fields covered by Union law." On the concept of effective judicial protection under EU law, succinctly but in an informative and thoughtful fashion, see Biondi (2023).

[21] See, for example, Case C-432/05 *Unibet (London) Ltd, Unibet (International) Ltd v Justitiekanslern* EU:C:2007:163, para 37; Case C-93/12 *ET Agrokonsulting-04-Velko Stoyanov v Izpalnitelen direktor na Darzhaven fond 'Zemedelie'—Razplashtatelna agentsia* EU:C:2013:432, para 59; and Case C-562/13 *Centre public d'action sociale d'Ottignies-Louvain-la-Neuve v Moussa Abdida* EU:C:2014:245, para 45.

its procedural side requires effective access to a fair hearing (before a court of law); whilst its substantive side embodies the right to an adequate legal redress.[22]

When unpacking the normative content of the right to an effective judicial remedy under EU law, it is key to keep in mind the extent to which the EUCFR is *anchored to the ECHR*. Where EUCFR rights correspond to rights laid down in the European Convention (and its Protocols), they are to be given the same scope and meaning (Article 52(3) EUCFR), also in accordance with the interpretations given by the European Court of Human Rights (ECtHR) in its case law. Ensuring the necessary consistency between the two European human rights catalogues means there is an opening towards higher standards when construing the precise contours of corresponding rights: the above requirement must "not prevent Union law providing more extensive protection" (Article 52(3) EUCFR, last sentence). In any event, the level of protection afforded by the EUCFR may never be lower than that guaranteed by the ECHR (Praesidium 2007).

Looking more closely at the common roots, the *first paragraph* of Article 47 EUCFR is based on *Article 13 ECHR*, which ensures the right to an "effective remedy before a national authority."[23] Hence, the EUCFR goes beyond that by requiring that the review be done by a tribunal.[24] The *second paragraph* of Article 47 EUCFR is based on *Article 6 ECHR*, which guarantees the right to a fair trial but only in the determination of civil rights or obligations, or any criminal charge.[25] This has precluded the application of Article 6 ECHR to immigration and asylum cases, since they do not involve the determination of a civil right or obligation.[26] Article 47 EUCFR, however, makes no such distinction. In view of the foregoing, the right to effective judicial protection encapsulated in Article 47 has an autonomous character under EU law: it "acquired a separate identity and substance … which are not the mere sum of the provisions of Articles 6 and 13 ECHR [and] that fundamental right goes on to acquire a content of its own".[27] The above also means that Article 47 EUCFR invariably applies to disputes arising in immigration and asylum matters.

From another vantage point, Article 47 is closely connected with the *right to good administration* which is binding on all EU Member States as a general principle of EU law[28] (and explicitly recognised by Article 41 EUCFR although only for actions of EU institutions and other Union entities[29]). The right to good administration

---

[22] See also, Aalto et al. (2014).

[23] For more on Article 13 ECHR, see, for example, Barkhuysen and van Emmerik (2018) and Rainey et al. (2021).

[24] Also noted in Praesidium (2007).

[25] For more on Article 6 ECHR, see, for example, Barkhuysen et al. (2018) and Rainey et al. (2021).

[26] *Maaouia v France* [GC] App no 39652/98 (ECtHR, 5 October 2000, paras 38–39).

[27] Opinion of Advocate General Cruz Villalón delivered on 1 March 2011 in Case C-69/10 *Brahim Samba Diouf v Ministre du Travail, de l'Emploi et de l'Immigration* EU:C:2011:102, para 39.

[28] In the migration context, see, for example, CJEU: Case C-604/12 *H. N. v Minister for Justice, Equality and Law Reform, Ireland, Attorney General* EU:C:2014:302, para 49.

[29] Also confirmed by the CJEU, see, for example, Joined Cases C-141/12 and C-372/12 *YS v Minister voor Immigratie, Integratie en Asiel*, and *Minister voor Immigratie, Integratie en Asiel v M and S* EU:C:2014:2081, paras 66–70.

operates as an enabling right that provides foundations for effective judicial review. The former incorporates the individual right to a *reasoned decision*, which serves as a prerequisite to fully guarantee one's access to justice when challenging that decision.[30]

Moving to the level of *secondary Union law*, the EU *data protection acquis* reconfirms that the right to an effective judicial remedy must be invariably provided[31] in relation to decisions by the 'data controller',[32] the 'data processor'[33] and the 'supervisory authority'[34] (the national data protection authorities). Data processed by AI-driven technologies is no exception. More specifically, all *large-scale EU IT systems* in the field of borders and migration, including in the context of their interoperability, guarantee the right to appeal before a court or a competent authority.[35]

As a consequence, the right to an effective (judicial) remedy should also cover decisions taken with the support of AI technologies.[36] It is to be noted, though, that the possibility to lodge an administrative complaint before a supervisory authority within the meaning of the General Data Protection Regulation[37] or the Law Enforcement Directive,[38] i.e., typically before national data protection authorities (DPAs), is not considered as an effective judicial remedy under Article 47 EUCFR.[39] Nonetheless, such complaint mechanisms can be complementary but cannot substitute judicial review with all the guarantees it involves. As a recent Council of Europe Committee of Ministers Recommendation (2020) underscores, "[j]udicial redress should remain available and accessible, when internal and alternative dispute settlement mechanisms prove insufficient or when either of the affected parties opts for judicial review or appeal."

---

[30] For an in-depth analysis of public authorities' duty under EU law to give reasons of their decisions in the context of automated decision-making, see Fink and Finck (2022).

[31] European Parliament and Council (2016a, Articles 78–79); European Parliament and Council (2016b, Articles 53–54).

[32] For the definition of this term, see European Parliament and Council (2016a, Article 4(7)); European Parliament and Council (2016b, Article 3(8)).

[33] For the definition of this term, see European Parliament and Council (2016a, Article 4(8)); European Parliament and Council (2016b, Article 3(9)).

[34] For the definition of this term, see European Parliament and Council (2016a, Articles 4(21) and 51); European Parliament and Council (2016b, Articles 3(15) and 41).

[35] For the legal references in the respective EU regulations, see EUFRA and ECtHR (2020).

[36] See also monographically, in the broader context of automated decision-making in the EU, Demková (2023).

[37] European Parliament and Council (2016a, Article 77).

[38] European Parliament and Council (2016b, Article 52).

[39] See also EUFRA (2020a).

2.2 *New (AI) Technologies—New Challenges to the Right to Judicial Review*

Algorithms/AI systems used for decision making by public authorities *can pose a challenge* to the right to an effective remedy in different ways. As a preliminary remark, the ensuing analysis takes the perspective of the right holder, the *individual* and not that of the judiciary when discussing challenges in ensuring effective judicial protection in this particular context.

Turning to the first challenge in the logical sequence, a crucial precondition to exercise the right to an effective remedy is that a person *must be aware* that their personal data are processed with the help of an algorithm/AI tool. In practice, this is not always the case, especially if personal data is processed by law enforcement or intelligence agencies in the context of surveillance or fighting serious crime. As the CJEU clarified with respect to security measures affecting the rights to private life and the protection of personal data, individuals whose data have been collected by the intelligence agencies must be notified of this as soon as the notification no longer jeopardises the tasks for which those authorities are responsible, and they must have access to effective remedies before a judicial or quasi-judicial body if they believe their rights have not been respected.[40] It flows from the foregoing that the person concerned should be able to know to *what extent AI influenced the decision* affecting them and *what procedure* to follow, including where and how to complain. Without access to this information, individuals subject to algorithmic decision-making are unable to defend themselves, assign responsibility for the decisions affecting them (Gstrein et al. 2019; Yeung 2019), or appeal any decision in the event of alleged rights violations caused by such technologies. Only thorough information about the AI systems provides equality of arms to meaningfully challenge decisions (EUFRA 2020a).

Another prominent concern is that algorithmic/AI-driven decision-making is notoriously *opaque*: data collection, algorithm training, selection of data for profiling, error rates etc. are not transparently reported (Ferguson 2017). The ensuing *partial explainability* and *lack of transparency* of AI and the decisions based on that (the so-called 'black box' effect (Dallas Card 2017))—also the result of intellectual property rights[41]—can limit individuals' *right to a reasoned decision*, which is part and parcel of the right to good administration as a general principle of EU law, and also of fair trial rights.[42] With regard to this latter, the CJEU has consistently held that

[40] CJEU: Joined Cases C-203/15 and C-698/15 *Tele2 Sverige AB v Post-och telestyrelsen* and *Secretary of State for the Home Department v Tom Watson and Others* EU:C:2016:970, para 12. See also, mutatis mutandis, Case C-555/07 *Seda Kücükdeveci v Swedex GmbH & Co. KG* EU:C:2010:21, para 52; and Case C-362/14 *Maximillian Schrems v Data Protection Commissioner* EU:C:2015:650, para 95.

[41] Companies often use the 'shield' of copyright, patent and trade secret protection to safeguard their knowledge on AI (ITLA 2019). See also EUFRA (2020a) and European Parliament (2020b).

[42] On the ways how the right to a fair trial may be impaired when public administration uses AI-systems for decision-making, see concisely de Heer (2021).

reasons must be provided both in facts and in law which need to be sufficiently clear and unequivocal to permit the review of legality and at the same time to provide the person with sufficient information to "know whether the decision may be vitiated by an error enabling its validity to be challenged".[43] When the reasons why a certain decision was taken are not sufficiently clear, this significantly affects the possibilities of individuals to challenge it, hence their access to justice.[44] The context in which individual decisions are made is important in determining the extent of the duty to give reasons (Craig 2014). While complex methods for automated decision-making, especially machine learning algorithms, and the way they influence decisions might be hard to understand and explain in simple terms, there is always a way to provide "meaningful information about the logic involved"—to borrow the language used in the GDPR.[45] As a minimum, users and providers of AI-driven technology can always provide a basic set of descriptions about the data used to build algorithms, its basic functioning and technology as well as tests carried out on its performance.[46] The proposed AI Act likewise purports to address this issue by setting out certain—although not convincingly sufficient—transparency obligations in relation to 'high-risk' AI systems.[47]

The third problem is tied in with the *limited availability of specialised legal support*. The lack of expertise and special knowledge, notably amongst lawyers and judges, appears to be a major hindrance in practice when individuals seek access to effective remedies. This is already visible in relation to the *large-scale EU IT systems* and the fundamental rights risks arising out of their functioning.[48] A number of the EU large-scale databases are just coming into operation (e.g., ETIAS, the Entry-Exit System (European Parliament and Council 2017), and the European Criminal Records Information System for Third-Country Nationals (European Parliament and Council 2019)), and even experts are still discovering how several aspects of them will work together. Their potentially vast impact on fundamental rights therefore remains partly unknown (EUFRA 2023), as not many people beyond those entrusted to set them up are aware of the fundamental rights safeguards in the systems (EUFRA 2021)—the lack of specialised lawyers is a symptom of that lack of expertise and special knowledge about such systems' functioning and fundamental rights implications.

---

[43] Case C-521/09 P *Elf Aquitaine SA v European Commission* EU:C:2011:620, paras 148–150. See also similarly Case C-199/99 P *Corus UK Ltd v Commission of the European Communities* EU:C:2003:531, para 145; and Joined Cases C-189/02 P, C-202/02 P, C-205/02 P to C-208/02 P and C-213/02 P *Dansk Rørindustri A/S v Commission of the European Communities et al* EU:C:2005:408, para 462.

[44] See similarly Fink (2021).

[45] European Parliament and Council (2016a, Article 13(2)(f)).

[46] See also Reichel and Molnár (2023).

[47] European Commission (2021b, Article 13).

[48] To assist practitioners, including civil society organisations better understand the fundamental rights implications—and related safeguards—of the EU databases in the areas of borders and migration, the EU Agency for Fundamental Rights (EUFRA) published an online awareness-raising tool, launched in December 2024—available at https://e-learning.fra.europa.eu/.

The above-depicted challenges make access to effective judicial remedy—available primarily still at national level, via the general system of remedies under EU Member States' domestic laws—*more burdensome* against decisions supported by AI technology. This is paired with the difficulty for affected persons of rebutting the results of the algorithm, and that courts might not be in the position to render such remedy at present. Owing to a lack of expertise of courts, the intensity of judicial review may drop, i.e., there is a risk that courts employ deference to decisions of public authorities even more widely when complex AI systems are used by such authorities.[49] In view of the lack of specialised knowledge by judges, their empowerment and training on the matter is invariably of central importance. A connected issue is how to ensure that the judiciary does not place inappropriate weight on the assumed or perceived accuracy of an AI system—which warrants addressing the so-called '*automation bias*' (when human decision-makers ascribe defining authority to AI-produced outcomes and thus disregard other available information, even in the face of 'warning signals') (Fink 2021).[50] Equally important is to make sure that available legal remedies provide the *equality of arms* between the victim and the defendant in cases concerning human rights violations caused by AI systems. The proposed EU AI Act envisages countering this automation bias by requiring human oversight in the case of 'high-risk AI systems'—such as the large-scale EU IT systems—to enable the person assigned this task to be able to correctly interpret the algorithmic output and be aware of the potential for such bias.[51] As concerns equality of arms, shifting the burden of proof to the law enforcement authority concerned, or at least sharing this onus between the applicant and the respondent[52] is an option to empower the individual who is in a weak position vis-à-vis the public authorities employing AI. This legal solution already applies in EU non-discrimination law[53] and in ECtHR case law on equal treatment,[54] which could equally inform the refining of the procedural aspects of the right to an effective remedy in this specific context at hand.

Considering the role played by the CJEU and its case law in this respect, one may question whether its existing jurisprudence already guarantees sufficient criteria and safeguards to effectively exercise the right to an effective remedy against such new forms of automated decision-making (including the outcome of AI-driven risk

---

49 Compare with Wolswinkel (2022).

50 For more on 'automation bias', see, for example, Skitka et al. (2000) and Alon-Barkat and Busuioc (2023).

51 European Commission (2021b, Article 14(3)(b)-(d)). Also noted by Fink (2021).

52 'Shared burden of proof' means that the claimant needs to bring sufficient evidence to suggest that a particular right violation may have occurred due to the AI-assisted decision making. This will raise a presumption of unlawful action, which the respondent public authority then has to rebut.

53 See Council (2000a, Article 8); Council (2000b, Article 10); Council (2004a, Article 9); European Parliament and Council (2006, Article 19).

54 See *Nachova and Others v Bulgaria* [GC] App nos 43577/98 and 43579/98 (ECtHR, 6 July 2005), para 147. This has been repeated in *Timishev v Russia*, App nos 55762/00 and 55974/00 (ECtHR, 13 December 2005), para 39; and *D.H. and Others v the Czech Republic* [GC] App no 57325/00 (ECtHR, 13 November 2007), para 178.

assessment). The *Ligue des droits humanins* ruling, analysed below in Sub-Sect. 3.3, has brought some—but not full—clarifications on that front.

3 (EU) Law in Context: Case Studies from the Field of Migration and Security and Their Implications on the Right to an Effective Remedy

The three case studies below, selected from new and emerging fields of 'big data-driven' state action in the area of 'freedom, security and justice', look more in-depth into the challenges individuals face when they want to enforce their right to effective (judicial) remedies in cases in which AI-powered technologies used for the purposes of border management and law enforcement infringe upon their fundamental rights protected under EU law.

3.1 ETIAS and Its 'Screening Rules'

The forthcoming *European Travel Information and Authorisation System (ETIAS)*, established by Regulation (EU) 2018/1240 and set to start operating from mid-2026,[55] is a pre-border checks system for visa-free travellers from non-EU countries.[56] The automated EU system, similar to the ESTA in the United States[57] or the ETA in Australia,[58] will pre-screen nationals from visa-free third countries to establish whether or not they should be allowed to enter the Schengen area for visits of up to 90 days in any 180-day period (short-term stays). It will use an online application tool to collect personal data of visa-free travellers prior to their arrival at the EU's external borders; then Frontex (its ETIAS Central Unit) and competent Member State(s)' border control authorities (as ETIAS national units) will cross-check those data against all relevant—EU and national—databases. If the checks conclude that the person does not pose a security, irregular migration or public health (e.g., epidemic) risk, the individual will receive an automatic [electronic] authorisation to travel to the EU. Otherwise, the application will be referred to manual checks by competent authorities; and can be finally rejected by them (EUFRA and ECtHR 2020).

---

[55] See at Frontex, ETIAS, https://frontex.europa.eu/what-we-do/etias/about-etias/.

[56] For the list of visa-free 'third countries' and other entities, see European Parliament and Council (2018b), Annex II.

[57] Electronic System for Travel Authorization. See its official website (the online application platform) at https://esta.cbp.dhs.gov/.

[58] Electronic Travel Authorization. See its official website (the online application platform) at https://immi.homeaffairs.gov.au/visas/getting-a-visa/visa-listing/electronic-travel-authority-601.

To conduct the above checks, ETIAS will use '*screening rules*' (EUFRA 2021),[59] which are driven by an algorithm that compares the data submitted in a visa-free traveller online application with specific risk indicators corresponding to security, irregular migration or public health risks.[60] As is well known, the functioning of algorithms implies a high degree of generalisation and uncertainty. The methods used to develop the above risk indicators, especially if these are construed in a rather broad fashion, may result in travel authorisations being automatically denied to a sizable number of applicants who actually do not represent a risk. Under EU law, ETIAS screening rules include safeguards to prevent discrimination on protected grounds,[61] and national authorities will ultimately decide whether or not to grant an authorisation to travel, thus ensuring human control. Nonetheless, risks of indirect discrimination and unjustified profiling[62] could arise from the algorithmic combination of criteria and proxies; or built-in bias. For instance, a certain ethnic group typically working in an economic sector (e.g., in agriculture) and from a certain country, region or city could be refused the authorisation to travel (EUFRA 2018).

The ETIAS Regulation expressly guarantees *access to remedy* for applicants against decisions affecting them, albeit by simply referring back to the system of remedies available under national law.[63] This provision, however, needs to be read in conjunction with Article 47 EUCFR—as recital (68) of the ETIAS Regulation (Parliament and Council 2018a) also instructs[64]—which then requires, at least ultimately, *judicial review* in cases in which an appeal is lodged. The problem lies in that challenging these decisions might be difficult. The person concerned should *be able to know* to what extent the output of the algorithm (the screening rules) influenced the negative decision affecting her/him (namely the refusal of the authorisation to travel or the annulment or revocation of an already issued authorisation), and the procedure to follow in such cases (Reichel and Molnár 2023). As a result, national

---

[59] European Parliament and Council (2018a, Article 33). For a critical assessment, see, for example, Gugliotta and Elbi (2023).

[60] The EUFRA is currently running a research project to provide evidence on potential algorithmic bias in ETIAS (via the 'screening rules') through simulation and testing of selected cases. See at https://fra.europa.eu/en/call-for-tender/2023/negotiated-procedure-middle-value-contract-assessing-potential-algorithmic.

[61] These include the person's sex, age, colour, race, ethnic or social origin, genetic features, language, political or any other opinion, religion or philosophical belief, trade union membership, membership of a national minority, property, birth, disability or sexual orientation. Parliament and Council (2018a, Article 33(5)).

[62] By virtue of Article 4(4) (European Parliament and Council (2016b)), 'profiling' means any form of automated processing of personal data consisting of the use of personal data to evaluate certain personal aspects relating to a natural person, in particular to analyse or predict aspects concerning that natural person's performance at work, economic situation, health, personal preferences, interests, reliability, behaviour, location or movements.

[63] European Parliament and Council (2018a), Articles 37(3) [in the event of refusal], 40(3) [in the event of annulment] and 41(7) [in the event of revocation].

[64] "This regulation respects fundamental rights and observes the principles enshrined in the Charter of Fundamental Rights of the European Union."

implementing legislation should regulate with care these issues in order to avoid violations of EUCFR rights, including Article 47.

Added to this, it appears that the ETIAS Central Unit is *not* obliged to *explain* the ground(s) for refusal or provide individualised information: a mere mention seems sufficient pursuant to Article 38(2)(c) of the regulation.[65] Therefore, it is likely that issuing negative ETIAS decisions will be simply a 'box ticking' exercise—and the refusal grounds are very broad themselves, covering a wide range of situations—; hence applicants will not be able to understand the actual reasons behind the negative decision when it comes to challenging it. Does that meet the requirement that everyone must be issued with a reasoned decision, with sufficient detail as part of the right to good administration? Answering in the negative prompts the conclusion that safeguards are insufficient when they undermine the applicant's right to an effective judicial remedy. One recent mitigating measure is worth mentioning, however: the Commission Implementing Decision laying down forms for refusal, annulment or revocation of a travel authorisation[66] requires the ETIAS National Units, besides 'ticking the box', to insert a statement of relevant facts and additional reasoning underpinning their decision. Hopefully, this can provide sufficient information to individuals to enable them to meaningfully exercise their right to an effective remedy.

3.2 Law Enforcement Using Real-Time Facial Recognition Technology and Dealing with 'False Positives'

Facial recognition technology (FRT) makes it possible to compare individuals' digital facial images to determine whether they are of the same person. FRT does this, first, by detecting and measuring various facial features, extracting these from the digitally captured facial image and then comparing them with features taken from other faces (EUFRA 2019).[67] Such technologies are being tested, piloted, and deployed by public authorities for law enforcement and border management purposes in a growing number of EU countries.[68]

This sub-section examines more closely a specific form of FRT: the so-called '*live facial recognition technology*'. In essence, it compares footage obtained from video cameras (e.g., CCTV) against electronic databases of facial images (e.g., a police 'watchlist', meaning a database of offenders wanted by the police and those who pose a risk to public order, national security etc.) for law enforcement and

[65] See also Derave et al. (2022); Brouwer (2021).

[66] European Commission (2022a, Annexes I–III).

[67] For more detail on how facial recognition technology works, see, for example, Christakis et al. (2022).

[68] See, for example, EUFRA (2019); INCLO (2021); European Parliamentary Research Service (2021b).

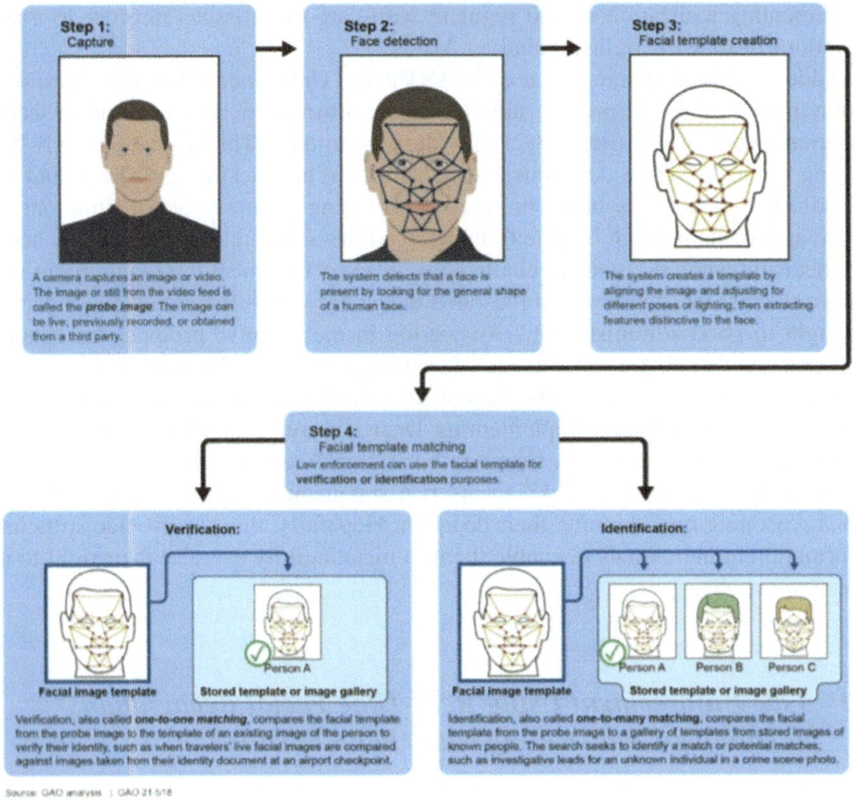

Fig. 1 Facial recognition technology search process. *Source* U.S. Government Accountability Office, GAO 21 518

border-management purposes. This is a form of 'one-to-many' comparison (identification) by FRT, which returns a score for each comparison indicating the likelihood [percentage] that two images indicate the same person (EUFRA 2019). Figure 1 below visualises the gist of how live facial recognition typically works.

While live FRT has real benefits for public safety and security, such technology is intrusive, pervasive and susceptible to error, which gives rise to a number of fundamental rights concerns (European Parliamentary Research Service 2021b). Focusing on one type of error FRT makes, a '*false positive*' match refers to the situation where an image is falsely matched to another image on the watchlist.[69] When false positives occur while (immigration) law enforcement agencies use facial recognition technologies, this means that a person is *wrongly identified* as being on the watchlist by the system. Questions of access to effective remedies arise in the event of police stops or arrests that have *solely* or *significantly* been *informed* by the output produced by a FRT system that the law enforcement agency has relied upon.

[69] For more, see, for example, Buolamwini et al. (2020).

As referred to earlier, a key precondition to exercise the right to an effective remedy is that a person concerned *must be aware* that his/her facial image is processed by live FRT. This occurs when law enforcement authorities populate a 'watchlist' with a great number of facial images; or when a public area is under live FRT surveillance.[70] As mentioned above, the CJEU has found that notification is, in fact, necessary to enable the persons affected by such FRT-enabled measures to exercise their right to an effective judicial remedy guaranteed under Article 47 EUCFR.[71]

Those affected by police stops, arrests or searches etc. due to live FRT-triggered false positives might want to *challenge* why their facial image has been included in the 'watchlist'; and why it has been done so in a non-transparent way and without their consent. In a similar vein, they might seek redress for a false positive match that entailed negative consequences for them (e.g., in case of an unlawful stop, search or arrest), including seeking compensation for any damage suffered, as foreseen in EU data protection acquis.[72] To give some everyday-life examples, such damage materialises when the individual subject to an FRT-generated false match missed a flight connection, or a non-EU national was wrongly prevented from entering an EU country and missed a business meeting (EUFRA 2019). In the best case, more legal clarity in this regard will come with the upcoming EU AI Act, which will govern—and ban at least some forms of—live FRT used for law enforcement purposes.

3.3 The Passenger Name Records (PNR) Directive and Decisions Based on Algorithmic Risk Assessment/Profiling

Passenger name record (PNR) data is personal information provided by all air passengers and collected by air carriers for their operational and commercial purposes in providing air transportation services. PNR data includes various information such as the name of the passenger, travel dates, itineraries, seats, baggage, contact details, dietary requirements and means of payment, etc.[73] As these data are provided by the passengers manually, they are thus unverified information and not necessarily accurate. This 'declaratory' nature of PNR data distinguishes it from Advance Passenger

---

[70] See also EUFRA (2019).

[71] Joined Cases C-203/15 and C-698/15 *Tele2 Sverige AB v Post-och telestyrelsen and Secretary of State for the Home Department v. Tom Watson and Others* EU:C:2016:970, para 12.

[72] See European Parliament and Council (2016a), Preamble, Recital (146) and Article 82; European Parliament and Council (2016b), Preamble, Recital (88) and Article 56.

[73] For more on PNR data, from an international (aviation) law perspective, see ICAO (2010), notably sections 2.1 and 2.5 and Appendix 1 [PNR data elements]. See also ICAO (2020), Amendment 28 to Annex 9 [Facilitation] to the 1944 Chicago Convention on International Civil Aviation, notably its Chapter 9, Section D which relates specifically to PNR. These standards are, in principle, legally binding on all ICAO member countries.

Information (API),[74] which is basic information of the passengers' and the crew's identity, contained in the machine-readable zone of travel documents and collected during the check-in process (verified data) (European Commission 2020d; OSCE 2019).

In the European Union, resonating with developments at United Nations level (ICAO 2010 and 2020; United Nations 2014 and 2016),[75] the *PNR Directive* (European Parliament and Council 2016c)[76] regulates the *transfer* of such data, both from extra-EU flights ('shall clause') and intra-EU flights ('may clause'), by air carriers—using the 'push method'[77]—to Member States' law enforcement authorities; and their processing for the purposes of preventing, detecting, investigating and prosecuting *terrorist offences*[78] and other forms of *serious crime*[79] (essentially corresponding to the 'crimes list' of the European Arrest Warrant Framework Decision (Council 2002)). The PNR Directive obliges each Member State to establish or designate a *Passenger Information Unit (PIU)* as part of their law enforcement structures, which is responsible for collecting, storing and processing the PNR data, and transferring the data or the results of the processing to the competent national authorities; as well as exchanging PNR data with other EU Member States and Europol.[80] When processing such data for the above-mentioned two purposes, i.e., fighting terrorism and other forms of serious crime, this must remain within the confines of the following specific actions: 1) *pre-arrival assessment* of passengers against pre-determined risk criteria (powered by algorithms) and relevant—international, European and national—law enforcement databases; 2) *specific investigations/prosecutions*; and 3) using the data as input in the *development* or *updating of risk assessment criteria*.[81] Figure 2 herewith summarises the PNR data flow, in comparison with the Advanced Passenger Information data transfers.

Without going into the complexities of the operation of the PNR Directive and the processing of PNR data thereunder (including 'datamining'[82]), only selected aspects are highlighted here which are of key relevance for the exercise of the right to a judicial remedy by any passenger whose rights have been allegedly infringed by querying PNR data under this scheme. The PNR Directive itself does not mention

---

[74] In the EU, the collection of API by air carriers and its transmission to Member State authorities is governed by Council Directive 2004/82/EC (Council, 2004b).

[75] United Nations (2014) and (2016) were then followed and complemented by United Nations (2017) and (2019), adopted under Chapter VII of the UN Charter, hence compliance with the obligations laid down therein is mandatory for all UN Member States.

[76] For academic commentaries and its critique, see, for example, Wojnowska-Radzińska (2023), Glouftsios and Leese (2023), and Vavoula (2016).

[77] ICAO (2010, para 2.7.1); European Parliament and Council (2016c, Article 8(1)).

[78] For the definition of 'terrorist offences', see European Parliament and Council (2016c, Article 3(8)).

[79] For the definition of 'serious crime' and the list of such criminal offences, see European Parliament and Council (2016c, Article 3(9) and Annex II).

[80] European Parliament and Council (2016c, Article 4).

[81] European Parliament and Council (2016c, Article 6(2)).

[82] See Korff and Georges (2015).

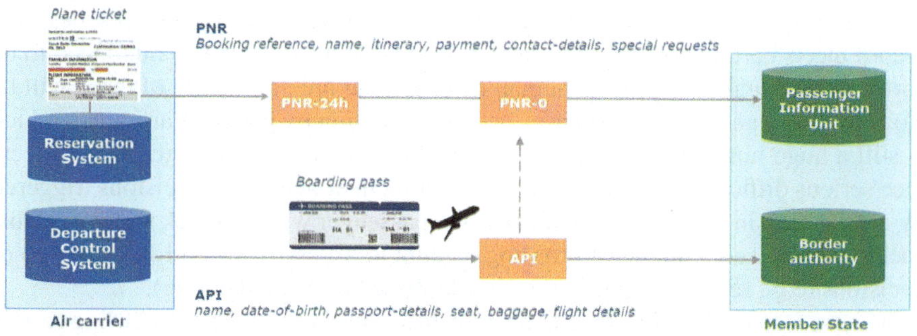

Fig. 2 Comparison of PNR and API data transfers from initial collection. 2022b *Source* European Commission

the right to appeal or judicial remedy in general, as a horizontal fundamental rights safeguard in the event of police action triggered by PNR hits: only the right to judicial redress as part of the more specific data subjects' rights in application of the EU data protection acquis[83] features therein (although seemingly the CJEU has interpreted the material scope of this 'redress' broadly in *Ligue des droits humains*—see below). Notwithstanding the wording on redress—and its coverage—in the PNR Directive, Article 47 EUCFR kicks in, as it is without a shadow of a doubt that Member States' authorities act within the scope of EU law when taking measures as a result of processing PNR data. Therefore, judicial review of such measures must be accessible under the general systems of legal remedies available in each Member State justice system. Yet, effectively challenging PNR-related police actions significantly affecting or having an adverse legal effect on a passenger (e.g., the person is taken to a second-line check at the airport or even put into short-term police custody due to wrong flagging/hit [false positive]; discriminatory profiling by reason of built-in bias in the algorithm, etc.) can be extremely cumbersome. The reasons are manifold.

To start with, some are similar to those described with respect to ETIAS, notably the person concerned should *be able to know* to what extent the output of the algorithm—meaning the use of pre-determined criteria for automated filtering/analysis of PNR data—influenced the measure taken against her/him. Given that algorithms run the *pre-determined criteria* and check PNR data against relevant *databases*, these programs are supposed to identify 'unknown' suspects by, for instance, extrapolating patterns and conclusions from an individual's flight habits or personal data to ascertain whether they are a suspected or potential offender. The PNR Directive follows a 'bottom-up' approach by casting the net as wide as possible: *all air passengers* are automatically monitored (not only third-country nationals, but also EU citizens and

---

[83] Article 8 EUCFR, the primary EU law provision providing for specific data protection-related remedies, expressly stipulates: "[e]veryone has the right of access to data which has been collected concerning him or her, and the right to have it rectified." The GDPR (European Parliament and Council, 2016a) and the Law Enforcement Directive (European Parliament and Council, 2016b) and other sectorial EU legislation (e.g., the regulations setting up large-scale EU IT systems) unfold this specific remedy in more detail and in a context-specific manner.

Member States' own nationals), as a result of which there are many 'hits' (if a personal record meets certain criteria). This also implies that many of these 'hits' need to be sorted out manually, by way of human review,[84] but only a fraction of those will be 'followed-up', and even fewer cases need intervention by police at airports—which is still a huge number, however.[85] In the latter scenarios, law enforcement officers face serious difficulties in sufficiently explaining their actions or decisions triggered by a PNR hit[86] in cases in which an affected passenger wants to seek redress against such measures (e.g., unlawful profiling leading to excessive second-line checks) or decisions (e.g., refusal of entry at the border based on PNR flagging).

Most recently, the CJEU shed some light on the legal permissibility of using certain forms of algorithms/AI for PNR purposes also from the vantage point of exercising the *right to an effective remedy*. In the June 2022 *Ligue des droits humains* ruling, the CJEU underscored, in agreement with the Advocate General, that "the opacity which characterises the way in which artificial intelligence technology works" might make it "impossible to understand the reason why a given program arrived at a positive match", thus depriving affected passengers of their right to an effective judicial remedy under Article 47 EUCFR.[87] Differently put, those algorithms/AI-driven tools whose results cannot be translated into clear criteria and are not discrimination-proof by design are incompatible with the EUCFR right to an effective remedy. This interpretation suggests that unexplainable and unchallengeable AI tools, such as 'self-learning' systems (machine learning) might face much broader limitations in their applicability across the board—i.e., in all areas of EU competence—than those only flowing from, in this case, the PNR Directive itself (Korf 2022; Mügge 2023). This can lead to a situation when AI systems regarded as lawfully marketable under the future AI Act may not actually be put into operation because operators (here: law enforcement agencies) fear a violation of EUCFR rights. Moreover, the CJEU went on to prescribe that "[national judges] reviewing the legality of the decision adopted by competent authorities… and the persons concerned themselves must have

[84] European Parliament and Council (2016c, Article 7(6)).

[85] For instance, the afore-cited 2020 Commission Staff Working Document (European Commission, 2020d) states that 0.59% of all passengers whose data have been collected were identified through automated processing as requiring further examination; then 0.11% of passengers were subsequently transmitted to competent authorities for further checks. This implies that false matches (such as those based on the same name) were among the reasons for the difference between the two figures. It does not, however, further clarify whether all these 0.11 % of cases (this corresponds to an estimated 1 million cases transferred to the national competent authorities in one year) were relevant—and if so to what extent—to the PNR Directive's overarching purpose of "preventing, detecting, investigating and prosecuting terrorist offences and serious crime". Neither does it show whether this number included other passengers flagged on the basis of false matches and other data quality issues. For more on the probabilities of flagging innocent passengers and those of flagging terrorists/other offenders, see EDRi (2019).

[86] As Korff (2021) pointedly opined: "[i]n the more developed 'artificial intelligence' … systems, the computers operating the relevant programmes create feedback loops that continuously improve the underlying algorithms—with almost no-one in the end being able to explain the results".

[87] Case C-817/19 *Ligue des droits humains ASBL v Conseil des ministres* EU:C:2022:491, para 195. See also Irion (2022); Zandstra and Brouwer (2022); Duroy (2023).

had an opportunity to examine both the grounds and the evidence on the basis of which the decision was taken…, including the … operation of the programs applying [pre-determined] criteria."[88]

In view of infusing more transparency into the functioning of PNR systems, the CJEU appears to set out even *notification requirements* in case of positive matches. These warrant that upon finishing the relevant administrative procedures (e.g., law enforcement querying the PNR system and checking the person in databases), the affected passenger subject to a 'hit' must be enabled "to understand how the [pre-determined] criteria and the [algorithms] work" in order to "decide with full knowledge of the relevant facts whether or not to exercise his or her right to the judicial redress".[89] This crucial procedural safeguard of transparency and explainability, an emanation of the right to good administration, is an important step in the right direction to address some of the above-mentioned challenges in AI-dominated environments and to put individuals in a position to have meaningful recourse to legal remedies in the context of PNR systems. Notwithstanding all this, and more generally, one might ask: do effective remedies actually exist against the very high number of (built-in) non- rights-compliant outcomes of such algorithm-based data mining and mass profiling?[90]

4 Conclusions—With an Outlook on the Future

The genuine availability of the right to an effective remedy, notably judicial review against any measure taken by public authorities is an essential prerequisite to upholding the *rule of law* in any legal order—which is a foundational value of the EU legal system (Article 2 TEU). As an enabling right, the right to an effective judicial review constitutes, at the same time, the backbone of *holding public authorities accountable* for any wrongdoings infringing people's fundamental rights. It comes as no surprise that some leading scholars contend that the right to an effective (judicial) remedy is perhaps the most important right in the EUCFR (Aalto et al. 2014). Set against this backdrop, this contribution has attempted to shine more light on the *role* of this fundamental right of central importance in AI-driven decision-making in select EU policy areas in migration and security and the *multiple challenges* associated with making access to effective remedies a reality for all affected by AI-enabled law enforcement measures. As noted in the introduction, this is all the more important in view of the relatively little scholarly attention paid so far to the development of tailored-made effective legal remedies in this specific digital context.

[88] Case C-817/19 *Ligue des droits humains ASBL v Conseil des ministres* EU:C:2022:491, para 211.

[89] Case C-817/19 *Ligue des droits humains ASBL v Conseil des ministres* EU:C:2022:491, para 201. Also noted by Thönnes (2022).

[90] Korff and Georges (2015) answer this question clearly in the negative.

As the above three case studies on ETIAS, live facial recognition technologies used for law enforcement purposes, and the EU PNR system demonstrated, AI-technologies can considerably alter the *nature of the decisions* that affected individuals might want to contest (European Parliament 2020a). The crux of the matter is that effective legal remedies must rely on *transparency* and *explainability*, paired with sufficiently *reasoned* decision-making (this latter being, at the same time, an inherent component of the right to good administration). All of this warrants that complainants have enough information to understand how a decision about them was made or a measure affecting them was adopted. Each of the three AI use-cases demonstrated significant gaps, unanswered questions and grey zones in this regard. As of now, such algorithms/AI-tools seem be too opaque to allow for effective judicial remedy against their recommendations or outputs, as it is often impossible to understand from the outside how they work.

Turning to upcoming EU legal developments, the *new AI Act*, once enters into force, will—to some extent—carry positive implications for individuals' access to an effective remedy, by creating more transparency and enhancing individuals' right to information. However, the politically agreed text of the AI Act merely embraces, in express terms, a timid reference to the *right to effective (judicial) remedies*—but not specifically for victims of alleged fundamental rights violations which result from AI-supported decision-making.[91] It would be highly desired to expressly refer to the right to an effective remedy in the new AI Act in this context, too—and not only in relation to challenging the decisions (penalties) of the market surveillance authorities. Equally important would have been not to carve out exceptions from the material scope of the new regulation, unlike both the original European Commission proposal and the politically agreed compromise version, according to which large-scale EU IT systems would, in principle, escape from the standards and safeguards of the new EU legislation governing AI (temporal exception).[92]

A robust and context-specific EU-level regulation of how individuals can make use of their right to an effective judicial remedy is needed, as these questions should not be entirely left to be worked out by litigation.[93] The forthcoming AI Act may

[91] See Article 71 [Penalties] and the new para 8a which was inserted during the trialogues: "[t]he exercise by the market surveillance authority of its powers under this Article shall be subject to appropriate procedural safeguards in accordance with Union and Member State law, including effective judicial remedy and due process."

[92] Article 83 of the original draft AI Act and the politically agreed text of January 2024 both exclude from the scope of the new regulation AI systems that are components of the current and upcoming (before the new Act's entry into effect) EU large-scale IT systems in the area of 'freedom, security and justice'. Added to this, when registering high-risk AI systems in the central EU database by virtue of Articles 51 and 60 of the politically agreed AI Act, providers or appointed authorities would be obliged to make public certain information pursuant to Annex VIII. The compromise version, however, exempts from some of the transparency requirements high-risk AI applications in the field of law enforcement as well as migration, asylum and border management (see Article 51(1c) and Annex VIII). Article 83(1) of the politically agreed text of January 2024 stipulates, however, that large-scale EU IT systems listed in Annex IX (including ETIAS) will have to be brought into compliance with the requirements under the AI Act by the end of 2030.

[93] See similarly Fink (2021) and Brouwer (2021).

actually not be able to fulfil its role if it does not sufficiently clarify the implications of affected fundamental rights protected by the EUCFR.

Quality legislation is only one side of the coin. Individuals subject to AI-facilitated decisions/measures by law enforcement agencies, as well as lawyers and judges alike have to be adequately *empowered* on these matters, including basic technological knowledge, with the aim to turn 'law in books' into 'law in action' when effective judicial protection is at stake in an ever-digitalising area of 'freedom, security and justice' within the Union. At the end of the day, making use of genuine and meaningful judicial remedies against AI-supported decision-making can greatly contribute, with the power of the courts and their interpretation, to carefully responding to the essential question of how to strike the *right balance* between fundamental rights and states' security interests in the digital age.

References

Aalto P, Hofman HCH, Holopainen L, Pauino E, Pech L, Sayers D, Shelton D, Ward A (2014) Article 47—Right to an effective remedy and a fair trial. In: Peers S, Hervey T, Kenner J, Ward A (eds) The EU Charter of Fundamental Rights. A commentary. Hart

Alon-Barkat S, Busuioc M (2023) Human-AI interaction in public sector decision-making: "automation bias" and "selective adherence" to algorithmic advice. Journal of Public Administration Research and Theory 33(1):153–169

Barkhuysen T, van Emmerik M (2018) Right to an effective remedy (Article 13). In: P van Dijk, F van Hoof, A van Rijn L Zwaak (eds), Theory and practice of the European Convention on Human Rights. Intersentia.

Barkhuysen T, van Emmerik M, Jansen O, Fedorova M (2018) Right to a fair trial (Article 6). In: P van Dijk, F van Hoof, A van Rijn, L Zwaak (eds), Theory and practice of the European Convention on Human Rights. Intersentia.

Biondi A (2023) Effective judicial protection. In: Garben S, Gromley L (eds) The Oxford encyclopaedia of EU law. Oxford University Press

Buolamwini J, Ordóñez V, Morgenstern J, Learned-Miller E (2020) Facial recognition technologies: a primer. https://assets-global.website-files.com/5e027ca188c99e3515b404b7/5ed1002058516c11edc66a14_FRTsPrimerMay2020.pdf

Brouwer E (2021) Schengen and the administration of exclusion: legal remedies caught in between entry bans, risk assessment and artificial intelligence. European Journal of Migration and Law 23(4):487–507

Christakis T, Bannelier K, Castelluccia C, Le Métayer D (2022) Mapping the use of facial recognition in public spaces in Europe—part 1: a quest for clarity: unpicking the 'catch-all' term. https://doi.org/10.2139/ssrn.4110512

CJEU: Court of Justice of the European Union, Research and Documentation Directorate (2021) Fact sheet—field of application of the Charter of Fundamental Rights of the European Union. https://curia.europa.eu/jcms/upload/docs/application/pdf/2018-05/fiche_thematique_-_charte_-_en.pdf

Council (2000a) Council Directive 2000/43/EC of 29 June 2000 implementing the principle of equal treatment between persons irrespective of racial or ethnic origin. OJ L 180, 19.7.2000, pp 22–26

Council (2000b) Council Directive 2000/78/EC of 27 November 2000 establishing a general framework for equal treatment in employment and occupation. OJ L 303, 2.12.2000, pp 16–22

Council (2002) Council Framework Decision 2002/584/JHA of 13 June 2002 on the European arrest warrant and the surrender procedures between Member States. OJ L 190, 18.7.2002, pp 1–20
Council (2004a) Council Directive 2004/113/EC of 13 December 2004 implementing the principle of equal treatment between men and women in the access to and supply of goods and services. OJ L 373, 21.12.2004, pp 37–43
Council (2004b) Council Directive 2004/82/EC of 29 April 2004 on the obligation of carriers to communicate passenger data. OJ L 261, 6.8.2004, pp 24–27
Council (2024) Proposal for a regulation of the European Parliament and of the council laying down harmonised rules on artificial intelligence (Artificial Intelligence Act). Institutional file. https://data.consilium.europa.eu/doc/document/ST-5662-2024-INIT/en/pdf
Council of Europe (2020) Recommendation CM/Rec(2020)1 of the Committee of Ministers to member States on the human rights impacts of algorithmic systems. https://rm.coe.int/09000016809e1154
Craig P (2014) Article 41—right to good administration. In: Peers S, Hervey T, Kenner J, Ward A (eds) The EU Charter of Fundamental Rights. A commentary. Hart
Dallas Card (2017). The "black box" metaphor in machine learning. https://dallascard.medium.com/the-black-box-metaphor-in-machine-learning-4e57a3a1d2b0.
Demková S (2023) Automated decision-making and effective remedies. The new dynamics in the protection of EU Fundamental Rights in the Area of Freedom, Security and Justice. Elgar
Derave C, Genicot N, Hetmanska N (2022) The risks of trustworthy artificial intelligence: the case of the European Travel Information and Authorisation System. European Journal of Risk Regulation 13(3):389–420
Duroy S (2023) Case C-817/19, Ligue des Droits Humains v. Council of Ministers (C.J.E.U.). Int Leg Mater, 62(4):611–670
EDRi: European Digital Rights (2019). Why EU passenger surveillance fails its purpose?. https://edri.org/our-work/why-eu-passenger-surveillance-fails-its-purpose/
EU Network: EU Network of Independent Experts on Fundamental Rights (2006) Commentary on the Charter on Fundamental Rights of the European Union. https://sites.uclouvain.be/cridho/documents/Download.Rep/NetworkCommentaryFinal.pdf
EUFRA: EU Agency for Fundamental Rights (2018a) Preventing unlawful profiling today and in the future: a guide. Publications Office of the EU
EUFRA: EU Agency for Fundamental Rights (2018b) Applying the Charter of Fundamental Rights of the European Union in law and policymaking at national level. Guidance. Publications Office of the EU
EUFRA: EU Agency for Fundamental Rights (2019) Facial recognition technology: fundamental rights considerations in the context of law enforcement. Publications Office of the EU
EUFRA: EU Agency for Fundamental Rights (2020) Getting the future right: artificial intelligence and fundamental rights. Publications Office of the EU
EUFRA: EU Agency for Fundamental Rights (2021) Fundamental Rights Report 2021. Publications Office of the EU
EUFRA: EU Agency for Fundamental Rights (2022) Bias in algorithms—artificial intelligence and discrimination. Publications Office of the EU
EUFRA: EU Agency for Fundamental Rights (2023) Fundamental Rights Report 2023. Publications Office of the EU
EUFRA: EU Agency for Fundamental Rights and Council of Europe (2016) Handbook on European law relating to access to justice. Luxembourg. Publications Office of the European Union.
EUFRA: EU Agency for Fundamental Rights and ECtHR: European Court of Human Rights (2020). Handbook on European law relating to asylum, borders and immigration—Edition 2020. Publications Office of the EU.
European Commission (2020a). Directorate-General Migration and Home Affairs. Opportunities and challenges for the use of artificial intelligence in border control, migration and security—Volume 1: Main report. https://data.europa.eu/doi/10.2837/923610

European Commission (2020b) Directorate-General Migration and Home Affairs. Feasibility study on a forecasting and early warning tool for migration based on artificial intelligence technology. https://data.europa.eu/doi/10.2837/222662
European Commission (2020c) Directorate-General Migration and Home Affairs. Management plan 2020. https://commission.europa.eu/publications/management-plan-2020-migration-and-home-affairs_en
European Commission (2020d) Commission staff working document accompanying the document 'Report from the Commission to the European Parliament and the Council on the review of Directive 2016/681 on the use of passenger name record (PNR) data for the prevention, detection, investigation and prosecution of terrorist offences and serious crime'. SWD(2020) 128 final
European Commission (2021a) A strategy towards a fully functioning and resilient Schengen area. COM(2021) 277 final
European Commission (2021b) Proposal for a regulation of the European Parliament and of the council laying down harmonised rules on artificial intelligence (Artificial Intelligence Act) and amending certain union legislative acts. COM(2021)206 final
European Commission (2022a) Commission implementing decisions laying down forms for refusal, annulment or revocation of a travel authorisation, COM(2022)366 final
European Commission (2022b) European Commission staff working document, Impact Assessment Report, SWD(2022) 422 final
European Parliament (2020a) Directorate General for Internal Policies, Policy Department for Citizens' Rights and Constitutional Affairs. Artificial intelligence and law enforcement. Impact on fundamental rights. Study requested by the LIBE Committee. Brussels, PE 656.295
European Parliament (2020b) Resolution of 20 October 2020 on intellectual property rights for the development of artificial intelligence technologies. https://www.europarl.europa.eu/doceo/document/TA-9-2020-0277_EN.html
European Parliamentary Research Service (2021a) Artificial intelligence at EU borders: overview of applications and key issues. Brussels, PE 690.706
Europan Parliament and Council (2006) Directive 2006/54/EC of the European Parliament and of the Council of 5 July 2006 on the implementation of the principle of equal opportunities and equal treatment of men and women in matters of employment and occupation (recast). OJ L 204, 26.7.2006, pp. 23–36
European Parliament and Council (2016a) Regulation (EU) 2016/679 of the European Parliament and of the Council of 27 April 2016 on the protection of natural persons with regard to the processing of personal data and on the free movement of such data, and repealing Directive 95/46/EC (General Data Protection Regulation). OJ L 119, 4.5.2016, pp 1–88
European Parliament and Council (2016b) Directive (EU) 2016/680 of the European Parliament and of the Council of 27 April 2016 on the protection of natural persons with regard to the processing of personal data by competent authorities for the purposes of the prevention, investigation, detection or prosecution of criminal offences or the execution of criminal penalties, and on the free movement of such data, and repealing Council Framework Decision 2008/977/JH. OJ L 119, 4.5.2016, pp 89–131
European Parliament and Council (2016c) Directive (EU) 2016/681 of the European Parliament and of the Council of 27 April 2016 on the use of passenger name record (PNR) data for the prevention, detection, investigation and prosecution of terrorist offences and serious crime. OJ L 119, 4.5.2016, pp 132–149
European Parliament and Council (2017) Regulation (EU) 2017/2226 of the European Parliament and of the Council of 30 November 2017 establishing an Entry/Exit System (EES) to register entry and exit data and refusal of entry data of third-country nationals crossing the external borders of the Member States and determining the conditions for access to the EES for law enforcement purposes, and amending the Convention implementing the Schengen Agreement and Regulations (EC) No 767/2008 and (EU) No 1077/2011. OJ L 327, 9.12.2017, pp 20–82

European Parliament and Council (2018a) Regulation (EU) 2018/1240 of the European Parliament and of the Council of 12 September 2018 establishing a European Travel Information and Authorisation System (ETIAS). OJ L 236, 19.9.2018, pp 1–71

European Parliament and Council (2018b) Regulation (EU) 2018/1806 of the European Parliament and of the Council of 14 November 2018 listing the third countries whose nationals must be in possession of visas when crossing the external borders and those whose nationals are exempt from that requirement. OJ L 303, 28.11.2018, pp 39–58

European Parliament and Council (2019) Regulation (EU) 2019/816 of the European Parliament and of the Council of 17 April 2019 establishing a centralised system for the identification of Member States holding conviction information on third-country nationals and stateless persons (ECRIS-TCN) to supplement the European Criminal Records Information System and amending Regulation (EU) 2018/1726. OJ L 135, 22.5.2019, pp 1–26

European Parliamentary Research Service (2021b) Regulating facial recognition in the EU – In-depth analysis. Brussels, PE 698.21

eu-LISA: European Union Agency for the Operational Management of Large-Scale IT Systems in the Area of Freedom, Security and Justice (2020) eu-LISA hosts its first working group meeting on artificial intelligence. https://www.eulisa.europa.eu/Newsroom/News/Pages/eu-LISA-Hosts-Its-First-Working-Group-Meeting-on-Artificial-Intelligence.aspx

eu-LISA: European Union Agency for the Operational Management of Large-Scale IT Systems in the Area of Freedom, Security and Justice (2021) Artificial intelligence in the operational management of large-scale IT systems. Perspectives for eu-LISA. Research and technology monitoring report. https://www.eulisa.europa.eu/Publications/Reports/AI%20in%20the%20OM%20of%20Large-scale%20IT%20Systems.pdf

Ferguson AG (2017) Policing predictive policing. Washington University Law Review 94(5):1109–1189

Fink M (2021) The EU Artificial Intelligence Act and access to justice. https://eulawlive.com/op-ed-the-eu-artificial-intelligence-act-and-access-to-justice-by-melanie-fink/

Fink M, Finck M (2022) Reasoned A(I)dministration: explanation requirements in EU law and the automation of public administration. European Law Review 47(3):376–392

Frontex: European Border and Coast Guard Agency (2021) Artificial intelligence-based capabilities for the European Border and Coast Guard—Final Report. https://www.frontex.europa.eu/publications/artificial-intelligence-based-capabilities-for-the-european-border-and-coast-guard-final-report-CYyjoe

Glouftsios G, Leese M (2023) Epistemic fusion: passenger information units and the making of international security. Rev Int Stud 49(1):125–142

Gstrein O J, Bunnik A, Zwitter A (2019) Ethical, legal and social challenges of predictive policing. Católica Law Review—Direito Penal 3(3): 77–98

Gugliotta L, Elbi A (2023) Will AI 'subtly' take over decision-making in the EU migration context? Warnings and lessons from ETIAS and VIS. Jean Monnet Network on EU Law Enforcement Working Paper Series. https://jmn-eulen.nl/wp-content/uploads/sites/575/2023/06/7.-WP-Gugliotta-Elbi.pdf

de Heer S (2021) Administrative automated decision-making: what about the right to an effective remedy?. https://ohrh.law.ox.ac.uk/administrative-automated-decision-making-what-about-the-right-to-an-effective-remedy

ICAO: International Civil Aviation Organization (2010) Guidelines on Passenger Name Record (PNR) Data. Approved by the Secretary General and published under his authority, Doc, p 9944

ICAO: International Civil Aviation Organization (2020) Amendment 28 to Annex 9 [Facilitation] to the 1944 Chicago Convention on International Civil Aviation. Adopted on 23 June 2020, communicated by State letter EC 6/3-20/71

HLEG: High-Level Expert Group on Artificial Intelligence (2019) Ethics guidelines for trustworthy AI. https://digital-strategy.ec.europa.eu/en/library/ethics-guidelines-trustworthy-ai

INCLO: International Network of Civil Liberties Organizations (2021) In focus—facial recognition tech stories and rights harms from around the world. https://inclo.net/pdf/in-focus-facial-recognition-tech-stories.pdf

Irion K (2022) Repairing the EU Passenger Name Record Directive: the ECJ's judgment in Ligue des droits humains (Case C-817/19). https://europeanlawblog.eu/2022/10/11/repairing-the-eu-passenger-name-record-directive-the-ecjs-judgment-in-ligue-des-droits-humains-case-c-817-19/

ITLA: International Technology Law Association (2019) Responsible AI: a global policy framework. https://www.itechlaw.org/ResponsibleAI2019

Jones K (2023) AI governance and human rights. Resetting the relationship. https://www.chathamhouse.org/sites/default/files/2023-01/2023-01-10-AI-governance-human-rights-jones.pdf

Korff D (2021) Opinion on the broader and core issues arising in the PNR Case currently before the CJEU (Case C-817/19). https://www.ianbrown.tech/wp-content/uploads/2021/12/KORFF-FREE-Paper-on-Core-Issues-in-the-PNR-Case.pdf

Korff D (2022) Opinion on the implications of the exclusion from new binding European instruments on the use of AI in military, national security and transnational law enforcement contexts. https://ecnl.org/sites/default/files/2022-10/ECNL%20Opinion%20AI%20national%20security_exec%20summary_0.pdf

Korff D, Georges M (2015) Passenger Name Records, data mining & data protection: the need for strong safeguards. https://rm.coe.int/16806a601b

Krenc F (2020) Article 47. Droit à un recours effectif et à accéder à un tribunal impartial. In : F Picod, C Rizcallah, S Van Drooghenbroeck (eds), Charte des droit fondamentaux de l'Union européenne. Commentaire article par article. Bruylant

Mügge D (2023) Squaring the triangle of fundamental rights concerns: The CJEU's PNR ruling and AI governance. https://verfassungsblog.de/pnr-fundamental-rights/

OSCE: Organization for Security and Co-Operation in Europe (2019) Overview of the use of Advance Passenger Information (API) and Passenger Name Record (PNR) in the OSCE Area. SEC.GAL/14/19

Ozkul D (2023) Automating immigration and asylum: the uses of new technologies in migration and asylum governance in Europe. https://www.rsc.ox.ac.uk/publications/automating-immigration-and-asylum-the-uses-of-new-technologies-in-migration-and-asylum-governance-in-europe

Praesidium: Praesidium of the European Convention (2007) Explanations relating to the Charter of Fundamental Rights. OJ C 303, 14.12.2007, pp 17–35

Rainey B, McCormick P, Overy C (2021) The European Convention on Human Rights. Oxford University Press

Reichel D, Molnár T (2023) Big data, big responsibility—fundamental-rights implications of using artificial intelligence in migration management: a European perspective. In: Rango M, Sievers N, Laczko F (eds) Harnessing data innovation for migration policy: a handbook for practitioners. International Organization for Migration

Skitka LJ, Moser K, Burdick MD (2000) Accountability and automation bias. Int J Hum Comput Stud 52(4):701–717

Thönnes C (2022) A directive altered beyond recognition: on the Court of Justice of the European Union's PNR decision (C-817/19). https://verfassungsblog.de/pnr-recognition

UNESCO (2021) Recommendation on the ethics of artificial intelligence. SHS/BIO/REC-AIETHICS/2021

United Nations (2014) Security Council Resolution 2178 (2014) https://www.un.org/securitycouncil/s/res/2178-%282014%29

United Nations (2016) Security Council Resolution 2309 (2016) https://undocs.org/Home/Mobile?FinalSymbol=S%2FRES%2F2309(2016)&Language=E&DeviceType=Desktop&LangRequested=False

United Nations (2017) Security Council Resolution 2396 (2017) https://www.un.org/securitycouncil/content/sres23962017

United Nations (2019) Security Council Resolution 2482 (2019) https://undocs.org/Home/Mobile?FinalSymbol=S%2FRES%2F2482(2019)&Language=E&DeviceType=Desktop&LangRequested=False

Van Den Meerssche D (2022) Virtual borders: international law and the elusive inequalities of algorithmic association. European Journal of International Law 33(1):171–204

Vavoula N (2016) 'I travel, therefore I am a suspect': an overview of the EU PNR Directive. https://eumigrationlawblog.eu/i-travel-therefore-i-am-a-suspect-an-overview-of-the-eu-pnr-directive/?print=print

Vavoula N (2022) Immigration and privacy in the law of the European Union: the case of information systems. Brill/Nijhoff

Veale M, Borgesius F (2021) Demystifying the draft EU Artificial Intelligence Act: analysing the good, the bad, and the unclear elements of the proposed approach. Computer Law Review International 22(4):97–112

Wojnowska-Radzińska J (2023) Implications of pre-emptive data surveillance for fundamental rights in the European Union. Brill/Nijhoff

Wolswinkel J (2022) Artificial intelligence and administrative law. https://www.coe.int/documents/22298481/0/CDCJ%282022%2931E+-+FINAL+6.pdf/4cb20e4b-3da9-d4d4-2da0-65c11cd16116?t=1670943260563

Yeung K (2019) A study of the implications of advanced digital technologies (including AI systems) for the concept of responsibility within a human rights framework. https://rm.coe.int/a-study-of-the-implications-of-advanced-digital-technologies-including/168096bdab

Zandstra T, Brouwer E (2022) Fundamental rights at the digital border: ETIAS, the right to data protection, and the CJEU's PNR judgment. https://verfassungsblog.de/digital-border

How Algorithmic Policing Challenges Fundamental Rights Protection in the EU: Lessons from the United Kingdom

Adam Harkens

Abstract Police in the United Kingdom are quickly emerging as global pioneers in the design and use of technologies employed for the purposes of algorithmic policing: i.e., the use of one or more algorithmic tools to generate outputs capable of supporting decisions taken by policing authorities in pursuit of their public duties and obligations to protect the public and/or to detect, prevent and investigate criminal and/or administrative offending. The range of technologies employed for these purposes include live facial recognition tools, geographical 'hotspot' mapping tools, and tools which allow predictive risk assessment of an individual's likelihood of future offending. These technologies are often framed as efficient and effective means by which to overcome such resourcing pressures, whereby digital data is increasingly viewed as a valuable 'strategic asset' through which to streamline and improve the precision and pace of policing interventions. However, despite widespread use of these tools, two significant regulatory challenges remain. Firstly, how to best ensure safeguards for the fundamental rights of individuals, when very little is known about how these tools are designed and intended to operate—even though multiple controversies have proven that their use is a threat to the ongoing protection of fundamental rights? Secondly, how to ensure accountability for the actions of law enforcement authorities, where violations of such rights might have occurred, or may be likely to occur in future: a problem that extends beyond UK, to the operation of algorithmic tools by law enforcement authorities within the EU? This chapter seeks to evaluate the regulatory landscape of algorithmic policing in Europe, including developments relating to the EU's AI Act, using examples drawn from the United Kingdom. It begins by defining 'algorithmic policing', before presenting and working through key regulatory challenges in this context: i.e., the 'naming' and 'claiming' fundamental rights. It demonstrates that algorithmic policing tools have a reach beyond law enforcement as such, incorporating wider administrative agencies into policing practices, and vice-versa, whereby tools may be presented as benevolent or beneficial to those being algorithmically profiled and/or evaluated. It ultimately argues that complex

A. Harkens (✉)
Strathclyde Law School, University of Strathclyde, Glasgow, UK
e-mail: adam.harkens@strath.ac.uk

M. Varju and K. Mezei (eds.), *The Challenges of Artificial Intelligence for Law in Europe*, Data Science, Machine Intelligence, and Law 6,
https://doi.org/10.1007/978-3-031-86813-9_9

webs of administrative relationships developed as part of these programmes, both technical and institutional, further complicate the already-complicated process of 'naming' and 'claiming' fundamental rights within an algorithmic decision-making process, and that existing regulations—including the AI Act—may not adequately acknowledge this complexity in a way that appropriate safeguards affected persons from harm.

1 Introduction

Police forces in the United Kingdom are quickly emerging as global pioneers in the design, deployment, and use of algorithmic tools for pre-trial decision-making purposes: i.e., the prevention, detection, and investigation of criminal offending. Technologies enabling live facial recognition (Oswald and Babuta 2020; Fussey et al. 2021), geographic 'hotspot' mapping (Chainey et al. 2008; Sandhu and Fussey 2021)—and the predictive risk assessment of an individual's likelihood of future offending (Oswald et al. 2018)—can, and are, being used to make police decisions about whether to initiate surveillance and intelligence-gathering activities, whether to stop, question and/or search specific persons or their property, and/or whether to arrest and detain individuals suspected of criminal offending or of having significant risk of future offending.[1]

Algorithmic tools used in this way can be considered under a broad definitional umbrella of 'algorithmic policing,' referring to a range of policing techniques centred around the use of data-intensive technologies, deployed in an effort to tackle the increasingly complex and resource-intensive demands of law enforcement in a digital world.[2] As explained in Sect. 2, however, ideas of law *enforcement* do not quite capture the entirety of possible applications and functions of algorithmic policing tools, which police in European Union Member States are also beginning to experiment with.

Concerns have been raised by academics, civil society, and the public alike, regarding the risk of bias in algorithmic policing decisions, potential threats to the rule of law and human rights, and an overall lack of transparency surrounding these technologies and their use, of both a technical and institutional nature (Yeung and Harkens 2023). These concerns have been raised in relation to algorithmic decision-making in the public sector more broadly, but they are at their most stark where

[1] See Amnesty International report (Amnesty Internationa 2018) on range of decisions that the Gangs Matrix tool supported and enabled in London. See Brayne (2021) for an ethnographical perspective on the ways in which algorithmic tools have transformed front-line police work in the United States.

[2] By data-intensive technologies, I mean a broad category of technologies that rely upon the use of large digital databases, to generate actionable outputs that inform and influence organisational decision-making. In the public sector context, these technologies may make use of existing, yet disparate, administrative data—or this data may be combined with private sector data and/or datasets bespoke to a particular application.

they pertain to the exercise of policing powers and hence directly relate to powers of coercive intervention with a direct impact upon fundamental rights (Yeung and Harkens 2023).

In the absence of targeted regulation, courts in Germany, the Netherlands and the UK have been required to rule on questions relating to the lawfulness of algorithmic policing, requiring judges to find coherence in otherwise sometimes disparate legal frameworks.[3] Various algorithmic policing tools in all three of the aforementioned jurisdictions have been made subject to judicial controls or outright prohibitions following the finding of clear conflicts between public law principles including fundamental rights—and technical and institutional practices in the design and/or use of these technologies.

The European Union, recognising the need for targeted regulation to develop legal clarity—particularly in response to concerns for the protection of fundamental rights—has pro-actively proposed to regulate the use of artificial intelligence (AI) systems including algorithmic policing tools, through the Artificial Intelligence Act (AI Act) (European Commission 2021; European Parliament 2023a). Following the successful passing of the legislative text by a vote in the European Parliament, the AI Act has, at time of writing, been considered and revised within trilogue discussions between the European Parliament, the Council of the EU, and the European Commission, and is subject to continuing negotiations. The final text of this legislation is yet to be written, but its underlying approach to regulation will remain the same: i.e., that it takes a 'risk-based approach' towards AI systems that intends to impose "regulatory burdens only when an AI system is likely to pose high risks to fundamental rights and safety", or indeed, unacceptable risks meriting prohibition (European Commission 2021).

Fundamental rights 'at risk' may include those protected under the EU Charter of Fundamental Rights (EUCFR). For instance, the right to human dignity (Article 1 EUCFR), respect for private life and right to protection of personal data (Articles 7 and 8 EUCFR), non-discrimination (Article 21 EUCFR), and rights to a fair trial, defence and presumption of innocence, and an effective remedy (Articles 47 and 48 EUCFR). The regulatory 'burdens' to be put in place in order to safeguard against violations of these rights currently include outright prohibitions on certain AI systems being placed on the market or put into service, incorporating those used for "the social scoring, evaluation or classification of groups and individuals leading to detrimental or unfavourable treatment",[4] those which subliminally exploit the vulnerabilities of an individual or group of individuals so as to distort their behaviour in ways that are likely to cause harm,[5] and the use of real-time biometrics for law enforcement purposes.[6] Further restraints are placed on AI systems identified as being 'high risk'

[3] *R v Bridges* [2020] EWCA Civ 1058; *NJCM* et al. *v The Dutch State* (2020) The Hague District Court ECLI:NL:RBDHA:2020:1878 (*SyRI*). See, for the German case, Koltzch (2023).

[4] European Parliament (2023a, Article 5(1)(a)).

[5] European Parliament (2023aArticle 5(1)(b)).

[6] The prohibitions pertaining to algorithmic policing practices, and related definitions, are set out more completely in Sect. 2.2 below.

under Title III, which sets out mandatory requirements for any such high risk systems to be lawfully placed on the market or put into service within the EU. This applies to two main categories: AI systems intended to be used as a 'safety component' of products subject to third-party conformity assessments with technical standards,[7] and the focus of this chapter, 'stand-alone' AI systems that pose a high risk to fundamental rights. The latter two are explicitly listed and defined under Annex III of the AI Act.

This chapter seeks to evaluate the regulatory landscape of algorithmic policing in the UK and Europe, with three purposes in mind. Firstly, it defines algorithmic policing by sketching out the current and policy context of the development, deployment, and use of these tools by police in the United Kingdom, which is becoming increasingly prevalent.

Secondly, it presents and works through two significant regulatory challenges relating to algorithmic policing, using the examples of tools deployed and used in the UK: the 'naming' and 'claiming' of fundamental rights. It demonstrates that algorithmic policing tools have a reach beyond law *enforcement* as such, incorporating wider administrative agencies into policing practices, and vice-versa, whereby tools may be presented as benevolent or beneficial to those being algorithmically profiled and/or evaluated. It argues that complex webs of administrative relationships developed as part of these programmes, both technical and institutional, further complicate the already-complicated process of 'naming' and 'claiming' fundamental rights within an algorithmic decision-making process.

Thirdly, using the examples of tools already deployed in the UK, the chapter evaluates the potential effectiveness of the AI Act as a regulatory mechanism for the protection of fundamental rights through the lens of 'naming' and 'claiming.' It asks whether the AI Act might be a quite blunt measure that fails to fully capture the full range of applications of algorithmic policing, which in its current form does not provide appropriate fundamental rights protection, particularly because it hinders the ability of affected persons to challenge decisions and achieve redress. It finishes with policy recommendations aimed at improving fundamental rights protection in the context of algorithmic policing, specifically targeted at the ongoing development and negotiation of the AI Act.

2 What is Algorithmic Policing?

2.1 A Complex Patchwork of People, Policy, and Machines

Algorithmic policing tools are one form of a range of technologies broadly defined as 'AI systems' under the EU's proposed AI Act. That is, in other words, *machine-based systems* "designed to operate with varying levels of autonomy and that can, for

[7] European Parliament (2023a, Article 6).

explicit or implicit objectives, generate outputs such as predictions, recommendations, or decisions that influence physical or virtual environments."[8] In practice, what one may outwardly perceive as a unified 'AI system' may not in fact be a singular software application, but instead a combination of multiple algorithmic tools serving as components in broader decision-making processes, 'sociotechnical systems' or 'assemblages' (Jasanoff 2017; Redden et al. 2020; Cobbe et al. 2021). These assemblages may incorporate a range actors and software packages from both the private and public sectors simultaneously.

See for example the SyRi system previously used, and then ruled to be unlawful, in the Netherlands. SyRi enabled public authorities, including police, to create administrative partnerships for the purposes of building flexible, customisable, risk profiling tools, to identify individuals that showed 'heightened risk of irregularities' amongst their personal data and to inform the investigation of criminal and administrative offences.[9] As found by the District Court of the Hague, this enabled database linkage and digital surveillance to a disproportionate and unlawful degree, rendering the system incompliant with the right to privacy in Article 8 of the European Convention on Human Rights.

However, to focus on the use of algorithmic tools deployed to detect criminal and/or administrative offending is to miss the full breadth of their potential application, which further extends into cases that can be loosely characterised as attempts to protect and safeguard both the public and individuals against harm on a preventive basis (Ashworth and Zedner 2014). Multi-agency partnerships (like those enabled by SyRi) can be formed between various law enforcement and public administrative agencies with the goal of identifying potential *victims* of crime—or otherwise vulnerable individuals—using an algorithmic tool, to guide action in an effort to *prevent* harm.[10] This may involve a broad variety of interventions that do not necessarily or inherently correspond to understandings of law *enforcement.* Indeed, in certain contexts, options for intervention by law enforcement and non-law enforcement agencies may be simultaneously designed into decision-making processes, informed by the output of an algorithmic tool, where they become entangled and sometimes inseparable.

All of this accords to general trends in policing towards the idea of *preventive justice*—which, as set out by Andrew Ashworth and Lucia Zedner (2019) refers to "the proliferation of state security laws, preventive measures, policies, and practices that are in different ways, all motivated by the same preventive impetus to minimize risks and forestall harms." This includes the use of, by police and other public authorities, coercive measures "intended to impose sufficient pressure on a person to force or make a person act in a certain way" (Ashworth and Zedner 2014). In this sense

---

[8] European Parliament (2023a, Article 3(1) and Annex I(a)).

[9] *NJCM* et al. *v The Dutch State* (2020) The Hague District Court ECLI:NL:RBDHA:2020:1878 (*SyRI*).

[10] This includes the Gangs Matrix, but also other that *are* data-intensive, but *not* automated, such as the County Lines Intelligence Collection Matrix. See, in this regard, MOPAC (2021).

preventive justice may entail either or both physical coercion (i.e., preventive detention or physical removal of a person from a given public space) or rational compulsion (i.e., the use of law to require individuals to undertake specific actions, or to refrain from acting in a certain way), under the threat of further coercion (Ashworth and Zedner 2014).

Even where other administrative agencies are not involved, algorithmic tools can allow police forces to combine coercion and rational compulsion in practice. For example, see the Harm Assessment Risk Tool, which previously used by Durham Constabulary to provide individuals algorithmically assessed as being 'medium risk' the opportunity to complete an 'out-of-court-disposal' and avoid formal charges, under agreed conditions: e.g., undergoing substance abuse treatment (Oswald et al., 2018). If these conditions were not met, this could lead to further prosecution.

For the purposes of this chapter, algorithmic policing can therefore be defined as the use of one or more algorithmic tools to generate outputs capable of supporting decisions taken by policing authorities in pursuit of their public duties and obligations to protect the public *and/or* to detect, prevent and investigate criminal and/or administrative offending. What it means to 'protect' the public can be taken broadly to include prevention of exploitation or personal harm, and also to provide assistance in times of personal need such as a mental health crisis (Syal 2023). Depending upon the context and specific use case, this may or may not involve other public authorities and administrative agencies with statutory duties and obligations that on the face of things sit tangentially to those of the police, yet when entangled within an algorithmic decision-making process, form part of an attempted algorithmic solution to loosely defined social problems (Redden et al. 2020).

The chapter uses emphasises the use of algorithmic tools by 'police' over the term 'law enforcement authorities'—the latter of which is the standard terminology used by the EU in relation to the AI Act and the Law Enforcement Directive (European Parliament and Council 2016a). It does so to draw a clear distinction between the various civil functions of the police, which contrast starkly with duties pertaining to national security. It takes an expansive view towards the functions of police, at least within the UK, where their role is defined in the common law:

(a) in addition to law *enforcement*, policing is a public *service* designed to offer methods to protect the public by reducing and preventing violence, resolving civil disputes, and to act as an organisational force for public demonstrations, and in times of crisis, which may or may not involve the exercise of coercive force; and
(b) police as a constitutive element of the administrative state whereby forces are required to, and often do, pro-actively form relationships with other public authorities in order to tackle complex social and political problems. In this latter role, police are governed and regulated by administrative rules, principles, and doctrine.

How algorithmic policing is legally governed and regulated, therefore, may have a significant impact upon the governance and regulation of administrative decision-making by public authorities more generally—and hence, standards of constitutional and administrative law within a given jurisdiction. As discussed below in Sect. 3, it is within these liminal administrative-policing spaces that algorithmic policing is becoming established as a policy tool in the UK. Even though it still involves policing decisions that can have a significant and serious effect on fundamental rights, the concept of law *enforcement* lacks sufficient breadth to explain why and how these tools are being commissioned and used.

Algorithmic policing does not connote an entirely automated process free of human intervention, but one in which multiple discretionary decisions combine, and are incorporated into, wider decision-frameworks containing a range of solely human, solely automated, and partly-automated decision-making (Bellanova and de Goede 2022; Cobbe et al. 2023). In other words, algorithmic policing is a process whereby the intuition of human police officers is often combined with and/or informed by, the outputs of an algorithmic tool—which are further influenced by the design choices of technical designers, and technical input and data manipulation of data analysts (who may or may not have capacity to frame decision choices) (Cobbe et al. 2021; Veale et al. 2023; Yeung and Harkens 2023). The latter two actors in this process themselves perform roles and functions novel to the police decision-making process, that merit separate research into their discretionary power outside of the scope of this chapter.

2.2 *The Regulatory Context of Algorithmic Policing Within the European Union*

As discussed above, the final text of the AI Act has not been formally agreed. However, this does not harm its position as a potentially world-leading regulatory instrument pertaining to algorithmic policing (among other uses of 'AI systems'). Initial drafts contained dedicated restrictions upon both (a) the development of 'AI systems' for the purposes of 'placing on the market'—and (b) the deployment of algorithmic tools by public authorities, including the police ('putting into service'). This framing will shepherd questions relating to fundamental rights protection into both the public and private sector.[11]

The AI Act takes a risk-based approach to regulation that combines broad principle-based requirements, with the imposition of targeted legal constraints upon specific kinds of algorithmic tools and related use cases, which are framed as 'regulatory burdens.' As such, it differs from the 'technology neutral' approaches of the General Data Protection Regulation (European Parliament and Council 2016a) and Law Enforcement Directive (European Parliament and Council 2016b).[12]

[11] European Parliament (2023a, Articles 3(10) and (11)).

[12] See Hildebrandt and Tielemans (2013). In other words, by focusing on *tasks* such as data collection, data processing and data retention etc., as Hildebrandt and Tielemans (2013) have put it on, the legal effect of data protection law "should not depend on the particular technology that is used by the addressees of the law."

While technology neutral approaches acknowledge that the normative effect of human rights should not depend upon the technologies used, the AI Act instead recognises that certain technologies—or specific use cases—may prohibit enjoyment of specific human rights in their entirety and therefore their deployment into live environments should not be legally authorised. Indeed, it could possibly be argued that the AI Act serves as much as a legal instrument as it is a political statement of red lines pertaining to what the minimum level of fundamental rights protection in the European Union should be, by categorising, classifying, restricting, and prohibiting, actual and *potential* risks. Such red lines are intended to contribute to the achievement of a well-balanced trade-off between the protection of fundamental rights within the single market, and the promotion of innovation, to serve market and industrial policy objectives. It remains to be seen whether this trade-off will be satisfactory in practice.

The primary 'regulatory burdens' present in the current text of the AI Act are organised into two categories: 'prohibited' and 'high risk' AI practices.[13] Prohibited practices refer to those AI systems identified by the AI Act that are deemed to generate 'unacceptable' levels of risk to fundamental rights, and therefore deemed to require an outright ban to prevent fundamental rights violations.[14] In the context of algorithmic policing, such practices include prohibitions on the use of algorithmic tools to undertake individual risk assessments of natural persons concerning their predicted risk of offending or re-offending,[15] emotional state detection,[16] the use of 'real-time' biometric identification systems (e.g., live facial recognition), and the indiscriminate 'scraping' of biometric data from CCTV for the purposes of retrospective facial recognition.[17] These prohibitions are contained under Article 5 of the AI Act, and are therefore given prominence within the core text of the AI Act itself, unlike 'high-risk' practices that are set out in Annex III.

High risk systems pertaining to algorithmic policing practices include evidence evaluation,[18] profiling in the course of detection, investigation or prosecution of criminal offences (distinct from risk assessment pertaining to an individual's likelihood of offending or re-offending), and quite vaguely, general forms of profiling and analytics to identify otherwise hidden or unknown patterns in large data sets that pertain to natural persons.[19] The list of AI systems contained within Annex III is not immutable. Rather, it can be updated over time to respond to newly identified risks via measures adopted by the Commission, which has been empowered under Article 7 AI Act to add additional high risk systems, if they are (a) intended to be used in the areas listed in Annex III (point 1 to 8); and (b) pose a risk to health and safety or fundamental rights at a level equivalent to, or greater than, AI systems already

[13] European Parliament (2023a, Annex III(6)(a)).

[14] European Parliament (2023a, Article 5).

[15] European Parliament (2023a, Annex III(6)(b)).

[16] European Parliament (2023a, Annex III(6)(c)).

[17] European Parliament (2023a, Article 5(1)(d)).

[18] European Parliament (2023a, Annex III(6)(d)).

[19] European Parliament (2023a, Annex III(6)(f)-(g)).

identified in Annex III.[20] Additional AI systems may therefore be added if deemed suitable by the Commission, who must demonstrate that they have taken into account characteristics of the AI systems related to, among others, their intended purposes, the extent to which they are to be used, the potential extent of harm or adverse impact caused by their use, and the vulnerabilities of affected individuals in relation to the user of the systems, caused by imbalances in power, knowledge, economic and social circumstances, and age.[21]

If identified in Annex III, high risk systems must both (a) meet a set of essential technical requirements, and (b) there must be organisational controls in place throughout their lifecycle. For instance, Article 8 imposes the need to complete and register a 'conformity assessment' demonstrating that the AI system complies with the provisions of the AI Act, the enabling of human oversight of the AI system, the development of a 'risk management' system,[22] and production of documentation relating to technical aspects of the tool,[23] data governance,[24] logging pertaining to the use of the tool,[25] and registration in a public database.[26] Some tools that have not been explicitly identified as prohibited or high risk will also be required to comply with certain requirements, such as limited transparency requirements under Article 52, if they involve emotional state detection, or if they interact with a natural person. Specifically, Article 52 requires providers to design AI systems which interact with natural persons in such a way to ensure that it is obvious to the person in question that they are interacting with an AI system. This obligation does not apply to policing applications.[27]

The precise contours of the Article 8 requirements will differ depending on a person's relationship to the AI system, i.e., dependent on whether they are a 'provider' (natural or legal person, or public authority who *develops* an AI system or who has an AI system developed with a view to putting it on the market or into service); or a 'deployer' (natural or legal person or public authority who is using an AI system under its authority).[28]

In the context of algorithmic policing, it is important to consider the outlined prohibitions and legal requirements alongside the EU's Law Enforcement Directive (European Parliament and Council 2016b), which regulates data protection in the specific context of law enforcement purposes (transposed as parts 3 and 4 of the Data

---

[20] European Parliament (2023a, Article 7).

[21] European Parliament (2023a, Annex III).

[22] European Parliament (2023a, Article 9).

[23] European Parliament (2023a, Article 11).

[24] European Parliament (2023a, Article 10).

[25] European Parliament (2023a, Article 12).

[26] European Parliament (2023a, Article 51).

[27] European Parliament (2023a, Article 52(1)).

[28] The term deployer has replaced the word 'user' to improve regulatory clarity by preventing possible confusion between the person or agency who deploys the tool for their own purposes, and an individual who may also interact with said tool in certain situations (and thus may also be called the 'user').

Protection Act 2018 in the UK). Both legal instruments ought to be read together, due to the intimate relationship between the collection, processing and analysis of personal data in digital formats, necessary for the design and use of algorithmic policing tools. As recognised by Veale and Borgesius (2021), the AI Act serves as *lex specialis* to the Law Enforcement Directive by generating rules for specific technologies, e.g., through the introduction of specific prohibitions in some areas, which can and likely will, determine whether a given system or practice is compliant with the data protection principle of 'lawfulness'. In addition, it is to be welcomed that the AI Act provides a richer tapestry of requirements for AI systems involved in the generation of 'semi-automated decisions', that are otherwise relatively non-existent in the Law Enforcement Directive.

Nonetheless, despite the many commendable elements to the AI Act some significant gaps remain in the legislation that may leave open opportunities for the unlawful or disproportionate interference with fundamental rights, by weakening safeguards introduced by the AI Act itself. Crucially, these gaps do not persist because they relate to a lack of technical knowledge about AI systems, but rather, because the administrative realities of policing and law enforcement have been misrepresented in four key areas, as set out below. Section 3 explores dangers that can arise in practice should these identified regulatory gaps persist. By using the example of the UK, it highlights how quickly, and easily algorithmic policing can lead to harmful outcomes, even where introduced with the best of intentions.

2.2.1 Negative Potential Impact(s) of Overly Broad Exemptions

Following the trilogue negotiations for the AI Act, significant exemptions to law enforcement use of AI systems have been inserted for which we do not have clear legal text. This includes, for example, exemptions for 'national security purposes,' and exemptions for the prohibition of real-time biometric identification systems including live facial recognition (Leufer et al. 2023).

Further, it is now expected that the final text will include a 'filter' whereby AI systems otherwise considered high-risk (and thus subject to heightened legal control and transparency requirements) can be self-exempted by AI developers provided that the AI system in question undertakes 'a narrow procedural task' and/or is used to 'confirm or improve an accessary factor of a human assessment,' or to 'perform a preparatory task.' Concerns have been raised by the European Parliament's legal service regarding the high degree of subjectivity in this process, which may generate significant legal uncertainty, and inequality in the legal obligations that apply. Most algorithmic policing tools known to have been used in practice could be included under one or more of the above filters, though it is important to note that tools involving 'profiling' will retain their high-risk classification (Bertuzzi 2023).

Taken altogether, this means that policing authorities may be capable of exercising the legal authority to commission algorithmic tools while simultaneously exercising a significant degree of authority to frame the operational policy purpose of these tools in way that facilitates the inappropriate self-exemption from the regulatory requirements pertaining to prohibited and 'high-risk' algorithmic policing tools. Where this occurs, it will render legal controls found within the AI ineffective, with a significant danger of undermining fundamental rights protection on a systemic level.

2.2.2 Vague Restrictions on Social Scoring

Secondly, although social scoring is prohibited by the AI Act, this does not mean that it prohibits the use of algorithmic tools by public authorities for the purposes of analysing data and profiling to inform pre-emptive interventions into the lives of individuals to prevent harm. For instance, this may include tools used to determine whether a vulnerable child requires interventions by social care, or whether a person is at significant risk of violence from their spouse.[29] As stated in Recital (28), the prohibition on social scoring also does not extend to the use of risk profiling by tax authorities to determine administrative offending—a use case reminiscent of the SyRI system.[30] In both of these situations, police and other law enforcement authorities may be involved both in one or more elements of the decision-making process, and the intervention process, including the exercise of coercive authority where necessary that may directly engage the fundamental rights of affected persons (Ashworth and Zedner 2014).

2.2.3 Omission of Safeguarding for Individuals Classified as 'Migrants'

Thirdly, AI systems intended to be used for the purposes of informing decisions pertaining to migration have been classified by the AI Act as a distinct set of technologies from those used for 'law enforcement'. As such, prohibitions such as those relating to individual risk assessment have not been extended to migrants, despite the risk to their fundamental rights.[31] It is law enforcement authorities, particularly police, who will primarily deal with migrants when they are 'on the move' within urban areas, and it ought to be recognised that the exercise of policing power may extend to individuals *suspected* of having entered a Member State irregularly or illegally (even if this is not the case).

---

[29] See Veale and Borgesius (2021) arguing that: "The Commission anticipates that a system which 'identifies at-risk children in need of social care' would be out of context if 'based on insignificant or irrelevant social 'misbehaviour' of parents, e.g. missing a doctor's appointment or divorce."

[30] *NJCM* et al. *v The Dutch State* (2020) The Hague District Court ECLI:NL:RBDHA:2020:1878 (*SyRI*).

[31] See for example the use of biometric tools to scan and track migrants in Greece (Human Rights Watch 2022). See further European Parliament (2023b).

2.2.4 Omission of Safeguards for Hotspot Mapping

Fourthly, generalised 'hotspot' mapping of geographical locations where the occurrence of crime may be deemed 'likely' within a defined time period has not been included in this list. Hotspot mapping does not relate to data about a natural person, and instead includes practices that may target a collective group or geographical area (Brayne 2021; Smuha et al. 2021). Although an individual's rights are not specifically at risk, in that they are not being individually profiled or surveilled (nor might any personal data be being analysed), there is still a danger of over-policing in particular areas, which may be worsened by feedback loops generated from poor training data and other policing practices (Ensign et al. 2018).

2.2.5 Failure to Implement Requirements for Robust Mechanisms of Accountability, Challenge and Redress

Finally, previous drafts of the AI act have not provided clear rules or guidance regarding direct processes for accountability, complaint, and redress where there is reason to believe that unlawful interference with fundamental rights may have occurred or be likely to occur. As we wait for a new legal text, there is no explicit indication or expectation that this situation will improve.

There is a clear need not only for a clear and robust complaints mechanism enabling affected individuals with rights concerns to complain to their relevant national supervisory authority—having responsibility for the application of the AI Act in a given Member State—but also for the development of mechanisms enabling access to judicial or administrative processes, with clarity and without undue delay (Smuha et al. 2021). It has been confirmed in trilogue discussions that individuals will have a right to complaint, but the associated powers of supervisory authorities to take action where legal requirements have not been met, is unclear (European Parliament 2023b). There is also no confirmation that there will be a right to appeal or take this complaint further, if the complainant is not satisfied with the outcome of the process.

Failure to provide clear processes of robust and clear accountability mechanisms would be to significantly hinder the ability of individuals affected to assert and defend their rights, which would seem to undermine its effectiveness from a public law perspective, and indeed, potentially the entire purpose of the AI Act. Accountability mechanisms ought to be considered on a systematic basis, considering that gaps in legal control in one part of the AI Act (e.g., via overly broad exemptions, or the introduction of a complaints mechanism without the ability to follow this up via formal legal claims), may harm the overall effectiveness of the regulation.

Clear processes of challenge and accountability are the only way that the complex entanglement of machine analysis and human discretion can be unravelled, to determine its necessity and lawfulness in policing. This is particularly so if the police authority in question is not forthcoming regarding necessary transparency, or they have not adequately informed an individual about how their rights have been balanced against operational priorities in each case. The requirement to implement fundamental rights impact assessments—as agreed in the trilogue negotiations—may mitigate some potential dangers here, but it remains to be seen precisely how this impact assessment will be structured, and which specific legal requirements will apply (European Parliament 2023b). In addition, there is little value in the development of an impact assessment, without accountability mechanisms that ensure their proper and appropriate completion and monitoring.

An important contrast can be made here with the Council of Europe's 'Committee on Artificial Intelligence' (CAI)'s draft for a 'Convention on Artificial Intelligence, Democracy and the Rule of Law' (Council of Europe 2023). At time of writing, this has reached the stage of 'consolidated working draft' meaning that it has only been agreed to at a very provisional stage, with its final content and actual enactment likely a number of years away (if at all). Article 13 of the current draft generates a requirement for measures to allow for effective remedies for violations of human rights and freedoms "resulting from the use of artificial intelligence systems." In doing so, it recognises that the effectiveness of rights protections depend upon access to effective legal remedies.[32] Relevant measures include the necessary maintenance of records pertaining to the use of the AI system, a right of access to oversight bodies authorised in domestic law, and the need for communication with affected persons where appropriate and applicable. It also requires a route for affected persons to contest (a) the general use of the system; and (b) specific decisions made or 'substantially informed' by the system. In this sense, the draft convention speaks to affected individuals directly, unlike the AI Act which speaks more directly to providers and deployers, and thus, the market.

3 Algorithmic Policing in Practice: What Makes UK Police 'Pioneers' in Algorithmic Policing?

Algorithmic tools have contributed, and are likely to continue to contribute, towards changes in the decision-making and policy formulation processes of police and related public authorities, including the prioritisation of resource allocation. All such decisions necessarily involve balancing the fundamental rights protection against operational priorities. If the AI Act is to be successful in protecting fundamental rights, it is then necessary that real, practical examples of algorithmic policing are studied on an ongoing basis, to enable the assessment and (re-)evaluation of existing, and proposed, regulatory measures.

It is only through the study of existing operational AI systems that legislators and policymakers, police, other public authorities, and regulators alike, can come to an understanding of the complexities of algorithmic policing in practice. Though the EU has taken the driver's seat in terms of initiating regulation, it is in fact in the UK where the pace of development, deployment and use is at its highest in Europe—even

[32] Council of Europe (2023, Articles 14 and 15).

if the UK's regulatory landscape remains underdeveloped and relatively sparse. The AI Act follows a risk-based regulatory approach, and as such, it ought to remain attuned to developments in practice, including those that take place outside of the direct jurisdiction of the EU.

3.1 Sense Number One: Grasping at Capacities

Algorithmic policing is not directly regulated via targeted legislation in the UK. It is instead (loosely) controlled through a range of directly indirectly relevant statute in the form of statutory powers and regulatory regimes including data protection and equality law, common law powers and duties of the police to investigate, detect and prevent crime, and general public law principles.[33] This regulatory regime, taken as a whole, requires significant discretionary interpretation to determine how both (a) laws developed without algorithmic policing in mind (e.g., existing policing powers); and (b) laws that are only indirectly related to *aspects* of algorithmic policing (e.g., data protection law), apply to practical use cases. As this section will show, policing authorities in the UK retain significant scope to shape the acceptable limits of such discretionary interpretation.

Police forces in the UK are pioneers in algorithmic policing in two senses. Firstly, policing policy—set by those in leadership positions including Chief Constables of each regional force who retain significant operational independence and discretionary power to do so—now clearly demonstrates a willingness to experiment with algorithmic law policing techniques in live environments. Police in the UK are being 'nudged' to develop, procure and test new technologies by three confounding factors: ongoing government-mandated economic austerity that has produces a reduction in general policing funding (Syal and Dodd 2022), the introduction of new incentivised funding for 'innovation' that has been made available in the funding vacuum caused by austerity (Home Office 2020), and a policy need for police to respond to increasingly complex societal challenges which has necessitated an expansion in the social role of police and their public responsibilities.[34]

UK government policy does not—yet, at least—*require* police to develop or procure algorithmic tools, but rather *encourages* police, through innovation funding and policy statements, to exercise their discretion to develop or procure *some kind of* digital technologies that may help support police interventions to reduce of resource

---

[33] See *R v Bridges* [2020] EWCA Civ 1058 and Gangs Matrix legal mandate (Metropolitan Police), https://www.met.police.uk/SysSiteAssets/media/downloads/force-content/met/about-us/gangs-violence-matrix/legal-mandate-for-the-met-to-use-the-gangs-violence-matrix.docx#:~:text=%E2%80%9CThere%20shall%20be%20no%20interference,disorder%20or%20crime%2C%20for%20the.

[34] See the adoption of the 'Right Care, Right Person' model for mental health interventions (Metropolitan Police), https://www.met.police.uk/notices/met/introduction-right-care-right-person-model/.

pressures and the production of 'smarter' decisions.[35] This is the case even despite the lack of clear and categorical evidence capable of demonstrating that algorithmic tools can actually improve policing in these ways (Dressel and Farid 2018).

Though not necessarily directly a reason for the introduction of algorithmic policing techniques, the (in)actions and decisions of police forces in the UK, are also increasingly being scrutinised by the public following multiple scandals pertaining to accusations of institutional racism, misogyny and other forms of discriminatory and harmful behaviour—including allegations of negligent failures of police leadership to prevent its occurrence.[36] Multiple police forces have additionally been placed under 'special measures' due to various failures in decision-making and/or limitations in capacities.[37]

As such, there is now a very active public debate regarding the functions and powers of police in the United Kingdom, with many seeking a rethink of what policing should be for—including the roles and functions of Chief Constables and Police and Crime Commissioners.[38] In relative terms, the (potential) changes that algorithmic policing can bring to public understandings of police functions have received comparatively little attention, beyond debates relating to the use of live facial recognition—thus missing the significant impacts that algorithmic tools based around data analysis can have, even if these transformations in decision-making are not externally perceptible.

All of this is not to say, however, that forays into algorithmic policing are driven purely by factors external to the police. Even within police forces, digital data is additionally increasingly viewed as a valuable 'strategic asset' that can improve and streamline the precision and pace of policing interventions (National Police Chiefs 2020). Commissioner Sir Mark Rowley of London's Metropolitan Police Service (MPS), the UK's largest police force, has even gone so far as to state that "there is a profound truth here that better understanding of trends in crime data can help save lives" (Rowley 2022). It has further been claimed that the use of algorithmic policing—and data analytics in policing more generally—will enable less biased, and more efficient policing practices (Department for Science, Innovation and Technology 2023).

Innovation is therefore occurring at the institutional level, where it is police forces who are helping to drive this algorithmic turn. Algorithmic policing, predicated on the greater exploitation of readily-available digital data, is presented as a generally benevolent development—if not unproblematic—and a response to frustrations amongst the forces that they are not properly equipped to fulfil their legal duties to

---

[35] See, for example, the Police STAR fund operated by the Office of Police Chief Scientific Adviser (OPCSA), https://science.police.uk/opportunities/police-star-fund/, and Defence Science and Technology Laboratory: Police futures: a taste of the future, https://science.police.uk/delivery/resources/police-futures-a-taste-of-the-future/. See further Philp (2023).

[36] See the Baroness Casey Review (Metropolitan Police 2023).

[37] See Letter of engagement (Cook 2023).

[38] The latter of which is an elected role.

protect the public from harm (broadly conceived) and to prevent criminal offending more generally in an increasingly digital and networked world.

3.2 Sense Number Two: Crossing Rights Frontiers

Police in the UK are also pioneers in a second sense, in that they are stepping across a foggy frontier of unknowns for fundamental rights, whereby the limits of existing laws, principles, and safeguards for affected individuals are being tested and challenged. In the absence of clear, dedicated, legislation pertaining to algorithmic policing, or indeed the use of algorithmic decision-making in the public sector more generally, police are exercising their discretionary powers, provided via a combination of the common law and statute, to develop novel algorithmic policing techniques without any legal or policy guidance from central government (Ní Loideáin 2024). This is not to say that police forces are deliberately interfering with, or seeking to interfere with, fundamental rights, but rather that they are not necessarily equipped to make difficult decisions centring around the balancing of fundamental rights against operational priorities.

Algorithmic tools are being designed and used on a discretionary and unsystematic basis, dependent upon the decisions and claimed needs of each regional police force—with little to no transparency, nor clear evidence surrounding their effectiveness (Birks et al. 2023). What you may expect in one regional area (e.g., London), is not necessarily what you should expect in another (e.g., Scotland or Greater Manchester).

As seen in the judgment in *Bridges*—which centred on the lawfulness of live facial recognition tools in policing—there is a significant lack of explicit legal control over the police use of algorithmic tools in the UK. Legal authorisation for algorithmic policing arises from an uneasy, vague and sometimes complex amalgamation of common law powers, data protection rules (which, as discussed, are 'technology neutral' and thus unsuitable to the hitherto discussed unique legal problems with algorithmic policing), and policy documents providing few assurances regarding fundamental rights protection.[39] Nonetheless, this has not prevented police forces from self-determining that they have struck the correct balance between rights protections and operational priorities.[40]

[39] *R(Bridges) v South Wales Police* [2020] EWCA Civ 1058.

[40] *R(Bridges) v South Wales Police* [2020] EWCA Civ 1058. See further the legal mandate written by the Metropolitan Police for the Gangs Matrix (https://www.met.police.uk/SysSiteAssets/media/downloads/force-content/met/about-us/gangs-violence-matrix/legal-mandate-for-the-met-to-use-the-gangs-violence-matrix.docx#:~:text=%E2%80%9CThere%20shall%20be%20no%20interference,disorder%20or%20crime%2C%20for%20the), which contains a very limited statement of relevant powers, and an incomplete proportionality assessment of the algorithmic decision-making process supported by the tool, with no explicit consideration of, potential risks and consequences resulting from its use.

Legal certainty around algorithmic policing has not been improved by the UK's proposed 'pro-innovation' approach to AI regulation, announced in a white paper produced by the Department for Science, Innovation and Technology. This approach tasks existing regulators—who currently operate disparately and within the confines of their legal remit and specialisms—to develop a 'principles-based approach' towards the regulation of AI, without a clearly stated definition of AI, nor the creation of any statutory duties nor powers for regulators and public authorities seeking to deploy AI systems alike (Yeung and Ahmed-Rengers 2023). There is therefore no clear nor obvious path around how algorithmic policing practices will develop in the UK in future, nor what kinds of police decisions that citizens ought to expect to made be made about then, with the use of algorithmic tools.

As algorithmic policing becomes more prevalent, novel forms of decisions are being taken using digital technologies to perform novel functions in the policing context. For example, the use of the Gangs Matrix by London Metropolitan Police involves data sharing (with 'partner agencies') and data analysis at a speed and scale that would not previously have been possible for police without the availability of algorithmic software capable of self-learning (Amnesty International 2018; MOPAC 2018). This does not automatically mean, however, that the outcomes for individuals being assessed by such tools are automatically improved, or desirable.

Even where algorithmic tools are used with the intent of informing safeguarding or harm prevention, such as the Gangs Matrix, their use is primarily targeted towards informing the exercise of discretionary and coercive policing powers, including powers to surveil, stop, search and arrest.[41] In the UK, this has led to harmful outcomes, even where the initial intentions of the system have been largely good, and further, even where the harmful actions were undertaken by partner agencies (Amnesty International 2018; Sardjo 2022). For instance, potential 'victims' of the Gangs Matrix were incorrectly included as 'gang nominals' on the Gangs Matrix system, and the data of individuals profiled as having a 'zero-harm' score by the Matrix itself was shared with other administrative agencies who took punitive measures against them such as deportation, school expulsion and refusal of housing, because of the stigma attached to the label 'gang nominal', attributed by virtue of having their name on the database (Amnesty International 2018; ICO 2018).

Additionally, even algorithmic tools that incorporate little to no automated learning, may lead to harm where due care is not taken. As seen in *Bridges*, it was not a simple case of finding that the use of the technology itself was unlawful and lacking sufficient legal control, but rather it was the reliance of this of this technology upon sets of 'watchlists' (i.e., databases of persons of interest) compiled by human officers on a discretionary and unsystematic basis, with little oversight, nor any clear governance as to how an individual finds themselves on the list. Additionally, because the lists were deleted after each deployment, there was no method of legal evaluation *ex post.* Any form of automated tool is therefore capable of automating such discretionary practices of questionable legality, without an obvious route to challenge or oversight. Legal questions relating to fundamental rights protection thus do not

[41] *R v Bridges* [2020] EWCA Civ 1058, [91]–[97].

necessarily hinge upon the technical capacities of a given algorithmic tool, but upon the ways in which police forces decide to use it.

In the absence of clear legal or regulatory control of specific decision types, police authorities ought to think more carefully about how to appropriately make use of technologies capable of enhancing and expanding their discretionary decision-making powers, sometimes perhaps beyond what was initially envisaged when conferred upon them. Legal boundaries regarding the extent and scope of discretionary policing powers in the context of algorithmic policing remain unclear—particularly where this involves the introduction of actors such as data analysts, designers, and private technology consultants into the criminal justice decision-making process. Clear guidance is needed regarding the designation of the appropriate authority to commission, design and use an algorithmic tool, and how that authority ought to be structured where any resulting decision may impact upon fundamental rights.

Robustly regulating algorithmic policing therefore requires a comprehensive and context-specific understanding of the potential scope of transformation that *might* occur in conventional understandings of policing powers and decision-making, should algorithmic tools be deployed, including whether particular tools facilitate novel exercise(s) of said powers. Despite seemingly widespread use of algorithmic policing tools in the UK, there is still currently a distinct lack of publicly available information regarding their design, use and evaluation—making it difficult to discern basic details including where, when, how, by whom, upon whom or what, and why they are being used (Yeung and Harkens 2023).

Policing in the UK has therefore now reached a point where the roles and functions of police are being challenged socially, legally, and politically—with unclear solutions to deal with said challenges. Police are being required to return to the drawing board, and to find such solutions to complex problems within an unclear and unhelpful legal and policy landscape. Police forces have a desire—and indeed are being incentivised—to turn towards developing algorithmic tools, on a relatively unsystematic basis, to fulfil their legal duties and obligations to a very basic level. In response, the UK's 'AI White Paper', takes an unsatisfactory 'principles-based approach' in lieu of concrete legal guidance and safeguards for both algorithmic policing actors *and* individuals whose rights may be, or are being, interfered with (Yeung and Ahmed-Rengers 2023).

4 What is the Problem of *Naming*?

Algorithmic policing generates novel legal questions by enabling novel methods of profiling, analysing, and deciding about individuals and populations made subject to the coercive powers of the police to make interventions. This chapter has so far shown in the context of the UK that those legal questions are particularly pertinent where there is a significant risk of unlawful interference with fundamental rights. It is thus incumbent upon legislators, policymakers—and police who make use of these tools—to reduce these risks. This is clearly not a simple task however, given that there are limited regulatory examples from which to model best practices, and indeed, to understand how potential negative impacts on fundamental rights protections ought to be identified, mitigated, and where appropriate, eliminated. As the examples of the UK and EU demonstrate, any attempt at regulating algorithmic policing will come up against two related regulated challenges: the 'naming' and 'claiming' of fundamental rights.

The process of 'naming' fundamental rights in the context of algorithmic policing refers to two inter-related steps within a broader regulatory approach. Firstly, how to identify risks of potential rights interferences in a quickly evolving situation of information asymmetry whereby the public knows very little about how these tools are designed and intended to operate? And secondly, how to best ensure the implementation of safeguards for the fundamental rights of individuals, to prevent *potential* rights violations from actualising in practice?

4.1 Which Rights Are Engaged? and Which Processes Generate Risks and Threats to These Rights?

A subtle but crucial challenge to fundamental rights protection in algorithmic policing, is the difficulty of discerning whether a fundamental right is engaged by a particular decision process, and which right is engaged if so, particularly given the relative novelty of these technologies, and the experimental nature of their deployment and use. This applies equally for affected persons and regulators alike, and has been made more difficult by the actions of deployers and lawmakers (in the EU and beyond) because of the combination of:

(a) complexity in decision-making, in terms of decision volume and shared responsibilities of administrative actors;
(b) opacity in decision process and technical operations; and
(c) imprecise or non-existent legal safeguards, exacerbated by law enforcement exemptions exist regarding communication with affected persons.

Some rights may seemingly be clearly engaged by certain algorithmic policing practices (e.g., the right to privacy and/or associated data protection laws), if the decision involves the processing of personal data and/or profiling in the reasoning process. The picture becomes murkier however for other rights including the right to liberty, presumption of innocence and right to an effective remedy where administrative partnerships are formed between the police and other public authorities involving and harmful decisions are taken that do not amount to formal prosecution yet may generate significant legal and social consequences for affected individuals. This occurred, for example, with the Gangs Matrix, where individuals could find themselves expelled from school, losing access to social housing, and in some cases, even deported from the country, because of their inclusion on the Gangs Matrix database (ICO 2018).[42] Additionally, it is significantly unclear whether and how fundamental rights will apply to algorithmic tools that do not pertain to individuals—for example, geographical hotspot mapping. Such technologies can have an impact on fundamental rights, by directing the exercise of policing powers upon communities, even if the output of the algorithmic tool has explicitly profiled a specific person or directed a human officer to coercively intervene on a particular person.

There is a clear need here for greater and more explicit procedural safeguards for algorithmic policing decisions, even where they do not necessarily amount to formal prosecution. Police and other administrative authorities ought to be aware of the risk that developing such technical systems can generate for affected persons, at scale, and on an emergent and automated basis. Appropriately attending to these risks may necessitate the development of new fundamental rights, or at least a targeted (re-) formulation of certain rights within the context of algorithmic policing.

4.2 *Who Has the Authority to Identify Rights, Risks, and Threats (and How)?*

It is imperative that the identification of rights in the algorithmic policing decision-making processes—and appropriate measures to safeguard those rights—is not left entirely to developers or deployers based on processes of self-assessment. Examples from the UK, discussed above, demonstrate that the development and use of these algorithmic tools involves the exercise of significant discretionary authority on behalf of the police and other administrative agencies. The exercise of this power ought to be accompanied by strong checks and balances, as is appropriate where any discretionary exercise of executive power has occurred. Therefore, the EU ought to consider whether independent bodies like the national supervisory authorities and the AI office might be strengthened with greater powers to inspect the activities of deployers, and to issue guidelines holding legal effect, in order to improve clarity and coherence of the law and restrict the capacity for deployers to avoid legal responsibility and/or prevent the potential over-expansion of law enforcement exemptions.

5 What is the Problem of *Claiming*?

Even where relevant rights can be named—and safeguards prioritised within decision-making processes—claiming those rights remains a significant challenge. Claiming is used here to refer to two somewhat distinct, but related, problems: Firstly, the challenge for organisations (i.e., providers and deployers of AI systems, to use the terminology of the AI Act) of implementing positive duties of transparency that seek

[42] See the discussion in ICO (2018) of the 'Al Capone approach' to data sharing.

to ensure high-levels of accountability where there is a risk of unlawful interference with fundamental rights—i.e., the improvement of policing transparency standards may provide explanations to the public as to how their rights may be affected, and assurances that the risk of adverse impact are limited. To exempt police forces from such transparency standards, is to hinder accountability in a domain where adverse impacts flowing from unlawful interference with fundamental rights are at their most acute. Secondly, even where such positive duties of transparency have been developed, members of the public ought to remain empowered to obtain further assurances regarding the legality of the tool, or redress where unlawful interference with a right has occurred, through routes to initiate legal or administrative challenges.

When thinking about the protection of fundamental rights, it is important that we centre our thought around the design of institutional and regulatory processes of accountability, as opposed to the technical characteristics of AI tools. As argued by Veale et al. (2023), issues of accountability relating to algorithmic tools cannot be separated from the wider socio-technical system within which they are embedded, and thus to frame a problem as purely technological is to fail to tackle the broader social and legal problems in which these issues arise. Given that algorithmic policing tools are embedded within a policing context, questions relating to their regulation ought to be primarily centred on normative and legal questions of policing power, its lawful exercise, and the appropriate distribution of lawful discretionary authority to make decisions regarding the commissioning, design and use of these tools. The regulatory answers to these questions ought not be diluted for the purposes of facilitating innovation, given the significant adverse impacts that policing decisions can have on the lives of affected persons.

5.1 Enhanced Procedural Protection by Design

The design of automated and semi-automated decision processes ought to ensure the active safeguarding of fundamental rights on both a prospective and retroactive basis. Institutional mechanisms of accountability ought to be designed to minimise unlawful interference with fundamental rights, *and* to make the process of bringing a claim simple, clear, and with a lower burden to challenge than a court process where interferences do occur (EDRi 2022). To reduce the burden of taking a legal claim where an affected person feels it necessary to raise a challenge, administrative complaint processes should be prioritised ahead of recourse to judicial processes The quality of these administrative processes ought not sacrifice standards of natural justice in an effort to save operational resources, and regulatory responses ought not leave the burden of constructing a legal challenge from other, disparate, areas of law (e.g., data protection law, equality law etc.) to affected persons. Constructing a regulatory measure in such a way, as agreements around the AI Act suggest that it has—and the UK's 'principles-based-approach' to AI regulation will—only serves to obstruct simple and appropriate access to justice.

Further, members of the public ought to know—at the point at which they become aware of an algorithmic policing decision being made about them—which rights apply in a given decision-making process, including where, when and how they apply (i.e., at which decision-points?). Any notice given in this way should also include communication of relevant and identifiable legal controls that apply to the given process that are capable of being legally *enforceable*, to enable the affected person to assess whether deployer obligations are being met (EDRi 2021; Smuha et al. 2021; EUFRA 2022). To avoid overlooking any potential risks to fundamental rights, deployers ought to consider and prioritise the form of notice procedures and subsequent accountability mechanisms during the design process of the algorithmic tool itself. Decisions made regarding the form of these processes ought to be factored into, and justified within, the relevant fundamental rights impact assessment, including the publication of reasons where transparency, or the capacity to challenge an algorithmic policing decision, has been made.

5.2 *Who is Responsible Where Things Go Wrong, or a Decision Unlawfully Interferes with a Fundamental Right?*

Institutions ought to develop clear 'chains of responsibility' regarding each stage of the design and decision-making process, which are recorded on a systematic basis, particularly where an algorithmic tool has been developed in co-operation with the private sector, or licensed via the use of a 'software as-a-service (SaaS)' tool.[43] Considering the coercive nature of the majority of police decisions, and the duty that police have to exercise these powers carefully and in lawfully limited ways, it is crucial that ultimate responsibility for the deployment of algorithmic tools lies with them, and with minimal sub-delegation of powers to private developers, who do not have domain expertise, and may not be subject to standards of constitutional and administrative law in a judicial review process. Any sub-delegation of said powers, ought to identified and justified by police as a matter of public record, to enable future scrutiny. The importance of such a process was demonstrated in *Bridges*, where South Wales Police were found to have failed to meet the requirements of the Public Sector Equality Duty under the Equality Act 2010, by failing to properly interrogate and evaluate whether NeoFace Watch—a private Live Facial Recognition tool—*may* have been biased.

It should not suffice for policing authorities to claim that they have acted lawfully, by shifting responsibility to private developers and failing to provide a substantive evaluation of a given algorithmic tool. Considerations relating to the distribution of responsibility should also be factored into any relevant fundamental rights

---

[43] See Beckers and Teubner (2022) regarding the significantly complex and unsolved nature of attributing legal liability within a decision-making process involving algorithmic tools. See further Cobbe et al. (2021).

impact assessment. Policing authorities ought to retain ultimate responsibility for any unlawful interferences with fundamental rights, as the 'deployer' in practice. This is particularly the case where a private tool has been customised or developed in a bespoke format for a particular police force or use case, therefore differing from the initial software package placed on the market by the software provider.

Failure to achieve the above, would amount to the development of a legal framework that generates opportunities for regulatory escape on the part of policing authorities (and other public authorities), where algorithmic policing decisions are being generated without robust legal control(s) (Lynskey 2019). In doing so, this would replicate and exacerbate existing problems of accountability and legal enforcement that persist in other statutes including the Law Enforcement Directive (European Parliament and Council 2016b), relating to the police processing of personal data (Lynskey 2019).

5.3 *Who is Responsible for the Enforcement of Accountability Measures?*

Member States ought to avoid taking a 'minimalist' approach to the development of national supervisory authorities, and instead ought to develop regulators with clear responsibilities for the enforcement of legal controls, and powers to ensure effective enforcement of said controls, including the stewarding of mechanisms of accountability. In addition, cases ought not need to go to court for the reasoning processes of policing authorities around rights-balancing and determination of necessity, to be publicised and scrutinised. National supervisory authorities ought to play a pro-active role in ensuring that every deployment of a high-risk algorithmic tool, in the policing context, has been appropriately and publicly justified, so that these justifications can be scrutinised and legally evaluated without undue burden.

6 Conclusion: What is to Be *Done*?

Drawing from research into the use of algorithmic policing in the UK, this chapter has identified normative lessons for the regulation of algorithmic policing in Europe. It argues for improved, systematic, approaches to regulation that prioritise and centre fundamental rights safeguarding at the heart of the design process for all algorithmic tools used in the policing context—recognising the enhanced potential for harm where decisions are made by the sharp end of the state, including where the policing decisions extend beyond the mere investigation of criminal offending. The EU's AI Act provides commendable prohibitions and restrictions for practices including individual risk assessment based on actual or potential criminal offending. However, amongst other areas, it still falls short on the regulation of algorithmic policing in the liminal spaces between decisions of a criminal and administrative nature, where the police may serve as only one of several administrative partners, and has failed to provide mechanisms for complain, review, or redress, on a systematic basis, and without undue burden on behalf of affected persons.

In order to more robustly safeguard fundamental rights for EU citizens against unlawful or interference with their fundamental rights, caused by algorithmic policing practices, there is a need for regulatory changes including a clear framework of directly enforceable rights (for the public) and duties (for public authorities), whether novel in nature, or reformulated from existing rights and duties. These rights and duties must be capable of being *named*—i.e., identified in the early stages of the design and implementations process—and must be capable of being *claimed* by both public officials to effect and realise appropriate standards of safeguarding on a proactive basis, and by potential/actual affected individuals and groups, to be capable of asserting their rights via administrative or judicial processes where they feel that their fundamental rights have been unjustly interfered with. It is only through the creation of such processes that the AI Act can achieve its stated aim of protecting the fundamental rights of individuals affected by these systems, and ensuring accountability where said rights have been violated, or are capable of being violated.

References

Amnesty International (2018) Trapped in the matrix: secrecy, stigma, and bias in the Met's gangs database. https://www.amnesty.org.uk/files/reports/Trapped%20in%20the%20Matrix%20Amnesty%20report.pdf

Ashworth A, Zedner L (2014) Preventive justice. Oxford University Press

Ashworth A, Zedner L (2019) The rise and retreat of the preventive state. Annual Review of Criminology 2:429–450

Beckers A, Teubner G (2022) Three liability regimes for artificial intelligence. Hart.

Bellanova R, de Goede M (2022) The algorithmic regulation of security. Regulation and Governance 16(1):102–118

Bertuzzi L (2023) AI Act: EU Parliament's legal office gives damning opinion on high-risk classification "filters". https://www.euractiv.com/section/artificial-intelligence/news/ai-act-eu-parliaments-legal-office-gives-damning-opinion-on-high-risk-classification-filters/

Birks D, Townsley M, Hart T (2023) Predictive policing in an Australian context: Assessing viability and utility. Trends & issues in crime and criminal justice no. 666. Canberra: Australian Institute of Criminology. https://doi.org/10.52922/ti78870

Brayne S (2021) Predict and surveil: data, discretion and the future of policing. Oxford University Press

Chainey S, Tompson L, Uhlig S (2008) The utility of hotspot mapping for predicting spatial patterns of crime. Secur J 21:4–28

Cobbe J, Seng Ah Lee M, Singh J (2021) Reviewable automated decision-making: a framework for accountable algorithmic systems. FAccT '21: Proceedings of the 2021 ACM conference on fairness, accountability, and transparency. https://doi.org/10.1145/3442188.3445921

Cobbe J, Veale M, Singh J (2023) Understanding accountability in algorithmic supply chains. FAccT '23: Proceedings of the 2023 ACM Conference on Fairness, Accountability, and Transparency. https://doi.org/10.1145/3593013.3594073

Cook A (2023) Her Majesty's Chief Inspector Andy Cook, Letter of engagement: Enhanced monitoring decision. https://s3-eu-west-2.amazonaws.com/assets-hmicfrs.justiceinspectorates.gov.uk/uploads/letter-from-hmci-andy-cooke-to-pcc-simon-foster.pdf

Council of Europe (2023) Working Draft: Convention on AI, human rights, democracy and the rule of law. https://rm.coe.int/cai-2023-18-consolidated-working-draft-framework-convention/1680abde66

Department for Science, Innovation & Technology (2023) A pro-innovation approach to AI regulation. https://assets.publishing.service.gov.uk/media/64cb71a547915a00142a91c4/a-pro-innovation-approach-to-ai-regulation-amended-web-ready.pdf

Dressel J, Farid H (2018) The accuracy, fairness, and limits of predicting recidivism. Sci Adv 4(1). https://doi.org/10.1126/sciadv.aao5580.

EDRi: European Digital Rights (2021) An EU Artificial Intelligence Act for fundamental rights: a civil society statement. https://edri.org/wp-content/uploads/2021/12/Political-statement-on-AI-Act.pdf

EDRi: European Digital Rights (2022) Ensure rights and redress for people impacted by AI systems. https://edri.org/wp-content/uploads/2022/05/Rights-and-Redress-AIA-Amendments-for-online.pdf

Ensign D, Friedler S, Neville S, Scheidegger S, Venkatasubramanian S (2018) Runaway feedback loops in predictive policing. Proceedings of the 1st conference on fairness, accountability and transparency. Proceedings of machine learning research, 81, 160–171.

EUFRA: European Union Agency for Fundamental Rights (2022) Bias in algorithms: artificial intelligence and discrimination. https://fra.europa.eu/sites/default/files/fra_uploads/fra-2022-bias-in-algorithms_en.pdf

European Commission (2021) Proposal for a regulation of the European Parliament and of the Council laying down harmonised rules of artificial intelligence (Artificial Intelligence Act). COM(2021) 206 final

European Parliament (2023a) Artificial Intelligence Act, amendments adopted by the European Parliament on 14 June 2023 on the proposal for a regulation of the European Parliament and of the Council on laying down harmonised rules on artificial intelligence (Artificial Intelligence Act) and amending certain Union legislative acts. COM(2021)0206—C9–0146/2021—20216(COD)

European Parliament (2023b) Artificial Intelligence Act: deal on comprehensive rules for trustworthy AI. https://www.europarl.europa.eu/news/en/press-room/20231206IPR15699/artificial-intelligence-act-deal-on-comprehensive-rules-for-trustworthy-ai

European Parliament and Council (2016a) Regulation (EU) 2016/679 of the European Parliament and of the Council of 27 April 2016 on the protection of natural persons with regard to the processing of personal data and on the free movement of such data, and repealing Directive 95/46/EC (General Data Protection Regulation). OJ L 119, 4.5.2016, pp 1–88

European Parliament and Council (2016b) Directive (EU) 2016/680 of the European Parliament and of the Council of 27 April 2016 on the protection of natural persons with regard to the processing of personal data by competent authorities for the purposes of the prevention, investigation, detection or prosecution of criminal offences or the execution of criminal penalties, and on the free movement of such data, and repealing Council Framework Decision 2008/977/JH. OJ L 119, 4.5.2016, pp 89–131

Fussey P, Davies B, Innes N (2021) 'Assisted' facial recognition and the reinvention of suspicion and discretion in digital policing. Br J Criminol 61(2):325–344

Hildebrandt M, Tielemans L (2013) Data protection by design and technology neutral law. Comput Law Secur Rev 29(5):509–521

Home Office (2020) Police funding for England & Wales: 2015–2021 (TSO, 2020), Statistical Bulletin 16/20. https://assets.publishing.service.gov.uk/government/uploads/system/uploads/attachment_data/file/900017/police-funding-england-and-wales-2015-to-2021-hosb1620.pdf

Human Rights Watch (2022) Greece: new biometrics policing program undermines rights. https://www.hrw.org/news/2022/01/18/greece-new-biometrics-policing-program-undermines-rights

ICO: Information Commissioner's Office (2018) Enforcement notice to the commissioner of police of the metropolis. https://www.met.police.uk/SysSiteAssets/media/downloads/force-content/met/about-us/gangs-violence-matrix/ico-enforcement-notice.pdf
Jasanoff S (2017) Virtual, visible, and actionable: Data assemblages and the sightlines of justice. Big Data & Society 4(2). https://doi.org/10.1177/2053951717724477
Koltzch T (2023) The federal government does not want police software ordered by Bavaria. https://www.golem.de/news/palantir-bund-will-von-bayern-bestellte-polizeisoftware-nicht-2306-175446.html
Lynskey O (2019) Criminal justice profiling and EU data protection law: precarious protection from predictive policing. International Journal of Law in Context 15(2):162–176
Leufer D, Rodelli C, Hidvegi F (2023) Human rights protections…with exceptions: what's (not) in the EU's AI Act deal. https://www.accessnow.org/whats-not-in-the-eu-ai-act-deal/
Metropolitan Police (2023) Baroness Casey review. An independent review into the standards of behaviour and internal culture of the Metropolitan Police Service. https://www.met.police.uk/SysSiteAssets/media/downloads/met/about-us/baroness-casey-review/update-march-2023/baroness-casey-review-march-2023a.pdf
MOPAC London Mayor's Office for Policing and Crime (2018) Review of the MPS Gangs Matrix. https://www.london.gov.uk/sites/default/files/gangs_matrix_review_-_final.pdf.
MOPAC London Mayor's Office for Policing and Crime (2021) Rescue and response county lines project: supporting young Londoners affected by county lines exploitation. https://www.london.gov.uk/sites/default/files/rescue_and_response_strategic_assessment_2021.pdf
National Police Chiefs' Council and Association of Police and Crime Commissioners (2020) National policing digital strategy: digital, data and technology strategy 2020–2030. https://pds.police.uk/wp-content/uploads/2020/01/National-Policing-Digital-Strategy-2020-2030.pdf
Ní Loideáin N (2024) Lawfulness and police use of facial recognition in the UK: Article 8 ECHR and Bridges v South Wales Police. In R Matulionyte, M Zalnieriute (eds) Facial recognition in the modern state. Cambridge University Press
Oswald M, Babuta A (2020) Machine learning predictive algorithms and the policing of future crimes: governance and oversight. In J.L.M. McDaniel, K. Pease (eds), Policing and artificial intelligence. Routledge
Oswald M, Grace J, Urwin S, Barnes GC (2018) Algorithmic risk assessment policing models: lessons from the Durham HART model and 'Experimental' proportionality. Information & Communications Technology Law 27(2):223–250
Philp C (2023) Chris philp MP and the home office. Police urged to double AI-enabled facial recognition searches. https://www.gov.uk/government/news/police-urged-to-double-ai-enabled-facial-recognition-searches
Redden J, Dencik L, Warne H (2020) Datafied child welfare services: unpacking politics, economics and power. Policy Studies 41(5):507–526
Rowley M (2022) Comments of sir mark Rowley at the 'exceptional policing conference' on 12 Oct 2022. https://www.youtube.com/watch?v=_4aaJ_tIY1E
Sandhu A, Fussey P (2021) The 'uberization of policing'? How police negotiate and operationalise predictive policing technology. Polic Soc 31(1):66–81
Sardjo D (2022) My sons were profiled by a racist predictive policing system—the AI Act must prohibit these systems (28 Sep 2022, Fair Trials). https://medium.com/@FairTrials/my-sons-were-profiled-by-a-racist-predictive-policing-system-the-ai-act-must-prohibit-these-b2ea66a9a763
Smuha N, Ahmed-Rengers E, Harkens A, Li, W, MacLaren J, Pisello R, Yeung K (2021) How the EU can achieve legally trustworthy AI: a response to the European Commission's proposal for an Artificial Intelligence Act. Available on SSRN: https://papers.ssrn.com/sol3/papers.cfm?abstract_id=3899991
Syal R (2023) Police in England and Wales dealing with more mental health crises than ever (21 Feb 2023, The Guardian). https://www.theguardian.com/uk-news/2023/feb/21/mental-health-crises-police-england-and-wales

Syal R, Dodd V (2022) Police chiefs blame Tory cuts for fall in crime detection and charge rates (31 August 2022, The Guardian). https://www.theguardian.com/uk-news/2022/aug/31/police-chiefs-blame-tory-cuts-for-fall-in-detection-and-charge-rates

Veale M, Borgesius F (2021) Demystifying the draft EU Artificial Intelligence Act: analysing the good, the bad, and the unclear elements of the proposed approach. Computer Law Review International 22(4):97–112

Veale M, Matus K, Gorwa R (2023) AI and global governance: modalities, rationales, tensions. Annual Review of Law and Social Science 19:255–275

Yeung K, Ahmed-Rengers E (2023) 'The smartest, healthiest, safest and happiest place:' a response to the UK's "Pro-Innovation" AI White Paper. https://papers.ssrn.com/sol3/papers.cfm?abstract_id=4487346

Yeung K, Harkens A (2023) How do 'technical' design-choices made when building algorithmic decision-making tools for criminal justice authorities create constitutional dangers? (Part I). Public Law, Apr, 265–286.

How to Regulate the Use of Algorithms in Sentencing? *De Lege Ferenda* Postulates

Konrad Burdziak

Abstract The aim of this chapter is to answer the question of how to regulate the use of algorithms, or more precisely algorithm-based tools, when courts adjudicate in the course of criminal proceedings. The paper proposes specific legal solutions that should be introduced into the legal systems of individual countries in the Central and Eastern European region. At the same time, it does not focus on all the necessary changes, but only on those that, in the opinion of the author of the work, seem to be the most relevant from the perspective of guaranteeing the rights of the individual and society in the procedure for granting conditional early release. The (general) method used in this study is the contextual method and the specific research method is (primarily) the dogmatic-legal method. Therefore, the use of algorithm-based tools in criminal proceedings was studied (primarily) through a comprehensive analysis of the normative material relating to all the issues raised. This analysis was carried out—it is worth adding—primarily using the derivational concept of legal interpretation developed by Zieliński.

1 Introduction

The aim of this work is to answer the question of how to regulate the use of algorithms, and more specifically the tools based on algorithms, during adjudication by courts in the course of criminal proceedings. The issue of adjudication in criminal proceedings is, of course, exceptionally extensive; there are many cases where the algorithms could be, and are, used. As is rightly indicated in the literature (Ugwudike 2022): "The algorithms are increasingly informing high stakes decisions across several areas, from policing and sentencing to conditional early release. They are also determining the intensity of probation and post-release supervision. Indeed, the technologies are proliferating across justice systems and could revolutionise the systems". Because

K. Burdziak (✉)
Faculty of Law and Administration, University of Szczecin, Szczecin, Poland
e-mail: konrad.burdziak@usz.edu.pl

M. Varju and K. Mezei (eds.), *The Challenges of Artificial Intelligence for Law in Europe*, Data Science, Machine Intelligence, and Law 6,
https://doi.org/10.1007/978-3-031-86813-9_10

of this, it would not be possible to discuss the issue in a possibly comprehensive way in a single work.

Thus, in this work, we will focus on only one part of the judicial practice of criminal courts, which is adjudication in cases for granting a convict conditional early release from serving the rest of the imprisonment term. This issue appears to be exceptionally important, as the decisions taken in this area are crucial from the perspective of the safety of society (which would not want to release people from prison who are not yet ready to be released) and the requirement to provide the convicted offender with justice to the full extent (not only before and during sentencing, but also when deciding whether or not they can leave prison at a certain point). Considerations on the above issue are also justified by the fact that in European countries we are already dealing with cases which use tools based on algorithms in cases concerning granting conditional early release. In the United Kingdom and Estonia, for example, appropriate versions of the OASys system (Offender Assessment System) are used, which is a fourth-generation tool developed to increase the protection of society by reducing the risk of recidivism among adult offenders of prohibited acts. The system was developed in the United Kingdom during pilot studies conducted in 1999–2001 and implemented there in 2001. It has been continuously researched and developed since then; the results of the system evaluation are published on an ongoing basis as part of the so-called OASys research compendiums.[1] As a fourth-generation tool, OASys uses actuarial models to predict reoffending, based on both static and dynamic risk factors, while integrating other offender-specific factors that are important for treatment and enable the planning and monitoring of intervention. The system is designed for many tasks, but the issue of assessing the probability of reoffending by the perpetrator appears to be particularly important (Moore 2015; Burdziak and Rüütel 2022).

Before proceeding to analyses of a strictly substantive nature, it should be emphasised that the author of this work is a supporter of the use of tools based on algorithms in the course of criminal proceedings, and in particular, is a supporter of the use of such tools in the course of proceedings for granting conditional early release to convicts. This is due to the fact that the courts, in particular Polish courts, are not always able to make an adequate criminological prognosis, which is exceptionally important in the above-mentioned cases. The results of the examination of the act conducted under the supervision of the author of this work (Burdziak et al. 2019) showed, among others, that: (1) in more than 36% of cases, in the justifications of decisions on conditional early release, the courts did not clearly indicate which circumstances argued in favour of granting conditional early release and which did not; (2) in 31% of cases, in the justification of the decision on conditional early release, the courts did not clearly indicate why conditional early release should ultimately be granted; (3) in the overwhelming majority of cases the justifications of decisions on conditional early release did not take into account all the factors required by the legislator; (4) the decisions of the courts in the vast majority of cases were

[1] See Moore (2015).

based on a small number of factors that could affect the decision on granting conditional early release. This type of situation is unacceptable and needs to be changed, and tools based on algorithms can help this change.

Of course, the author of this work is far from considering that algorithms and the tools based on them are a remedy for all the ills of criminal proceedings, ills which include, among others, the courts' lack of knowledge, experience or reliability, a lack of time to properly analyse the case or individual organs' need to improve their competence. It should be emphasised, however, that when faced with the choice of whether to use all possible means that may affect the adequacy of the decision to grant (or not) conditional early release, or to stick to the traditional way of deciding in this regard, responsibility for society and the individual requires that the former be opted for. Only then will it be possible to believe that everything that can be done has been done to avoid violating those interests which are important for society and the individual.

Thus, this work proposes specific legal solutions that should be introduced into the legal systems of individual countries of Central and Eastern Europe in the context of tools based on algorithms. At the same time, it does not focus on all the necessary changes, but only on those which, in the opinion of the author of the work appear to be the most important from the perspective of guaranteeing the rights of the individual and society in the proceedings for granting conditional early release. In the context of other solutions, or rather their outline, the author refers to the excellent policy paper by Fair Trials (Fair Trials 2002) entitled Regulating Artificial Intelligence for Use in Criminal Justice Systems in the EU.

The (general) method used in this work is the contextual method, due to two circumstances: (1) it allows for a multilateral approach to the studied phenomena; (2) it aims to define all relevant contexts: genetic, historical, functional, logical, axiological and others (Tokarczyk 2008). As Tokarczyk (2008) points out: "contextualism leads to obtaining (...) rich (...) analytical material (...). It aims to (...) take into account not only the internal content of the legal phenomena under study, but also the circumstances of their creation, development and end, personality traits of legislators and creators of legal ideas, [and] connections between laws and legal views with other social phenomena. Contextualism makes it possible to achieve (...) well-established and (...) scientifically valuable (...) results of cognitive processes". The detailed research method used in the publication is (primarily) the dogmatic and legal method.[2] The study of the issue of use of algorithm-based tools in criminal proceedings was therefore (primarily) carried out through a comprehensive analysis of the normative material relating to all the issues raised. This analysis was carried out—and this is worth adding—primarily with the use of the derivational concept of interpretation of law developed by Zieliński.[3]

[2] See Cross et al. (1995); Cross (2009); Yule (2009); Walton et al. (2020).

[3] See Bogucki (2020).

2 Why Should One Use Algorithms in the Criminal Law?

Imagine the following factual circumstances: the court convicts the perpetrator of a robbery (theft through the use of violence) and hands down a sentence of imprisonment for 10 years. The judgment comes into force and the convicted offender is sent to prison. After a period of 5 years, during which the convict behaves in a fully correct manner and undergoes the process of social rehabilitation, they obtain the possibility to apply for conditional early release from serving the rest of their term and submit an application for this probation measure to be applied to them. The first application is rejected; however, after an appropriate period of time, the convict submits a second application. The meeting at which the request is to be considered is scheduled for June 30, 2023, at 12:30. On this day, from the morning (from 8:00 am), the court considers similar cases, but a short lunch break is scheduled for immediately after the application of the convict in question has been considered. The judges of the court are becoming more and more hungry and bored with the analysis of repeated cases on the same subject. There are signs of fatigue. When it comes to considering the case of the convict in question, the court has had enough, wants to quickly finish another case and go to lunch. The case files are quickly reviewed and a negative decision is issued; the court does not agree to grant the convicted offender conditional early release.

The presented factual circumstances are entirely fictitious (although, of course, nothing prevents them from happening in reality). However, this hypothetical situation is exceptionally important, due to the fact that it perfectly reflects the problems that may arise in connection with the judicial practice of courts issuing decisions on conditional early release. In the context of the above factual circumstances, doubts may finally arise as to whether the decision issued by the court was indeed a correct and fair decision from the substantive point of view. After all, the court's view of reality could be falsified by non-objective factors, and consequently also non-substantive ones.

What factors could these be? For example, factors such as hunger or fatigue. Such a statement appears to be justified. After all, as Danziger et al. (2011) point out: "(…) the likelihood of a favorable ruling is greater at the very beginning of the work day or after a food break than later in the sequence of cases. (…) The plot shows that the likelihood of a ruling in favor of a prisoner spikes at the beginning of each session—the probability of a favorable ruling steadily declines from ≈0.65 to nearly zero and jumps back up to ≈0.65 after a break for a meal. Figure 2 A and B presents a histogram of the probability of a favorable ruling for cases of similar legal characteristics that appeared in one of the three ordinal positions at the beginning versus at the end of a decision session; from the perspective of the prisoner, there is a clear advantage to appearing at the beginning of the session (i.e., either at the beginning of the day or immediately following the break)".[4] Of course, these authors do not directly suggest that it is hunger or fatigue that influence court decisions. However, as they (Danziger et al. 2011) state: "our results do indicate that extraneous variables can influence

[4] Compare this with Glöckner (2016).

judicial decisions, which bolsters the growing body of evidence that points to the susceptibility of experienced judges to psychological biases (19, 20; for a review, see ref. 21). Finally, our findings support the view that the law is indeterminate by showing that legally irrelevant situational determinants—in this case, merely taking a food break—may lead a judge to rule differently in cases with similar legal characteristics".

The court's view of the convict's case could also be falsified by the unconscious use by the court of one of the heuristics distinguished in psychology, and more specifically the heuristics referred to as the status quo bias. Status quo bias may arise from an individual's desire for consistency, including achieving consistency in decisions. Past choices are rationalised by the individual while rejecting or suppressing information that indicates that the past decision was wrong. The process of rationalisation extends to present and future choices, leading—ultimately—to the maintenance of existing choices. According to attitude self-perception theory, individuals establish their basic attitudes and preferences by observing their own behaviour, just as they do in the context of third parties. So, in making present and future choices, they refer to their past decisions, thinking: "If it was good enough for me then, it is (must be) good enough for me now". This kind of reasoning leads to upholding a previously made choice, and thus to maintaining the status quo.[5]

As indicated above, the application rejected by the court on June 30, 2023 was the second application submitted by the convict in the same case. It is very possible that considering the previous negative decision, the court decided to make a similar decision again, primarily due to the desire to be consistent. The court's reasoning could be as follows: "If I previously made a negative decision, and little has changed since then, I should be consistent and make the same decision again." Of course, it is impossible to deny the legitimacy of this kind of reasoning. It should be emphasised, however, that a situation in which this type of argumentation would be the main basis for the decision of the judges of the court that are not fully aware of that fact, cannot be accepted.

It may also happen in any case, regardless of fatigue or hunger, that the court, when making a decision in a given case, will not take into account all the circumstances that it should take into account in order for the decision to be considered rational and just. According to an empirical study on the judicial practice of Polish courts, when making criminological prognoses, Polish courts take into account a low number of risk factors, the description of factors used in the justifications of decisions of Polish courts on conditional early release is laconic and superficial, Polish courts do not attempt to adequately interpret the factors provided for in Article 77, Section 1 of the Polish Criminal Code[6] or assess their prognostic value, and moreover, they do not perform a real and in-depth analysis of the convict's behaviour and personality, and often ignore circumstances that are inconvenient for them (Burdziak and Rüütel 2022). This does not bode well for the Polish courts and clearly leads to the conclusion

---

[5] See, in this regard, Burdziak (2021a). See also Samuelson and Zeckhauser (1988).

[6] Polish Criminal Code (Criminal Code of June 6, 1997).

that they require support in making decisions in the field of conditional early release from serving the rest of the imprisonment.

Thus, the question arises—what should be done? Can we, or must we, approve the possibility for courts to make decisions that are not fully rational and are based (at least partly) on non-substantive arguments (because perhaps this is a situation that cannot be changed), and if we do not have to do this, and perhaps even cannot accept this situation, is there an alternative?

In the opinion of the author of this work, court decisions based on non-substantive arguments cannot be accepted. Decisions of this kind may, firstly, undermine the principle of equality before the law, i.e., the principle according to which individual members of society should be treated in the same way if they are in a similar situation. Secondly, they may violate the principle of justice, according to which—as Hervada (2011) claims—everyone should be guaranteed what they are entitled to. It is difficult to talk about the possibility of guaranteeing a man what he is entitled to in a situation in which the decisions made by the courts will be based not on reason, but on various physiological reactions of the body, heuristics or cognitive bias. Hervada (2011) rightly points out that justice is a kind of obligation relationship in which one party is entitled to a right, and the second party must ensure the implementation of this right (through appropriate action or omission of a certain type of action). This type of obligation relationship is possible only where relationships between people are governed by reason, and not by instincts, physical or biological forces. In other words, such relations can only exist in the world of rational and not irrational human actions.

But what is an alternative in this regard? One of the alternatives is to support the courts by introducing into the legal systems of individual countries the obligation to use tools based on algorithms in the course of making decisions on granting or not granting conditional early release from serving the rest of the prison sentence, as is the case in Estonia or the United Kingdom, where the OASys (Offender Assessment System) system is used. These are tools that have been designed, among other things, to overcome the limitations of the human mind, incapable of effectively processing large amounts of information and susceptible to the aforementioned heuristics or cognitive bias. The results of the use of such tools in Estonia encourage serious consideration of this alternative. The latest evaluation of the Estonian version (Estonian Ministry of Justice 2020) of the OASys system shows the predictive efficiency of this tool at a level of approximately 70%, which—as it seems—is a better result than what would be achieved based solely on human intuition.[7]

It should be emphasised, however, that the use of algorithms may also pose a risk to the reasonableness of decisions made by courts. The author of this work has already noticed that in the event of ill-considered and careless use of algorithms there may occur, for example, the so-called anchoring heuristic,[8] which in this case could appear as follows: a judge (as in Poland, cases for conditional early release are considered by a single judge) uses the OASys system to obtain a percentage

[7] Compare with Dressel and Farid (2018).

[8] See Boz (2019).

result; put simply, the degree of risk that the convict will relapse to crime in the future. Suppose this result is 70%. The judge then assesses the risk of the relapsing to crime based on the clinical method, i.e., assesses the perpetrator based on the circumstances relating to the commission of the criminal offence, the personality of the offender, their previous personal history and conduct during the service of the sentence, their living conditions and the consequences which release on parole may bring about for the offender. The risk assessment determined by the judge in this way may be different, i.e., higher or lower. Nevertheless, due to the fact that the number 70 was previously anchored (reflected in the mind), it can be expected that it will be similar to this number, although—substantively—it may be unjustified (Burdziak 2021b). In other words, the assessment of the judgment, in a situation of uncertainty, would be similar to the number-based result resulting from the use of a tool based on an algorithm, which would not be a fully conscious decision (and perhaps not a fair decision), but one resulting primarily from the psychological conditions of the human mind.

The above, however, is not the only potential threat related to the use of algorithms. Further risks include in particular:

First, courts and other participants in court proceedings may lack an understanding of the rules of operation of algorithms. The development of each of the tools based on algorithms requires the involvement of theoreticians (scientists) and practitioners who, based on the conducted research and collected data, will be able to develop algorithms that predict the future in an adequate way. The conducted research attempts to identify the indicators that will predict in the best way possible the likelihood of reoffending by a convicted person, to determine whether they are to be considered only static or also dynamic indicators, to determine the weights for individual indicators, to determine the formula to which individual indicators will be substituted with data. For example, one of the measures used in the Estonian version of the OASys system (Estonian Ministry of Justice 2020) has the following form: RH-V 2a = EXP((0.0649*sum of independent variables)- 5.1448)/(1 + EXP((0.0649*sum of independent variables)- 5.1448)))/, determining the descriptive power of the model or proper fit of the model based on the AUC index. The indicated research and its results can only be understood by persons with at least a basic knowledge of statistics, criminology, sociology or psychology. It is difficult to expect that judges (or lawyers in general), and especially 'ordinary' citizens, could possess such knowledge or acquire it ad hoc at the time when tools based on algorithms were used in their case;

Secondly, information about algorithm-based tools may not be considered publicly available information and thus the fundamental human right to defence may be restricted. Regardless of who will produce the algorithm-based tool, be it a private company (in the case of the COMPAS system, the manufacturer is the private company Northpoint) or a public entity (as is the case with the UK's OASys system, developed by Newcastle University in cooperation with the British Police), access to information on the indicators or formulas used may be either concealed (due to the commercial nature of the tool and the desire to maximise profits, or due to the broadly understood security of the state) or publicly available (at least for people against whom the tool will be used). The first solution, i.e., a solution that assumes no access to key information regarding the tool based on algorithms, will be an extremely dangerous solution. First, it will then be impossible to evaluate the tool on an ongoing basis by independent specialists not employed by a given company, which may lead to the use of a tool that is in fact incapable of achieving its intended purpose, or to one that it is useful, but only to a limited extent. Second, it will be impossible to verify whether the use of the tool does not discriminate against any population group, e.g., people of a certain skin colour or people of a certain nationality. Third, the authorities using algorithms will not be able to fully understand the principles of the tool's functioning and the results obtained as a result of its application, nor will they be able to independently assess whether it should be used at all in a given, specific case. Fourth, and most importantly, the lack of information on the tool used will prevent the person against whom the proceedings are pending from properly preparing their defence, including in particular the possibility of actual verification of the result obtained as a result of the use of the tool and the possibility of effectively undermining it. The above will limit the right of the said person to defence by violating the principle of equality of arms, which states that both the prosecutor and the accused should be able to prove their arguments in the same way and to the same extent. Palmiotto (2020) rightly points out that: "according to the case-law of the European Court of Human Rights (ECtHR) on Article 6§3(d), the right to confrontation not only requires that defendants should be in a position to challenge the probity and credibility of evidence against them, but that they should also be able to test their truthfulness and reliability. Nevertheless, in order to do so, it is necessary to comprehend how the software works and how it is used".

Thirdly, it is possible to unjustifiably treat a group of people with certain characteristics less favourably. Imagine that out of a thousand identified perpetrators of crimes (police data), the vast majority are people of Polish nationality. Also, imagine that people of Polish nationality constitute a definite minority of perpetrators of crimes prohibited under the law, but their crimes are definitely more often frequently detected or they are much more often wrongly suspected by the police of committing such crimes (data inadequacy). If a tool based on an algorithm uses in its calculations an indicator in the form of the perpetrator's nationality and gives it a high weight, and at the same time the police data is used in the algorithm, then the next perpetrator of Polish nationality will be much more likely to be a person with a negative criminological prognosis under proceedings before a court, even though in a given case it could be absolutely unjustified (a false positive result). Such a situation would directly lead to discrimination against the persons concerned on the basis of their nationality, which, of course, could not be accepted.

It is worth adding that the literature (Ugwudike 2022) indicates that:

> Some studies have (…) found that risk of recidivism algorithms can over-predict risks in cases involving Black people (e.g., Angwin et al. 2016; Hao and Stray 2019; Lowder et al. 2019). Predictive policing algorithms can also expose Black communities in the US to over-policing (e.g., Ensign et al. 2018; Lum and Isaac 2016; Richardson, Schultz and Crawford 2019). Studies suggest that algorithmic bias can affect Indigenous populations in Australia (Allan et al. 2019; Shepherd et al. 2014) and Canada (Cardoso 2020). A reason for this is

> that predictor data based on Western values (such as those relating to family circumstances) can be culturally insensitive and, as such, capable of over-predicting the risks posed by these populations. (see also, Maurutto and Hannah-Moffatt 2006)

Fourthly, there may be a sense of harm on the part of the offender. One of the tasks of the courts in criminal law cases is to ensure a sense of justice for three parties: (a) society as a collective party; (b) the aggrieved party; and (c) the perpetrator. The need to ensure the perpetrator's belief that they have been treated fairly appears to be crucial, taking into account the need to convince them of the legitimacy of the position taken by the court, to submit to the imposed penalty in a way that may lead to the achievement of its goals, to make an attempt to reconcile with the aggrieved party and to enforce the adjudicated compensatory measures, etc. The fact that the court made a decision primarily on the basis of a tool based on algorithms may meanwhile lead to a misunderstanding by the perpetrator of the grounds for the issued decision, it will make it difficult for them to appeal against it, and above all, they will feel aggrieved for the reasons indicated and experience unfair treatment in the administration of justice. This may lead to the perpetrator's lack of willingness to submit to the judgment issued against them and make it difficult for them to return to society.

All the threats described above should be taken seriously due to the possibility of limiting fundamental human freedoms and rights as a result, including in particular the right to defence or the right to privacy. If a decision is made to introduce tools based on algorithms to the legal systems of individual countries, legal regulations enabling their use in individual cases should therefore be constructed in such a way as to limit the potential negative effects of their use to a minimum, or at least to a socially acceptable level and to provide legal and other protection for individuals against the violation of their rights and other protected interests. In the next part of this study, therefore, *de lege ferenda* postulates will be formulated that can be used by the individual countries of Central and Eastern Europe in which solutions based on algorithms have not been introduced so far. We will limit ourselves to the tools used in the context of conditional early release.

3 How to Regulate the Use of Algorithms in the Criminal Law?

To set out the context for further considerations, it is worth starting the analysis of the method of regulating the possibility of using algorithms in the course of criminal proceedings in cases for granting conditional early release with a short presentation of the procedure that has been provided in Poland for proceedings in this type of cases. It should also be noted that solutions similar to the Polish ones are provided for by other legal orders, including the Czech,[9] Slovak[10] and Hungarian.[11] Considerations concerning the Polish procedure can therefore be easily transferred to the legal orders of other Central and Eastern European countries.

First, it should be pointed out that, according to the current wording of the Polish Criminal Code, a court may conditionally release a person sentenced to imprisonment from serving the rest of the imprisonment only if their attitude, characteristics and personal conditions, circumstances of committing the crime, and behaviour after committing it and during the sentence justify the belief that the convict, after being released, will comply with the imposed penal or preventive measure, and observe the legal order; in particular, they will not commit a crime again (Article 77, Section 1 of the Polish Criminal Code). This is the so-called substantive premise in the form of a positive criminological prognosis.

The formal condition for conditional early release of a convict is that they have served the appropriate part of the sentence of imprisonment imposed on them. Usually this means serving at least half of the sentence. The time remaining to serve the sentence constitutes a probation period for the convict who was granted conditional early release. This period may not, in principle, be shorter than two years or longer than five years (Article 80 of the Polish Criminal Code).

The convict's situation will differ, depending on their behaviour during the probation period. In the event of inappropriate conduct, the conditional early release will be revoked. In the event of proper conduct and no revocation of conditional early release during the probation period and within six months of its completion, the sentence will be deemed as served at the time of conditional early release (Article 82 of the Polish Criminal Code).

Pursuant to the Polish Penal Enforcement Code (Article 161 of the Polish Penal Enforcement Code), a conditional release is decided by a (penitentiary) court composed of one judge at a session that should be held in a penal institution. The prosecutor, the convict and the defence lawyer have the right (and not the obligation) to participate in the meeting, as well as other persons who are entitled to submit an application for conditional release, if they have submitted such an application (application for conditional release may also be submitted by the director of the penal institution or the court-appointed professional probation officer).

If the request was submitted by the director of the penal institution, they also send an opinion drawn up by the penal institution administration, including in particular a criminological and social prognosis. In other cases, this opinion is sent by the director of the penal institution at the request of the penitentiary court or at the request of the convict applying for conditional release. The criminological and social prognosis is prepared for the duration of the convict's stay outside the institution and consists of a written justification of the assumption that the convict will comply with the legal order during this stay. This justification should include, in particular, an analysis of factors characterising: (1) family environment; (2) personality traits, including the degree of

---

[9] See https://www.euprobationproject.eu/national_detail.php?c=CZ.

[10] See https://www.euprobationproject.eu/national_detail.php?c=SK.

[11] See https://www.euprobationproject.eu/national_detail.php?c=HU.

self-discipline and the tendency to use violence; (3) the convict's alcohol addiction or addiction to narcotic drugs or psychotropic substances; (4) past addiction treatment, as well as motivation to maintain abstinence; (5) the path of social derailment along with the determination of the extent of the lack of a moral sense; (6) the type of crime for which the convicted person is serving a sentence; (7) behaviour during previously served penalties, with particular emphasis on the use of the permission to leave the facility; (8) the environment in which the convict will stay during their temporary release.

In the course of the proceedings, the penitentiary court hears a representative of the administration of the penal institution, and a court-appointed professional probation officer, if they have applied for conditional early release, and takes into account the settlement reached as a result of mediation. It is generally not necessary to consult experts (Article 162 of the Polish Penal Enforcement Code).[12]

In the above-mentioned procedure, as can be seen, there is no place for the use of tools based on algorithms. Their use would even constitute unlawful (illegal) conduct and a potential basis for undermining the decision issued in relation to a specific person. After all, state authorities may act only on the basis and within the limits of the law. Thus, if there is a desire to use algorithms in the Polish or similar to the Polish legal order, appropriate changes should be made to the content of the applicable legal provisions or appropriate new legal provisions should be added to the applicable legal acts. Proposed new solutions will be listed below under the following points.

First of all, general regulations providing for the possibility of using algorithms in criminal proceedings should be introduced into the legal systems of individual Central and Eastern European countries. Such regulations should be included in legal acts of the highest rank in individual legal systems (most often they will be the constitutions of individual countries), as tools based on algorithms can and, in a sense do, violate the most important freedoms and human rights, including, inter alia, the right to privacy, freedoms and rights which are regulated in the indicated acts.

The content of the proposed regulations could be as follows:

> Article X. Section 1. Algorithms and tools based on them may be used in criminal proceedings only when the possibility of their use is expressly provided for by the law and only when their use is necessary in a democratic state.
>
> Section 2. Algorithms and tools based on them cannot be the sole basis for a decision taken in criminal proceedings.
>
> Section 3. The use of algorithms may not lead to violation of the essence of freedom and human rights.
>
> Section 4. Full characteristics of algorithms and tools based on them used in criminal proceedings constitute public information.

The proposed regulations would make tools based on algorithms subsidiary (auxiliary) in relation to the analyses of authorities involved in criminal proceedings, and at

[12] See, in this regard, Burdziak and Rüütel (2022).

the same time would clearly indicate that their use should be limited to a minimum; i.e., to cases where their use would actually be necessary to ensure that the court is able to issue an adequate procedural decision. After all, it is difficult to justify the possibility of using algorithms in all cases, even the most obvious ones. The possibility, and perhaps even the necessity, of using algorithms in all cases could even lead to 'lazy' courts and a situation in which algorithms, and not judges, would make key decisions in individual cases. At the same time, the proposed regulations ensure universal access to data related to algorithms and tools based on them, in order to ensure that the public can verify and evaluate them on an ongoing basis. Social control over such tools is crucial from the perspective of preventing software errors potentially dangerous to participants in criminal proceedings; errors—it should be added—that are unnoticed, and perhaps even intentionally introduced by the software producer, its user or a third party.

The second proposed amendment is inspired by British legislation. According to Section 14 of the UK Data Protection Act, applicable in the United Kingdom, for material decisions based solely on automated processing that is permitted by law and is subject to the safeguards of the data subject's rights, freedoms and legitimate interests, i.e., for decisions that produce legal effects concerning the data subject or similarly significantly affects the data subject, the following requirements must be met: (a) the controller must notify the data subject in writing as soon as possible, that the decision was taken solely on the basis of automated processing, (b) the data subject may, within one month of receiving the notification, ask the controller to reconsider the decision or to take a new decision not based solely on automated processing. At the same time, if the request referred to the above is submitted to the administrator, the administrator is obliged to consider the request, including any information provided by the data subject that is relevant to them, and comply with the request, and inform in writing the data subject about the steps taken to comply with the request and the result of compliance with the request.

Similar regulations should be introduced in the legislation of Central and Eastern European countries, if they decide to introduce the procedure for adjudicating on conditional early release using tools based on algorithms. Of course, in the case of decisions on conditional early release, one cannot expect the introduction of the possibility of making decisions based solely on the use of one or another algorithm. As it will be shown later, the best method is a mixed method, which assumes a combination of a clinical method with a statistical method. However, even in the case of a decision-making process supported only by algorithms, it is necessary to properly protect the freedoms and rights of the convict. Thus, it is proposed to introduce the following solution:

> Article X. Section 1. The court informs the convict in writing about the result of using an algorithm-based tool in their case. The information should include a clear instruction on the basic principles of the algorithm-based tool and an explanation of the meaning of the result obtained.
>
> Section 2. The convict may, within one month of receipt of the information referred to in Section 1, ask the court to re-use the tool based on algorithms or raise objections as to the legitimacy or manner of using the algorithm.

Section 3. If the application referred to in Section 2 is submitted, the court is obliged to consider it, taking into account all information provided by the convict, and inform the convict about the position taken within one month. The information should contain a comprehensive justification.

The solution proposed above seems to be a key element of the procedure in which tools based on algorithms are used. The convict must have official information about the use of such tools in their case. Only then will they be able to properly defend their freedoms and rights. They have to also be equipped with basic information on the principles of operation of tools based on algorithms and with instructions on how to understand the result obtained as a result of their application. Imagine that the convict receives a letter with information that the result of the application of the algorithm obtained in their context is 70 (or some other specific number). What does this information mean? For a person who has not dealt with algorithms before, it will be useless. In this regard, instruction appears to be not only desirable, but even necessary. This type of instruction will also be a starting point for the convict to submit reservations as to the legitimacy or manner of using the algorithm, and thus, for a discussion on the use of the algorithm in their case; a discussion, which, in principle (due to the court's mandatory answer), may lead to the convict becoming convinced of the legitimacy of using tools based on algorithms in cases for granting conditional early release and of the potentially beneficial effects of their use in such cases (especially in their case). Of course, it may happen that a given, specific convict will not understand the instruction sent to them at all. It should be emphasised, however, that it will at least give them a chance to take action to protect their interests by seeking opinions in this regard from specialists, theoreticians and practitioners who, at least to some extent, will be able to determine whether the tool used in the case of a convicted perpetrator was used reasonably, properly, etc.

Of course, there may be an objection that the convicted person may not have sufficient financial resources to consult appropriate specialists. It should be emphasised, however, that the solution proposed in the first point, providing universal access to data on algorithms and tools based on them, gives a chance for publicly available opinions on these tools prepared by researchers or non-governmental organisations to appear in the public space (especially on the Internet). Such materials could be of sufficient assistance to the convict in preparing for their case.

Thirdly, it is necessary to inform the public and individual convicts about the possibility of applying the algorithms to their case (before the algorithms are applied). The following legal amendment is therefore proposed:

> Article X. Section 1. A person sentenced to imprisonment may be conditionally released by the court from serving the rest of the sentence only if the criminological prognosis formulated in its context justifies the belief that after release, the convicted person will comply with the adjudicated criminal or security measure and comply with the legal order; in particular, they will not commit a crime again.
>
> Section 2. When making a criminological prognosis, the court takes into account all of the following circumstances: the convict's attitude, their characteristics and personal conditions, the circumstances of the offence, behaviour after the commission of the crime and while serving the sentence, the opinion of an expert psychologist, information about the

> convict collected through an environmental interview conducted by a probation officer, and a criminological prognosis prepared by the prison administration.
>
> Section 3. When making a criminological prognosis, the court may use tools based on algorithms. At the request of the convict, the court makes a criminological prognosis using the tool referred to in the first sentence.
>
> Section 4. An application for the use of an algorithm-based tool may also be filed in an appeal against a court decision not agreeing to conditional release from serving the rest of the sentence.

The proposed regulation has already been proposed (Burdziak and Rüttel 2022) by the author of this work. Initially, however, the author assumed that the use of algorithms in the procedure of making a criminological prognosis for the purposes of proceedings for granting conditional early release should be obligatory, and at the same time that the use of a tool based on algorithms should be dealt with by the administration of the prison (State Prison Service officials), and not the court. At this point, the author suggests different solutions: first, the use of tools based on algorithms should be dealt with primarily by the court (which does not, however, exclude the use of algorithms by the State Prison Service officials); secondly, the use of these tools should be limited to cases in which either the court considers that it requires support in making an adequate decision (principle of proportionality), or the convict considers that the use of algorithms will favour the objectification of the proceedings in their case and their interest. The first solution was dictated by the need to ensure that the court hearing the case will know what algorithm-based tools are, what they can be useful for, how they work, what indicators they take into account, what the result of using such tools means, etc. Of course, the possibility of using tools based on algorithms solely by entities other than the court would not preclude the court from knowing about them. However, granting such competence directly to the court would force the court to gain knowledge on this subject directly through appropriate training in statistics, criminology, sociology or psychology. This, in turn, is by all means desirable not only from the perspective of using algorithms, but also from the perspective of evaluating the other factors referred to in the proposed regulation.

The second solution, i.e., the optional use of tools based on algorithms, is dictated by the desire to ensure that the results of their application will be treated as only subsidiary, auxiliary to the court's own assessment. If the proposed solution is adopted, the court would firstly be obliged to make a preliminary criminological prognosis of the convict based on the factors listed in the proposed regulation, and only then to assess whether the use of tools based on algorithms would be appropriate in a given case justified (from their, i.e., the court's, perspective). The opposite solution, i.e., starting the prognosis process by determining the result of using tools based on algorithms, would be unacceptable. The latter solution would be extremely dangerous. However, the author of this paper noticed (Burdziak 2021b) the risk of courts treating the results of the use of tools based on algorithms in a binding way, perhaps releasing them from responsibility for the decision in a certain sense. Above all, they can be a source of various heuristics used by the courts. There is a certain risk that tools based on algorithms will take real control over the decisions of the courts, depriving them of any autonomy (or at least significantly limiting this autonomy). This type of situation can be prevented by treating the use of algorithm-based tools as an option, not an obligation.

At the same time, it seems desirable to grant the convict the right (at each stage of examining their application) to use algorithms in a case concerning them. It needs to be emphasised that a convict with no confidence in the judiciary (or for other reasons), may demand the objectification of these proceedings; and algorithms can provide this kind of objectification. Basing the court's decision on the result of using tools based on algorithms may also be much more convincing for the convict. If both factors (i.e., the assessment of the court based on the clinical method and the assessment made by the algorithms) are consistent with each other, then even a negative decision may meet with appropriate understanding on the part of the convict. However, if the indicated factors are contradictory, then the convict will have reasonable grounds to appeal against the decision and will be given a chance to discuss their case in the proceedings before the second instance authority. At the same time, the proposed solution will, to a large extent, provide the convict with an influence on the grounds for the decisions made against them.

It should also be pointed out that the proposed solution ensures that the court will use other means of evidence in the form of a psychologist's opinion, a criminological prognosis prepared by the State Prison Service officials and an environmental interview. Including these elements would be obligatory, but they would not constitute either the main or the most important reason for the court's decision. Placing them at the end of the list could even indicate that they are purely ancillary in relation to the prognosis made freely by the court, based on all the circumstances related to the convicted person and their past, present and potential future situation, that is, on the basis of the circumstances listed in the first part of the list.

The proposed regulation would also be an element of introducing into the Polish legal order the most desirable mixed method of making a criminological prognosis, which would consist of a clinical method (coming from an assessment based on the knowledge and experience of specialists—experts, probation officers, prison administration), a statistical method (i.e., risk assessment based on algorithms) and a free decision based on the court's own conviction (although developed with the support of the two previously mentioned elements).

Finally, the proposed change would inform both the public and convicts about the grounds for decisions on conditional early release, including in particular the possibility of including in this process a risk assessment prepared by the court with the use of tools based on algorithms, and would impose on the drafter a duty to prepare an appropriate justification for the act amending the Criminal Code (or another relevant act) and an appropriate information campaign in this regard to accompany the change. Otherwise, this change could meet not only with misunderstanding, but also with opposition from society (Burdziak and Rüttel 2022).

It is also worth mentioning that the proposed regulation would fully comply with Article 22 of the EU General Data Protection Regulation (GDPR) (European Parliament and Council 2016a), according to which "1. The data subject shall have the right not to be subject to a decision based solely on automated processing, including profiling, which produces legal effects concerning him or her or similarly significantly affects him or her. 2. Paragraph 1 shall not apply if the decision: (…) 3. is based on the data subject's explicit consent", and analogous solutions provided for in the Law Enforcement Directive (European Parliament and Council 2016b).

Fourthly, it is necessary to strive to avoid the use of heuristics and cognitive errors by the courts; this also requires legal changes. For obvious reasons, the impact of the indicated circumstances on the decisions of the courts is much more likely where decisions are made by one person. After all, in the case of one-person benches of judges, there are no entities or factors that could draw the decision-maker's attention to the defectiveness of the reasoning adopted by them or the result of this reasoning at the decision-making stage. It is also much more likely that such factors as the pressure of subjects or external entities will have an effective impact on the court. Therefore, the following regulation is proposed:

Article X. In cases of conditional release, the court adjudicates in a panel of three judges.

At the same time, they should be experienced judges, trained in psychology, sociology, criminology, statistics, etc., and these requirements should be directly indicated in the act regulating the system of common courts in a given country.

Of course, group decision-making has not only advantages but also disadvantages (Lunenburg 2010). It seems, however, that in the context of such serious matters as early release of a convict from a penal institution, broad knowledge, life experience, and different perspectives on the case are necessary; all this can be ensured by having decisions made in collegiate panels of judges. The possible shortcomings of group decision-making, at least to some extent, can be overcome through the use of algorithm-based tools, as well as by discussing the possibility of conditional early release with specialists and taking into account their written opinions. Hence the need for the court to take into account the opinion of an expert psychologist, information about the convict collected through an environmental interview conducted by a probation officer, and a criminological prognosis prepared by the administration of the penal institution. In this context, it is also proposed to introduce a requirement to prepare comprehensive justifications for court decisions before they are issued. It is, of course, common practice that the reasons for judgments are not always prepared, and if they are, only after the decision has been issued. The author of this work proposes to change this order. Preparing the justification for the decision before it is issued (the justification describing the course of the court's thought process) allows the decision-maker's attention to be drawn to potential errors in their reasoning at the stage when they are able to do something about it.

It should be added that the author of this work (Burdziak and Rüttel 2022) previously proposed adjudication in a panel of one judge and two lay judges. It should be emphasised, however, that the composition of three professional judges will prevent the disadvantage of groupthink in the form of potential dominance of an individual, a defect described (Lunenburg 2010) as follows: "Often one person will dominate the group because of difference in status or rank from other members or through force of personality. This can cause resentment among other group members who are prevented from participating fully. The problem is that what appears to emerge as a group decision may actually be the decision of one person".

Fifthly, it is proposed that the method of making criminological prognoses by the State Prison Service officials needs to be standardised. The new regulation could have the following form, proposed and justified earlier by the author (Burdziak and Rüttel 2022):

> Article X. Section 1. The criminological prognosis consists of a written justification of the assumption that the convict will comply with the legal order during this stay.
>
> Section 2. The criminological prognosis for the purposes of conditional early release includes the characteristics of the convict, including the assessment of the likelihood of their reoffending, the degree of risk on their part and the possibility of their conditional release.
>
> Section 3. The risk assessment is prepared taking into account the convict's previous criminal record, their behaviour while serving the sentence, the execution of an individual plan of execution of the sentence while serving the sentence, interviews with the convict, other State Prison Service officials and relevant specialists, and information obtained from databases and other relevant information. The risk assessment should include an analysis of the convict from the perspective of: 1) criminal behaviour; 2) danger on their part; 3) the use of addictive substances and problem behaviours; 4) dealing with economic problems; 5) living conditions; 6) employment and education; 7) health and emotional state; 8) thinking and behaviour; 9) attitudes; and 10) relations with the environment.
>
> Section 4. The description of the inmate is made on the basis of the convict's risk assessment, and its purpose is primarily to assess the degree of threat posed by the convict and the probability of their committing a new crime and the circumstances contributing to it. The characteristics should include: 1) personal data of the convict; 2) information about the committed crime and the imposed penalty; 3) activities carried out in the penal institution in order to reduce the risk and their results; 4) a summary of the risk assessment related to the personality, life and behaviour of the convict; 5) the degree of threat on the part of the convict and the level of risk at the time of release; and (6) an opinion on the probationary period and applicable obligations.
>
> Section 5. Together with the criminological prognosis, the penal institution shall transfer the convict's personal files to the court.
>
> Section 6. The risk assessment referred to in Section 2 may be prepared using tools based on algorithms.
>
> Section 7. The director of the penal institution informs the convict in writing about the result of using an algorithm-based tool in their case. The information should include instruction on the basic principles of operation of the tool based on algorithms and an explanation of the meaning of the result obtained.
>
> Section 8. The convict may, within one month of receiving the information referred to in Section 7, request the director of the penal institution to re-use the tool based on algorithms or raise objections as to the legitimacy or manner of using the algorithm.
>
> Section 9. If the application referred to in Section 2 is submitted, the direction of the penal institution is obliged to consider it, taking into account all information provided by the convict, and inform the convict about the position taken within one month. The information should contain a comprehensive justification.

As can be seen, the proposed regulation provides for the optional use of tools based on algorithms by the prison administration. Previously, the author proposed the obligatory use of the indicated tools. The change of position is dictated by the desire to ensure that the results of the application of algorithms will be treated as only subsidiary and auxiliary, in relation to the prison administration's own assessment. At the same time, the proposed regulation ensures that the convict will have official information about the use of tools based on algorithms in their case and will be provided with basic information on the principles of their operation and instructions on how to understand the result obtained.

In the context of the above, it is also worth pointing out that it would be desirable if the persons responsible for making the assessment using tools based on algorithms were specialised in this issue, and not randomly, ad hoc obliged to make the assessment. Therefore, it is postulated to create an additional position responsible only for making criminological prognoses, having appropriate knowledge (in the field of law, psychology, sociology, social rehabilitation, pedagogy and statistics) and obliged to cooperate with educators and psychologists operating within penal institutions. A person holding such a position should be characterised by social maturity, communication skills, self-confidence, analytical and synthesising skills, ability to cope with stress and pressure, high morals, a sense of justice and a sense of mission, a high degree of independent thinking, discretion and reflection on how best to do their job. It seems that the creation of the discussed position would relieve the State Prison Service officials responsible for social rehabilitation of the convict from the obligation to make criminological prognoses, and at the same time would allow the persons holding the position to focus on only one issue (specialisation) and devote the appropriate amount of time to self-improvement in this area (excellence) (Burdziak and Rüttel 2022).

Finally, it is recommended to introduce into the legislation of individual countries (if it has not already been done) solutions analogous to the provisions of Articles 13–15 GDPR. Protection of the convict's data is an important condition for ensuring proper protection of their freedoms and rights. The convict must know that someone wants/wanted to obtain data about them, for what purpose these data will be/were used, from what perspectives they will be/were assessed, how long they will be processed, etc. In the case of convicts, these data will usually be additionally obtained from third parties, and not from themselves, hence the need to protect their interests requires qualified solutions and is even necessary.

The introduction of a regulation such as the regulation of Article 14 GDPR would also be advisable. The aforementioned regulation could take the following form:

> Section 1. If in the case of a convicted person in which tools based on algorithms were used, data relating to them were not obtained from them, the entity obtaining the data provides the convicted person with the following information: a) the identity and contact details of the data obtainer and, where applicable, the representative of the data obtainer; b) contact details of the personal data protection officer; c) the purposes of processing for which the personal data will be intended, as well as the legal basis for processing; d) the categories of personal data that have been obtained; e) information about possible recipients or categories of recipients of personal data.
>
> Section 2. In addition to the information referred to in Section 1, the entity obtaining the data shall provide the convict—the data subject—with the following information necessary to ensure fair and transparent processing: a) the period for which personal data will be stored; b) legitimate interests pursued by the entity obtaining the data or by a third party;

c) information on the existence of the right to demand rectification, deletion or limitation of processing from the entity obtaining the data and the right to object to processing; d) the right to lodge a complaint with the supervisory entity; (e) information on where the personal data come from and, where applicable, whether they come from publicly available sources.

Section 3. The entity obtaining the data shall provide the information referred to in Sections 1 and 2 within a reasonable time after obtaining the personal data, but not later than within one month from the moment of obtaining the personal data and not later than two months before entering the obtained data into the tool based on algorithms.

Section 4. The request and objection referred to in Section 2 letter c, may be submitted to the entity obtaining the data within a week from the date of obtaining the information referred to in Sections 1 and 2.

Section 5. The entity obtaining the data considers the request and objection referred to in Section 2 letter c, within three days from the date of receipt of the request and objection and informs the convicted person about the manner of considering the case no later than within seven days from the date of receipt of the request and objection.

Section 6. The complaint referred to in Section 2 letter d, the convict may submit through the entity obtaining the data within a week from the date of obtaining the information referred to in Section 7.

Sections 4, 5 and 6 of the proposed regulation appear to be particularly important. They extend the scope of protection of the freedoms and rights of the convict, including, above all, their right to defence. However, they may demand verification of the obtained data, giving a chance to obtain in their case the result of using a tool based on algorithms as close as possible to reality. There is no denying that this type of effect is an effect desired not only by the convict themselves, but also by the court and the whole of society, which also demands, above all, justice, not unjustified ailment.

The solutions proposed above do not, of course, exhaust all the necessary changes that should be made as part of the process of introducing tools based on algorithms in Poland or in another country. It seems, however, that these are the most important changes and reflect the idea of a new way of deciding on the possibility of conditional early release of a convict from serving the rest of their imprisonment. At the same time, these are proposed solutions referring directly to the key aspects highlighted in the 2022 Fair Trials policy paper. The issues are: "a) making it a legal requirement for decision-makers to be adequately alerted and informed about the risks associated with AI systems; b) making AI systems' assessments intelligible to decision-makers; c) requiring decision-makers to provide full, individualised reasoning for all decisions influenced by an AI system; and d) making it easy for decision-makers to overrule AI assessments that produce unfavourable outcomes for defendants" (Fair Trials 2022).

4 Summary

Considering the above, it should be stated that algorithms are not so much an alternative to the hitherto used methods of deciding in cases of conditional early release from serving the rest of a term of imprisonment, but rather support judges in making decisions in this regard. Algorithms are a unique way of achieving objectivity within the conducted proceedings; they give a chance to avoid cognitive bias or heuristics that may occur in the decision-making process of a human being, but never in a machine/program. However, they cannot be the only basis for decisions made in the course of criminal proceedings, as their use is also associated with certain risks, at the very least, the possibility of racial or national discrimination. The uncontrolled introduction of algorithms into criminal procedure can lead to violations of fundamental constitutional freedoms and human rights. Human dignity may be violated by de-individualising the accused and reducing his or her live to statistics (algorithms are, after all, pure statistics, whereas we should be interested in the individual case of a given accused). A person's right to defence may be violated if the accused does not understand what the algorithm is about, what criteria it uses or how it is applied. Indeed, if he or she does not understand how algorithm-based tools work, how will he or she be able to challenge their application in his or her case. Finally, a person's right to have his or her case heard by an independent court may be violated. As it turns out, there are mechanisms that can be triggered by the use of algorithm-based tools and that will lead to a limitation of the judges' freedom to make decisions in criminal cases. An example of this type of mechanism is anchoring, which can lead to a court being biased by the percentage score given by an algorithm-based tool.

When deciding to introduce algorithms and tools based on them into the legal systems of individual countries, one should approach the method of regulating this issue in national legislation with great care. Appropriate regulations will make it possible to fully use the potential of a human being (in court) and a machine/program (algorithm), and at the same time they will duly protect the freedoms and rights of a human being who is the subject of criminal proceedings. Proposed solutions of such regulations have been included in this work, hoping that they will facilitate the work of lawyers and legislators from the countries of Central and Eastern Europe, or at least become the basis for further discussion on the issues indicated.

References

Bogucki O (2020) The derivational theory of legal interpretation in Polish legal theory. Int J Semiot Law 33:617–636. https://doi.org/10.1007/s11196-019-09628-1

Boz H (2019) Anchoring effect: a myth or reality? The International Journal of Economic and Social Research 1(15):33–47

Burdziak K (2021a) Organ donation in the context of human tendency to be consistent. Considerations with reference to law and psychology. Probacja 3:118–119. https://doi.org/10.5604/01.3001.0015.2711

Burdziak K (2021b) Can the use of algorithms enhance judicial independence? Reflections in the context of The Hague Declaration. Biuletyn Kryminologiczny 28:9–17. https://doi.org/10.5281/zenodo.6810541

Burdziak K, Rüütel E (2022) *Prognoza kryminologiczna. Porównanie rozwiązań estońskich i polskich*. TYGIEL.

Burdziak K, Jankowski M, Kowalewska-Łukuć M (2019) Diagnostyka sądowokryminalna w orzekaniu i wykonywaniu warunkowego przedterminowego zwolnienia w teorii i praktyce sądowej—raport z badania. Prawo w Działaniu 39:50–52

Cross F (2009) The theory and practice of statutory interpretation. Stanford University Press

Cross R, Bell J, Engle, G (1995) Cross: statutory interpretation. Oxford University Press.

Danziger S, Levav J, Avnaim-Pesso L (2011) Extraneous factors in judicial decisions. Proc Natl Acad Sci 108(17):6889–6892. https://doi.org/10.1073/pnas.1018033108

Dressel J, Farid H (2018) The accuracy, fairness, and limits of predicting recidivism. Sci Adv 4(1). https://doi.org/10.1126/sciadv.aao5580

Estonian Ministry of Justice (2020) Eestis kasutatavate retsidiivsusvalemite koondanalüüs. Uuringu telli ja: Justiitsministeerium. Analüüs: Turu-uuringute AS (Vaike Vainu). Unpublished. Made available to the author as a courtesy of the Estonian Ministry of Justice

European Parliament and Council (2016a) Regulation (EU) 2016/679 of the European Parliament and of the Council of 27 April 2016 on the protection of natural persons with regard to the processing of personal data and on the free movement of such data, and repealing Directive 95/46/EC (General Data Protection Regulation). OJ L 119, 4.5.2016, pp 1–88

European Parliament and Council (2016b) Directive (EU) 2016/680 of the European Parliament and of the Council of 27 April 2016 on the protection of natural persons with regard to the processing of personal data by competent authorities for the purposes of the prevention, investigation, detection or prosecution of criminal offences or the execution of criminal penalties, and on the free movement of such data, and repealing Council Framework Decision 2008/977/JH. OJ L 119, 4.5.2016, pp 89–131

Fair Trials (2022) Regulating artificial intelligence for use in criminal justice systems in the EU—Policy paper. https://www.fairtrials.org/app/uploads/2022/01/Regulating-Artificial-Intelligence-for-Use-in-Criminal-Justice-Systems-Fair-Trials.pdf

Glöckner A (2016) The irrational hungry judge effect revisited: simulations reveal that the magnitude of the effect is overestimated. Judgm Decis Mak 11(6):601–610. https://doi.org/10.1017/S1930297500004812

Hervada J (2011) Wprowadzenie do prawa naturalnego. Petrus

Lunenburg F C (2010) Group decision making. Natl Forum Teach Educ J 20(3). http://www.nationalforum.com/Electronic%20Journal%20Volumes/Lunenburg,%20Fred%20C.%20Group%20Decision%20Making%20NFTEJ%20V20%20N3%202010.pdf

Moore R (2015) The Offender Assessment System (OASys) and the 2009–2013 research projects. In: Moore R (ed), A compendium of research and analysis on the Offender Assessment System (OASys) 2009–2013. Ministry of Justice Analytical Series 2015. https://assets.publishing.service.gov.uk/government/uploads/system/ uploads/attachment_data/file/449357/research-analysis-offender-assessment-system.pdf.

Palmiotto F (2020) Regulating algorithmic opacity in criminal proceedings: an opportunity for the EU Legislator? Maastricht Law, Faculty of Law WP. https://doi.org/10.2139/ssrn.3697173

Samuelson W, Zeckhauser R (1988) Status quo bias in decision making. J Risk Uncertain 1(1):7–59

Tokarczyk R (2008) Komparatystyka prawnicza. Wolters Kluwer Polska

Ugwudike P (2022) Predictive algorithms in justice systems and the limits of tech-reformism. Int J Crime Justice Soc Democr 11(1):85–99. https://doi.org/10.5204/ijcjsd.2189

Walton D, Macagno F, Sartor G (2020) Statutory interpretation: pragmatics and argumentation. Cambridge University Press

Yule K (2009) Statutory interpretation: general principles and recent trends. Nova Science

The FemTech Jacquerie: Situating Co-creation for Efficient Stewardship in Women's Health *Vis-À-Vis* the European Union Artificial Intelligence Act

Pin Lean Lau

Abstract This chapter offers a critical assessment of the under-represented gendered dimensions of techno-science, specifically focusing on technologies driven by artificial intelligence (AI) within the context of women's healthcare in the European legal space. Firstly, it enquires into the gendered dimensions of medicine and healthcare, and demonstrates the centrality of androcentrism and the existence of biases in women's healthcare and medical data. Secondly, it highlights the FemTech revolution and the harmful implications of AI algorithmic biases against women, and investigates whether existing supranational AI legislation or legal frameworks adequately protect the fundamental rights of patients in health or medical FemTech and AI. This assessment looks to the European Union Artificial Intelligence Act and the Council of Europe Zero Draft Framework Convention on Artificial Intelligence, Human Rights, Democracy, and the Rule of Law for this purpose. Thirdly, it seeks to recommend the co-creation of effective stewardship as one of the solutions to health equality for women. Viewed through the lens of data feminism, effectiveness means acknowledging privilege versus oppression in the access to and quality of women's healthcare, and identifying approaches that look towards dismantling inequitable power structures that influence the dynamics of bias and under-representation in women's healthcare.

1 Introduction

The integration of artificial intelligence (AI) into modern healthcare and biomedicine has ushered in a transformative era, revolutionising techniques, tools, and methods of healthcare delivery and treatment. For instance, cutting-edge rehabilitative robotics have emerged as a pivotal force, empowering patients to reclaim their motor skills

P. L. Lau (✉)
Brunel Law School, Brunel University of London, London, UK
e-mail: PinLean.Lau@brunel.ac.uk

M. Varju and K. Mezei (eds.), *The Challenges of Artificial Intelligence for Law in Europe*, Data Science, Machine Intelligence, and Law 6,
https://doi.org/10.1007/978-3-031-86813-9_11

through the implementation of highly efficient robot strategies that serve as "trainers" for the human sensory motor systems (Colombo and Sanguineti 2018). Furthermore, AI has found diverse applications in biomedical health, encompassing patient monitoring, genetic algorithms, optimisation techniques, and other advanced machine learning methodologies that enable the processing of vast amounts of data for diagnostic purposes.

Many contemporary reports on AI-related findings highlight that data-driven approaches have shown immense promise in clinician-facing applications, particularly in image analysis and interpretation in radiology (Lau and Staccini 2019). Contemporary emphasis has been squarely placed on transcending the outdated paradigm of paternalistic medicine, and instead fostering collaborative partnerships between medical professionals and patients, augmented by disruptive technologies. A pivotal aspect of this paradigm shift is the imperative to make AI in healthcare more patient-centric. Indeed, a meaningful integration of AI into the patient or consumer experience is crucial for realising a brighter digital future in healthcare.

As healthcare technology companies venture into the realm of health data, either through acquisitions or collaborations with health-focused entities to "manage" data, the need for profound ethical solutions becomes even more pressing (Copeland et al. 2020). Striking a delicate balance between individuals' rights in biomedicine and the non-opt-out nature of health-search tools demands meticulous attention. Hence, it is irrefutable that the practical applications of AI in biomedicine continue to hold paramount importance in the realm of medical treatments, research, and diagnostics (Lee and Yoon 2021).

Despite these notable advances, the utilisation of AI in healthcare fails to adequately represent the diverse communities it serves. Unlike AI technologies in other industries, the application of AI in healthcare warrants special consideration due to its profound implications on public and individual health, and even lives. For instance, the utilisation of large datasets of health data, including personal data, to train AI algorithms for healthcare systems presents significant challenges. The quality of health data is often compromised by its unstructured nature, inaccuracies stemming from measurement errors in self-reported health or medical records, and biases resulting from the absence of inclusive clinical data and underrepresentation of minorities. Such inaccuracies in the training datasets may lead to biased outcomes that can result in personal harm or even loss of life. Racial and gender biases in AI algorithms may lead to inaccurate diagnoses and further exacerbate existing socioeconomic disparities. The fundamental right of patients to have full knowledge and informed consent to medical treatment is threatened by a lack of transparency and explanation of algorithms, findings, and techniques resulting from AI, with vulnerable groups being disproportionately at risk of harm.

In the context of women's health, the focus of this chapter, the existing literature review reveals a glaring gender data gap in AI technologies and data science fields (Hariharan 2021). Traditional evaluations of women's healthcare, including prospective applications of AI in these domains, have largely overlooked the biological differences between men and women, with a few exceptions for gynaecological specifics and breast cancer. Consequently, the available data in women's healthcare also suffer from the pervasive problem of a gender gap. This gender data gap in women's healthcare perpetuates algorithmic gender bias when AI systems are employed to evaluate the data, significantly impacting women's healthcare experiences, treatment protocols, and ultimately, their rights in the realm of health (Smith and Rustagi 2021).

We should also consider the role of FemTech in this discussion. Whilst it is unclear whether the FemTech burst onto the technological scene was a response to the under-representation of women in healthcare, its purpose, in theory, aims to advance technological innovations specifically for women. It has been defined in the Cambridge dictionary as "female technology: electronic devices, software, or other technology relating to women's health."[1] The term in itself has courted controversy, but the intentional creation of FemTech is a noble one, warranting deeper ruminations on the subject of health or medical AI for women.

On this basis, the main inquiries in this paper are three-fold. Firstly, it enquires into the gendered dimensions of medicine and healthcare, and demonstrates the existence of biases in women's healthcare *vis-à-vis* AI. Secondly, it analyses the FemTech revolution, and investigates whether existing supranational AI legislation or legal frameworks adequately protect the fundamental rights of patients in health or medical FemTech and AI; and thirdly, it seeks to recommend effective legal stewardship as one of the solutions to health equality for women. Viewed through the lens of data feminism, effectiveness means acknowledging privilege versus oppression in the access to and quality of women's healthcare, and identifying approaches that look towards dismantling inequitable power structures that influence the dynamics of bias and under-representation in women's healthcare.

2 Un(Gendering) Medicine and Healthcare

2.1 Gender in(Equality) in Medicine and Healthcare

On 8 March 2023 just past, the celebration of the United Nations International Women's Day 2023 dramatically proclaimed a theme most befittingly matched to our contemporary scientific and technological advancements. Despite the bravado of DigitALL: Innovation and Technology for Gender Equality (United Nations 2023), it was highlighted that women still experience digital inequalities, with only 22% of women making up the global percentage of work in AI, and at least 44% of 133 AI systems across industries found to demonstrate gender bias (UN Women 2023). The World Bank pronounces its commitment through its #AccelerateEquality campaign, to "close gender gaps and promote women and girls' empowerment to drive transformative change, unlocking trillions of dollars in economic potential" (World Bank

[1] https://dictionary.cambridge.org/dictionary/english/femtech.

2023). Whilst we might choose to be grateful for the diminutive increases in gender equality over the decades, the lack of gender parity is similarly reflected in medicine and healthcare. This should not be surprising, considering the traditional exclusion of women from science and medicine from as early as 2600 BC (Kushner 2008)—but the knowledge that this still continues in our day and age is both shameful and staggering.

Throughout the course of history, the 'otherness' of woman has been acutely felt, and in the twenty-first century, 'othering' continues to be a problem. Defined as "a set of dynamics, processes and structures that engender marginality and persistent inequality across any of the full range of human differences based on groups' identities" (Powell and Menendian 2017), 'othering' is a consequence of systemic discrimination and prejudice. Manifesting in various ways, including overt expressions of prejudice, 'othering' is unfortunately more insidiously embedded in "institutionalization and structural features", where "individual acts of discrimination have a cumulative and magnifying effect that may help explain many group–based inequalities" (Powell and Menendian 2017). In this chapter, the author argues that 'othering' and gendered dimensions in medicine and healthcare have a dual effect on women, making them voiceless, invisible, and seen as deviant when medicine fails to find a male comparative for women's illnesses and diseases. This phenomenon is a result of the way that gender inequality is embedded within medical structures, which can perpetuate the 'othering' of women in medicine.

Consider the report issued by the British Medical Association (2021) in 2021, finding that there are still significant pay gaps between men and women in the medical profession in England: 18.9% for hospital doctors, 15.3% for GPs and 11.9% for clinical academics, with these figures being adjusted once for differences in working hours. The same is true for gender inequalities in medicine; with more serious consequences that result not only in under-representation of women patients, but also increased risks of mortality, misdiagnosis, and sub-par treatment (Brierley 2019). Cultural historian, Elinor Cleghorn, in her remarkable book (2021), highlights the long-term misogyny and gender biases against women in medicine and healthcare, with horrifying examples of cases and case studies enumerating the way in which medicine and healthcare have failed women.

It is also all too striking that it is mostly women, throughout time immemorial, who have sought to (and needed to) claim their rights over bodily autonomy, over their own health, and over their reproductive functions, in the courts system. Take the landmark case of *Roe v. Wade*[2] in the United States, signifying a woman's constitutional right to abortion; now disingenuously overturned by the Supreme Court in 2022 in *Dobbs v Jackson's Women Heath Organization.*[3] We should also consider the plethora of reproductive rights cases at the European Court of Human Rights: *L.F. v Ireland* (App. no. 62007/17), *K.O. v Ireland* (App. no. 61836/17) and *W.M. v Ireland* (App. no. 61872/17), where the (women) applicants had been subject to surgical symphysiotomy. The plight of the Roma women, forcibly sterilised against their will, have

[2] *Roe v. Wade*, 410 U.S. 113 (1973).

[3] *Dobbs v. Jackson Women's Health Organization*, 597 U.S. 215 (2022).

been magnified in cases, such as *K.H. and others v Slovakia* (App. no. 32881/04) and *V.C. v Slovakia* (App. no. 18968/07). In addition, women's access to safe and legal abortions continues to pose challenges, as evidenced in cases such as *S.F.K. v Russia* (App. no. 5578/12) and *G.M. and others v the Republic of Moldova* (App. no. 44394/15). In most (if not all) of these legal cases, the continued discrimination against women in medical treatment is evident.

2.2 *Androcentricity & Gender Medicine*

Technoscience and techno-cultural studies have historically been dominated by men—not only from a scientific perspective, but also through cultural and sociological practices (Lan 2012). The pervasiveness of androcentricity (Merone et al. 2022) in medicine contributes to this exclusion, highlighting the likelihood that "ongoing discrepancies in the care of female patients" (Merone 2022) do have a significant impact on patient care through the experience of female patients.

Androcentricity is the name given to the phenomenon, popularised by Charlotte Perkins Gilman in 1911, to mean "a state of having men or males at the centre" (Perkins Gilman 1911). Perkins Gilman (1911) states: "The man was accepted as the race type without one dissentient voice; and the woman—a strange diverse creature, quite disharmonious in the accepted scheme of things—was excused and explained only as a female." In other words, society's treatment of men, male, and masculinity through androcentric practices, equates their superiority as the benchmark of standards and norms which all societal practices should adhere to. Women, female, and femininity were (and continue to be) impacted as a direct result of androcentric activities, and whilst this might be thought to be archaic (given the contemporary efforts to increase gender equality globally), these stereotypical legitimations of man's power and privilege do not disappear overnight.

As a consequence, it also results in androcentricity in medicine and healthcare—translating consequentially into medical and clinical data. As Kate Young and her co-authors (2019) highlight:

> Medicine defines the female and male bodies as distinct but not equal; analyses of medical texts throughout history reveals the male body to be constructed as superior and the template against which bodies are judged. Any aspect of the female body that differs from the male or that cannot be given a male comparative (exemplified by the uterus) is viewed as evidence of deviation or "fault".

An illustration of this deeply systemic androcentricity can be seen in clinical trials for drugs (medication). Studies have demonstrated that a gender gap in drug trials have resulted in women experiencing adverse drug reactions (ADRs) twice as often as men (Anwar 2020). This is particularly because a one-size-fits-all approach was often used, based on male-dominated clinical trials, without considering the fundamental biological differences between men and women. Hence, whilst women were given the same dosage of a particular drug, they reacted differently to the same drug, metabolised the drugs in different ways and always almost had a higher concentration of the drugs in their system (Zucker and Pendergast 2020). The exclusion of women from clinical trials which "neglects sex differences in pharmacokinetics and dimorphisms in body weight, risks overmedication of women, and contributes to female-biased adverse drug reactions" (Zucker and Pendergast 2020).

The gender data gap in medicine and healthcare also risks misdiagnosis in women. An example of this is the way women with acute myocardial infarction (MI) present their symptoms (which are different from men's) (Merone et al. 2022). Because women's symptoms are different from men's, they are less likely to be identified as suffering from MI during an angiogram, which therefore does not leave space for the condition to be appropriately managed or monitored. In the long-term, women were therefore more likely to suffer adverse reactions, over-complications and even increased overall mortality, due to this oversight (Merone et al. 2022).

Whilst significant attention is now increasing to ensure that the gender equality gaps in technologies and medicine are addressed, and ultimately, closed, there is much that still needs to be done. The European Institute for Gender Equality report (2020) supports the reality of gendered patterns in technologies, and the power relationships that exist in gender and technology, particularly if "technological change is shaped and structured according to societal norms and relations, which are in turn influenced by technological transformations" (EIGE 2020). It is almost no wonder, that in modern technologies, traditional technoscientific practices believed in the need to govern a woman's body and how this body interacts with technological tools. As AI-driven technologies proliferate the realm of medicine and healthcare, what kind of inequalities will continue to be exacerbated, and do we need to anticipate novel forms of bias and discrimination against women?

Whilst unrelated to the advancement of AI, it may also be worth considering gender medicine, which was established as a subject in response to Yentl syndrome (Healy 1991). Similarly, Yentl syndrome has its historical roots in medicine, where "medicine is tailor-made for men's physiologies, and women simply have to make do with a healthcare system made by men for men" (Rajesh 2021). As a subject, gender medicine attempts to study and give importance to the effects of sex and gender on health and medicine. Indeed, many existing studies (in addition to those mentioned above) already demonstrate sex and gender disparities in fields such as epidemiology, pathophysiology, clinical manifestations, disease progression, and response to treatment (Mauvais-Jarvis 2020). It has also been recorded that the "genetic, epigenetic, and hormonal influences of biological sex can influence physiology and disease, and how the social constructs of gender affect the behaviours of the community, clinicians, and patients in the healthcare system and interact with pathobiology" ((Mauvais-Jarvis 2020). These are also important factors that need to be taken into account when considering existing healthcare and medical data used in AI-driven technologies.

3 The FemTech Revolution: A Paradoxical Reaction

3.1 Algorithmic Gender Bias

A growing kind of bias and discrimination against women in healthcare and medicine is already apparent *vis-à-vis* AI-driven technologies. AI systems are, in essence, fuelled by the methods of machine learning and algorithms used to train the systems, so that a certain function or task can be performed independently and in an automated way. However, it may never be possible to generate outcomes that are pure and completely fair (Samuel 2022), because the value systems of human persons are activated when programming the systems. The notion of fairness may also be arbitrary and differ from one perspective to another depending on the contextual framework (Samuel 2022). Hence, when AI systems are first 'taught', not only is it vital that the relevant machine learning method used is appropriate; it is also crucial that the data sets (training data) that would allow the system to learn and diffuse patterns, are also of good quality, and are representative and inclusive.

Algorithms, the means by which AI-driven technologies process data and arrive at outcomes, are the backbone of how these processes arrive at a particular decision or outcome (Müldner 2002). Any machine learning system or algorithm that is trained with human-generated data will only be as effective and fair as the data it has been trained with. It is therefore important that all stakeholders in the lifecycle of an AI type of technology are aware of the potential biases that they might face during each development stage. They should also consider the various factors that they might use to train their systems, such as their quality and diversity (Manyika et al. 2019). Data can be 'tainted' with bias, built in with historical prejudices that translate into the inequalities in society. Data can also be inadequate and unrepresentative—for example, as illustrated above, where women are deliberately excluded from medical or clinical trials, resulting in a gender gap in medical data. For many years, too, men's bodies were regarded as the standard for any form of medical testing—and the exclusion of women from medical research and trials meant that women's health was and continues to be at risk (Westervelt 2015)—no less so in AI-driven systems as well, due to inadequacy of data. Hence, the phrase 'rubbish in, rubbish out' has been used to describe this kind of phenomenon.

Algorithms, which have been referred to as "weapons of math destruction", can and do perpetuate inequalities in daily living, affecting aspects of daily life such as credit scoring and risks of recidivism (O'Neill 2016). Algorithms can specifically affect certain segments of population groups, essentially claiming to quantify the essential and desirable traits for society (Lamb 2016), and excluding others such as the poor, the homeless, persons of colour, and other marginalised groups. Such is the power of an algorithm, and whilst there are groups in the scientific community that believe in the neutrality of technologies (Welchel 1986), such as AI and its algorithms, this chapter wishes to point out that neutrality is often misconstrued with the nature of such technologies versus the human use of technologies.

The problem of algorithm bias, therefore, is a very real one, even within the realm of women's healthcare. In a recent study on AI-driven technologies and women's healthcare, Lau et al. conducted a systematic literature review to determine whether AI-driven technologies adequately represented medical data and research into women's healthcare. One key finding from this research was that there was clearly a lack of representative data on women's healthcare conditions (Lau et al. 2023). The authors divided the research inquiry into five thematic clusters (Lau et al. 2023), comprising, amongst others, gender equality and health AI. It is unsurprising that the findings of this study point to the need for a much more significant body of required research for the improvement of AI risk prediction models for many aspects of women's healthcare (Lau et al. 2023). In addition, the authors note that the representation of women's healthcare conditions are low and uneven in comparison to other available general health data (Lau et al. 2023), and even if sparsely available, this representation has been limited to disease-specific interventions. Hence, when AI-driven technologies or systems are deployed in medicine and healthcare, based on the limited availability of good quality and representative data regarding women, any resulting outcomes will clearly be skewed.

For example, because women have been excluded from many clinical trials (Deziel 2016), this may result in incomplete data sets to train systems for disease and illness suffered by women. Algorithmic biases present themselves *vis-à-vis* false diagnosis, and if this false diagnosis is relied upon, wrong treatment protocols can further exacerbate the situation (Gerke et al. 2020). Deploying AI-driven technologies that do not account properly for differences and diversity means we are ultimately releasing into healthcare delivery, high level risks of lack of safety and inadequacy (Fosch-Villaronga et al. 2022). Therefore, what is clear is that even 'good' algorithms (algorithms intended to be used for altruistic and noble reasons) can become sexist in their outcomes, based upon the kind and quality of data that is used to train the AI systems (Smith and Rustagi 2021). This explains the urgent actions and measures currently being undertaken at the governmental level to address the problems of AI biases (Alake 2020).

3.2 Enter FemTech: Situational Irony?

As stipulated in the Introduction of this chapter, FemTech's emergence in the technological landscape may have been a deliberate response to the under-representation of women in healthcare, and in particular, technologies that formed part of these healthcare dimensions. Since 2021, there has been a significant increase in the FemTech industry, with most FemTech companies and start-ups hailing from the United States—although there are also indications of large successful investment and funding rounds emerging from within Europe (Mansour 2020). Encompassing technologies that range from assisting in tracking conditions such as fertility, menstruation, and menopause, to precision AI and genetic testing in contraception, FemTech was seen as the much-needed response to women's healthcare needs and services.

In our contemporary setting, it is now more critical than ever to push the FemTech agenda globally, and look into ways of fostering greater diversity and inclusivity in growing the FemTech industry. Notwithstanding the good intentions in the grand scheme of raising the profile of FemTech, there are also debates that surround the emergence of FemTech, and inquiries into whether it may have the unintended effect of furthering the 'othering' narratives regarding women.

This author notes two main concerns. Firstly, whilst the FemTech industry continues to grow, with large health corporates looking towards banking innovative FemTech start-ups (Mansour 2020), one cannot help but note that FemTech almost exclusively caters to women's reproductive or gynaecological needs. Whilst it is true that these tend to be exclusive to women, this only addresses a small part of the wider biases in healthcare systems. Only focusing on mostly women's reproductive or gynaecological functions does little to mitigate the other forms of under-presentation of women in healthcare—for example, relating to clinical trials and research, research and development of cardiovascular diseases affecting women, mental health conditions, drugs and pharmaceuticals, insurance, costs and accessibility, and neurological diseases, amongst others. Some FemTech companies have devoted themselves to providing rich data to improve women's health, as this would certainly be a step in the right direction to bringing balance to available health or medical datasets. However, more support is needed to ensure the FemTech industry can not only thrive, but withstand the waves of both technological and societal development, as FemTech is still lagging behind in terms of accessing venture capital funding (Mansour 2020).

Secondly, it is possible that FemTech's focus on only women's health may be seen as exclusionary, and exclusion often typically has close connections to 'othering'—which is a paradoxical reaction and could be seen as situationally ironic (FemTech Insider 2023). In addition to further 'othering' narratives, critics of FemTech have lashed out at its terminological exclusion of transgender or non-binary individuals. These individuals can, and may, have the same biology as cisgender women—and at the same time, they may also choose not to identify as women or female (Mansour 2020), or choose to identify as queer or gender-fluid. In these instances, so as not to perpetuate the continued discrimination against transgender and non-binary communities, FemTech's role and purpose must continue to be emphasised, whilst simultaneously ensuring inclusivity, diversity, equity, and equality.

Nonetheless, these concerns notwithstanding, the role of FemTech in our technological epoch is an important one: one that we still need. Perhaps it may be necessary to view FemTech as a social and political movement, where there is a long trudge on the path to gender equality. As FemTech supporters have proclaimed: "Why are we afraid to claim our way to mainstream technology?" (FemTech Insider 2023). Indeed, like other social-political movements during recent times: the #Metoo movement, #BlackLivesMatter, the Women's Marches—FemTech seeks not to ostracise but to highlight the discrimination and under-representation of women in the health and medicine landscape—and like all worthy social-political movements, necessitates distinction to place women's health as a priority in technological developments.

4 The Regulatory Framework for AI and Health in Europe

For the purposes of this section, the focus is now turned to reviewing the current regulatory efforts of the European Union (EU) and Council of Europe (CoE) and analysing the extent to which these efforts adequately protect the interests and rights of patients in FemTech and health AI, particularly women. For clarification, the specific legislation analysed in this section is the EU Artificial Intelligence Act (AI Act) (European Commission 2021), and the CoE's Zero Draft Framework Convention on Artificial Intelligence, Human Rights, Democracy and the Rule of Law (CoE AI Convention) (CAI 2023).

4.1 The European Union Artificial Intelligence Act

When the European Commission published the first proposal of the AI Act in April 2021, no one looked towards this with as much anticipation as those working in the field of AI, law, and governance, as well as in industries where AI systems are implemented, deployed, or manufactured. Whilst it has now been some time since that first proposal, the AI Act has gone through substantial deliberations, with the most recent draft dating from 9 May 2023 (European Parliament 2023a). More importantly, on 11 May 2023, the Committee on the Internal Market and Consumer Protection and the Committee on Civil Liberties, Justice and Home Affairs voted for the endorsement of new transparency and risk management rules for AI systems in the EU (European Parliament 2023b), as per the aforesaid recent draft. When it is ultimately passed, the AI Act will be one of the most comprehensive horizontal legislation proposals for a governance framework for risk posed by AI products and services in the EU, and is likely to be regarded as the first global law enacted by a major regulator.

The risk-based approaches in the AI Act correspond with the relevant compliance and conformity assessments imposed on primarily AI "providers"[4] (which may include various AI developers, manufacturers, processors, and those who put the AI systems on the market), and "importers" and "distributors".[5] Obligations are also imposed on "users", although the clarity on what amounts to "users" would be better made apparent (since it does not have the same meaning of "users" as it does in the General Data Protection Regulation (GDPR) (European Parliament and Council 2016). Each of the risk categories would be subject to different requirements (proportionate to the risks posed), such as codes of conduct, transparency obligations, or conformity assessments.

Because the AI Act is very much focused on risks as its main object and justification, thereby establishing rules that are proportionate and seek to be effective (Mahler

[4] European Commission (2021, Article 3).

[5] European Commission (2021, Articles 26 to 28).

2022), it is easy to question how its scope would be effective in protecting the interests of the ‘end users’ of AI systems and technologies. Experts that have evaluated the AI Act also wonder whether, even though “this scheme has worked relatively well for tangible products, where the manufacturer of a product is the analogue of the provider in the Act, this top-down allocation of duties will be more challenged in a world of ‘upstream’ AI services, which can be re-used downstream in a wide variety of unforeseeable contexts” (Edwards 2022).

Further evaluation is needed on these issues, based on the transparency and risk management approaches that have been recently voted upon, and how AI systems that may be used for a number of different purposes may be categorised. In the medical or healthcare landscape, it is therefore possible that AI systems used for personalised medicine and patient engagement applications could be classified as general-purpose AI, but could simultaneously be regarded as high-risk AI systems if licensed for other specific uses (Sidley Austin 2022). It is questionable how these categorisations will then impact on compliance, conformity and other requirements under the Act. For example, one question that arises regarding FemTech might be that it could be simpler to classify a menstruation and ovulation cycle application as a low-risk general-purpose AI than it might be to classify FemTech for use in reproductive technologies such as preimplantation genetic testing to screen embryos,[6] and the evaluation of genetic mutation propensity based on personal genetic information, which are likely to be classified as medium to high-risk.

Further consideration in this chapter should also look at Article 37 of the AI Act. An earlier version of the Act (European Commission 2021) provides that some AI systems deserve special consideration, particularly because of “the access to and enjoyment of certain essential private and public services and benefits necessary for people to fully participate in society or to improve one’s standard of living”. Health or medical AI was not then addressed as part of this special consideration. The Article goes on to declare that AI systems should not lead to “discrimination of persons or groups and perpetuate historical patterns of discrimination……or create new forms of discriminatory impacts.” The use of AI in specific areas, such as critical infrastructure (Article 34), education or vocational training (Article 35), employment (Article 36) and law enforcement (Article 38), were expressly identified—whereas health or medicine (including FemTech) was markedly missing. Indeed, as pointed out by Palmieri and Goffin (2023):

> Although the AI Act is not intended to be applied specifically to the health sector but is intended to be applied horizontally, it aims to solve *ab origine*, risks that could seriously impact the health of the patient who comes into contact with an AI. Health, as is often said, is wealth and represents the necessary precondition for the enjoyment of all other rights recognised in the European Union. Therefore, while exploring the suitability of the AI Act to, *lato sensu*, protect fundamental rights, the health sector deserves special attention.

However, the revised version of the AI Act (European Parliament 2023a) now includes some references to healthcare within the purview of Article 37, namely that “healthcare services, and essential services, including but not limited to housing,

[6] See Basille et al. (2009).

electricity, heating/cooling and internet" have now been included to acknowledge the importance of AI impacts within Article 37. If this is ultimately adopted and approved, this at least signals the recognition that AI technologies in health and medicine do, indeed, deserve special consideration. Nevertheless, whilst this recognition may be provided, it is important that it must be fully implemented and not just exist in theory alone.

Another important consideration of the AI Act is its relationship with medical devices, as some AI systems can also be medical devices. Under the Act, all systems in Annex III, as well as those falling under the regulations listed in Annex II requiring third-party conformity assessments, will be classified as high-risk AI systems (van Oirschot and Ooms 2022). To date, the only regulations that would fall within the criterion of Annex II that would require third-party conformity assessments are the Medical Devices Regulation (MDR) (European Parliament and Council 2017a) and the In-Vitro Diagnostic Medical Devices Regulation (European Parliament and Council 2017b). There is concern, therefore, that the scope of the AI Act does not particularly value the implications ensuing from the use of health or medical AI systems, and it is not clear which AI systems would therefore qualify as medical devices (given also that the MDR broadly defines medical devices) and therefore also be subject to third-party conformity assessments under the MDR (van Oirschot and Ooms 2022). Arguably, this means that AI systems (for health and medicine) could ultimately possibly fall under the low-risk, high-risk, or unacceptable risks categories. This is disconcerting as this implies that some AI systems used in health and medicine will not be regarded as high risk, so are not subject to conformity assessments under the Act. Concurrently, it seems to be that "only software which is used to diagnose patients, make therapeutic decisions, monitor physiological processes or which is used for contraceptive purposes, is classified as a Class IIa medical device or higher, and hence subject to third party conformity assessment and classified as a high-risk AI system" (van Oirschot and Ooms 2022). On this basis, classification of AI systems falling under the low-risk category, even if they are used for health or medical purposes, risks a complete lack of oversight—and does not present a set of mandatory obligations for providers, manufacturers, and developers to comply with (van Oirschot and Ooms 2022).

Hence, whilst the AI Act was seen as pre-eminent in setting out (to a certain extent) harmonised rules for the market placement and use of AI in the EU, critics were of the opinion that its scope is too broad and does not adequately factor in fundamental rights protections.[7] The revised version of the Act reveals that a new Article 29a in Annex III is in place, that is, a fundamental rights impact assessment for high-risk AI systems must be carried out. This is a welcome revision, and is required to be in addition to the data impact assessment under the GDPR, if applicable for some systems.

For those who work within the field of health or medical AI, the AI Act could still provide greater clarity, notwithstanding the slight recognition that AI in healthcare services deserve special consideration. Gender equality should also be one of the

[7] See the Chapter by Grozdanovski in this volume.

aspirations in the AI Act, and could arguably be treated as a 'special consideration'. However, the main parameters of how these special considerations would be carried out in reality will still need to be deliberated. Whilst it is necessary for the AI Act to be read in conjunction with other horizontal EU-level regulations or legislation, the particularities of health or medical AI need to be considered to protect patient interests, which include women's healthcare interests and FemTech too. It remains to be seen, due to the internal market demands and technical harmonisation measures in the EU, how gender considerations or vulnerabilities may be *internalised vis-à-vis* appropriate legislation.

4.2 *The Council of Europe Zero Draft Framework Convention on Artificial Intelligence, Human Rights, Democracy and the Rule of Law*

In an exciting unfolding of events, the CoE, in January 2023, published its Zero Draft Framework Convention on Artificial Intelligence, Human Rights, Democracy and the Rule of Law (CAI 2023). Although it cannot be said that this was not foreseeable, scholars in the field are optimistic regarding this new framework from the CoE, believing that this framework may become a critical companion to the EU's AI Act. Where the AI Act featured its risk-based approaches and categorical obligations as part of the EU market, the CoE AI Convention, in its current, draft form, is expected to enhance the fundamental rights protections (van Kolfschooten 2023) offered under the AI Act. These include, amongst others, as rights to privacy, data protection, respect for human dignity, and most importantly, prohibition against discrimination, as contained in Article 3.[8]

The CoE AI Convention, however, is an extremely new instrument currently being negotiated (at the current time of writing this chapter), involving the CoE members, and observer countries, stakeholders from civil society and the private sector. Whilst the presently available version online is a zero-draft version, this is going to be irrelevant in due course (CAI 2024). Nevertheless, a first reading of the zero-draft version provides some optimism where health or medical AI such as FemTech is concerned. Chapter III (application of AI systems in provision of goods, facilities and services), Article 8, Section A, for example, provides obligations for public and private actors to ensure compatibility with national and international laws "in provision of goods, facilities and services in essential areas, such as but not restricted to, *health* [author's emphasis], family care, housing, energy consumption, transport,

[8] Article 3 reads: "The implementation of the provisions of this Convention by the Parties shall be secured without discrimination on any ground such as sex, gender, sexual orientation, race, colour, language, age, religion, political or any other opinion, national or social origin, association with a national minority, property, birth, state of health, disability or other status, or based on a combination of one or more of these grounds."

food supply, education, employment, finance, environmental protection, digital information, media and communication…". Arguably, this would encompass AI-driven applications of FemTech.

In the meantime, Chapter IV of the CoE AI Convention encompasses fundamental principles of AI systems. These include principles relating to equality and anti-discrimination (Article 12); privacy and personal data protection (Article 13); accountability, responsibility and legal liability (Article 14); transparency and oversight (Article 15); safety (Article 16); safe innovation (Article 17), and public consultation and additional measures (Article 18).

Whilst it may be too early to speculate and interpret the provisions of the zero-draft version, the CoE AI Convention, at this infant stage, may placate those who have been concerned about the human rights implications of AI. It is possible to interpret that the combination of Articles 3, the specific mention of health in Article 8, Section A, and the fundamental principles in Articles 12 to 18, are likely to provide a measure of comfort regarding the use of AI and protective human rights mechanisms that are available to individuals. Conversely, the CoE AI Convention is also likely to address and counter the existing issues faced in women's healthcare and medical treatment in a more dignified manner, and may encourage the proliferation of FemTech in more inclusive ways.

5 Co-Creation for Efficient Stewardship in Women's Healthcare

For efficient stewardship in women's healthcare to be brought to fruition, this requires the twin reflections, not only on the existing failings of healthcare systems that have historically excluded women, but also on developing an empathetic approach to experiences and narratives of privilege and oppression within healthcare. The process of co-creation in healthcare (Fusco et al. 2023), employed as part of intersectionality discourse (Crenshaw 2013), will necessitate conscious, holistic, and ethical employment of the use of AI-driven technologies in every aspect; fabricating a comprehensive ecosystem of women's health that no longer look towards men's biological bodies as the standard in medicine and healthcare.

In this chapter, the author's view is that embracing co-creation hinges on two specific limbs: firstly, on the conceptual notions of intersectionality and data feminism (D'Ignazio and Klein 2020); and secondly, by incorporating analogical dimensions of regulation of medical products through the five 'P's: products, persons, premises, practices, and processes (WHO 1999).

5.1 The First Limb of Co-Creation: Intersectionality and Data Feminism

In addressing the first limb of co-creation, which is the intersectionality and data feminism perspectives, it is also important to acknowledge the twin diametric of privilege versus oppression in the under-represented picture of women in healthcare systems, management, quality of services and available data. In intersectionality theory, it is critical to acknowledge that oppression does not occur in a vacuum and all types of oppression are interconnected to each other. In essence, considering intersectionality means that we understand how "the interconnected nature of social categorisations such as race, class, and gender, [are] regarded as creating overlapping and interdependent systems of discrimination or disadvantage."[9]

An acute awareness of how intersectionality also affects women in oppression is necessitated when considering women's healthcare as part of the qualitative nature of medical data and medical treatment. As stated by feminist Zoe Samudzi (2018), "intersectionality is such a vital framework for understanding systems of power, because 'woman' is not a catch-all category that alone defines all our relationships to power." This situates oppression on the opposite spectrum from 'privilege' (where even 'privilege' for women does not equate to the same kind of 'privilege' for men).

What does this mean for women's healthcare more broadly? A very insightful direction is provided by scholars Catherine D'Ignazio and Lauren F. Klein (2020), who proffer intersectionality in a concept they term "data feminism". Data feminism, according to D'Ignazio and Klein (2020), is one of the approaches employing feminist theory, that may overcome the "overwhelming white, male, techno-heroic" model in big data, data science and AI. In essence, data feminism emphasises the employment of black feminism (including that of Kimberle Crenshaw) as a lens by which to view how power structures operate in society, especially in relation to women. In an interview with Nightingale, the journal of the Data Visualization Society (Forrest 2019), D'Ignazio offers this food for thought:

> We try to ask questions like: How do these structural inequalities permeate the data science process? How did they infect every stage of the pipeline? What kind of questions even get asked? Right on down to what kinds of colors you choose to represent different things in your chart. So that's kind of the intentionally broad focus on power while still being focused on gender throughout, but like, power writ large.

Hence, power differentials between men and women; as well as between white women and Black women, academic researchers and indigenous communities, and people in the Global North and the Global South—these are all intersecting systems of power in a society.

In an idealised world, intersectionality and data feminism may be one of the solutions to address algorithm biases in women's healthcare in a mindful way—with the core of the theory providing specific strategies to data scientists in working towards attaining ethical, equitable, equal data justice. Embracing the 7 principles of

---

[9] 'Intersectionality, n.' https://www.oed.com/dictionary/intersectionality_n.

data feminism (examine power; challenge power; elevate emotion and embodiment; rethink binaries and hierarchies; embrace pluralism; consider context; and make labour visible) is also a starting point when considering how AI is used in women's healthcare and how better data can be gathered. This can also extend to machine learning methods in AI, and designing experiments and research for data, whilst simultaneously working towards intentionality to improve women's healthcare and AI in holistic ways.

5.2 The Second Limb of Co-Creation: The Five 'P's

The second branch of co-creation for effective stewardship is to mimic and use by analogy the five Ps of regulating medical products—but in this case, steering the regulation of FemTech and other AI-driven technologies in the following distinct ways—that is, through the following elements: firstly, products (licensing of FemTech, and issuance of marketing authorisations for FemTech); secondly, personnel (authorising or licensing manufacturers, developers, manufacturers, importers, exporters, distributors, etc. of FemTech); thirdly, premises (encompassing standards, quality control, safety and FemTech product liability in the supply chain); fourthly, practices (employing only the highest standards, including standards of care, licensing of specific institutions that may provide FemTech products and services and providing standards of FemTech healthcare provision); and finally, processes (indicating clear and transparent processes to implement, monitor, evaluate, survey, audit and enforce FemTech).

Besides the five specific dimensions, effective stewardship can be encouraged by horizontally looking towards regulation or guidelines that overlap with the health profession and general good practices, specific protocols for healthcare facilities and personnel, and training, education and development of a FemTech stewardship system. For instance, one of the first measures that can be undertaken in the co-creation endeavour concerns education, continuing professional development, and specific targeted education on FemTech and AI-driven technologies for medical and health professionals. Because regulations and legislation is critical to ensure a functional and independent regulatory agency, it would also be helpful to designate a specific FemTech or women's health task force in each national system. Without these bodies, the necessary stewardship actions cannot be undertaken in a coordinated way. In addition, to target the under-representation of women in clinical trials, clinical stewardship based on feminist legal approaches could reflect on questions such as the following:

(i) Are there FemTech stewardship requirements for healthcare providers/hospitals?
(ii) Are there FemTech stewardship requirements for healthcare professionals (physicians/pharmacists/doctors/dentists/nurses/community healthcare workers)?

(iii) Are there rules on record keeping and the submission of information to the competent authority on the use of FemTech?
(iv) Are there specific standards related to the use of FemTech for medical professionals and healthcare workers?
(v) Are there elements on FemTech stewardship that need to be part of the formal education for all medical professionals and healthcare workers?
(vi) Are there specific standards related to training on FemTech or FemTech stewardship?

It would appear that these two aspects to foster effective co-creation are not unattainable, and given adequate political and social will, are reasonable measures that can be implemented to address the proliferation of FemTech in an ethical and responsible manner, vis-à-vis any existing forms of regulations. This necessitates working in complementarity with other existing EU-level regulations or directives that also include the recognition and protection of fundamental rights, although we must also realise practical realities that the EU has functionally restricted competencies to regulate technologies, such as the competence available under Article 114 TFEU in harmonising national technological regulation in the interest of EU market integration.[10] Enabling and fostering genuine co-creation will be a difficult task, especially when the parties interested in such practices are not industry participants or holders of other business interests.

6 Conclusions

In essence, systemic biases in women's healthcare will continue to permeate, unless specific, concentrated, and intentional measures are taken to dismantle the patriarchal model of medicine and healthcare. In concert with the co-creation limbs for effective stewardship of women's healthcare, a joint measure proposed in this chapter is to look towards the creation and advancement of a women's health ecosystem. An ecosystem in the healthcare setting, or of health systems are not new ideas, but their success has rarely been documented due to low implementation of ecosystem models (Pidun et al. 2021). This chapter recommends that a specific women's health ecosystem, and embracing fundamental rights values, intersectionality, and data feminism, can be built on a smaller scale with an identified number of vested stakeholders, using inclusive FemTech as the tool by which assessments can begin. A women's health ecosystem is "the optimal governance model when a high level of modularity (offerings of different players can be flexibly combined) meets a significant need for coordination in order to align stakeholder activities" (Pidun et al. 2021). Besides the clear stakeholders such as healthcare providers, insurers, pharmaceutical companies, policy makers, suppliers, and regulators, the added dimensions of intersectionality and data feminism mean that this women's health ecosystem can also incorporate civil society representative groups, patient groups for under-represented women,

[10] See, in this regard, the Chapter by Varju in this volume.

feminist data scientists and data engineers, bioethicists, and more. A women's health ecosystem could likely advance the proliferation of AI to reduce women's health inequalities, whilst advancing equality, no longer looking towards men's biological bodies as the standard in medicine and healthcare, but consciously and intentionally investing in health or medical AI design, research, technology, deployment, ethics, and use that is fair, unbiased, representative, and equitable.

Beyond this, it is important to recognise and acknowledge that the simplest ways to begin striving for gender equality in medicine and healthcare only requires (at the beginning) education and reorientation. These might include, the inclusion of a higher percentage of women in healthcare and STEM decision making, from research to policy making, to leadership (Hilman 2020). Including critical modules of gender, including new disciplines such as gender medicine (Shai et al. 2021), and studies of other intersectional and historical inequalities as part of the healthcare and medical curriculum is equally impactful. Finally, practising a more dynamic form of informed consent (Rao 2016) in women's healthcare, listening to their voices and needs to eradicate the barriers that cause their societal invisibility, allows co-creation and cooperation that may fully leverage the benefits of AI-driven technologies.

References

Alake R (2020) Algorithm bias in artificial intelligence needs to be discussed (and addressed). Medium. https://towardsdatascience.com/algorithm-bias-in-artificial-intelligence-needs-to-be-discussed-and-addressed-8d369d675a70

Anwar Y (2020) Lack of females in drug dose trials leads to overmedicated women. https://news.berkeley.edu/2020/08/12/lack-of-females-in-drug-dose-trials-leads-to-overmedicated-women/

Basille C, Frydman R, El Aly A, Hesters L, Fanchin R, Tachdjian G, Steffann J, LeLorc'h M, Achour-Frydman N (2009) Preimplantation genetic diagnosis: state of the art. Eur J Obstet Gynecol Reprod Biol 145(1):9–13

BMA: British Medical Association (2021) BMA commentary on mend the gap: the independent review into gender pay gaps in medicine in England. https://www.bma.org.uk/media/3617/bma-commentary-on-medicine-gender-pay-gap-dec-2020.pdf

Brierley R (2019) Gender equality in medicine: change is coming (editorial). The Lancet Gastroenterology & Hepatology 4(12):893. https://doi.org/10.1016/S2468-1253(19)30351-6

CAI: Council of Europe Committee on Artificial Intelligence (2023) Zero draft framework convention on artificial intelligence, human rights, democracy, and the rule of law. https://rm.coe.int/cai-2023-01-revised-zero-draft-framework-convention-public/1680aa193f

CAI: Council of Europe Committee on Artificial Intelligence (2024) Draft framework convention on artificial intelligence, human rights, democracy, and the rule of law. https://search.coe.int/cm/Pages/result_details.aspx?ObjectId=0900001680af0734

Cleghorn E (2021) Unwell women: misdiagnosis and myth in a man-made world. Penguin

Colombo R, Sanguineti V (eds) (2018) Rehabilitation robotics. Academic Press

Copeland R, Mattioli, D, Evans, M (2020) Inside Google's quest for millions of medical records. Wall Str J (11 Jan 2020). https://www.wsj.com/articles/paging-dr-google-how-the-tech-giant-is-laying-claim-to-health-data-11578719700

Crenshaw KW (2013) Close encounters of three kinds: on teaching dominance feminism and intersectionality. Tulsa l. Rev. 46(1):151–189

Deziel S (2016) How medical research has failed women. Chatelaine. https://www.chatelaine.com/health/women-medical-research-bias/
D'Ignazio C, Klein LF (2020) Data feminism. MIT Press
Edwards L (2022) Expert explainer- the EU AI Act: a summary of its significance and scope. https://www.adalovelaceinstitute.org/wp-content/uploads/2022/04/Expert-explainer-The-EU-AI-Act-11-April-2022.pdf
EIGE: European Institute for Gender Equality (2020) Gendered patterns in use of new technologies. Gender equality index 2020. https://eige.europa.eu/publications-resources/toolkits-guides/gender-equality-index-2020-report/gendered-patterns-use-new-technologies?language_content_entity=en
European Commission (2021) Proposal for a regulation laying down harmonised rules on artificial intelligence. COM(2021) 206 final
European Parliament (2023a) Compromise amendments on the draft report proposal for a regulation of the European Parliament and of the council on harmonised rules on artificial intelligence (Artificial Intelligence Act). https://www.europarl.europa.eu/meetdocs/2014_2019/plmrep/COMMITTEES/CJ40/DV/2023/05-11/ConsolidatedCA_IMCOLIBE_AI_ACT_EN.pdf
European Parliament (2023b) AI Act: a step closer to the first rules on artificial intelligence. https://www.europarl.europa.eu/news/en/press-room/20230505IPR84904/ai-act-a-step-closer-to-the-first-rules-on-artificial-intelligence
European Parliament and Council (2016) Regulation (EU) 2016/679 of the European Parliament and of the Council of 27 April 2016 on the protection of natural persons with regard to the processing of personal data and on the free movement of such data, and repealing Directive 95/46/EC (General Data Protection Regulation). OJ L 119, 4.5.2016, pp 1–88
European Parliament and Council (2017a) Regulation (EU) 2017/745 of the European Parliament and of the Council of 5 April 2017 on medical devices. OJ L 117, 5.5.2017, pp 1–175
European Parliament and Council (2017b) Regulation (EU) 2017/746 of the European Parliament and of the Council of 5 April 2017 on in vitro diagnostic medical devices. OJ L 117, 5.5.2017, pp 176–332
FemTech Insider (2023) FemTech: controversial or necessary?. FemTech Insider. https://femtechinsider.com/femtech-controversial-or-necessary/
Forrest J (2019) None of us are free if some of us are not: Catherine D'Ignazio on Data Feminism. Nightingale. https://medium.com/nightingale/catherine-dignazio-on-data-feminism-ce3b3c65f04a
Fosch-Villaronga E, Drukarch H, Khanna P, Verhoef T, Custers B (2022) Accounting for diversity in AI for medicine. Comput Law Secur Rev 47:105735. https://doi.org/10.1016/j.clsr.2022.105735
Fusco F, Marsilio M, Guglielmetti C (2023) Co-creation in healthcare: framing the outcomes and their determinants. J Serv Manag 34(6):1–26
Gerke S, Minssen, T, Cohen, G (2020) Ethical and legal challenges of artificial intelligence-driven healthcare. In: Bohr A, Mermazadeh K (eds) *Artificial intelligence in healthcare.* Academic Press
Hariharan K (2021) How will AI affect gender gaps in health care?. https://www.mmc.com/insights/publications/2021/june/how-will-ai-affect-gender-gaps-in-health-care.html
Healy B (1991) The Yentl syndrome. N Engl J Med 325(4):274–276
Hillman S (2020) Why women are still 'the other' in medicine?. https://warwick.ac.uk/newsandevents/knowledgecentre/health/patient-care/women_in_medicine/
Kushner H (2008) The art of medicine. Medical historians and the history of medicine. Lancet 372(9640), 710–711
Lamb E (2016) Review: weapons of math destruction. https://blogs.scientificamerican.com/roots-of-unity/review-weapons-of-math-destruction/
Lan K W (2012) Technofetishism of posthuman bodies: representations of cyborgs, ghosts, and monsters in contemporary Japanese science fiction film and animation. University of Sussex DPhil Thesis. https://sussex.figshare.com/articles/thesis/Technofetishism_of_posthuman_bodies_representations_of_cyborgs_ghosts_and_monsters_in_contemporary_Japanese_science_fiction_film_and_animation/23387660

Lau AYS, Staccini P (2019) Artificial intelligence in health: new opportunities, challenges, and practical implications. Yearb Med Inform 28(1):174–178

Lau PL, Nandy M, Chakraborty S (2023) Accelerating UN Sustainable Development Goals with AI-driven technologies: a systematic literature review of women's healthcare. Healthcare 11(3):401. https://doi.org/10.3390/healthcare11030401

Lee DH, Yoon SN (2021) Application of artificial intelligence-based technologies in the healthcare industry: opportunities and challenges. Int J Environ Res Public Health 18(1):271. https://doi.org/10.3390/ijerph18010271

Mahler T (2022) Between risk management and proportionality: the risk-based approach in the EU's Artificial Intelligence Act Proposal. Nordic Yearbook of Law and Informatics 2020–2021: Law in the Era of Artificial Intelligence, 247–270. https://doi.org/10.53292/208f5901.38a67238

Mansour K (2020) How femtech is shifting our approach to women's health. Early Metrics. https://earlymetrics.com/rise-of-femtech-womens-health/

Manyika J, Silberg J Presten B (2019) What do wed do about the biases in AI?. Harvard Business Review. https://hbr.org/2019/10/what-do-we-do-about-the-biases-in-ai

Mauvais-Jarvis F, Bairey Merz N, Barnes P J, Brinton R D, Carrero J J, DeMeo D L, De Vries G J, Epperson C N, Govindan R, Klein S L, Lonardo A, Maki P M, McCullough L D, Regitz-Zagrosek V, Regensteiner J G, Rubin J B, Sandberg, K, Suzuki A (2020) Sex and gender: modifiers of health, disease, and medicine. Lancet 396(10250): 565–582. Erratum in Lancet 396(10252): 668

Merone L (2022) Exploring androcentricity in medicine, medical research and education, and the impacts on the experiences of female patients. James Cook University PhD Thesis. https://researchonline.jcu.edu.au/77806/1/JCU_77806_Merone_2022_thesis.pdf

Merone L, Tsey K, Russell D, Nagle C (2022) Sex inequalities in medical research: a systematic scoping review of the literature. Womens Health Rep (New Rochelle), 3(1): 49–59. Erratum in: Womens Health Rep (New Rochelle) 3(1): 344

Müldner T (2002) An algorithm for explaining algorithms. https://www.researchgate.net/publication/228425886_An_Algorithm_for_Explaining_Algorithms#fullTextFileContent

O'Neil C (2016) Weapons of math destruction. Crown Books

Palmieri S, Goffin T (2023) A blanket that leaves the feet cold: exploring the AI act safety framework for medical AI. Eur J Health Law 30(4):406–427

Perkins Gilman C (1911) The man-made world; or, our androcentric culture. Gutenberg

Pidun U, Knust N, Kawohl J, Avramakis E, Klar, A (2021) The untapped potential of ecosystems in health care. https://www.bcg.com/publications/2021/five-principles-of-highly-successful-health-care-ecosystems

Powell J A, Menendian S (2017) The problem of othering: towards inclusiveness and belonging. http://www.otheringandbelonging.org/the-problem-of-othering/

Rajesh A (2021) Ladies, it's not you, modern medicine is made for men. https://www.thequint.com/fit/her-health/gender-gap-in-medicine

Rao R (2016) Informed consent, body property, and self-sovereignty. J Law Med Ethics 44(3):437–444

Samudzi Z (2018) Afro-diasporic feminism and a freedom in fluidity. In J E Udorie (ed), Can we all be feminists?. Penguin

Samuel S (2022) Why it's so damn hard to make AI fair and unbiased?. Vox. https://www.vox.com/future-perfect/22916602/ai-bias-fairness-tradeoffs-artificial-intelligence

Shai A, Koffler S, Hashiloni-Dolev Y (2021) Feminism, gender medicine and beyond: a feminist analysis of "gender medicine." Int J Equity Health. 20(1):177. https://doi.org/10.1186/s12939-021-01511-5

Sidley Austin (2022) Proposal for EU artificial intelligence act passes next level—where do we stand and what's next?. https://www.sidley.com/en/insights/newsupdates/2022/12/proposal-for-eu-artificial-intelligence-act-passes-next-level

Smith G, Rustagi I (2021) When good algorithms go sexist: why and how to advance AI gender equity. Stanford Social Innovation Review. https://doi.org/10.48558/a179-b138

United Nations (2023) DigitALL: innovation and technology for gender equality—UN observance of International Women's Day 2023. https://media.un.org/en/asset/k1m/k1mpovmzy5

UN Women (2023) In Focus: International Women's Day (UN Women—Headquarters, 1 March 2023). https://www.unwomen.org/en/news-stories/in-focus/2023/03/in-focus-international-womens-day

van Oirschot J, Ooms G (2022) Interpreting the EU Artificial Intelligence Act for the health sector. https://haiweb.org/wp-content/uploads/2022/02/Interpreting-the-EU-Artificial-Intelligence-Act-for-the-Health-Sector.pdf

van Kolfschooten H (2023) The Council of Europe's artificial intelligence convention: implications for health and patients. https://blog.petrieflom.law.harvard.edu/2023/04/18/council-of-europe-artificial-intelligence-convention/

Whelchel RJ (1986) Is technology neutral? IEEE Technol Soc Mag 5(4):3–8

Westervelt A (2015) The medical research gender gap: how excluding women from clinical trials is hurting our health. The Guardian. https://www.theguardian.com/lifeandstyle/2015/apr/30/fda-clinical-trials-gender-gap-epa-nih-institute-of-medicine-cardiovascular-disease.

WHO: World Health Organization (1999) National drug regulatory legislation: guiding principles for small drug regulatory authorities. Technical Report Series, No. 885

World Bank (2023) International Women's Day 2023: accelerating equality and empowerment. https://www.worldbank.org/en/topic/gender/brief/international-women-s-day-2023-accelerating-equality-and-empowerment

Young K, Fisher J, Kirkman M (2019) "Do mad people get endo or does endo make you mad?": clinicians' discursive constructions of medicine and women with endometriosis. Fem Psychol 29(3):337–356

Zucker I, Prendergast BJ (2020) Sex differences in pharmacokinetics predict adverse drug reactions in women. Biol Sex Differ 11(1):32. https://doi.org/10.1186/s13293-020-00308-5

Copyright Evaluation for Content Generated by Artificial Intelligence

Anikó Grad-Gyenge

Abstract In this chapter, we aim to establish that neither the current applicability, nor the future extensibility of copyright should be completely discarded in certain, well-defined cases regarding the results produced by AI. Certain aspects of the results produced by AI are already subject to copyright. At the same time, however, to enforce well-defined social interests, bringing additional sub-areas under the scope of legislation would not be without significance. Since in some situations the operation of AI may lead to serious disruptions in the functioning of the copyright markets (if it has not already done so, it may have been overlooked), it is necessary to consider the possibilities for a balanced protection of interests in situations in which AI products are competing in the market with works created by humans. To this end, extending copyright legislation and at least assessing the situations in which the results of AI compete with human creations should not be summarily discarded. A ban would not be effective. Further development of the copyright toolbox, including the creation of a new related right, could be a powerful way to strike a balance between the interests of the author and those of the AI developer and user. The chapter examines several aspects of the relationship between copyright and AI, with a particular focus on the introduction of a possible neighbouring right, which would be owned by the person using AI and would exist in respect of certain results produced with AI.

1 Introduction

Supplementing and replacing human creativity by artificial intelligence (AI) is not an event in the distant future. It is part of our immediate reality. Publishing some of the articles and news available on news-generating websites no longer requires

---

A. Grad-Gyenge (✉)
Faculty of Economic and Social Sciences, Budapest University of Technology and Economics, Budapest, Hungary
e-mail: grad-gyenge.aniko@gtk.bme.hu

M. Varju and K. Mezei (eds.), *The Challenges of Artificial Intelligence for Law in Europe*, Data Science, Machine Intelligence, and Law 6,
https://doi.org/10.1007/978-3-031-86813-9_12

human input. Writing editorials (at least the texts that appear to be so) or even poems[1] by AI is no longer impossible.[2] Critical reports on the outcome of both composing and performing with AI can be read both in classical and popular music news.[3] AI is also gaining more and more ground in many other creative fields (Hart 2020). Moreover, a very significant proportion of these services are freely available, so their development is extremely fast, and their reach is growing rapidly.[4]

The relationship between AI and copyright has recently been the subject of several studies, also cited below. Strategy documents have been drafted by national strategy making platforms[5] and in the European Union's legislative bodies and their advisory think-tanks.[6] The dominant approach is that results generated by AI are largely outside the scope of copyright law, and consequently they cannot be brought under the scope of such laws. However, several aspects need to be considered: in particular, the ownership of AI, the identity of the author, the appropriate remuneration, as well as questions related to potential market concentration/extension of any monopoly arising.[7]

The primary argument against copyright protection is that AI itself cannot be encouraged to create new works by granting copyright protection to the results it creates. Another important argument is that the protection criteria that a work must meet cannot be identified in relation to the results produced by AI (Mezei 2023).

In this chapter we aim to establish that—essentially in agreement with the above—neither the current applicability nor the future extensibility of copyright should be completely discarded in certain, well-defined cases regarding the results produced by AI. Certain aspects of the results produced by AI are already subject to copyright. These include, for example, the various activities of text or data mining and the free uses that have recently been incorporated into EU law and national legislations in connection with them. This study does not deal with the question of whether the software or data set/database underlying the operation of AI may themselves be subject to copyright or related rights protection. In our understanding, this issue is not currently at the heart of the debate, and their copyright and related rights protection is adequately recognised by the legislation (European Parliament 2020). At the same time, however, to enforce well-defined social interests, bringing additional sub-areas under the scope of legislation would not be without significance.

AI may be relevant to copyright, in part because it endows machines with capabilities like those possessed by humans, such as learning, planning, reasoning, organising, and ultimately—albeit this is still highly contested—autonomous creativity.

---

[1] See Editorial (2020).

[2] See GPT-3 (2020).

[3] AI has created the music for Symphony X based on Beethoven's earlier works: https://www.beethovenx-ai.com/. The pop song Break Free was composed by AI with lyrics written and performed by singer Taryn Southern: https://www.youtube.com/watch?v=XUs6CznN8pw.

[4] See OpenAI's Jukebox: https://openai.com/blog/jukebox/, and Porter (2019).

[5] See, for example, the AI strategy of Hungary (MIK et al. 2020).

[6] See Drexl et al. (2019); Hartmann et al. (2020); European Commission (2022).

[7] European Parliament (2020, para 14).

The AI software enables the machine to sense what is going on around it, solve any problem arising when it is challenged and plan its individual steps in advance (Ződi 2018). A different AI software may not process its environment in the same way and may not get the same results from that processing. This can be of decisive importance in terms of the AI's market success. The AI may not only be able to receive the data, but also to process (interpret) it and react to it, possibly even by revising its previous reactions. This may vary among different AI software programmes. According to the Oxford Dictionary, AI is a computer system that performs tasks usually performed by humans: it can compose and perform music, but it can also record music in a sound recording (not only the mechanical recording itself, but also any necessary mastering of the recording) (Cubert & Bone 2018).

It is also necessary to state in advance that the aim of AI systems is generally not to create works of authorship (or products that appear to be works of authorship). They are usually created to serve a special purpose which traditionally cannot be achieved by the human mind or even with previously used computer tools, or only at much greater expense. Nevertheless, these systems also include those whose primary aim is to produce, through some kind of processing, analysis and 'learning' of existing intellectual outputs, products that may even become replacement products/services in the market for cultural products. The products created by this type of AI system enter the market of cultural products and compete with 'real' works. Examples of such AI algorithms are Google's DeepDream,[8] which creates visual results, or Magenta,[9] which creates musical content, or Sony's Flow Machines AI,[10] which also provides 'assistance' in composing music.[11]

An examination of the copyright aspects is necessary because AI products are already substitutes for human creations in some areas (e.g., music), and in other areas it is only a matter of time before AI products become of sufficient quality to compete with human creations. Today, human perception is not always capable of distinguishing between them. Thus, in our understanding, the question to be addressed is not only whether AI products can be protected at all, but whether copyright (or other) protection today is effective in filtering out non-human products and fulfilling its primary purpose of encouraging human creation. Focusing on this problem, the study looks for answers as to how AI products could be 'pulled closer' to the real works of authorship by means of the copyright law, thus ensuring the proper enforcement of interests, or, alternatively, how to level the playing field for different works so that the spread of AI does not threaten to reduce or eliminate human creation.

It is also necessary to deal with the question of what can happen to products that build heavily (either by learning the style or by learning and incorporating specific

[8] https://deepdreamgenerator.com/#gallery.

[9] https://magenta.tensorflow.org/.

[10] https://www.flow-machines.com/.

[11] European Parliament (2020), Point J ("whereas the development of AI and related technologies raises questions about the protection of innovation itself and the application of IPRs to materials, content or data generated by AI and related technologies, which can be of an industrial or artistic nature and which create various commercial opportunities; whereas in this regard it is important to distinguish between AI-assisted human creations and creations autonomously generated by AI").

pieces of art) on existing, human-made works. In these cases, the moral and material interests of the authors may be harmed at least as much as when a human being imitates their works.[12]

Taking all of this into consideration, this chapter examines the question of whether the general incentive functions of copyright are suitable for the protection of certain results created by AI. If so, who can be the right holder/beneficiary of the existing copyright-like protection of AI produced results? Furthermore, the question of which type of AI-created products may be justifiably considered as suitable for granting copyright-like (supplementary) protection, should also be examined.

2 The Incentive Role of Copyright as an Exclusive Right in Relation to AI Systems

The fundamental principle of the copyright paradigm is that the monopoly it provides is intended to serve, support and encourage the individual as a creator.[13] However, modern copyright laws, regional and international rules also recognise several legal constructions more or less distant from this original goal and which are no longer exclusively intended to motivate the creative person.[14]

Copyright is a legal instrument with a double effect: its primary goal from the beginning has been to provide the creator with material recognition for his or her existing works, while ensuring that he or she has a stable financial basis for future works (Pogácsás 2017). In cases where the copyright (or at least the economic rights as part of it) belongs to a legal entity, the exclusive right and the income from its exercise contribute to ensuring the effective functioning of the legal entity, not of the creator (He 2019).

The requirement of the author's moral recognition is a legislative aim that came later in the development of copyright but has now become an integral part of protection (Sundara Rajan 2012). In this respect, the Anglo-Saxon and continental legal systems offer regulatory solutions with a more characteristically different emphasis.

[12] See Christie's (2018).

[13] According to the preamble of the Hungarian copyright act (Act LXXVI of 1999 on copyright): "Modern copyright law, keeping pace with technological progress, plays a decisive role in encouraging intellectual creation, preserving the values of national and universal culture; it strikes and maintains a balance between the interests of authors and other right holders, and those of users and the general public." See also, on the basic functions of copyright, Lontai et al. (2012) and Grad-Gyenge (2022).

[14] In addition, regional and international rules also take into account the fact that different national regulators grant different rights for different interested non-natural persons to different extents. Here, it is sufficient to think of the Software Directive (European Parliament and Council 2009), which allows EU national legislators to designate the legal entity with an interest in the development of the software as the original copyright owner of the software (see Article 2(1) of the Software Directive). But this may also be supported by the fact that international copyright rules avoid regulating the question of who the original owner of copyright may be, leaving the possibility open for the contracting parties to adopt rules according to their own legal, cultural and economic criteria.

Attribution or integrity protection may also be influenced by whether copyright is primarily thought of as a means of personal expression or as a means of increasing the efficiency of business operations.

Where, and to the extent to which, the copyright does not attach to the person of the author, that is, it is transferable to a certain degree either through legislation or private law contract, the primary legislative objective is to protect the investment of the right holder.

The more technical and functional the creation is, the more all copyright regimes easily allow the transfer of the right (and with it the work). The more the use of the work serves some functional business purpose, the less practical (and ideological) importance the actual creator, the human being behind the work, will have. In the case of software or a database, it is much less important for the audience (or in the case of a functional work, rather the user) who created it than in the case of a painting or a novel (Dreier and Hugenholtz 2006).

Within the context of copyright-related protections, except for the protection for performing artists, the aim of protection has never been personal, creative performance, but rather the legal recognition of the financial and human investment, as well as the organisational effort as an expenditure (Békés 2021).

There are, of course, many ways for someone (whether a legal entity or a natural person) to secure the result of their investment, without necessarily having some kind of monopolistic right. At the same time, there is no doubt that for decades the copyright monopoly has been an attractive means for the legislator in all cases where there is a minimum level of intellectual activity and a need to ensure the creator the income.

It cannot be denied that the prevalence of this approach is leading to the transformation of copyright law into industrial copyright and the erosion of the idealistic layer of the monopoly that was meant to celebrate the creative mind. Nevertheless, development in this direction is not provoked by AI, but has been witnessed since the introduction of copyright (and copyright-related, then related) rights of films, software, and databases. Moreover, in the listed examples, the focus is increasingly less on individual creativity and more on protecting the interests of the person primarily involved in the production.

In the case of products created by AI, similar interests can be identified as in the case of traditional works of authorship. The creator of AI—which is part software and part database—has specific interests which are currently recognised by copyright law. In the case of results created by AI, similarly to technically defined works, it is of great importance which person's business activity the result belongs to, if it belongs anywhere, and whether the legislation can ensure that the products can be linked to these identifiable persons. An important and in some way appreciable consideration may also be whether the interest of other persons operating the AI is stronger and whether any legal protection should be granted to them. The introduction of such means can ensure both fair economic exploitation of the results and the identifiability of these results.

The copyright(-like) protection of products created by AI that compete with copyrighted works can ensure identifiability as a moral (or market safety) expectation, as well as protection against unfair market practices. In particular it may also be in the interest of those for whom the products generated by the AI are created to prevent misuse (exploitation by others). For this reason, in our understanding, copyright protection in this area can provide a sufficient incentive.

3 The Person Entitled to the Result Generated by the AI System

The author or holder of related rights as a point of reference is decisive for legal personality, while the author's identifiability is the key to the exercise of the right (and to the enforcement of the right in the case of civil procedures). If the right holder cannot be identified, copyright cannot be exercised, or only with crutches. Considering the occasional transferability and the length of the protection period, copyright legislation now provides several solutions to allow rights to be exercised even if the author's identity would otherwise not be known (Ballardini et al. 2019).

Of course, there is a difference between who the right is vested in (i.e., who the right holder is) and who the right to exercise the right is vested in (i.e., who can act on behalf of the right holder) (Margoni 2018).

The cases where the two regulatory elements are separated show the purposes for which this may be necessary. The right holder and the exerciser of rights are separated if the creator is a minor under the age of 14 and also if, as an adult, his or her capacity to act is partially or completely restricted. The right holder and the exerciser of the right are different even if the right is exercised in collective management or if the right holder appoints another representative (e.g., agency, lawyer). This is also the case with works of unknown authorship and orphan works. In these cases, the identity of the right holder does not change, but he or she does not exercise his or her rights himself/herself.

The situation is different when the natural person who is the right holder can transfer his or her rights and another person becomes the right holder. In comparison, the inheritance of rights can be considered an intermediate situation. Here, the successor in title finally takes the place of the right holder but differs in person from the actual creator. This also includes the case of works created during the employment relationship, in respect of which the employer is entitled to the existing (property) rights on the created work by virtue of the employment relationship.

Based on the above, it can be concluded that the copyright law has many constructions where the natural person creator is deprived of the right to exercise the rights. So, even if the original purpose of copyright is to encourage the natural person to create, it is not unusual for copyright law to provide that rights do not already exist in favour of a natural person or to separate the right holder from the exerciser of the rights. This is the purpose of the concept of a co-authored work and the definition of its right holder, which is based on certain copyright directives in the EEA countries.[15]

From a legal point of view, it is therefore not inconceivable that the creator of AI, or rather the person in whose interest AI works, becomes the copyright owner of the product that AI produces. This may be justified by the circumstance that the new information/results managed, collected, processed, and produced by AI are usually of a kind that would not be produced in either quantity or quality without the application of AI.

The question may arise as to whether it is necessary to separate the creator of AI software from the owner of the result produced by the software. Considering that the product created by AI is typically no longer in the interests of the creator/creators of the software, it may be considered that the owner of the result produced by the software should be the person for whose benefit AI works. This may either be the creator of AI itself or another person. In the former case, it may happen that the creator of AI enjoys two types of protection, even if protection will not be based on the same performance. (The cumulation of certain forms of protection is already well-known.)

The operation of AI allows the data it processes to be organised into a database, even if this is not strictly necessary, but the software developer does not necessarily acquire the copyrights or the related rights of producer on the database. Based on the above, the protection of the product created by AI does not necessarily have to be understood as an extension of the software developer's existing copyright in the software.

Nevertheless, authorship is still typically associated with the person who contributed creatively to the achievement. In most cases, this will be the user of AI instead of its developer. Furthermore, in the case of commercial AI systems, it is particularly likely that the developer does not wish to share authorship (and liability) with the users of the AI (Hugenholtz et al. 2020).

As long as there is no independent regulation on this issue, there is also a position in the literature that considers the presumption of authorship set out in Article 5 of the Enforcement Directive (European Parliament and Council 2004) to be a suitable means for establishing entitlement for those AI results that are artistic in nature and those that are not. According to the presumption of authorship, the person whose name is indicated as such on the work shall be considered the author until proven otherwise (Arguijo and Gervais 2020). However, in my view, the presumption of authorship may only apply if there is a work at all. It is not possible to apply the presumption of authorship to results that are not known to be works, but only appear to be works.

Identifying the right holder is also closely linked to the content of the entitlement, which is why the identifiability of the right holder will be revisited in the next part.

---

[15] Section 6 of the Hungarian copyright act (Act LXXVI of 1999 on copyright); Article 4(2) of the Database Directive (European Parliament and Council, 1996); Preamble, Recitals (28)-(30), Article 2(1), second sentence, and Articles 2(2) and 3 of the Software Directive (European Parliament and Council 2009; Article 1(3)) and Preamble, Recital (13) of the Term Directive (European Parliament and Council 2006).

4 The Possible Related Rights Protection of the Product Created by AI Systems

It is also necessary to examine whether it is sufficient to provide related rights protection for the result created by AI. When considering AI-generated products, we would not primarily want to assess the extra financial and organisational investment, but the effort that goes into introducing the data into AI and protecting the associated result. An important benefit of such separate protection is that the right holder does not have to share the right with someone else but would leave the copyright protection (of the software or database) intact.

As mentioned in the introduction, I do not address whether AI software can be protected. The analysis focuses on the question of whether the results created by AI can be protected for the benefit of someone in particular. In my view, it is worth addressing the question of whether the results created by AI should be protected in favour of the operator of AI, and whether this protection lies within the field of related rights.

It does not matter whether the human producers of a radio and television organisation create non-individual unoriginal programmes or programme streams, or whether the person using AI creates non-individual unoriginal results. If the producer produces a non-individual unoriginal result, it does not matter whether the producer is human or a machine. However, the financial investment in relation to the producer may justify the monopoly right.

The transferability of rights and the protection of the investor's interests are much easier to manage regarding the holders of related rights achievements which are now widely recognised and applied. To be protected, creators of related rights achievements have traditionally not been required to make the same creative contribution as authors of copyright works (Lauber-Rönsberg & Hetmank 2019).

In the case of performing artists, some literary sources assume that they are entitled to protection only in the case of some individual achievement (an approach which the author of this article can agree with), but no legal basis for this can be found. However, in the case of related right holders who typically operate as legal entities (database producers, phonogram producers, film producers, radio and television organisations and, more recently, publishers of press products), the right is not conferred on the right holders in return for creativity but in return for the financial resources invested and, in some cases, for organisational expenditure. Their connection to copyright varies in extent and content: while in the case of phonogram publishers and film producers, the protected subject matter typically also contains copyrighted works, that is, the sound recording and film typically also contain a copyrighted work (belonging to other right holders), in the case of radio and television organisations, as well as publishers of press products, the protection covers a higher proportion of results that are not protected by copyright at all: not all programmes or press releases are individual and original. And in a much larger percentage of cases, the achievement of the database producer is not protected by copyright at all: the importance of a database producer's independent protection is precisely that it should also apply to databases which are not otherwise considered to be collective works, but which require and result in monopoly protection for the significant effort required to create them.

If the result created by AI is some kind of sound material, phonogram producer protection may be considered, or if the result is an audio-visual material, film producer protection may be considered as well (Hugenholtz et al. 2020), but these related rights protections ultimately honour the organisational and material expenditure rather than the activity carried out by the operator of AI.

It is important to emphasise that this protection can exist alongside the copyright protection of AI software. This originally belongs to the developer of the software and the rights can only be transferred to someone else (e.g., the developer's employer or client). However, if the result produced by AI software is no longer generated from information, data, or works in the possession of the developer of the software, or if the software does not work for his or her benefit, claims may be raised by the person for whose benefit the AI was developed and operated (de Cock Buning 2018).

In summary, it can be said that even if the result produced by AI does not necessarily have to be protected by copyright, the means of related rights may well be applicable to it. The related rights protection may therefore be granted to a person who does not make an individual, original achievement, but who makes that achievement for his or her business or economic interests.

5 Assessment of the Achievements Appearing in the Product Created by AI Systems

The question of whether the result created by the software can be protected by intellectual property rights has been examined for a long time: the implementation of inventive activity by AI has already raised the question of whether the resulting invention can be protected by a patent (Hugenholtz et al. 2021). Copyright case law also provides guidance: for example, the criteria developed by the European Court of Justice in the *Painer* case can contribute to determining whether an individual and original creative activity is taking place. In *Painer*, in distinguishing among the creative phases, it was established that an activity may deserve protection if there is a human contribution to the 'conception' and 'execution' of the work (Hugenholtz et al. 2020).

The impact of the contribution of machines on a work's individual and original character has been examined in the literature (Whitford Committee 1977) for a relatively long time, and in Great Britain there is explicit legislation that answers the question. Accordingly, a work created by a machine must be considered a work not created by a human being, and authorship should be granted to the person who undertook to take the necessary steps to create the work.[16] Although the purpose of the legislation in this case is to determine the right holder in respect of works in which

[16] In Section 178 of the UK Copyright Designs and Patent Act (CDPA), a computer generated work is defined as a work that is generated by a computer such that there is no human author. Under

the software is used as a tool, it is still important to see that in this case also the issue of who should be granted that right is decided on the basis of the interest involved (Maggiore 2018).[17]

Even before the era of computer software, no one denied that being an author does not preclude the use of performance assistants for the implementation/execution of the work. By definition, a performance assistant is a person who does not have an intention of his or her own, does not perform for his or her own purpose or benefit, but performs his or her activities under the direction of the creator. That is why the liability for his or her work is primarily borne by the creator, and the activity itself must be assessed as if it had been carried out by the creator himself/herself. Although the recognition of master-apprentice relationships varies in certain eras and in certain fields of art, it is known that many artists produced pictures and sculptures essentially and ultimately by the hands of their apprentices who worked under the guidance of their 'masters'. In the field of music, this kind of tradition is much poorer, given that the role of the students was more likely to be copying the music, and this practice is not known at all in the field of literature.

The use of material tools during artistic creation was also never excluded as an activity. In this sense, chisels, tape measures, supports used for sculpture, and the design software used for modern architectural planning fall under the same category. The design process has obviously always involved the designer making some elements from previously available pieces, and not always designing the previously available elements himself/herself. There is no need to enter the triad in C major into the composing software either, as it is available as a built-in element.[18] However, this does not preclude the individual and original thought of the creator from being expressed in some other way during the creative process and being reflected in the result.

Generally speaking, therefore, as long as the creator (human) controls the process from beginning to end, regardless of the means he or she uses, the result can be a work of authorship if the process and the result include the individual's original intellectual activity.

A very important element of copyright is the demonstrability of the relationship between the author and the work, i.e., the manifestation in the work of the creator's individual original intellectual activity. The Turing test, which is designed to determine whether a given machine can give answers like a human being, will be of particular importance here. As is well known, the test consists of the assessor asking questions, via a keyboard and monitor, to two test subjects, who are thus neither seen nor heard. One of the two subjects is a human being, while the other is a machine, and both try to convince the interviewer that they are thinking humans. If the interviewer cannot clearly determine which of the two subjects is the machine even after

Section 9(3), authorship of such work is given to the person by whom the arrangements necessary for the creation of the work are undertaken.

[17] See further Hugenholtz et al. (2020).

[18] Furthermore, not only unprotected elements can be 'prefabricated', but also elements that are themselves protected.

five minutes of questioning, the machine has passed the test. Twisting this a bit: if, after five minutes, it cannot be determined whether the given product is a work of authorship or not, i.e., whether a human being is behind it or not, the machine has successfully passed the test. If the machine passes the test, the question is whether the result it creates becomes worthy of copyright protection or not?

In relation to AI, the question arises as to whether the programmer or the legal entity for whose benefit AI works and the self-learning, developing ability of AI, as well as the resulting 'end product' are far from the creator's original ability to influence it, that is, whether loss of control also means loss of eligibility for protection. The looseness of the link may be a reason to deny copyright protection.

There is a well-known view that the results of AI operations cannot be protected due to the so-called 'black box' effect (Hugenholtz et al. 2020). However, creation has not always been a conscious activity in all its elements. Of course, this does not only refer to (often highly successful) works created under the influence of various mind-altering drugs, but also to cases where the intentionality of the creative activity is manifested precisely in the fact that the result is produced with less control or even without control (see improvisation or aleatoric composition). It is not so far from this if the author of the software opens up the possibilities of assembling the building blocks of the given genre and allows the algorithm to vary them according to certain rules, partly by letting go of the creative decision-making process, and partly by leaving these steps to the software. Thanks to this, creating a result using AI can also be a creative process worthy of copyright/related rights recognition.

Finally, it is also important to consider that as the threshold for copyright and related rights protection is now very low, very little intellectual effort may be sufficient to establish copyright protection. Thanks to the development of technology, it is not difficult to produce any visual or audio results today.

The instructions (prompts) the AI user gives to the algorithm is clearly the point in the process at which a creative choice can still be made and, as a result, it can be individual and original. Very often, these instructions (or their order) can be modified and adapted so that the end result indeed produces the desired effect or comes closest to it. This is one way in which it can be considered an effort protectable by related rights.

6 The Involvement of Human Creations Underlying the Product Created by AI Systems

Finally, it should be examined as a separate, extremely important issue whether the copyright of the person whose music, lyrics and/or films serve as the basis for a work produced by AI is affected by this activity and whether it is necessary for him or her to have any claim to these products. Although some authors consider it to be ethically very objectionable for the algorithm taught by their works to create new products based on them, which may be like theirs, it may also be the case that this is done without their knowledge or without it being obvious to an outside observer that their works, in small 'chunks', have also been used as 'feed' for the algorithm.[19]

It is important to assess what the purpose of the AI's activity is in such cases. If the AI operates with the express purpose of 'getting under the skin' of a particular creator, in his or her style, or using elements of his or her works to create previously non-existent works that the public can then enjoy by attributing them to the creator (at a much lower cost than the original works), the issue arising is similar to the long-standing (and already addressed) problem of creating and distributing fake paintings (Miernicki and Ng 2021).

Copyright law does not currently provide a remedy for these situations: in such cases, the use of the author's name may be challenged under the general privacy law on names. Furthermore, if elements of the author's genuinely existing works are used which are protected in their own right, action may be taken against their use, for example for infringement of the rules on quotation, or, if the use exceeds the scope of the quotation, for infringement of the right of reproduction. In these cases, infringement occurs even if the resulting product is not an independent work of authorship. Thus, the infringement is independent of whether the product created by AI is ultimately considered to be a work of authorship or a related rights achievement. In these cases, the lawfulness of the product created by AI can be ensured by obtaining prior permission to attribute the name of the original author and to use the individual parts.

Although arguments can be found in the literature that opt-out rather than opt-in would be the practical solution in such cases, copyright law, apart from the possibility of opting out of free use of text and data mining for commercial purposes, does not generally support this. Furthermore, there are already developments for authors to be able to exercise their licensing rights.[20]

The applicability of the text and data mining exception introduced when the CDSM directive was transposed into the Copyright Act is questionable in several respects.[21] Free use only allows the reproduction of works, which means that if there is no reproduction (or other use), it cannot be understood under the copyright rules, and also, if there is other use, free use does not apply. What is/may be significant here is that legal protection extends not only to the whole work but also to a part of it sufficient to recognise the authorship, and that the dismemberment of a work and its 'assembly' as the final step is not an obstacle to establishing use, as the CJEU decision classifying torrent file sharing has established.[22]

---

[19] See Mastrangelo (2023).

[20] For an example, see https://haveibeentrained.com/, on which the data that feeds AIs can be browsed by searching for any term.

[21] Section 35/A(1) of the Hungarian copyright act (Act LXXVI of 1999 on copyright): "Free use is the reproduction necessary for text and data mining covering works, if (a) the work concerned by the use has been lawfully accessed, (b) the right holder has not objected to the free use in advance, in an appropriate manner—in the case of content made publicly available electronically—in a machine-readable form, and (c) the copies necessary for text and data mining are kept only for the time necessary for the purpose of text and data mining.".

[22] Case C-597/19 *Mircom* EU:C:2021:492.

It is clear that the free use cannot be lawful if the author has not given his or her prior consent and the reproduction of the data does not fall under the scope of free use. However, the question of whether, when AI learns the data, there is reproduction or other copyright relevant use, is something that should be carefully examined. The legal availability of freely available works online requires special consideration. Their simple reproduction on other platforms is not permitted and making them available by linking them to other platforms does not fall within the scope of relevant free use, since it is at most a case of making them available for downloading.

Furthermore, the above-mentioned exception only allows reproduction as free use, it does not allow the dissemination of the result of the reproduction to the public, or any adaptation that goes beyond reproduction.

Unfortunately, the text of free use only excludes works from commercial 'learning' (where teaching the AI can be considered reproduction at all) if the right holder has not objected to such use in advance. However, it is arguable whether, if the author only becomes aware of the activity after a work is fed into AI, he or she can still act or object on this basis. It may be a question whether the legislator had previously considered this at all. If so, it may seem that the free flow of data has taken precedence over copyright interests (European Parliamentary Research Service 2020).

The situation is different when AI creates products that are not otherwise composed of elements of the creator's previous works (protected or not protected), but the machine masters the compositional methods or authorial style based on earlier works and creates new products using that authorial or compositional method. The style is not protected by copyright: the protection extends to the specific works formulated in the given style. It cannot be disputed that the individual and original nature of the work is, of course, partly due to the style, so that if specific solutions can be identified in it, certain elements of the style may be protected. In such a case, however, there is a chance that the identification and application of the style also provides a basis for asserting a copyright claim. However, in the case of imitating the style itself, one can only rely on the developers allowing opt-out, on ethical grounds, or in some cases feeding the algorithm with works of consenting authors (opt-in).

As a result, the use of an author's works as 'learning data' by AI to create new works is still subject to numerous prohibitions. Nevertheless, if the AI operates for the benefit of a person independent of the author of the original works and his or her contribution to the operation of AI is worthy of the related rights protection as described above, his/her rights can be expected to be enforced in accordance with the interests of the right holders of the original works.

7 Conclusions

AI is a general technology that has an impact on our lives in countless areas. Only a small fraction of this is now clearly visible in its impact on the copyright system. Many of the problems can be addressed under existing legislation. However, several problems remain to be solved. Since in some situations the operation of AI may lead to serious disruptions in the functioning of the copyright markets (if it has not already done so, it may have been overlooked), it is necessary to consider the possibilities for a balanced protection of interests in situations in which AI products are competing in the market with works created by humans. To this end, extending copyright legislation and at least assessing the situations in which the results of AI compete with human creations should not be summarily discarded. A ban would not be effective. Further development of the copyright toolbox, including the creation of a new related right, could be a powerful way to strike a balance between the interests of the author and those of the AI developer and user.

References

Arguijo VR, Gervais D (2020) Study on trends and developments in artificial intelligence: challenges to the IPR framework. https://ipkitten.blogspot.com/2020/12/guest-post-study-on-trends-and.html

Ballardini RM, He K, Roos T (2019) AI-generated content: authorship and inventorship in the age of artificial intelligence. In: Pihlajarinne T, Vesala J, Honkkila O (eds) Online distribution of content in the EU. Elgar

Békés G (2021) Az előadóművész. Iparjogvédelmi És Szerzői Jogi Szemle 126(3):7–39

Christie's (2018) Is artificial intelligence set to become art's new medium? https://www.christies.com/features/A-collaboration-between-two-artists-one-human-one-a-machine-9332-1.aspx

Cubert JA, Bone RGA (2018) The law of intellectual property created by artificial intelligence. In: Barfield W, Pagallo U (eds) Research handbook on the law of artificial intelligence. Elgar

de Cock Buning M (2018) Artificial intelligence and the creative industry: new challenges for the EU paradigm for art and technology by autonomous creation. In: Barfield W, Pagallo U (eds) Research handbook on the law of artificial intelligence. Elgar

Dreier T Hugenholtz PB (2006) Concise European copyright law. Kluwer Law International

Drexl J, Hilty R, Beneke F, Desaunettes-Barbero L, Finck M, Globocnik J, Gonzalez Otero B, Hoffmann J, Hollander L, Kim D, Richter H, Scheuerer S, Slowinski PR, Thonemann J (2019) Technical aspects of artificial intelligence: an understanding from an intellectual property law perspective. Max Planck Institute for Innovation & Competition Research Paper No. 19-13. https://doi.org/10.2139/ssrn.3465577

Editorial (2020) Interesting novels written by AI. https://medium.com/the-research-nest/interesting-novels-written-by-artificial-intelligence-d407e330fe07

European Commission (2022) Study on copyright and new technologies—copyright data management and artificial intelligence. https://data.europa.eu/doi/10.2759/570559

European Parliament (2020) Intellectual property rights for the development of artificial intelligence technologies. P9_TA(2020)0277

European Parliamentary Research Service (2020) STOA opinions brief. The impact of the General Data Protection Regulation (GDPR) on artificial intelligence. https://www.europarl.europa.eu/RegData/etudes/STUD/2020/641530/EPRS_STU(2020)641530(ANN1)_EN.pdf

European Parliament and Council (1996) Directive 96/9/EC of the European parliament and of the council of 11 March 1996 on the legal protection of databases, OJ L 77, 27.3.1996, pp 20–28

European Parliament and Council (2004) Directive 2004/48/EC of the European Parliament and of the Council of 29 April 2004 on the enforcement of intellectual property rights, OJ L 157, 30.4.2004, pp 45–86

European Parliament and Council (2006) Directive 2006/116/EC of the European parliament and of the council of 12 December 2006 on the term of protection of copyright and certain related rights, OJ L 372, 27.12.2006, pp 12–18

European Parliament and Council (2009) Directive 2009/24/EC of the European parliament and of the council of 23 April 2009 on the legal protection of computer programs, OJ L 111, 5.5.2009, pp 16–22
GPT-3 (2020) A robot wrote this entire article. Are you scared yet, human? https://www.theguardian.com/commentisfree/2020/sep/08/robot-wrote-this-article-gpt-3
Grad-Gyenge A (2022) Egy modern szerzői jog. MTMI
Hart M (2020) Google AI helps you write poetry like Poe. https://nerdist.com/article/google-ai-writes-poetry-like-legendary-poets/
Hartmann C, Allan J, Hugenholtz PB, Quintais JP, Gervais D (2020) Study on trends and developments in artificial intelligence—challenges to the IPR framework. https://data.europa.eu/doi/10.2759/683128
He T (2019) The sentimental fools and the fictitious authors: rethinking the copyright issues of AI-generated contents in China. Asia Pacific Law Review 27(2):218–238
Hugenholtz PB, Quintais JP, Gervais D (2020) Trends and developments in artificial intelligence: challenges to copyright. http://copyrightblog.kluweriplaw.com/2020/12/16/trends-and-developments-in-artificial-intelligence-challenges-to-copyright/?_ga=2.37878945.322916481.1647679777-2782912.1647679777
Hugenholtz PB, Quintais JP, Gervais D (2021) Trends and developments in artificial intelligence: challenges to patent law. http://patentblog.kluweriplaw.com/2021/01/27/trends-and-developments-in-artificial-intelligence-challenges-to-patent-law/
Lauber-Rönsberg A, Hetmank S (2019) The concept of authorship and inventorship under pressure: does artificial intelligence shift paradigms? J Intellect Prop Law & Pract 14(7):570–579
Lontai E, Faludi G, Gyertyánfy P, Vékás G (2012) Magyar polgári jog. Szerzői jog és iparjogvédelem. Eötvös Kiadó
Maggiore M (2018) Artificial intelligence, computer generated works and copyright. In: Bonadio E, Lucchi N (eds) Non-conventional copyright. Do new and atypical works deserve protection? Elgar
Margoni T (2018) Artificial intelligence, machine learning and EU copyright law: who owns AI? Create working paper 2018/12. https://doi.org/10.2139/ssrn.3299523
Mastrangelo D (2023) Getty sues AI art company in US over alleged copyright violations. https://finance.yahoo.com/news/getty-sues-ai-art-company-194457221.html?guccounter=1&guce_referrer=aHR0cHM6Ly93d3cuZ29vZ2xlLmNvbS8&guce_referrer_sig=AQAAAJAQCoxWCabBwIzR5NUmI9I3kuihgeF9oW0brcKqsaWu1pqI-xZmXKmKnBFE2f0c2fEYTIp2F0t_Zp4eFzzNEOCZs8wgxeMlry
Mezei P (2023) You ain't seen nothing yet—arguments against the protectability of AI-generated outputs by copyright law. In: Borghi M, Brownsword R (eds) Law, regulation and governance in the information society. Routledge
Miernicki M, Ng I (2021) Artificial intelligence and moral rights. AI & Soc 36:319–329
MIK: Mesterséges Intelligencia Koalíció, Digitális Jólét Program, Innovációs és Technológiai Minisztérium (2020) Magyarország mesterséges intelligencia stratégiája 2020 (Hungary's artificial intelligence strategy 2020). https://ai-hungary.com/api/v1/companies/15/files/137203/view
Pogácsás, A (2017) *Különbözőség az egységben*. PPKE.
Porter J (2019) 1000000 free AI generated headshots put stock photo companies on notice. https://www.theverge.com/2019/9/20/20875362/100000-fake-ai-photos-stock-photography-royalty-free
Sundara Rajan MT (2012) Moral rights. Principle, practice and new technology. Oxford University Press
Whitford Committee (1977) Whitford Committee on copyright designs and performers protection. Cmnd 6732 HMSO
Ződi Z (2018) Platformok, robotok és a jog. Gondolat

The Data Protection Issues of Smart Contracts as Possible Tools for Automated Decision-Making

Dániel Eszteri

Abstract In this chapter, some of the essential regulations of the European Union's (EU) data protection law will be presented that can be applied to 'smart contracts' which are automated applications embedded into blockchain technology. Smart contracts are automatically fulfilled if their previously specified contractual conditions are met; therefore, the contract is unbreachable. The fulfilment, security and inviolability of the contractual terms are secured by the computer network in which the parties created the contract. The personal data of contracting parties, executed operations and other information relevant in the context of the contractual conditions are recorded and logged in the blockchain in an unchangeable way. The GDPR has special provision for solely automated data processing operations in its Article 22. This chapter intends to test these provisions against automated applications such as smart contracts embedded into blockchain technology. Basically, the commands automatically executed by smart contracts do not have the kind of complexity that can be considered 'automatic decision-making' under the terms of the GDPR. Therefore, the privacy risks they pose do not justify the application of the special provisions in Article 22 in most cases. However, it also possible that automated contracting applications can be backed and optimised by machine learning based AI and these solutions can be suitable to develop robust yet effective automated decision-making systems falling under the special provisions of the EU regulation. Also, following a practical example of smart grids and smart metering, the chapter will attempt to separate the applicability of the rules of data protection law for simple and AI-backed smart contract types.

D. Eszteri (✉)
Hungarian National Authority for Data Protection and Freedom of Information, Budapest, Hungary
e-mail: eszteri.daniel@naih.hu

Artificial Intelligence National Laboratory, HUN-REN Centre for Social Sciences, Budapest, Hungary

M. Varju and K. Mezei (eds.), *The Challenges of Artificial Intelligence for Law in Europe*, Data Science, Machine Intelligence, and Law 6,
https://doi.org/10.1007/978-3-031-86813-9_13

1 Introduction

Blockchain and artificial intelligence (AI) are two fields of technological developments that are being heavily discussed in legal scientific literature nowadays. As of now legal literature tends to examine these topics separate from each other. However, these innovations can be applied jointly and will likely converge more often in the future.

One possible connection between these technologies could be that blockchain provides the infrastructure for data processing and sets up the rules of engagement, while AI automatises and/or optimises processes and rules (Sandner et al. 2020). Data can be collected by 'Internet of Things' (IoT) devices or just simply loaded into the system by the data controller as an already available training database. In this chapter I would like to identify and examine the connections of these apparently remote topics in order to strengthen the discussion on them in terms of the EU's General Data Protection Regulation (GDPR) (European Parliament and Council 2016). In the analysis I take it as a prerequisite that personal data should be processed in the blockchain and take the very practical phenomena of smart contracts—which are automated applications embedded into blockchain—as starting point of the analysis and their possible compliance with EU data protection law.

Smart contracts should not be mistaken with AI in general, however they can be made capable to carry out automated tasks or decisions which can heavily affect the fundamental rights and freedoms of data subjects. Blockchain-based data processing systems equipped with automated contracting applications could pose serious risks to the rights and freedoms of individuals because they could be built around these two quite new and less mature technologies. In the first part of the paper the nature of the two examined technologies will be presented from a data protection point of view, then in the second part, I shall attempt to present the problems stemming from the connection of the technologies.

2 The Nature of Data Processing Based on Blockchain Technology and Smart Contract Applications

2.1 Blockchain as a Network for Data Processing

Blockchain-technology is a representative of the so-called distributed ledger technologies. It has frequently been implemented in real practice during the last decade, mostly in the form of cryptocurrency networks. Distributed ledger is a transactional database which is distributed on a network of several computers; thus, it is not stored in a central place. The term blockchain stems from the attribute of the system that transactions are stored in groups in so-called blocks. The blocks form a chain connected to each other in chronological order (European Central Bank 2017).

Blockchain can be described, in an intentionally simplified way, as a data storing and authenticating system. A prerequisite of this system is a distributed network consisting of computers with no subordination or superiority to each other. Computers connected to the distributed network function as 'nodes' which are also connected with each other. In the end, every node is connected in some way to all of the others. The advantage of this network is that the disconnection of a node does not create any disruption in the system, because their tasks can be taken over by any other node (Győrfi et al. 2019).

Data packages in the blockchain can be suitable to store any type of information, so the technology can be used universally for nearly any kind of data processing purpose.[1]

2.2 *The Block as a Unit for Storing Data*

In networks built on blockchain technology, data is stored in so-called blocks. These blocks can be seen as a blank piece of paper, document or board on which any information can be written (Deloitte Legal 2022).

Depending on the purpose of the given blockchain's creation, blocks as data storing units can store any kind of data and related information. Blocks storing information are connected to each other in a chain-like, subsequently unchangeable way, which means that new blocks containing new data are always being connected to the end of the chain. The first created block at the beginning of the chain is called the 'genesis-block' (Győrfi et al. 2019).

Regarding data processing, there is no actual data transfer between blocks in the blockchain network. This means that the execution of data processing operations with data stored in the blocks occurs in such a way that the network only assigns the 'right of disposal' to the given dataset. Technically speaking, the network assigns the 'digital signature' (via hashing) of users to the stored datasets and in this way decides who will have the right to dispose of, access etc. the given data (NAIH 2017).

The network is built up like a chain and new data is added in newly created blocks which constitute the ever-growing network of the blockchain. The log and hashes of every data processing operation are also stored in the individual blocks alongside the data itself. The summary of transactions results in the so called Merkle-tree (Frankenfield 2021). The history of data processing operations is called the 'block-history'. The algorithmic verification of every single data processing operation with the data stored in the blocks is the task of the computers (the nodes) connected to the network (Kakavand et al. 2017).

During the approval of an operation, the following two elements will be verified by the nodes: Is the operation appropriately signed with the digital signature of the initiating party and does it have any authentic previous history on the blockchain?

[1] For example, blockchain can be used as a good tool for identity management purposes. See Shraddha (2018).

If the nodes (or a predetermined number of them) approve the operation, then it is recorded in the block which will be stored in the chain in an unchangeable way. A further guarantee of credibility is that every single node will download a copy of the blockchain so that they can continuously monitor each other for verification purposes and share the newest copy of the database with each other (Győrfi et al. 2019).

Based on the information above, we can describe blockchain in the simplest way as a data processing technology that enables processing of data on a joint, distributed network which is functional without the existence of any central verification body. The verification of data processing operations on the network is ensured by algorithmic based self-checking mechanisms.

2.3 *Automated Data Processing on the Blockchain by Smart Contract Applications*

It is possible to automatise data processing operations in the blockchain by running algorithms on the network. It was Nick Szabó who described for the first time—using the concept and term 'smart contract' in 1996—the automatisation of data processing operations in a distributed network.

According to Szabó, a smart contract is a contract that is automatically fulfilled if its previously specified conditions are met, therefore making the contract unbreachable. It is primarily built on the 'if–then' logical operation. When the contractual conditions are met, then the fulfilment, security and inviolability of the contractual terms are secured by the computer network in which the parties created it. Therefore, the contracting parties do not need to rely on the assistance of a third party, for example a lawyer, for authentication (Szabó 1996).

Blockchain is a fully viable technology for running smart contract applications: the possibility for users to enter into smart contracts was introduced by the blockchain-technology-based platform, Ethereum (Buterin 2013). In essence, the program running on the network automatically executes a certain, mostly predetermined, decision when the required conditions are met.

In the case of smart contracts, the verification of the operations and the processed data is the task of the network nodes. Verified data can include, for example, the bank account numbers of contracting parties, the amount, relevant dates (e.g., deadlines), other terms, related personal data (e.g., names), and even other textual information (e.g., statements, short messages), all of which can be recorded. Therefore, a smart contract embedded in blockchain is dependent on outside input. Data, executed operations and other information relevant in the context of the contractual conditions are recorded and logged in the blockchain in an unchangeable way (Filatova 2020). According to a more technical perspective, for example, the hash of a file and the owner's name can be stored as pairs in the code to achieve the functionality of proof of ownership. The hash of a file and the block's timestamp can also be stored as pairs to realise the proof of existence function (Xing and Marwala 2018).

The smart contract application runs on every node of the distributed network, so every user can benefit from it and use its functions. The code and algorithm of the smart contract application responsible for automatisation is available, accessible and usable by every participant in the network (Bacon et al. 2017).

Blockchain technology allows individual users to transfer any value (such as money, securities, real estate) to each other via the Internet, or to create any documents, or contracts among themselves—all without the involvement of third parties—confidentially, securely, automated and in near real time. Smart contracts are essentially commands that are automatically executed on the network when the pre-set conditions are met. From the perspective of smart contracts, blockchains can be considered smart contract platforms.

2.4 *Non-Deterministic Smart Contracts and Oracles*

Smart contracts can be separated to two groups: deterministic and non-deterministic smart contracts. A deterministic smart contract is a predetermined digital contract that obtains all the necessary information from the database of the blockchain for which it was developed. The other group of smart contracts is the non-deterministic smart contract type. Unlike the deterministic type, this requires information that appears outside the blockchain and is independent of it. In this case, the user will have to entrust an 'oracle' (third party) that has the information needed for fulfilment.

Thus, a smart contract is non-deterministic if the program's 'if–then' logical operation needs information that does not occur on the blockchain. In this case, it is also necessary to establish a connection that connects the program running on the blockchain with the necessary information that can be found in the outside world. The oracles provide a solution for this, channelling information onto the blockchain through secured channels (Labancz 2018). The oracle is connected to a data source from the outside world, which can contain information about the price of a stock, temperature, etc. (Labancz 2018).

The oracle should be a reliable source of information for non-deterministic contracts whether it is a natural person, a legal person or a database. The data transmitted by the oracles may be interpretable or unquestionable facts. The facts to be interpreted come into play when a smart contract needs information that requires discretion. This may be the case when the fact is not clear and various experts are needed to decide the matter (e.g., determining the extent of insurance in the event of a damages). On the other hand, unquestionable facts do not require a separate interpretation, as they are clear to all parties (Tulsidas 2018).

3 Optimising Smart Contracting on the Blockchain by Machine Learning Techniques

Smart contract applications should not be confused with AI techniques. These relatively simple automatised applications cannot be treated as AI applications on their own, because they do not make individual decisions based on data in the blockchain. The main purpose of smart contracts in most situations is only to automatise and authenticate transactions on the blockchain when certain conditions are met. In most cases, they do not feature a great deal of complexity (Schrepel 2021). In general, smart contracts are not considered AI themselves. However, AI and especially machine learning (ML) can enhance the efficiency of smart contracting applications. In the following, I will attempt to show how this could be possible.

3.1 The General Technological Background of Machine Learning

First, we need to briefly consider the general technological background of AI and ML, so than we can provide a technologically accurate legal analysis of the model of blockchain-based AI and ML. The report of the Norwegian Data Protection Authority[2] describes AI as a system capable of learning based on its own experience and applying the knowledge obtained in different situations to resolve complex problems. AI learns from the personal data it 'sees' (in practice the input data) and makes decisions or 'forecasts' (Datatilsynet 2018). AI, however, serves as an umbrella term, which covers all the procedures when a software programme makes a decision automatically (CNIL 2017). Relative to this, ML is a narrower concept, which constitutes one branch of AI development. The heart of this is that the system generates independent knowledge out of its own experience. Based on data examples and patterns, the system is able to recognise and determine regularities and rules independently or with human assistance and then makes decisions based on the regularities discovered in the acquired knowledge base (EUFRA 2019).

Data processing carried out by an AI system in the course of ML can be divided into three steps. First, a large quantity of data is entered into the system and the algorithm tries to find patterns and similarities in this data set. This data set is called 'training data'. If the algorithm finds identifiable patterns, it will record and save them for subsequent use. After this, the system generates a model on the basis of the recorded and saved patterns. Based on the already identified patterns, with the help of the model, the system is capable of processing data input later. As the second step, the AI system has new data uploaded, which are similar to the data used for training. Then, based on the model, the AI decides which new data are similar to which learned pattern. Finally, the system makes a decision based on the acquired patterns

[2] Datatilsynet.

with the new input data and informs the observer about the decision (Datatilsynet 2018; EUFRA 2019). It is also important to note that the model generated in the course of ML does not necessarily contain the source data, which served as the basis of its learning. In most cases, the AI system generated in the course of ML is able to operate independently of the data that served as the basis of learning (Datatilsynet 2018).

3.2 Blockchain-Based Machine Learning

In the specific technological context of blockchain, running an analyser software which is capable of identifying patterns in the stored data by ML techniques would definitely make the blockchain capable of making decisions automatically. As suggested by literature, blockchain-based data processing can be assisted or enhanced via various AI and ML techniques (Xing and Marwala 2018).

Essentially, there are two ways to run AI applications on the blockchain. The first one is *the blockchain-based machine learning approach:* AI analyses data processing operations carried out by users in the blockchain and tries to identify patterns. In this case blockchain means the storing form and source of the training data. The identified patterns constitute a model which can later be used to produce a decision based on the identified patterns and also to increase system efficiency. In this case, blockchain stored data should serve as input for AI-based data processing.

The second is called *the blockchain-based automated decision-making approach:* These methods entail the process when AI executes data processing operations on the blockchain and tries to optimise decisions at the same time. In this approach decisions made by the AI algorithm should also be logged in the blockchain itself (in fact: in the block-history and Merkle tree). In my opinion, it could also be possible to store a copy of the logs of the decisions in a separate (not necessarily blockchain-based) database as well, but it is not fundamentally necessary for the working mechanisms of such systems.

A collection of projects on applications or software capable of making automated decisions with processed data in the blockchain can be found in recent research papers[3] along with a collection of blockchain-based AI projects (Lopes and Alexandre 2019). According to these studies, blockchain-based automated decision-making applications search for patterns in the database and make decisions based on the identified model.

[3] See, for example, the study by Sankaran et al. (2018) on the concept of blockchain-based profiling for energy management purposes.

3.3 *The Synergy of Blockchain, Smart Contracts and AI: The Practical Example of Smart Grids and Smart Metering*

Having established that blockchain technology is suitable to serve as the basis of an automated decision-making system, we need to consider smart contract applications and how these three technological phenomena (blockchain, AI/ML and smart contracts) can come together. As highlighted in a recent research paper, blockchain and AI can operate together in relatively simple models. For example, in a smart city the network of streetlamps can be considered to constitute a blockchain and every lamp has its own identity (block) on the network. Since all lamps are connected to a blockchain, they will store data about their usage, performance and downtime. AI could analyse and learn from this data and optimise the network's maintenance. For example, the system could automatically suggest a more regular maintenance of more frequently used lamps etc. (Sandner et al. 2020).

We can apply this example to a system based more directly on the processing of personal data. For example, in the opinion of the Article 29 Working Party (WP29), smart grids and smart metering have been already analysed from a data protection point of view (WP29 2013). The antecedent of the opinion was the European Commission's recommendation on preparations for the roll-out of smart metering systems. In the context of the recommendation smart grid means "an upgraded energy network to which two-way digital communication between the supplier and consumer, smart metering and monitoring and control systems have been added."[4] Furthermore, smart metering means "an electronic system that can measure energy consumption, adding more information than a conventional meter, and can transmit and receive data using a form of electronic communication."[5]

Smart meters can actually be considered a digital version of conventional meters, except that smart-meters act as a two-way communication channel between consumers and service providers (e.g., electricity, water, gas). The advantage of smart meters is that they transmit detailed and real-time consumption information to the provider in a simple and direct way. Consumers will receive a very detailed statement of their energy consumption based on real-time quantitative data, which will make their consumption easily optimisable. This recommendation has already drawn much attention to the requirements and enforcement of the principles of 'data protection by design and default' in the context of planning and operation because a huge amount of personal data about consumers will be processed in such systems.[6]

If we apply the above-mentioned hypothetic example (blockchain-based streetlamps) to a smart grid and smart metering system, we can say that individual households could constitute the blocks of the network. They can store data about their consumption of water, gas, electricity etc. and send it in real time to the service providers. On the other hand, AI and ML technologies could also analyse the

[4] European Commission (2012), point 3. (a)-(b).

[5] European Commission (2012), point 3. (a)-(b).

[6] European Commission (2012), point 3. (d)-(e).

consumption data of households and identify 'consumption-patterns' in order to optimise energy distribution between customers. Individual service providers could also share the identified data-processing patterns with each other to synchronise their services for a better service distribution. In such systems, the history of consumption data will be recorded in the blocks (households) as well, and can be tracked back historically. The effectiveness of consumption optimisation by ML can also be followed in the blocks by tracking back consumption details of individual households. This could also make the system more transparent and help to develop further the applied AI and ML techniques for a better functioning smart grid and smart metering system.

On the other hand, smart contract applications can process the billing and service information of households. Smart contracts between consumers and individual service providers can constitute the legal links and represent contractual relations. For example, the smart contract application can follow the optimised, individual consumption data of consumers and issue 'smart bills' or even automatically initiate financial transactions towards the bank account or crypto wallet of the users. If third party data must be gathered to carry out the contractual transactions, oracles can also be set up in the system, for example to take into account means-tested beneficiary discounts for certain users. The recent report prepared for the European Commission and the European Investment Bank also took note that in the energy sector the synergy of these technologies can be used: AI to optimise energy use in buildings and blockchain to share data to across the energy industry to optimise network usage (Verbeek and Lundquist 2021).

4 The Applicability of the GDPR to Smart Contracts and Its Specific Provisions on Automated Decision-Making

4.1 Identifying the Data Controller and the Data Processor in Blockchain Environments

Based on GDPR terminology, a data controller is a person or organisation that determines the purposes and means of data processing, alone or jointly with others.[7] The data controller is the main entity that should be held accountable for personal data processing operations and has to comply with data protection law. Within the blockchain, the identification of data controllers and processors was also addressed in the report of the French Data Protection Authority (CNIL)[8] (2018) and in the resolution of the Hungarian Data Protection Authority (NAIH)[9] (2017).

[7] European Parliament and Council (2016, Article 4(7)).

[8] Commission Nationale de l'Informatique et des Libertés (CNIL).

[9] National Authority for Data Protection and Freedom of Information (NAIH).

According to the CNIL report (2018), in a blockchain-based data processing, a "participant" who has decided to register for the service and thus adds data to the database and then processes it in the network may qualify as a data controller. The CNIL points out that a natural person is considered to be a data controller only if he or she processes data not only for private purposes, but also for professional or business purposes (CNIL 2018). The NAIH's position on the identity of the data controller is largely the same as that of the CNIL. Based on the resolution, each participant that adds blocks and data stored in it to the system is also considered a data controller (NAIH 2017).

The above general statements do not necessarily mean that in a blockchain-based data processing environment, all users whose personal data is processed by the system will also be considered data controllers. This exceptional case can only occur in the case of public, unauthorised blockchains, where anyone is free to add data to the database without prior permission. However, in most cases, it is the organisation centrally operating the blockchain that determines the purposes and means of data processing, specifically, about whom, under what conditions and what data is processed in the system. In these cases, the operator will be considered a data controller based on the concepts of the GDPR. The rules and conditions of data processing in these cases are most often specified by the contractual provisions between the user and the data controller.

In addition to data controllers, the CNIL's report (2018) also deals with the identification of data processors. The GDPR defines a data processor as a person or organisation which processes personal data on behalf of the data controller.[10] In this regard, to identify data processors on the blockchain, CNIL highlights (2018) two cases as examples: the first one is cryptographic authentication of data processing operations, the second is development of applications for concluding and fulfilling smart contracts. In the first case, the operators of the nodes, who carry out the validation of operations ordered by another participant, are considered data processors, since they have not determined the purpose of data processing, but only participate in their validation due to the specificities of the technical regulatory medium. In the second case, during the fulfilment of the smart contract, the scope of the necessary personal data and the purpose of data processing are typically not determined by the application developer. The application developer only designs the tool for the data processing activity but does not decide on the purposes, hence they are considered data processors as well (CNIL 2018).

To use the example given by the CNIL (2018): A software development company develops and operates a smart contract application running on blockchain for an insurance company that automatically refunds the price of flight tickets to passengers if the flight is cancelled or delayed. In this case, the company operating the smart contract application is considered a data processor, and the insurer determining the purpose of data processing is considered a data controller.

[10] European Parliament and Council (2016, Article 4(8)).

The above findings of the authorities describe exactly who can qualify as a data controller and data processor on the blockchain. I note that in the case of a so-called private blockchain, it is easier to identify the data controller, since there the organisation that created it (e.g., the insurer in the example above) determines for what purposes it intends to create the blockchain-based database. The data of the data subjects are typically processed in accordance with the contractual conditions concluded between the data controller and the data subject in the system reserved by the data controller for this purpose.

If an organisation decides to operate a blockchain-based data processing system and to automatise some activities via smart contract applications, we can differentiate between the following two types regarding data controllers and processor. With the first type, the data controller and one of the contracting parties is the same entity: in this case the organisation sets up the blockchain environment on its own, and exclusively decides on the purposes and means of data processing, including the categories of data gathered from potential users. If smart contract applications are embedded into the system, the contracting parties are the organisation (setting up the environment) and the users. In this case we have only one data controller which is exclusively responsible for the system from a data protection point of view. For example, an electricity supplier company operates a blockchain-based smart grid for consumers. Billing and transactions of payment are automatised via smart contract applications. The contracting parties are the electricity supplier company—which is considered the data controller –, and the consumers—who are considered data subjects.

With the second type, the data controller and one of the contracting parties is not necessarily the same entity: in this case we also have an organisation setting up the blockchain environment but it does not decide on the purposes and categories of data stored in the network and processed by smart contract applications. Users can freely decide on and put in data to the blockchain and use smart contract applications for more flexible contracting purposes by their own decisions. In this case, the operator of the blockchain acts as a network service provider and the individual user decides on the purposes and means for data processing. In this case users putting data into the system and entering into various contracts for their own previously decided purposes are considered data controllers and the network provider is acting in most cases as a data processor.

It is also possible to set up more complex, hybrid-like data processing environments using blockchain, where the roles of data controllers, data processors and data subjects can overlap or complement each other regarding various separated operations with personal data. However, for the sake of simplicity and to keep the focus on more common practices, this topic will not be elaborated here further.

4.2 General Rules on Automated Decision-Making in the GDPR

The GDPR (European Parliament and Council 2016) does not define the concept of *automated decision-making*; however, it uses this expression several times in the normative text. According to the relevant guidance of Article 29 Data Protection Working Party (WP29), automated decision-making is a capability of making decisions with the help of technological instruments without human intervention (WP29 2017). That is to say, there is no human involvement in decision-making in the case of exclusively automated decision-making. Pursuant to Article 22(1) of GDPR, "the data subject shall have the right not to be subject to a decision based solely on automated processing, including profiling, which produces legal effects concerning him or her or has similarly significantly impact on him or her." This provision constitutes a general prohibition on decision-making based exclusively on automated data processing. Therefore, as a main rule GDPR sets forth a general prohibition on exclusively automated individual decision-making, which produces legal effects or similarly significant impact (Veale and Edwards 2018).

In order to qualify an activity as human intervention with regard to the decision and therefore establish that the general prohibition of Article 22 should not apply to it, the controller has to ensure that the human review of the decision be of merit and not only a symbolic gesture. It has to be done by a person who has the authority and the competence to alter the decision. In other words, to be exempt from the prohibition, the final decision must be made by a human, or the decision proposed by the algorithm has to be reviewed and approved by them (WP29 2017). Furthermore, the rules applicable to exclusively automated decision-making have to be applied only in cases in which the decision has legal effects or similar significant impact on the natural person. This wording of the regulation makes it clear that Article 22 extends only to effects involving severe consequences (Veale and Edwards 2018). The legal effect requires that the decision should influence the legal rights of a person. A legal effect may be something that will influence the legal standing of a person or his/her rights based on contract. According to WP29, examples of such effects include automated decisions concerning natural persons as a result of which: contracts are terminated, welfare benefits (such as child-related benefits or housing support) guaranteed by law are granted or rejected, entry to a country is refused, citizenship is denied etc. (WP29 2017).

In addition, however, there is the more vaguely worded "similarly significant" impact in Article 22, which is also a circumstance subject to the prohibition. Recital (71) of the GDPR's Preamble may contain some guidance concerning this notion as it lists the following examples: "refusal of an online credit application" or "e-recruiting practices without any human intervention". There are, however, exemptions from this general prohibition set forth in Article 22(2). Accordingly, the prohibition cannot be applied if the decision is: necessary for entering into or performing a contract between the data subject and the data controller; authorised by European Union or Member State law, to which the data controller is subject and which also lays down suitable measures to safeguard the data subject's rights and freedoms and legitimate interests; or based on the data subject's explicit consent (e.g., it was expressed in a written statement provided by the data subject). According to the European Data Protection Board (EDPB) (2020), in a digital or online context it may happen, for instance, that the data subject can issue this statement by completing an electronic form, uploading a scanned document containing his signature or using an electronic signature. It is also possible to gain assurance of the validity of the express consent through the two-step control of the consent (a good example of this is the use of two stage verification).

4.3 Applicability of the GDPR's Rules on Automated Decision-Making to Blockchains and Smart Contracts

Based on the earlier discussion, where personal data is processed in the blockchain for automatic decision-making purposes, the controller must comply with the above requirements of the GDPR, as well. Of course, it will always be the data processed, the specific purpose of the processing and its impact on the data subject that determines whether the rules of Article 22 apply or not. If so, data processing using automated decision-making is only possible on the blockchain if the controller can demonstrate the legitimate use of the exceptions above.

If we look at smart contract applications running on blockchain we can say that they are capable of executing commands automatically that can have legal effects on the data subjects because these automations influence the fulfilment of a contact. These automated actions are based on the personal data of users processed in the distributed network. However, in most cases the decision behind the application's working mechanisms is not based solely on automated data processing. The decision which has a legal effect was already made by the contracting parties (usually natural or legal persons), immediately before entering data into the system. The smart contract applications only automatically executes this (human) decision and in this way makes the contractual will of the parties fulfilled and the contract itself unbreacheable. In my opinion, in this case the decision influencing the data subject's rights is not made by the system; it only executes the decision of the contracting parties by automated actions. So, in general, we should differentiate between automated decisions and automated actions of a system.

Only more complex smart contract systems with solely automated individual decision-making behind the contractual actions or terms fall under Article 22 of the GDPR. This can be the case if we take the hypothetical example of blockchain-based smart metering from Sect. 2.3 of this chapter. Arguably, such data processing falls under the ruling of Article 22, because one of the essential parts of the contract, namely the quantity and pricing of resources, is based on a ML optimised network. These decisions regarding one of the contract's essential terms influence the legal rights of persons (e.g., the right to electricity supply). Moreover, the processing is based on a contract between the data subject (customer) and the data controller (e.g., the electricity service provider). Furthermore, smart contract applications automatically process and execute payments in the system, without any direct human intervention. Therefore, the data controller setting up such complex systems must comply with these provisions of the GDPR and should be capable of demonstrating that one of the exceptional legal bases listed in Article 22(2) applies.

Dynamic pricing systems can constitute another example. In these cases, the consumer accepts the purchase price automatically calculated through dynamic pricing based on his/her personal preferences (Brkan 2019). Here, the decision made on the basis of personal data (the calculation of the price based on the profile of the data subject) is made and is available well before it is accepted. The dynamically calculated price is based solely on automated data processing and also influences the essential terms (the price) of the future contract between the data subject (in this case the consumer) and the data controller (the provider of the service or product) so Article 22 should be applied. Such systems can be even developed using smart contract applications.

4.4 Informing the Data Subjects About Automated Decision-Making

The GDPR requires the controller to provide information in relation to decision-making based exclusively on automated personal data processing which has legal effects or similarly significant effects on the data subject. The regulation includes profiling based on such data processing in this category.[11] Under this, the following three items of information must be communicated with the data subjects: they must be informed of the fact of such data processing; they must be given meaningful information on the logic applied; and they must be informed of the significance of data processing and its expected consequences for the data subject.[12] The communication of the fact that automated individual decision-making is taking place suffices if the controller provides meaningful information about it. It is important that the data subject must also be aware if automated individual decision-making also implies profiling.

The mode of providing information on the logic applied raises a number of issues. This may be a substantial challenge for the controller in the case of ML methods as they are frequently based on exceedingly complex data processing processes that are very difficult to review. According to the GDPR, controllers must provide "meaningful information" on the logic applied, using clear and plain language. If a controller communicates only in general that, for instance, it is operating a system based on a neural network, this may not be sufficient in itself as the data subject will have little meaningful understanding of what is happening with his personal data in the course

[11] European Parliament and Council (2016, Article 15(1)(h)).

[12] European Parliament and Council (2016, Article 13(2)(f)).

of processing. The requirement of meaningful information does not necessarily mean that the controller should provide complicated explanations on the algorithm applied or present the algorithm in full. A detailed presentation of the technology would, in most cases, decrease the comprehensibility of the information and impede its reception (Péterfalvi et al. 2021). In addition, the GDPR itself declares that information on the logic applied does not affect business secrets or intellectual property, including the copyright guaranteeing the protection of the software.[13] Naturally, the complexity of the technology cannot be an excuse for completely avoiding the provision of information.

Regarding smart contract applications running on the blockchain, providing meaningful information about their logical operation should not be a difficult task in my opinion. In most cases, smart contract applications only execute quite simple automated commands in order to fulfil or terminate a contract and do not necessarily include more complex—for example, ML-based—data processing operations. The logic behind these simpler ('if–then') decisions can be communicated easily to the data subject with graphical illustrations or figures. It should be mentioned here again that in most cases, operation of simpler smart contract applications does not even fall under the rules of Article 22 of the GDPR because the decision affecting the rights of individuals was not based solely on automated means of processing, as was indicated in Sect. 3.3.

In more complex, ML-based systems, it was already recommended by the literature that the controller could provide an opportunity for the data subject to learn the operation of data processing by a public test system and by filling in fictional data. The reason for this is that most of the time data subjects are not really interested in how the logic operates, they are much more interested in how they themselves can improve the result established by the algorithm (Wachter et al. 2018). Making a test system accessible is a good solution not only for the applied logic, but also for demonstrating the effects on and significance for the data subject.

4.5 Requesting Human Intervention Against Automated Decisions

Pursuant to the GDPR provisions, the controller is under an obligation to enable the data subject to request human intervention in relation to the automated individual decision-making affecting him. This opportunity must be provided by the data controller.[14] That is to say, in this case human review of the course of the decision-making must be enabled as well as the amendment of the decision in the given case in order to eliminate eventual defective conclusions and errors. The data subject is entitled to express his position concerning the decision and to object to it

[13] European Parliament and Council (2016), Preamble, Recital (63).

[14] European Parliament and Council (2016, Article 22(3)).

in order to find a remedy to the erroneous decision affecting him (Péterfalvi et al. 2021).

The WP29 guidance underlines that human intervention must be carried out by a person who has the appropriate authority and capability to change the decision. The reviewer has to examine thoroughly all the relevant data, including any additional information made available by the data subject. One of the purposes of the human review of the decision-making may be that the data subjects should not be exposed to detrimental discrimination (Péterfalvi et al. 2021; WP29 2017). The guidance recommends the incorporation of periodic auditing algorithms as a general practical solution in relation to the prohibition of detrimental discrimination, although unfortunately it does not provide a specific example (Veale and Edwards 2018).

In my view, when exercising the request for human intervention, the review of the decision-making mechanisms should be approached from the viewpoint of the effect on the data subject. The person designated to carry out human intervention must examine exactly what data were included in the decision-making and what decision was made; this would then have to be compared to the objections submitted by the data subject. In such a case there is no need, necessarily, for the thorough exploration and understanding of the algorithmic process behind the decision. A person authorised to review would not really have a genuine opportunity for this in most cases, because mathematical, algorithmic operations carried out by AI on the data cannot be followed by a human observer beyond a certain level (Datatilsynet 2018). But the person authorised to review should consider first and foremost whether the decision would have the same result if it was not made by an algorithm.

Regarding smart contract applications, it is also important to highlight that human intervention should be granted only if the decision behind the contract affecting the rights of individuals is based solely on automated means of data processing. In most cases, the decision on the terms and nature of the contract was already set up by the contracting parties so the applications only automatically executes these terms. If the terms of the contract are set up solely by automated means based on personal data, or an essential part of the contract that has legal or similarly significant effect was influenced solely by automated decision-making based on personal data, then human intervention should be also provided to review these decisions.

5 Conclusions

We have seen that smart contracts are good solutions to efficiently automatise and also secure contractual agreements because the fulfilment, security and inviolability of the terms are secured by the computer network in which the parties created the contract. Blockchain, which usually serves as the technical background and platform for smart contract applications, is a data processing environment that uses a distributed network structure to ensure a high level of data security and manage distributed resources efficiently. This data processing environment can be made suitable to constitute the basis of smart contracting. It is important to highlight that most of the time smart contract applications are not on such a level of complexity that we can call them AI solutions at the same time. In most cases, smart contracts do not make individual decisions based on data in the blockchain; their main purpose is only to automatise and authenticate predetermined transactions on the blockchain when certain conditions met. However, we have also seen that it is possible to develop automated decision-making systems that can make decisions quickly and efficiently using patterns learned from personal data stored in the blockchain.

The two solutions—namely smart contracting and ML—can be mixed in order to develop robust and complex blockchain-based automatic contracting systems that can have serious impacts on the users'/consumers' rights. When we talk about these complex AI systems, data protection compliance is a key issue because of the very serious privacy risks posed by them to individuals and their personal data which is processed in the system. When these conditions meet, the applicability of Article 22 of the GDPR should be tested for data protection compliance under EU law. We can say that it should be ensured that the system operates in a transparent and accessible manner, where information on the logic used is one of the key elements. All in all, it can be said that from a general regulatory perspective the issue of AI and data-driven automated decision-making is still in its infancy; however, the concrete regulatory concepts developed in the recent period seem to be forward-looking. The key issue for the coming years will be the practical applicability and the efficiency of the regulation. From the perspective of data protection professionals, it is essential that developments occur not only in the technological domain, but also in regulation and legal practice.

References

Bacon J, Michels JD, Millard C, Singh J (2017) Blockchain demystified. Queen Mary school of law legal studies research paper No. 268/2017. https://papers.ssrn.com/sol3/papers.cfm?abstract_id=3091218

Brkan M (2019) Do algorithms rule the world? Algorithmic decision-making in the framework of the GDPR and beyond. Int J Law Inf Technol 27(2):91–121

Buterin V (2013) A next-generation smart contract and decentralized application platform. https://ethereum.org/en/whitepaper

CNIL: Commission nationale de l'informatique et des libertés (2017) How can humans keep the upper hand? The ethical matters raised by algorithms and artificial intelligence. https://www.cnil.fr/sites/default/files/atoms/files/cnil_rapport_ai_gb_web.pdf

CNIL: Commission nationale de l'informatique et des libertés (2018) Blockchain and the GDPR: solutions for a responsible use of the blockchain in the context of personal data. https://www.cnil.fr/sites/default/files/atoms/files/blockchain_en.pdf

Datatilsynet (2018) Artificial intelligence and privacy. https://www.datatilsynet.no/globalassets/global/english/ai-and-privacy.pdf

Deloitte Legal (2022) Blockchain: legal implications, questions, opportunities and risks. https://www.deloitte.com/content/dam/assets-shared/legacy/docs/dttl-tax-global-blockchain-wp-sept-20221.pdf

EDPB: European Data Protection Board (2020) Guidelines on consent under Regulation (EU) 2016/679. https://edpb.europa.eu/sites/edpb/files/files/file1/edpb_guidelines_202005_consent_en.pdf
EUFRA: European Union Agency for Fundamental Rights (2019) Data quality and artificial intelligence—mitigating bias and error to protect fundamental rights. https://fra.europa.eu/sites/default/files/fra_uploads/fra-2019-data-quality-and-ai_en.pdf
European Central Bank (2017) How could new technology transform financial markets? www.ecb.europa.eu/explainers/tell-me-more/html/distributed_ledger_technology.en.html
European Commission (2012) Recommendation on preparations for the roll-out of smart metering systems (2012/148/EU). https://eur-lex.europa.eu/legal-content/EN/TXT/HTML/?uri=CELEX:32012H0148&
European Parliament and Council (2016) Regulation (EU) 2016/679 of the European parliament and of the council of 27 April 2016 on the protection of natural persons with regard to the processing of personal data and on the free movement of such data, and repealing directive 95/46/EC (general data protection regulation), OJ L 119, 4.5.2016, pp 1–88
Filatova N (2020) Smart contracts from the contract law perspective: outlining new regulative strategies. Int J Law Inf Technol 28(3):217–242
Frankenfield J (2021) Merkle Root (Cryptocurrency). https://www.investopedia.com/terms/m/merkle-root-cryptocurrency.asp
Győrfi A, Léderer A, Paluska F, Pataki G Trinh AT (2019) Kriptopénz ABC. HVG
Kakavand H, Kost De Sevres N, Chilton B (2017) The blockchain revolution: an analysis of regulation and technology related to distributed ledger technologies. https://papers.ssrn.com/sol3/papers.cfm?abstract_id=2849251
Labancz A (2018) Innováció a szerződéses jogban: smart contract. In: Gellén K (ed) Gazdasági tendenciák és jogi kihívások a 21. században. Iurisperitus
Lopes V, Alexandre LA (2019) An overview of blockchain integration with robotics and artificial intelligence. Proceedings of the first symposium on blockchain and robotics, MIT Media Lab, Cambridge, MA, USA. https://doi.org/10.5195/ledger.2019.171
NAIH: Hungarian National Authority for Data Protection and Freedom of Information (2017) Opinion on blockchain technology in the context of data protection. https://naih.hu/data-protection/decisions
Péterfalvi A, Révész B, Buzás P (eds) (2021) Magyarázat a GDPR-ról. Wolters Kluwer
Sandner P, Gross J, Richter R (2020) Convergence of blockchain, IoT, and AI. Front. Blockchain 3:522600. https://doi.org/10.3389/fbloc.2020.522600
Sankaran S, Sanju S, Achuthan K (2018) Towards realistic energy profiling of blockchains for securing Internet of Things. 2018 IEEE 38th International Conference on Distributed Computing Systems (ICDCS), Vienna, Austria. https://doi.org/10.1109/ICDCS.2018.00148
Schrepel T (2021) Smart contracts and the digital single market through the lens of 'law + technology' approach. European commission, Brussels. https://ssrn.com/abstract=3947174
Shraddha K (2018) Building-blocks of a data protection revolution—the uneasy case for blockchain technology to secure privacy and identity. Munich Intellect Prop Law Center—MIPLC Stud 35(1). https://doi.org/10.5771/9783845294025
Szabo N (1996) Smart contracts: building blocks for digital markets. www.truevaluemetrics.org/DBpdfs/BlockChain/Nick-Szabo-Smart-Contracts-Building-Blocks-for-Digital-Markets-1996-14591.pdf
Tulsidas TU (2018) Smart contracts from a legal perspective. Final degree work. Alicante University. https://rua.ua.es/dspace/bitstream/10045/78007/1/Smart_Contracts_from_a_Legal_Perspective_Utamchandani_Tulsidas_Tanash.pdf
Veale M, Edwards L (2018) Clarity, surprises and further questions in the article 29 working party draft guidance on automated decision making and profiling. Comput Law Secur Rev 34(2):398–404

Verbeek A, Lundquist M (2021) Artificial intelligence, blockchain and the future of Europe: how disruptive technologies create opportunities for a green and digital economy. Main report. Publications office of the European union

WP29: Article 29 Data Protection Working Party (2013) Opinion 07/2013 on the data protection impact assessment template for smart grid and smart metering systems ('DPIA template') prepared by Expert Group 2 of the commission's smart grid task force (WP209). https://ec.europa.eu/justice/article-29/documentation/opinion-recommendation/files/2013/wp209_en.pdf

WP29: Article 29 Data Protection Working Party (2017) Guidelines on automated individual decision-making and profiling for the purposes of regulation 2016/679 (WP251rev.01). https://ec.europa.eu/newsroom/article29/items/612053

Wachter S, Mittelstadt B, Russell C (2018) Counterfactual explanations without opening the black box: automated decisions and the GDPR. Harvard Journal of Law & Technology 31(2):842–887

Xing B, Marwala T (2018) The synergy of blockchain and artificial intelligence. https://doi.org/10.2139/ssrn.3225357

Towards the Conceptualisation of Big Data Ethics

An Attempt to Visualise Ethical Data Usage by Adopting the Big Data Ethical Matrix

András Pünkösty

Abstract Automated (algorithm-driven) decision-making based on big data analysis encompasses an ever wider range of personal circumstances. Many innovative solutions and comfort-enhancing services have been achieved as a result of rapid digital development, but it is difficult to judge how the effects of technological development transform our society and affect the individual in the long run. A number of research studies have been launched to identify ethical artificial intelligence, and to clarify the legally explainable liability issues for technological innovation. The purpose of this chapter is somewhat different. It is to contextualise the ethical approaches towards big data analysis, and by building on the existing frameworks, to develop a big data ethical matrix that at an abstract level could serve as a tentative reference point for the emerging ethical issues in big data analysis. The starting point of the investigation is the dramatic appreciation of the significance of the data. The chapter claims that the digital transformation of our societies has reached a new reality that needs to be addressed legally in a holistic way, through the overlapping concepts of data protection, competition law and consumer protection.

1 Introduction

Digitalisation covers an ever-wider range of living conditions, according to our natural experience. The European level law making determined to give the adequate answers for the evolving digitalisation process. The main focus of th1e research and the ongoing European legislation deals with creating an environment that ensures fair and contestable markets even with respect to the gatekeeper platforms (the Digital Markets Act [European Parliament and Council 2022a]), the establishment of a clear

A. Pünkösty (✉)
Pázmány Péter Catholic University, Budapest, Hungary
e-mail: punkosty.andras@jak.ppke.hu

Ludovika University of Public Service, Budapest, Hungary

M. Varju and K. Mezei (eds.), *The Challenges of Artificial Intelligence for Law in Europe*, Data Science, Machine Intelligence, and Law 6,
https://doi.org/10.1007/978-3-031-86813-9_14

conditions for the digital services provided by very large platforms (the Digital Services Act [European Parliament and Council 2022b]), as well as a risk-based approach which can be adopted for regulating AI (the Artificial Intelligence Act [AI Act] [European Commission 2021]). This latter measure will become binding law and is the subject of heavy criticism claiming that regulation will reduce the incentive for innovation and will further hold back Europe's global position in the field.

This chapter does not aim to reflect on the discussion on regulation, examine the adoption of ex ante market legislative measures, or assess the risk-based intervention to AI regulation. Instead, it aims to show that the appropriate legal approach to modern technologies based on data analysis, necessarily goes beyond the traditional branches of law and strives for a complex adaption thereof. The emerging questions caused by digital transformation go beyond attitudes to enforcing data protection, competition law and consumer protection separately, yet the interplay of these legal areas is inevitable for addressing the issues effectively (third part).

After adopting this position, the fourth part of the chapter examines the underlining ethical narratives, among others, the background issue analysed by Mariarosaria Taddeo (2017), i.e., how to find the appropriate level of trust in the technology. The fifth part synthetises the conceptual framework of data ethics, in particular referring to the academic approach elaborated by Taddeo and Floridi (2016), and consequently simplified coordinate system is introduced to summarise at an abstract level the most compelling ethics-related characteristics of ethical big data analysis (the big data ethics matrix) in order to put the related notions in context.

The chapter thus seeks to contribute to the discussion of good ethical practices for dealing with large data sets. The approach surveys a broad landscape of changes that digitalisation (big data) has brought to the European legal landscape by reviewing the legal and regulatory responses to the societal challenges that have arisen. This stocktaking is necessarily haphazard in its nature. Nevertheless, it provides a point of departure for identifying the ethical narrative, for both practitioners and academics.

2 The Prerequisites of the Evaluation of the Ethical Framework

2.1 The Data-Driven Society

It is now a truism to say that data is the new oil (The Economist 2017). Europe is also catching up to the need to harness the economic potential of data.[1] The explicit aim of the European Union's own European Data Strategy (European Commission 2020a) is to make data generated in the government sector accessible to economic actors and to develop a framework for equitable access to data generated and managed by

[1] https://commission.europa.eu/strategy-and-policy/priorities-2019-2024/europe-fit-digital-age/european-data-strategy_en.

businesses. The need to exploit data's economic benefits is becoming more and more pronounced, alongside data protection, which is the underlining approach in Europe, based on the General Data Protection Regulation (GDPR) (European Parliament and Council 2016). Accordingly, the EU has recently adopted several legal instruments and draft legislations that seek to facilitate access to data while respecting the data protection aspects rooted in the European constitutional tradition based on European values. It remains to be seen how the emerging regulatory framework will strike a balance among the divergent legal interests; how the European regulator can reflect this emerging economic interest alongside the divergent legal interests of the GDPR's fundamental rights approach.

The EU Open Data Directive (European Parliament and Council 2019), which came into force on 6 July 2019 and replaced the previous Public Sector Information (PSI) Directive (European Parliament and Council 2003a), aims to promote the re-use of open and government data. The PSI Directive focused on the economic aspects of information re-use, encouraging EU countries to make as much information as possible available for re-use. This included information obtained by ministries, public agencies, municipalities and organisations funded mainly by or under the control of public authorities, such as meteorological institutes.[2] The Open Data Directive introduces the notion of high-value data sets, whose re-use can bring significant benefits to society and the economy. These are subject to specific rules to ensure that they are available free of charge, in machine-readable format, and that access is provided through application programming interfaces (APIs). The material scope of high-value data sets is set out in the Annex to directive.[3]

The draft Data Governance Regulation (European Commission 2020b) was adopted on 25 November 2020.[4] The regulation aims to make more data available and facilitate data sharing across sectors and EU countries in order to better harness the potential of data for European citizens and businesses.[5] The Data Act (European Parliament and Council 2023b) was adopted on 23 February 2022 and it aims to ensure fair access to the use of data generated by the Internet of Things and to empower SMEs to benefit from the economic potential of data through business planning and innovative solutions by safeguarding a fair and innovative data economy.[6]

---

[2] https://digital-strategy.ec.europa.eu/en/policies/legislation-open-data.

[3] The list of thematic categories of high-value data sets referred to in Article 13(1): 1. Geospatial data 2. Earth observation and environmental data 3. Meteorological data 4. Statistical data 5. Company and company ownership data 6. Mobility data.

[4] The Regulation entered into force 20 days after its publication and is applicable 12 months after its entry into force.

[5] https://digital-strategy.ec.europa.eu/en/policies/data-governance-act.

[6] https://ec.europa.eu/commission/presscorner/detail/en/ip_23_3491.

2.2 The Need for a Data Ethics Discourse

In a data-driven society, the ethical issues surrounding the use of data are increasingly coming to the fore. Data is a crucial source of input for companies, but it can also be used to streamline processes in public administration and even in policy making. Some technology companies' core business model is to provide convenience services by using personal data. The effectiveness of artificial intelligence-based solutions also depends to a large extent on the quality of the data used to teach them. It is, therefore, no coincidence that attitudes towards data are changing in Europe (European Commission 2022), and it is indicative that in the United States, as of 2016, the data scientist is consistently among the top three most sought-after jobs (Joubert 2023).

From a data protection perspective, personal data[7] is the subject of fundamental rights-inspired privacy protection. Data can be separated into personal and non-personal data; by definition, privacy protection relates to the former category. In this context, the anonymisation of data is proposed as a first step for compliance (ICO 2017). From a technical point of view, however, it is debatable how effective anonymisation is since it is easy to imagine the extraction of sensitive information and the recovery of data of a personal nature in the case of large data sets (ICO 2017). In the case of anonymised data from mobile phones alone, it is possible to predict a person's age with a difference of one year with an accuracy of 70%, and their gender with an accuracy of 70–80%, but also to determine their religion from the way they use their phone, based on an indication from an Indonesian service provider (Taylor 2016).

The UK's Information Commissioner's Office (ICO) has warned that anonymisation is becoming less and less effective recently with big data (ICO 2017). The success of the technique is fundamentally disputed. Cavokuian and Castro (2014) conclude that de-identification is possible. According to an MIT study, cited by the UK Information Commissioner's relevant report, 90% of the 1.1 million individuals in a dataset of credit card usage data over a three-month period could be identified by the dates and locations of only four transactions (ICO 2017). The efficiency of anonymisation is still debatable, but it would be highly challenging to exclude the possibility of post-identification in the era of big data, especially if data from other sources is available (ICO 2017). Data are typically obtained from data brokers in the market conditions of the data economy (Elvy 2017). The European Commission has repeatedly failed to give due weight to the competition assessment of accumulated data by merging firms precisely because data can be obtained from other sources.[8]

---

[7] According to Article 4(1) of the GDPR (European Parliament and Council 2016), personal data means any information relating to an identified or identifiable natural person ('data subject'); that an identifiable natural person is one who can be identified, directly or indirectly, in particular by reference to an identifier such as a name, identification number, location data, an online identifier or to one or more factors specific to the physical, physiological, genetic, mental, economic, cultural or social identity of that natural person.

[8] Case No. COMP/M.4731—Google/ DoubleClick, para 365.

Artificial intelligence-based solutions are also based on big data. Self-learning algorithms are able to perform a given operation using the data they are learning. These solutions inevitably have a growing impact on fundamental areas of life, such as human communication, business and administrative efficiency, the digital economy and, in general, supporting complex decisions (such as medical diagnoses and jurisdictional decisions). These all have a common input: data on which algorithmic decision-making and AI solutions are built.

The extent of human exposure in the online space and AI solutions is perhaps not yet fully clear to researchers. Media reports indicating the particular vulnerability of the human actor in machine-human interaction also need to be examined. According to a recent Belgian newspaper report, a man in crisis committed suicide due to a conversation with a chatbot (Eliza) with which he developed a regular 'relationship' (Walker 2023). The man's psychiatrist later confirmed the machine's involvement in his decision (Kéfer 2023).

Facebook's (Meta) 'emotional contagion experiment' is another textbook example of how research with data can raise ethical questions (Jouhki et al. 2016). In 2014, an experiment was published that illustrated that emotional states can indeed spread in the online environment (Kramer et al. 2014). The experiment was conducted by the Facebook Core Data Team and two academic researchers. The experiment consisted of manipulating the messages posted by friends in the news feed and reducing the amount of positive and negative content that appeared for two specific groups. The research aimed to see how this influenced the users in expressing their emotional state. The company involved 689,003 users in the experiment. The researchers found a significant correlation between the emotional content of the posts users are exposed to and the emotional content of the posts they generate. An analysis of around three million posts and 122 million words showed that those who had reduced positive content in their newsfeed shared more negative status updates and less positive content. Conversely, those for whom negative status reports were reduced shared more positive status and fewer negative status updates. Furthermore, the less emotionally charged content users were exposed to, the fewer words they used in their status updates (Jouhki et al. 2016). The research found that emotional statuses can be passed from one person to another through "emotional contagion" without the person being aware of it (Jouhki et al. 2016). The existence of emotional contagion has been demonstrated before, but it can happen outside of direct interaction between people and even through online social media platforms (Jouhki et al. 2016).

The Facebook experiment has raised serious ethical concerns, not only because of the attempted manipulation but also because of the lack of consent (Flick 2016). The experiment was conducted with reference to the terms and conditions of the contract, which included the term 'research', but it turned out that the consent to research was only included in the terms and conditions four months after the experiment had started (Hern 2014). Some have also raised the issue of human experimentation (Jouhki et al. 2016). In the professional community, the experiment has given rise to a heated debate on the research ethics of data science.

3 The Approach to Data Protection, Competition Law and Consumer Protection

3.1 Privacy Matters

3.1.1 The Principles of Data Protection Laws

Fundamental rights protection issues in theory establishing a clear boundary for big data technologies. The very concept of privacy originates from Anglo-Saxon legal thinking. At the same time the continental European tradition, including the domestic and EU law, is more reliant on the concepts of data protection law (Weichert 2012). The GDPR (European Parliament and Council 2016) provides the general framework of the binding law in Europe, while a number of guidelines have been adopted to address the constantly changing technological environment at both EU and Member State level. The European Data Protection Board (EDPB) issued guidelines, inter alia, on the territorial scope of the GDPR (EDPB 2020a), the interconnected vehicles (EDPB 2020b), data collection and types of data in connection with online services (EDPB 2019a), the data subject's consent (EDPB 2020c), and privacy by design and default (EDPB 2019b).

The challenge to respond to the data protection concerns of the evolving technology is still present, and some even claim that the GDPR does not provide any adequate answer to the technology-raised concerns (Ződi 2023). A draft E-privacy Regulation was also prepared in 2017 (European Commission 2017), which was originally due to enter into force at the same time as the GDPR. The UK ICO focused its attention, already back in 2014, on the data protection aspects of big data usage (ICO 2014). In 2017, the ICO discussed the links between big data, artificial intelligence, machine learning and data protection (ICO 2017). The former Article 29 Data Protection Working Party—the antecedent of EDPB—also adopted its guidelines on automated decision-making and profiling (WP29 2016). From these documents, it became clear which principles of data protection laws are most essential to protect privacy in the context of big data technologies.

3.1.2 Guidelines for Compliance with Data Protection Laws

Substantive European data protection legislation may be understood on the company's side as a requirement to comply with data protection regulations. Compliance with data protection rules may even create a stronger market position. For companies in technology industries, the extensive need for data is a general requirement.[9] The UK Information Commissioner (ICO 2017), which adopted a positive attitude toward technological development, stressed the necessity of striking a balance between enforcing the data protection laws and maintaining an environment that fosters technological innovation, by emphasising that *privacy* is not an end in itself but an *enabling right.* It noted that *privacy* and embedded data protection in *big data* analysis may not only bring social benefits, but also have benefits at the organisational level by promoting creativity, innovation and fostering trust (ICO 2017).

A frequently raised problem in *big data* analysis is the reuse or the secondary use of data for various purposes *(repurposing data).* It is not necessarily foreseeable for what other purposes the dataset may be used in the future, which may create quality tensions and, in similar cases, for which it is problematic to obtain an appropriate consent. The UK Information Commissioner (ICO 2017) emphasised, in particular, that the *fairness* principle needs to be observed. The data processing organisations should thus consider the potential effects of *big data* analysis on individuals (such as profiling) and examine whether it is carried out within the framework of the reasonable expectations of individuals.

The very existence of a *privacy policy* in a company is essential. Innovative solutions need to be entrenched in a clear policy so that they can be communicated unequivocally to stakeholders, whose consent must be valid. In a report, the relevant committee of the House of Commons in the UK Parliament pointed out, however, that if an average user read the terms of use of internet services (House of Commons 2014), it would take an average of one month out of the year. If users read through the privacy notices, they would spend more time on this than they spend on average using the application (Arnold et al. 2015).

Legal compliance is also facilitated by so-called *privacy impact assessment.* This tool can help to identify and reduce risks in the private sector. Based on the GDPR (European Parliament and Council 2016), the data protection impact assessment for *big data* analysis is essential when personal data processing is involved. The GDPR also requires integrated and default data protection[10] *(data protection by design and by default),* which creates a legal obligation for the entities to consider data protection compliance when designing a service in technical terms.

Certificates and markings *(privacy seals)* are a further adequate way of ensuring compliance. The UK Information Commissioner pointed out that the processing organisations should strengthen ethical considerations in their data management practices (ICO 2017), and therefore it is necessary to set up ethical committees at the organisational and at national levels to identify ethical issues and apply ethical principles. An ethical approach to personal data helps to build confidence on the individual's side and to develop appropriate standards for the application of *big data,* which can help to spread industry best practices.

---

[9] Margrethe Vestager, member of the European Commission in her speech 'Security and trust in a digital word' in Copenhagen on 13 September 2019 spoke about the data requirements of digital platforms (Vestager 2019a).

[10] European Parliament and Council (2016, Article 25(b)).

3.2 Competition Law Aspects: The Relationship Between Data and Market Power

The economic importance of *data* has dramatically increased in recent times. In the data-driven economy, the question of how competition law enforcement can adequately address the specific features of the digital economy has gradually been highlighted. At the same time, it has become apparent that the concepts of competition law need to be adapted in order to make sure that competition law objectives are realised in the digital economy.[11]

Initially, the policy and academic discourse focused on the shift of focus in competition policy from competition between undertakings to competition between business models. Digital markets are often characterised by the 'winner takes it all' phenomenon. National Competition Authorities (NCAs) took the initiative in Europe. The German and French competition authorities' leaders published an article jointly in the Italian competition authority's journal in 2017.[12] In this work, Lasserre and Mundt (2017) established that the *big data* phenomenon has three main implications: at first, data is an essential factor of market power; data may contribute to transparency between competitors, which may facilitate collusion; and thirdly, data may be a means of restricting competition.

Regarding the issue of *market power*, the use of accumulated datasets, as part of the incumbent's business model, may constitute a barrier to entry to the market if the new entrant cannot collect or buy data at the same scale. *Network effects* will further increase this phenomenon, and can result in extremely high differences in the *volume* of the available data. Not surprisingly, social media and internet search services will produce a very high *quality of data* in terms of the possibility of monetising it through online advertisement. This brings us to the phenomenon of a *two- or multi-sided market*, where one side of the market is the core service, while the other side monetises the data through online advertising. In such settings, companies such as Meta and Google share the vast majority of the sharply growing online advertising market.

The German NCA (Bundeskartellamt) initiated a hallmark antitrust procedure in March 2016 against Facebook (Meta) based on alleged abuse of a dominant position.[13] The French NCA (Autorité de la concurrence) and the British watchdog (Competition and Markets Authority)[14] also launched a sector inquiry on the online advertising market (Autorité de la concurrence 2016; Competition and Markets

[11] Margrethe Vestager at a conference on big data held in Brussels on 29 September 2016 called for an effective application of competition law to maintain the potential of big data (Vestager 2016).

[12] A direct background to this publication was the report produced jointly by the German and the French competition authority on 10 May 2016 entitled 'Competition law and data' (Autorité de la concurrence and Bundeskartellamt 2016).

[13] Bundeskartellamt, Facebook, Exploitative business terms pursuant to Section 19(1) GWB for inadequate data processing, B6-22/16. On 15 February 2019, the Bundeskartellamt established the abuse of dominant position by Facebook.

[14] The interim results (Competition and Markets Authority 2019) published on 18 December 2019 indicated that in 2018 Google had secured 90% of the advertisements related to internet searches

Authority 2019). Margrethe Vestager, former EU Competition Commissioner, and the Vice-President of the European Commission responsible for digital transformation, also raised awareness of the role of data in the digital economy (Vestager 2019b).

3.3 Consumer Protection in Digital Markets: The Hungarian Practice

The Hungarian Competition Authority (GVH) has been quite active in investigating consumer protection issues in the digital economy proceeding under the Consumer Protection Act (Act CLV of 1997). In its Booking.com decision, the GVH highlighted its general approach towards consumer protection in online markets (GVH 2020). According to the decision, the platform misled the consumers when it offered 'free cancellation' of accommodation reservations, while at the same, it used aggressive commercial practices by influencing consumers' decisions with messages that are capable of exerting psychological pressure. Furthermore, the company infringed the requirement of professional diligence when it indicated differently to certain accommodation operators whether the Széchenyi card—an alternative payment system used in Hungary—is acceptable.

The company sends strong messages to consumers during their hotel reservation procedure that the relevant accommodation they currently view is very sought after or restricted. According to the GVH, these messages that the company sends at each step of the reservation process aim to ensure that consumers not only consider starting the reservation process but also go ahead and make a reservation.[15] These messages could have put consumers in an imaginary or real competitive position, and they could therefore experience psychological pressure to complete their bookings as quickly as possible. In its decision, the GVH made a remarkable reference to the results of behavioural economics,[16] and ultimately examined whether 'urging messages' are capable of significantly restricting consumer choice. The GVH referred in a detailed way to the consumer behaviours known as *scarcity bias*, the *bandwagon* phenomenon, and the FOMO *(fear of missing out)* effect, which together could amplify the desire to seize the accommodation in a way that is outside the conscious sphere of perception of the consumer ('unconscious effect').

The *scarcity bias* is a form of consumer behaviour in which consumers tend to regard a product that appears to be available in limited quantity or time as more valuable. The *bandwagon* effect is a phenomenon in which if the consumer is exposed to as many positive opinions as possible, which is intensified by the design of the reservation system, then he is inclined to come to the same conclusion. The FOMO

(value: around GBP 6 billion), while Facebook had secured half of the total visual advertising revenue (value: GBP 2 billion).

[15] Decision in VJ/17/2018, para 545.

[16] Decision in VJ/17/2018, para 493.

effect is the basic human fear of missing out on something. The messages may trigger the feeling that if the user does not book the accommodation as soon as possible, they may miss their chance. In essence, the GVH criticised the fact that these techniques are complementary to one another, and act to make consumers behave in such a way that they have no chance of recognising the influencing mechanisms involved or of protecting themselves against them in a deliberate way.[17]

In its 2019 proceedings against Facebook (Meta), the GVH condemned some of Meta's practices (GVH 2019). The GVH examined whether Meta distorted consumers' transactions by claiming that its service was free of charge, which statement was available on the opening page and in the Help Centre. According to the GVH's findings, the business model Facebook operates is very complex, and the monetisation of the consumer's data clearly forms part of it.[18] Detailed user profiles are used to distribute targeted advertisements to end users, eventually selling advertisement space to third parties.[19] The GVH found that the users contribute to the platform with their data, attention and activity. The watchdog moreover emphasised that users' data compensate for the services that are promised to be free of charge.

In the context of this compensation, the GVH considered to be economically relevant, data which, in addition to consumers' personal data, concerned every aspect of consumer activity and their expressed opinions. The GVH considered that consumers, through the monetisation of their data, are in too complex a position to make any decisions about their activity and the management of their data when using Facebook, while they are likely to access and receive only limited information about the potential risks of the service. The actual weight of the consumer compensation is hardly transparent and perceptible to an average consumer, and accordingly could lead to a distortion of their behaviour.[20] The GVH's decision was later overturned by the Budapest-Capital Regional Court, which was upheld by the Kúria.[21]

3.4 Digitalisation as a New Reality?

Digitalisation results in a new and complex reality that cannot be adequately addressed by relying on individual branches of law on their own. The recently adopted *ex ante* regulations on the EU level are an answer to this very phenomenon. In the above, we have tried to illustrate the basic approaches of the regulations to the most relevant legal areas. First, there is the data protection approach, which seeks to safeguard privacy in a risk-based and fundamental rights protection approach, where personal data protection is a key concept. Secondly, competition law focuses on the market power, and looks at *big data* solutions from the perspective of market

[17] Decision in VJ/17/2018, para 495.

[18] Decision in VJ/85/2016, para 200.

[19] Decision in VJ/85/2016, para 253.

[20] Decision in VJ/85/2016, para 200.

[21] Kfv.II.37.243/2021/11.

dynamics, innovation and access to data. Third, the consumer protection approach protects consumers and their transactional (free) choices in the digital environment.

Digitalisation, as a predominantly technological innovation, through its impact on the economy and efficiency gains, can create new channels of economic activity and communication. It even influences societal expectations. This results in the rise of new (digital) organisational structures called online platforms (Vestager 2019c). These platforms work predominantly with large data sets and algorithmic decisions—so algorithms will become the new regulators operating within the platform (Vestager 2017). The link between the technological code, the language of the algorithm and the legal language currently shaping social life, is still to be elaborated. The challenge from a regulatory and compliance perspective is that no single market supervisory authority can control by using its own legal means the algorithmic operational structure of a platform. The translation of legal resolutions into an effective coding system within the algorithmic establishment of a platform is a precondition for effective regulation.

The European Data Protection Supervisor (EDPS) claimed in 2014 that data protection, competition and consumer protection aspects are inextricably linked in the digital world (EDPS 2014). The Supervisor analysed how competition law and data protection are linked together when gaining control over personal data and how online services achieve market potential. In his view, inadequate and inaccurate data protection policies help to extend this power further, and in addition, with the development of technology and invasiveness of this kind, the users might 'lock in' to a given service.

3.5 Recent Developments in the EU Court of Justice's Case Law

In its Meta Platforms ruling, the Court Justice of the European Union (CJEU) supported this above elaborated position.[22] The ruling prospectively has a chilling effect on the business model of many technological companies. In the data-driven economy, the monetising of (personal)data is a crucial business approach; however, the highly complex nature of the digital markets, and the built-in data trade posed a challenge to effective law enforcement. The CJEU now recognised the new reality of the digital economy.[23] The CJEU realised that the access and use of personal data are of great importance in the context of the digital economy.[24] In its ruling, the CJEJ affirmed that preventing the competition authorities from considering the data protection rules, while assessing competition cases would disregard this economic

[22] Case C-252/21, *Meta Platforms Inc., formerly Facebook Inc., Meta Platforms Ireland Limited, formerly Facebook Ireland Ltd, Facebook Deutschland GmbH v Bundeskartellamt*, EU:C:2023:537.

[23] Case C-252/21, *Meta Platforms Inc.*, EU:C:2023:537, para 50.

[24] Case C-252/21, *Meta Platforms Inc.*, EU:C:2023:537, para 50.

reality and undermine the effectiveness of competition law.[25] The legal uncertainty of the barter of the personal data and to access 'free' convenience services between the users and the technological companies is the other side of the same coin. This legal development and the new ex-ante regulations adopted on the European level can potentially give appropriate legal answers to the digitalisation-created reality.

4 Digitalisation and Technology Ethics

4.1 Human Dignity as the Core Norm

Following the EDPS's earlier mentioned position (EDPS 2014), digitalisation may indeed be addressed adequately by law when legal responses can match its complexity. This new reality nevertheless raises serious ethical questions regarding the big data usage as the basis of the entire development. In its opinion No. 4/2015 (EDPS 2015), the EDPS also made it clear that ethics should influence the regulatory responses given to the relevant challenges. This, however, requires the definition of a broader ethical narrative.

For the EDPS, the starting point, which follows from European constitutional traditions, is the protection of human dignity both as a value and a fundamental right (EDPS 2015). In its view, human dignity is inviolable and this should inform all technology regulation. The EDPS also asserted that the right to privacy and the protection of personal data have never been so important to ensure respect for human dignity. The EDPS declared that technology cannot dictate values or alternate rights, and it must also avoid misrepresenting them.

The EDPS stated further that, in today's digital environment, compliance with *legislation is not sufficient and that the ethical dimension of data processing needs to be reconsidered* (EDPS 2015). This has evident engineering, philosophical, legal and moral aspects. It proposed a four-step "big data protection ecosystem" to address digital challenges supported by ethical considerations. The critical factor, according to him, is the future-oriented regulation of data processing and the respect for the rights to privacy and data protection, accountable controllers who determine personal information processing, privacy-conscious engineering and empowered individuals.

[25] Case C-252/21, *Meta Platforms Inc.*, EU:C:2023:537, para 51.

4.2 A Trust-Based Approach to Technology

According to Mariarosaria Taddeo (2017), *trust*[26] is a factor that facilitates interactions between actors in a system, whether they are human actors, artificial actors, or a combination of the two (hybrid system). Trust is linked to and influences the relationships within a system, such as doing business, negotiating, communicating and placing orders. As Taddeo (2017) further explained, trust is not a relationship in itself but a property of relationships, something that changes how relationships work. In Francis Fukuyama's (2007) view, trust is one of the most essential social virtues, and he saw the development of a high level of trust as a key for the success of societies. In his reflection on crisis recovery (Fukuyama 2020), he argued that societies' efficiency depends on trust. Taddeo (2017) explained that trust, as a property of a given relationship, alters the functioning of the relationship by minimising the effort and commitment of an actor who chooses to trust to achieve a given goal. This can be done in basically two ways (Taddeo 2017). The trusting party does not have to take the action necessary to achieve the goal if it has reason to trust that the necessary collaborator will carry it out. On the other hand, it may decide not to monitor the intermediary's performance (saving the effort) in the context of the existing trust.

The facilitating role of trust is essential for a system to work. Without trust, delegation would be much more difficult and would require constant monitoring, and this would be an unnecessary interference in the division of tasks that is essential for a system to work (Taddeo 2017). Taddeo (2017) asked the question of what a society would look like without trust in doctors, teachers and drivers. In practice, this would require members of society to devote a significant amount of their time and resources to monitoring the performance of others' tasks, all at the expense of their own tasks. It is important to stress that not all systems require the same level of trust to function. In the short and long term, too little trust can have a limiting effect on the internal dynamics of a system, but too much trust can lead to the collapse of the system, as Taddeo (2017) clarified, in the absence of adequate control and coordination. Setting the correct level of trust is the real issue given the system's characteristics and the actor's expectations.

As digitalisation progresses, this broader system is the *information society*. In this system, developing the right level of trust is crucial, which implies a certain maturity. Luciano Floridi (2016) defined mature information societies as "societies in which digital opportunities are the expected backdrop to all aspects of society, as opposed to societies in which such opportunities are new or unexpected". The maturity of societies concerning information technologies can be basically defined by their expectations (Floridi 2016). Levels of analysis of the maturity of information societies can be based, among others, on the unreflected and implicit expectations of their members (Floridi 2016). In the context of expectations, Floridi (2016) considered education, understanding and innovation critical. Achieving the right level of

---

[26] As defined by Blackburn (2008), trust is an attitude of expecting good performance from another party, whether in terms of loyalty, goodwill, truth or promises. The importance of trust as a kind of invisible glue that binds society together is most visible when it is lost.

trust is a delicate issue. It needs to take into account the system itself (mature information societies), the expectations of the principal (the tasks delegated by people) and the nature of the delegated (e.g., digital technologies) (Taddeo 2017).

4.3 Basic Challenges to the Data Ethics Discourse

From a research ethics perspective, a fundamental challenge is that large data sets are primarily accumulated by private actors so academic considerations may only slowly and indirectly shape the ethics of technology development, marketing and use. It is no accident that large technology companies are able to carry out cutting-edge data science research. In this environment, some large technology companies are making significant efforts to influence the interpretative framework of data ethics. Facebook, for example, funds the Institute for Ethics in Artificial Intelligence at the Technical University of Munich (Shead 2019), but technology companies are also actively involved in developing normative regulation as stakeholders.

Thomas Metzinger, a philosopher and a former member of the European Commission's High-Level Expert Group on Artificial Intelligence, is not optimistic about the motivation of businesses in shaping the ethical foundations for regulation (Metzinger 2019). The European Union's draft proposal (European Commission 2021) for regulating artificial intelligence (the EU's AI Act) follows on from the ethics directive document (HLEG 2019) issued by the High-Level Group on 8 April 2019. According to Metzinger (2019), industry stakeholders have been involved in the panel's work with the motivation to delay the ethical discourse and thus delay the emergence of effective European normative regulation as much as possible. Metzinger pointed out that the expert group included only four academics who had received formal academic training in ethics. He argued that they had done their utmost to ensure that the ethical foundations on policy-making and regulation could be laid as soon as possible.

A further challenge to developing a valid ethical framework is the phenomenon of 'ethics washing'. This means that many market players in the technology sector publish ethical guidelines to "wash away" concerns about their activities (van Maanen 2022). Such an approach to ethics is not alien to the strategic selection (shopping) between principles that least constrains the action of the actor concerned, yet is able to communicate that it contributes to the public good (van Maanen 2022). According to Gijs van Maanen (2022), a pessimistic response to this problem is to impose alternative means and methods of enforcing ethical boundaries on the part of the technology sector, such as data justice, or the human rights approach as a safe space. While in the optimistic approach, a more precise explanation and definition of ethical boundaries can help avoid abuses by dominant actors (van Maanen 2022).

5 The General Framework of Data Ethics

5.1 Business Data Ethics

In their critical in-depth analysis, Linnet Taylor and Lina Dencik concluded that market actors' motivations for engaging in ethical discourse are fundamentally determined by the need to restore consumer trust (Taylor and Dencik 2020). In another approach, the companies' efforts to thematise data ethics can be used to communicate corporate social responsibility in a new way, which can lead to a competitive advantage (Hasselbach and Tranberg 2016).

According to Taylor and Dencik (2020), the market player's perspective on data issues generally can be described as defensive. In many cases, economic actors increasingly seek to influence ethical thinking on the use of data, an attitude typically defined by a technology-determinist view that innovation is, by definition, good and thus the focus is on exploiting the economic value of data (Taylor and Dencik 2020), although news on data leakage or the implementation of data management that has caused outrage is not uncommon.[27] In some cases, these may undermine the credibility of the corporate sector. However, there are also several initiatives to incorporate ethical considerations into corporate data projects at the design stage (ethical by design) (Jongen 2021).

From a corporate perspective, Taylor and Dencik (2020) distinguished between ethical issues at the micro and macro levels. At the micro level, this focuses on the level of the individual employee, with the question of how they approach data issues in their daily work. This will determine the internal procedures and ethical guidelines for businesses when dealing with data sets, and this approach is typically shaped by general research ethics issues. This does not reach the organisational level approach but emphasises the duty of the individual data scientist in the context of compliance (Taylor and Dencik 2020). However, this can also lead to paradoxical situations where the individual employee is complying with a narrowly defined obligation, but in a broader context, the company's data handling practices raise ethical issues (Taylor and Dencik 2020). The macro ethical level, on the other hand, is the private corporate sector policy level, which asks how technology should be regulated and addresses the policy perspective on data (Taylor and Dencik 2020).

5.2 Data Ethics as Applied Ethics

In many areas, data ethics can contribute to solving ethical dilemmas. Annika Richterich's (2018) attempt to collect its principles can serve as a basis to present some problem areas in the context of big data. These are: ensuring security and protecting

[27] See European Parliament (2018).

privacy, open data initiative, data philanthropy, informed consent, and algorithmic bias (Richterich 2018).

Ensuring Security and Protecting Privacy Protecting personal data is the basis for guaranteeing the right to privacy, but law enforcement agencies have a basic need for information to detect security risks.[28] The extensive literature on the subject also covers the accountability of services for using modern technologies and data.[29] However, Richterich (2018) argued that the dichotomy between security and privacy is false.

Open Data Initiative The tensions between security and privacy, government surveillance and similar business practices have triggered calls for a normative justification for the operational framework for big data. Promoting transparency requires the disclosure of information on a large scale, which implies the disclosure of procedures and technical solutions, whether academic, governmental, corporate or even individual. The concept of open data use is often linked to the concept of accountability. The concept of open data has also brought transparency to big data: open data is that which can be freely used, re-used and re-shared by anyone. The open data initiative has strong support in Europe.

Data Philanthropy In the corporate sector, sharing large datasets beyond their business uses is very rare. Data philanthropy is the initiative to share large data sets for this purpose. It is framed not only for its economic value but also as a contribution to the public good. One flagship initiative is the ENS Global Pulse initiative, whereby big data sets are shared for sustainable development and humanitarian action.

Informed Consent Informed consent is essential for human experimentation, but a similar requirement applies in data management. The consent of users should also legally cover the processing of data provided in the course of the provision of services by businesses. There is also a serious debate at the level of legal procedures on the validity of consent, especially in the case of dominant companies. The issue leads to the question of users' autonomy of choice in digital services.

Algorithmic Bias The issue of algorithmic bias arises in the context of bias in large data sets. In many cases, data sets implicitly contain patterns that exist in society. At the same time, the typical solution of either accepting the offered terms or not using the service may also have the consequence that the data of more privacy-aware individuals are excluded from the large patterns, also called the awareness paradox (Baruh and Popescu 2017).

[28] Pursuant to Article 2(2)(d) GDPR (European Parliament and Council 2016), the GDPR does not apply to the processing of personal data carried out "by competent authorities for the purposes of the prevention, investigation, detection, prosecution or execution of criminal penalties, including the protection against and the prevention of threats to public security."

[29] See Vadász & Ződi (2021).

5.3 Academic Takes on Data Ethics

The conceptual framework of data ethics was developed by Floridi and Taddeo (2016) in 2016, and they defined it as a new branch of ethics. According to them, data ethics has the ambition to explore and evaluate ethical issues related to data (data generation, capture, handling, use, dissemination, and sharing), including algorithms (artificial intelligence, artificial agents, machine learning and robotics) and their processes (responsible innovation, programming, hacking and coding) in order to develop and promote morally good solutions (good practices and values) (Floridi and Taddeo 2016). Data ethics builds on the foundations provided by computer science and information ethics while positioning the focus of its research from information-centricity to data-centricity in theorising ethical issues (Floridi and Taddeo 2016).

Floridi and Taddeo (2016) argued that data science has enormous potential for improving private, social and environmental life but that this potential also comes with serious ethical challenges. They noted that the extensive use of ever-increasing amounts of data, often personal if not sensitive big data, and the increasing reliance on algorithms to analyse data in order to identify choices and make decisions, as well as the gradual reduction of human intervention and even the abandonment of human supervision in many automated processes, raise pressing questions of equity, responsibility and respect for human rights (Floridi and Taddeo 2016). They argued that data science can effectively address these ethical challenges, and that the great challenge of data ethics is precisely to navigate the narrow path between social rejection and legal prohibition to maximise the ethical value of these data science solutions for societal benefit (Floridi and Taddeo 2016).

Floridi and Taddeo (2016) elaborated the following three branches of data ethics and defined them as follows.

Data Ethics Data ethics deals with ethical issues related to the collection and analysis of big data, such as using big data in biomedical research and social sciences, profiling, online advertising, data philanthropy, and open data. Key issues here include the re-identifiability of individuals through data mining, the leakage, aggregation and re-use of big data, and the potential for breaches of group privacy (group privacy). Trust and transparency also play an essential role in recognising the lack of general knowledge and awareness of data science in a large part of society (Floridi and Taddeo 2016).

The Ethics of Algorithms This branch of data ethics broadly addresses the increasing complexity of the autonomy of algorithms (including artificial intelligence, artificial agents, and internet bots), particularly machine learning-based applications. The challenge in this area is the moral responsibility and accountability of designers and data scientists for unforeseen and unintended consequences or even missed opportunities (Floridi and Taddeo 2016).

The Ethics of Process The third branch of data ethics deals with the processes, including professional ethics and ethics of duty. It addresses the issue of the responsibility of individuals and organisations to develop procedures and policies for data management, including those of data scientists, to set ethical frameworks and professional codes of conduct for responsible innovation, development and use, which can both provide a framework for the development of data science and ensure the rights of individuals and groups (Floridi and Taddeo 2016).

5.4 *The Big Data Ethics Matrix*

This chapter seeks to contribute to the discussion of the ethical challenges of digitalisation and provide an overview of data-related ethical issues. The starting point in the discourse has been to estimate the relevance of data in today's society and to endorse the position that digitalisation has created a rapidly changing new reality that creates an environment to identify fundamental ethical issues. Given that this is a complex reality, with aspects related to economic, social and technological development taking place under individual conditions, including all the relevant ethical aspects in a single framework is a significant challenge. This is attempted by the big data ethics matrix, which focuses on the individual's position, and employs visualisation to incorporate into a diagram the main assessment framework, which can provide a basis for formulating ethical issues as appropriate (Fig 1).

The matrix seeks to present the individual's position as a subject of personal data processing. The three axes illustrate the most notable characteristics of data processing, namely the level of transparency (A), the effectiveness of privacy protection (B), and the quality of consent by the individual (C). The intersection of these three abstract variables determines the most critical conditions for ethical evaluation. In this perspective, maintaining identity control is a crucial priority in the digital environment, based on awareness of the control of personal data (including the reduction

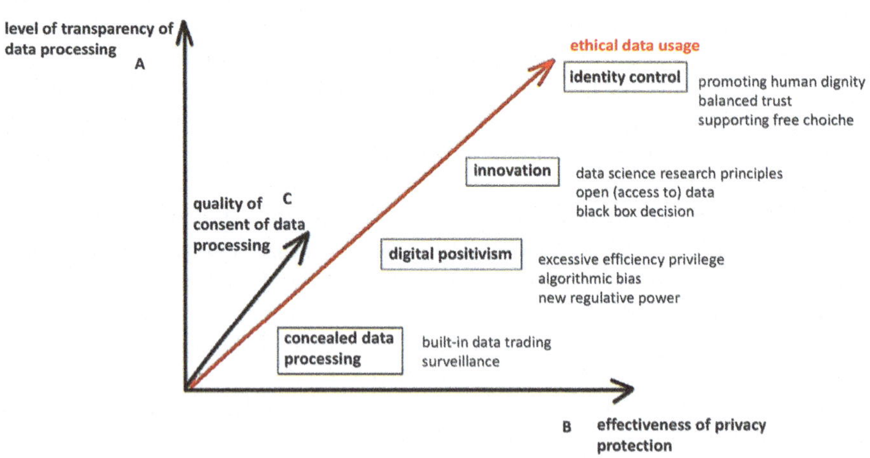

Fig. 1 Big data ethics matrix (created by author, 2023)

of exposure) and the conscious use of technical solutions to support (free) human decisions. It also includes the correct and critical trust in the big data (AI) solutions which are right for the purpose that the data is used for.

The opposite side of this value chain is the lack of control over personal data, and exposure to data processing that does not respect the identity elements of the individual represented by the given personal data, such as undeclared surveillance or built-in data trading by commercial entities. In between these two distinct phenomena further notions need to be assessed, bearing in mind that digitalisation is a complex reality whose potential effects need delicate discernment from an ethical perspective. Innovation is regarded as a desirable social benefit, supported by digitalisation in many ways; however, overestimating the efficiency gains by creating a regulatory framework that might intervene with life-related customs without due care for a space for equity should be considered as risk from a humanistic standpoint which in this respect can be referred to as digital positivism (Fuchs 2017; Richterich 2018).

6 Conclusions

In the contemporary world, data already has immense economic and social importance and value, and is essential for essential and high-value business operations. Technological development relies heavily on the use of data, especially when technology involves artificial intelligence-based solutions. In mature information societies, the expectations for technology are balanced and are based on solid trust that understands the emerging risks. Therefore, risk-based regulation plays a critical role in anchoring and maintaining trust in technology solutions.

This chapter has highlighted three basic assumptions. First, accelerated digitalisation is creating a new reality that requires the adaptation of law enforcement and also raises the need for regulation, which requires a more accurate understanding of the phenomenon and a framework in which it can be ethically evaluated. Second, individual branches of law and regulation, with their regulatory areas, are unable respond to the complex challenges effectively on their own; a coherent, holistic approach is needed, combining responses from data protection, competition law and consumer protection. Finally, it is essential to establish the ethical foundations for an effective regulation, especially given that it is a challenging task to assess the effects of technology-led development on society in the longer term.

However, in order to achieve the desired complex usage of legal-regulatory tools we need to clarify and adequately integrate the ethics of data usage. Data ethics is a branch of ethics that has emerged due to the widespread automated use of big data that points to the need to cultivate data ethics in our present society. In this chapter, we claimed that there is a need for a big data ethical matrix that can ensure the construction of mature information societies and promote a human-centred procession of data.

References

Arnold R, Hillebrand A, Waldburger M (2015) Personal data and privacy. Report for Ofcom. https://www.wik.org/fileadmin/Studien/2015/Personal_Data_and_Privacy.pdf

Autorité de la concurrence (2016) The Autorité de la concurrence begins, at its own initiative, gathering information in order to assess data processing in the online advertising sector. https://www.autoritedelaconcurrence.fr/en/communiques-de-presse/23-may-2016-autorite-de-la-concurrence-begins-its-own-initiative-gathering

Autorité de la concurrence, Bundeskartellamt (2016) Competition law and data. https://www.bundeskartellamt.de/SharedDocs/Publikation/DE/Berichte/Big%20Data%20Papier.pdf?__blob=publicationFile&v=4

Baruh L, Popescu M (2017) Big data analytics and the limits of privacy self-management. New Media Soc 19(4):579–596. https://doi.org/10.1177/1461444815614001

Blackburn S (2008) The Oxford dictionary of philosophy. Oxford University Press

Cavoukian A, Castro D (2014) Big data and innovation, setting the record straight: de-identification does work. Information and privacy commissioner Ontario, Canada. https://www2.itif.org/2014-big-data-deidentification.pdf

Competition and Markets Authority (2019) CMA lifts the lid on digital giants. https://www.gov.uk/government/news/cma-lifts-the-lid-on-digital-giants

Floridi L, Taddeo M (2016) What is data ethics? Phil Trans R Soc 374(2083):1–5

Fukuyama F (2007) Trust—The social virtues and the creation of well-being. Europe Books

Fukuyama F (2020) The thing that determines a country's resistance to the coronavirus. The Atlantic. https://www.theatlantic.com/ideas/archive/2020/03/thing-determines-how-well-countries-respond-coronavirus/609025/

EDPB: European Data Protection Board (2020a) Guidelines 3/2018 on the territorial scope of the GDPR (Article 3). https://www.edpb.europa.eu/sites/default/files/files/file1/edpb_guidelines_3_2018_territorial_scope_after_public_consultation_en_1.pdf

EDPB: European Data Protection Board (2020b) Guidelines 1/2020 on processing personal data in the context of related vehicles and mobility-related applications. https://www.edpb.europa.eu/our-work-tools/our-documents/guidelines/guidelines-012020-processing-personal-data-context_en

EDPB: European Data Protection Board (2020c) Guidelines 05/2020 on consent under regulation 2016/679. https://www.edpb.europa.eu/our-work-tools/our-documents/guidelines/guidelines-052020-consent-under-regulation-2016679_en

EDPB: European Data Protection Board (2019a) Guidelines 2/2019 on the processing of personal data under Article 6(1)(b) GDPR in the context of the provision of online services to data subjects. https://www.edpb.europa.eu/our-work-tools/our-documents/guidelines/guidelines-22019-processing-personal-data-under-article-61b_en

EDPB: European Data Protection Board (2019b) Guidelines 4/2019 on article 25 data protection by design and by default. https://www.edpb.europa.eu/our-work-tools/our-documents/guidelines/guidelines-42019-article-25-data-protection-design-and_en

EDPS: European Data Supervisor (2014) Privacy and competitiveness in the age of big data. https://www.edps.europa.eu/data-protection/our-work/publications/opinions/privacy-and-competitiveness-age-big-data_en

EDPS: European Data Supervisor (2015) Opinion 4/2015: towards a new digital ethics. Data, dignity and technology. https://www.edps.europa.eu/sites/default/files/publication/15-09-11_data_ethics_en.pdf

Elvy S-A (2017) Paying for privacy and the personal data economy. Columbia Law Rev 117(6):1369–1460

European Commission (2017) Proposal for a regulation of the European parliament and of the council on privacy and the protection of personal data in electronic communications (regulation on privacy and electronic communications). COM(2017) 010 final

European Commission (2020a) A European strategy for data. COM(2020)66 final

European Commission (2020b) Proposal for a regulation of the European parliament and of the council on European data governance (data governance regulation). COM(2020)767 final

European Commission (2021) Proposal for a regulation of the European parliament and of the council laying down harmonised rules of artificial intelligence (artificial intelligence act). COM(2021) 206 final

European Commission (2022) Commission staff working document on common European data spaces. SWD(2022) 45 final

European Parliament (2018) Facebook scandal: MEPs call on Zuckerberg to provide answers. https://www.europarl.europa.eu/news/en/headlines/society/20180418STO02004/facebook-scandal-meps-call-on-zuckerberg-to-provide-answers

European Parliament and Council (2016) Regulation (EU) 2016/679 of the European parliament and of the council of 27 April 2016 on the protection of natural persons with regard to the processing of personal data and on the free movement of such data, and repealing directive 95/46/EC (general data protection regulation), OJ L 119, 4.5.2016, pp 1–88

European Parliament and Council (2019) Directive (EU) 2019/1024 of the European parliament and of the council of 20 June 2019 on open data and the re-use of public sector information (recast), OJ L 172, 26.6.2019, pp 56–83

European Parliament and Council (2022a) Regulation (EU) 2022/1925 of the European parliament and of the council of 14 September 2022 on contestable and fair markets in the digital sector (Digital Markets Act), OJ L 265, 12.10.2022, pp 1–66

European Parliament and Council (2022b) Regulation (EU) 2022/2065 of the European parliament and of the council of 19 October 2022 on a single market for digital services (digital services act), OJ L 277, 27.10.2022, pp 1–102

European Parliament and Council (2023a) Directive 2003/98/EC of the European parliament and of the council of 17 November 2003 on the re-use of public sector information, OJ L 345, 31.12.2003, pp 90–96

European Parliament and Council (2023b) Regulation (EU) 2023/2854 of the European parliament and of the council of 13 December 2023 on harmonised rules on fair access to and use of data (data act), OJ L, 2023/2854, 22.12.2023

Flick C (2016) Informed consent and the Facebook emotional manipulation study. Research Ethics 12(1):14–28. https://doi.org/10.1177/1747016115599568

Floridi L (2016) Mature information societies—a matter of expectations. Philosophy & Technology 29(1):1–4

Fuchs C (2017) From digital positivism and administrative big data analytics towards critical digital and social media research! Eur J Commun 32(1):37–49. https://doi.org/10.1177/0267323116682804

GVH: Gazdasági Versenyhivatal (2019) GVH imposed a fine of EUR 3.6 M on Facebook https://www.gvh.hu/en/press_room/press_releases/press_releases_2019/gvh-imposed-a-fine-of-eur-3.6-m-on-facebook

GVH: Gazdasági Versenyhivatal (2020) Gigantic fine imposed on booking.com by the GVH. https://www.gvh.hu/en/press_room/press_releases/press-releases-2020/gigantic-fine-imposed-on-booking.com-by-the-gvh

Hasselbalch G, Tranberg P (2016) Data ethics. Publishare, The new competitive advantage

Hern A (2014) Facebook T&Cs introduced 'research' policy months after emotion study. The guardian. https://www.theguardian.com/technology/2014/jul/01/facebook-data-policy-research-emotion-study

House of Commons: Commons Science and Technology Committee (2014) Responsible use of data. https://publications.parliament.uk/pa/cm201415/cmselect/cmsctech/245/245.pdf

ICO: Information Commissioner's Office (2014) Big data and data protection. https://rm.coe.int/big-data-and-data-protection-ico-information-commissioner-s-office/1680591220

ICO: Information Commissioner's Office (2017) Big data, artificial intelligence, machine learning and data protection. https://ico.org.uk/media/for-organisations/documents/2013559/big-data-ai-ml-and-data-protection.pdf

HLEG: High-Level Expert Group on Artificial Intelligence (2019) Ethics guidelines for trustworthy AI. https://digital-strategy.ec.europa.eu/en/library/ethics-guidelines-trustworthy-ai
Jongen T (2021) How to make your data project ethical by design. https://towardsdatascience.com/how-to-make-your-data-project-ethical-by-design-99629dcd2443
Joubert S (2023) Data science careers shaping our future. https://graduate.northeastern.edu/resources/data-science-careers-shaping-our-future/
Jouhki J, Lauk E, Penttinen M, Sormanen N, Uskali T (2016) Facebook's emotional contagion experiment as a challenge to research ethics. Media Commun 4(4):75–85. https://doi.org/10.17645/mac.v4i4.579
Kéfer Á (2023) Öngyilkos lett egy fiatal családapa, miután hetekig beszélgetett a mesterséges intelligenciával. Index. https://index.hu/kulfold/2023/03/30/chatbot-chatgpt-openai-mesterseges-intelligencia-ongyilkossag-belgium
Lasserre B, Mundt A (2017) Competition law and big data: the enforcers' view. Antitrust & Public Policies 4(1):87–103. https://doi.org/10.12870/iar-12607
Metzinger T (2019) Ethik-Waschmaschinen made in Europe. Tagesspiegel. https://background.tagesspiegel.de/digitalisierung/ethik-waschmaschinen-made-in-europe
Richterich A (2018) The big data agenda. University of Westminster Press, Data ethics and critical data studies
Shead S (2019) Facebook backs university AI ethics institute with $7.5 million. Forbes. https://www.forbes.com/sites/samshead/2019/01/20/facebook-backs-university-ai-ethics-institute-with-7-5-million/
Taddeo M (2017) Trusting digital technologies correctly. Mind Mach 27:565–568
Taylor L (2016) The ethics of big data as a public good: which public? Whose good? Phil Trans R Soc A 374:20160126. https://doi.org/10.1098/rsta.2016.0126
Taylor L, Dencik L (2020) Constructing commercial data ethics. Technol Regul 1–10. https://doi.org/10.26116/techreg.2020.001
The Economist (2017) The world's most valuable resource is no longer oil, but data. https://www.economist.com/leaders/2017/05/06/the-worlds-most-valuable-resource-is-no-longer-oil-but-data
Vadász P, Ződi Z (2021) The accountability of intelligence and law enforcement agencies in information search activities. In: Edelmann N et al. (eds) Electronic participation. Epart 2021. Lecture notes in computer science(), vol 12849. Springer. https://doi.org/10.1007/978-3-030-82824-0_16
van Maanen G (2022) AI ethics, ethics washing, and the need to politicize data ethics. Digital Society 1(2):9. https://doi.org/10.1007/s44206-022-00013-3
Vestager M (2016) Big data and competition. Speech at the EDPS-BEUC conference on big data. Brussels, 29 September 2016. http://bit.ly/3bHHwPz
Vestager M (2017) Algorithms and competition. Speech at the Bundeskartellamt 18th conference on competition. Berlin, 16 March 2017. https://wayback.archive-it.org/12090/20191129221651/https:/ec.europa.eu/commission/commissioners/2014-2019/vestager/announcements/bundeskartellamt-18th-conference-competition-berlin-16-march-2017_en
Vestager M (2019a) Security and trust in the digital world. Speech before the CCBE standing committee. Copenhagen, 13 September 2019. https://dig.watch/updates/commissioner-vestager-calls-more-security-and-trust-through-regulation
Vestager M (2019b) Competition and the digital economy. Speech at the OECD/G7 conference. Paris, 3 June 2019. https://wayback.archive-it.org/12090/20191129200956/https:/ec.europa.eu/commission/commissioners/2014-2019/vestager/announcements/competition-and-digital-economy_en
Vestager M (2019c) New technology as a disruptive global force. Speech at the youth and leaders summit. Paris, 21 January 2019. https://wayback.archive-it.org/12090/20191129204150/https:/ec.europa.eu/commission/commissioners/2014-2019/vestager/announcements/new-technology-disruptive-global-force_en

Walker L (2023) Belgian man dies by suicide following exchanges with chatbot. Brussels times. https://www.brusselstimes.com/430098/belgian-man-commits-suicide-following-exchanges-with-chatgpt
Weichert T (2012) Privacy and data protection—a conflict between the US and Europe. https://www.datenschutzzentrum.de/artikel/675-Advanced-Topics-in-European-Privacy-Privacy-and-Data-Protection-A-Conflict-between-the-US-and-Europe-engl.html
WP29: Article 29 Data Protection Working Party (2017) Guidelines on automated individual decision-making and profiling for the purposes of Regulation 2016/679 (WP251rev.01). https://ec.europa.eu/newsroom/article29/items/612053
Ződi Z (2023) Platformjog. Ludovika

Bias, Machine Learning and Liability—Can EU Policy Improve the Development of AI Systems?

Miklós Zorkóczy

Abstract This chapter examines the policy and regulatory challenges of artificial intelligence (AI) from the perspective of the typical lifecycle of an AI-powered product, taking into account previous incidents of AI bias. It explores how the legal consequences of AI bias can be controlled in the case of both explainable and non-explainable algorithms. In this regard, the chapter analyses developments in EU policy, in particular those that aim to create a comprehensive policy response suitable for an 'algorithmic society'. It highlights that European policy-making faces difficult choices as on the one hand it needs to create sufficient controls for AI-risks, while on the other it needs to guarantee the competitiveness of European industry and societies.

1 Introduction

Alth ough speculations about the future of humans in the machine era are difficult to avoid when analysing past, present and potential future developments in technology regulation, this chapter will do exactly that and focus on concrete technological developments, their social, ethical and legal challenges, and the policy and regulatory responses that we can give to those challenges. The chapter will look at the technological background of artificial intelligence (AI) and machine learning operations (MLOps), consider their main challenges for developers, users and regulators, including risks of bias and problems with their explainability, and then examine how EU policy-making has attempted to respond to these challenges, trying to make sure that its relevant economic and industrial policy objectives are not jeopardised.

The lifecycle of an AI system usually consists of four phases: (i) design, data, and models, (ii) verification and validation, (iii) deployment and (iv) operation and monitoring (OECD 2019). Developing an AI tool or product is a complex workflow, which requires the work of a large and complex team of professionals. They need

M. Zorkóczy (✉)
Legalise Zorkoczy Law Office, Budapest, Hungary
e-mail: miklos@legalise.hu

M. Varju and K. Mezei (eds.), *The Challenges of Artificial Intelligence for Law in Europe*, Data Science, Machine Intelligence, and Law 6,
https://doi.org/10.1007/978-3-031-86813-9_15

to design and develop an AI system which its users can trust, and in a corporate environment, trust needs to come from multiple sources: from company managers, employees, and ultimately clients (Jägare 2022). Trust can be secured when the system, in this case the AI system, is transparent, accountable, reliable, explainable and adheres to a broad range of expectations, such as ethical design, being built on a fair database, being compliant with data privacy rights, and ensuring the protection of users and consumers. Already, a number of AI scandals have revealed that trust in AI systems was premature in these particular cases, as algorithms and their biased data sets discriminated against vulnerable people or minority groups in society.

The target.com case in 2012 was one such watershed moment indicating that the use of algorithms can lead to a gross violation of privacy (Hill 2012). The supermarket chain sent a 13-year-old girl an advertising magazine aimed at pregnant women. This was noticed by her father, who complained to the company; however, a week after the complaint, it turned out that the young girl was indeed expecting a baby. Apparently, the algorithm used by Target figured out the pregnancy sooner than the family. The algorithm was programmed to find pregnant women—by recognising patterns—who could be targeted with marketing and adverts on maternity products. It used a training database of individual histories of previous purchases and current web searches. The predictive outputs of the algorithm, which the family felt was excessively intrusive, could easily have been prevented. However, to achieve that the developer and its data scientists should have pursued a more responsible course of conduct, i.e., they could have cleaned the training database to include only those people who had already purchased maternity products. They could have integrated data risks into the assessment of business needs, and recommended developing a marketing system that does not single out individual consumers or groups of consumers so directly.

The era of big data has been marked by several similar examples of algorithmic intrusion (O'Neil 2016). Companies measuring the vital data of their employees, such as blood pressure, blood sugar and BMI, comparing these data with average population data, and rewarding or penalising them on that basis is just one of the injustices to have emerged (O'Neil 2016). In another case, the mayor of Washington D.C. decided to monitor underperforming schools and evaluate teachers using data and an algorithmic system. When previously well-performing teachers were fired based on these evaluations, it turned out that the lower scores produced by the algorithm resulted from data set distortions, i.e., that other teachers started to give better grades to students, fearing that poor performance by students would lead to them being fired (O'Neil 2016). Similar events happened in the context of granting bank loans, credit vetting, criminal sentencing, ranking in education, and giving investment advice, which all contradicted our social values and infringed upon the rights of individuals (O'Neil 2016). Tech giants have also been responsible for similar practices or developments. Google's algorithm failed to predict adequately the spreading of the flu virus, because its data set contained data on commercial interests, internet searches and movement, but not relevant health data (Lazer and Kennedy 2015). Amazon built a discriminative recruiting tool (Reuters 2018), Google Photos made an evident racist blunder (BBC 2015), Microsoft had to switch off its racist TayTweets (Hunt

2016), and Facebook was fined in a data scandal with Cambridge Analytica (Criddle 2020).

The danger of algorithms lies in their ability to amplify and institutionalise the inequalities and biases of human systems and cultures, and their potential, in such instances, to cause discrimination and injustice on a massive scale. Furthermore, their operation is difficult to control, as their learning and operating techniques may be extremely opaque and thus difficult to understand and assess. The training of algorithmic systems is key to mitigating their risks; however, training is just one component of the human control that we need to impose throughout the entire lifecycle of an algorithm. Beyond issues with their trustworthiness, the safety and security of algorithmic systems are also challenging to examine and evaluate. AI systems may produce results which we cannot explain; for instance, they may be able to predict the race and skin colour of the person concerned on the basis of X-ray images, without being programmed to do so (Nield 2022).

The central aim of this chapter is to investigate whether and how the European Union—an active and relevant regional technology policy actor—may intervene in this technology area and produce technology policy and regulation that is suitable for an 'algorithmic society' and still ensure competitiveness for Europe in the global economy. It has been predicted that advances in AI—through the weaponisation of the technology—pose a risk for democracy and liberal societies (Council of the European Union 2023). Competition for European firms comes from "Silicon Valley giants" that have an immense "data advantage" over their competitors (Pasquale 2015). The challenges are therefore fairly clear. We approach this question from the perspective of the technology itself, from how machine learning takes place and how MLOps can be developed. We then examine the key technological challenges and the challenges they pose for policy-making and regulation, such as ensuring the explainability of the algorithm, how ethical operation can be designed into the algorithmic system, and how data processing workflows need to be organised so that their effectiveness can be ensured without compromising data ethics and risking data bias. With this background, we will overview and analyse the EU regulatory measures which are being prepared or have just been adopted, focusing on whether they have managed to establish the desired balance between the economic and non-economic objectives of regulation.

2 Machine Learning Operations

Algorithms offer the possibility of processing immense quantities of data using technological means. However, when designing them data scientists need to look beyond the immediate technological questions and also consider the business challenge or other application that requires an algorithmic solution. Understanding both the algorithmic tool and its real-life application is imperative also for actors from the other side of development, including businesses, policy-makers and regulators, and ultimately users too. Without a complex understanding of how the development of algorithmic systems takes place, law and policy will have insufficient knowledge of when interventions need to be ordered, who can make those interventions, which contributor can make which intervention, and which contributor should bear responsibility for which harm.

In the process of multidisciplinary product development, development operations (DevOps) is a practice of designing, coding, building, testing, maintaining, and operating software systems. It is built on intensive communication among the participants so as to ensure adequate coordination in the development process. Recently, DevOps have started to integrate machine learning models into their processes. MLOps add further complexity to the already complex DevOps, but also enable a sufficiently complex management of the entire lifecycle of the machine learning model used (Jägare 2022). In MLOps, the data scientists who train and build the machine learning tool work closely with the team who will operate the model, and the aim of their cooperation is not simply the development of the machine learning system but to keep it in operation (Jägare 2022). MLOps, which includes components such as model training, evaluation, monitoring, versioning, validating etc., and also involves collaboration among multiple teams in the development process, including data engineers and scientists, IT developers (DevOps), other industry-specific experts, such as UX designers, and the compliance team responsible for the application of data protection rules and other legal regulation (Jägare 2022).

When the machine learning model has passed the necessary design phases, it is ready for deployment. In this second phase of machine learning development, the system is put into service and is then continuously monitored. The gaps between development, operation and deployment are bridged by continuous development and continuous training modules. During the workflow, data scientists have at least 14 distinct opportunities to make fundamental choices and/or intervene (Jägare 2022). These opportunities emerge when they gather the existing data sets, determine how the data relates to the products and/or services of the client, interpret and understand pain points and business needs, determine what new data is needed, choose what data sets needs to be compared and analysed, and select which models and algorithms to use. Further opportunities for intervention arise when they start engineering, test the model, measure its accuracy, and decide how to present the results and the model to the client (Jägare 2022).

The contracts for software development usually consist of two main parts. In one part, they define general contractual terms, such as the parties, the relevant rights and obligations, payment terms, confidentiality, IP rights, dispute resolutions, language, applicable law and jurisdictions. The other part contains all relevant technical requirements as specifications of the contracted work. Determining these specifications is a delicate part of the transaction, and lawyers need to understand the key logic and features of the software development, which assumes sufficient technical knowledge on their part. On the other hand, developers also need to understand the key legal milestones of the development process. Otherwise, the contract will not protect against disputes between the parties and unperformed software development deliveries. The specification of machine learning tools in contracts is even more challenging, considering that such products need to be developed from scratch and are rarely off-the-shelf products. Their architecture components include data acquisition specifications, feature management, frequency of model training, deployment and monitoring, management and governance, and service level of operations (Jägere 2022).

3 The Explainability Problem

Behind the issue of algorithmic explainability, which has become a central benchmark for policy-making and regulation,[1] there are a number of fundamental questions regarding the control of machine learning and AI. In particular, it is unclear whether we should trust data scientists to develop and control machine learning technology, or the law should be developed to impose external controls. Should regulation be entrusted with tech companies and their codes of conduct, and ultimately users and the market be left to decide which algorithmic solutions can be trusted?

An MLOps engineer has several roles in making machine learning systems explainable. These include tasks such as optimising, evaluating and retraining, version tracking, creating metrics and benchmarks, and providing best practices, proof of concepts and management (Jägere 2022). The MLOps engineer is therefore a key figure in the process. If they decide to leave the developer company, it loses not only the know-how, but also the ability to carry out these tasks and maintain, update or modify the AI-powered product, which then jeopardises the explainability of the system. MLOps engineers can use different toolkits to ensure explainability and control the algorithm. They can use algorithms for this purpose, such as those using the SHAP model (SHapley Additive exPlanations), the LIME technique (Local Interpretable Model-agnostic Explanations), or TensorBoard. Frameworks or toolkits, such as TensorFlor, PyTorch, Keras, or the Amazon or Microsoft toolkits are also available. When developers download and use an interpretable algorithm from an inventory, they receive the necessary documentation and they are also guaranteed an algorithm that is explainable.

So-called visualisation tools, which visualise outputs, such as the model-independent interpretation technique, can also be used to make a machine-learning model explainable (Spindler 2020). They are able to explain the prediction of any model by computing the contribution of each feature in the model to the prediction (Layer-wise Relevance Propagation, LRP). There are a number of available visualisation tools that can also be used to demonstrate the relationship between the database used and the outcome (the Tensorflow What-if Tool (WIT), the Google & Open AI

[1] Explainability is a requirement that aims to overcome the 'black box' problem of algorithms. The expression 'black box' was coined in connection with the US credit bureaus scandal. See Pasquale (2015).

activation atlases), and there is DeepLift which measures the contributions of the system's predictive elements (Mahajan 2021). The model developed by MIT can tell what a machine-learning model cannot do; for example, it can evaluate deviations and unexpected events, which then can be used to enhance and control the safety of the model (Matheson 2019). Using these solutions, and solutions such as supervised learning or a semi-supervised training model, developers can significantly increase the explainability and interpretability of a model. The cross-examination of (deep) neural networks is also possible, which makes it possible to audit and explain the system's logic, although the 'black box' problem of algorithms limits these possibilities.

It was reported in 2022 that most AI systems available are not put to use in an actual business environment (Jägere 2022). There are multiple reasons for this, such as the low accuracy of algorithms, the risk of biased and/or false data used, inadequate systems features, system variables and attributes that do not satisfy business needs, inappropriate programming language, and problems with system scalability (Jägere 2022). Perhaps the main problem with deploying AI systems in actual business environments is that their use may lead to discriminatory or biased outputs. In principle, by ensuring that the AI system is explainable and is thus transparent, the risk of discrimination and bias can be excluded. When we know what likely output the input data will yield, and how a change in the input data will affect the output, we have an explainable AI system. However, the needs of big data analysis push the development of more and more complex, and as a result less and less explainable, algorithms (compare the explainable 'linear regression algorithm with the complex 'random forest' algorithm, which uses a decision tree and where data further from the node will have a lesser impact on the output). The solution to this problem may follow from ethics-driven and/or responsible innovation and development, in other words technological development that excludes in advance the negative effects of the technology by embedding values into it (Coeckelbergh 2020).

The ethical design of algorithms requires intensive human involvement. The designer must know what the AI system is for, and what business uses it is going to serve. The designer must also understand what a particular data field will mean for output, and must ensure that the data is regularly clarified, updated, cleaned and structured. The designer must also oversee training, validation and testing, and must integrate follow-up mechanisms into the system. Human involvement and human overseeing also constitute general requirements of AI development if we accept the 'human-in-the-loop' concept (Zanzotto 2019) as valid. Human control, which covers coding, the input data selection, training etc., ensures a clear knowledge lifecycle in an AI system. The involvement of humans is also necessary because it provides the basis of the legal liability of the actions or inactions of AI systems (Kerrigan 2022). Human involvement also makes sure that compliance with regulatory requirements, such as obligatory documentation, the placement of disclaimers, and the informing of users and consumers, takes place.

4 Ethical Design

The ethical design of technologies is a commonly used notion. However, it is difficult to give a general definition of the notion. Instead, we need to rely on industry-specific uses to define what it means. In the healthcare field, a "human-centred design" usually means understanding the clinical task that needs to be supported with the technology, as well as the human and material conditions of that task, in particular as prescribed in regulations (Chen et al. 2022). As one important human condition, the capabilities and responsibilities of future users must be explored and understood. Only when these circumstances are understood can the algorithm's characteristics, properties, accuracy, explainability and interpretability be designed, and these need to be designed in advance (Chen et al. 2022). The next step is to establish acceptable assurance and transparency for the prospective user (the physician); otherwise, the technology will not be used (Chen et al. 2022). Practically, designers need to develop technologies (AI systems) that users will trust and will thus have a genuine market. The final component is making sure that the parameters established in the design face will be followed in the entire life-cycle of the technology, and users are assured that this is the case (Chen et al. 2022). This may include solutions, such as performance evaluation based on appropriate metrics, or the continuous evaluation and validation that the transparency and explainability tool built into the system is operational and effective. The latter may be the ultimate guarantor of users' trust and thus the economic success of the system.

Co-planning was identified by the EU's High-Level Expert Group on Artificial Intelligence in its ethics guidance for trustworthy AI as a solution for designing ethically acceptable AI systems (HLEG 2019). It entails involving in the development process the relevant actors and stakeholders and integrating into technological design their particular considerations and interests (Zicari et al. 2021). Nevertheless, such multi-participant development processes will have to address the problem of "many hands" (Schiff and Borenstein 2019)—the problem that with multiple participants and inputs it may become difficult to established who contributed what and who should bear responsibility for a particular component. To avoid this problem, the developer must document precisely every step, from training, testing, and database validation, to the modification and updating of versions and features. Quality assurance frameworks can also support users' trust in AI systems. Transparency cannot be achieved by publishing millions of lines of program code. However, a quality assurance system can ensure that the AI system is properly implemented and continuously monitored, and that its operation can be explained and, in case of doubt, the root cause of problems can be found by adequately documented reverse engineering in the causal chain (Bartneck et al. 2021). Generally speaking, developers, service providers and users should not treat AI systems with blind confidence, and even if the outcomes produced confirm our hypothesis, we must not exclude possibilities of algorithmic bias.

5 The Data Problem

AI systems cannot operate adequately without data of sufficient quality and quantity (European Commission 2018). For data engineers to work effectively, the data set must be as easy as possible to process, structured and organised. For the training and operation of the AI system to be adequate and the system to work accurately, the data must be large, correctly recorded and complete. From a legal and ethical point of view, the data set must be up to date, should comply with data protection requirements, and must be compiled and composed subject to the requirements of fairness and non-discrimination. The data set must also meet the expectations of users, in particular it must enable users to trust the technology. Hence, users must be able to understand what data is necessary in light of the intended use of the AI system, how it would be processed, and whether its processing meets the requirements of transparency and explainability.

There are further particular data protection and data management issues with the development and deployment of AI systems. First, the personal identity of the data controller may be difficult to establish. In the data processing workflow of AI systems that role could be fulfilled by the data engineer, the developer, or even the operator of the model. The machine learning development pipeline data engineering comes first, which starts with the setting up of the raw data. It is then followed by the data upload from off- or online resources, the preparing of the data by exploring and transforming them; after that comes the feature engineering, and finally the training, testing and validating of data sets (Jägare 2022). The data is uploaded continuously under the control of the data engineer. The data engineer needs to know the nature of the data, how it was collected and from what sources, how it was stored and structured, and for what purposes it can be used (Jägare 2022). The data engineer needs to be sure of the quality of the data record, having regard to the concrete business target and whether the data needs to be fed continuously into the system. The data engineer must also make sure that the data documentation complies with data protection requirements (Jägare 2022).

In cases in which the data flow is systematically automated, there is a data pipeline which enables and secures the processing of data from the phase of sourcing to the phase of data transfers, and also circulates the entire workflow, feeding back performance metrics to the system. Data sources in a data pipeline can automatically come from a data warehouse, batch files, real-time streaming, a cloud-based source, or an open-source. Data Operations (DataOps) is not simply a combination of extract, transform and load (ETL) activities; it involves a continuously developing framework of operations. Data Mesh is an approach that delivers data as a deliverable element (data as a product) to data processors (data consumers) for it to be used in their data pipelines (Data Infrastructure as a Platform). It works like an automated data factory. Human supervision and control are essential in such an environment; compliance with data protection requirements, responsibility for non-compliance, the prevention of data bias and other data faults must all be prevented.

6 Data Bias

Bias in data sets, which will lead to biased outcomes in the operation of an AI system, is incredibly difficult to exclude, since data sets are compiled or otherwise controlled by humans. Even when an unsupervised machine learning system collects the data, for example from social media, there will be a human being who decides on the features to learn from, or who evaluates the outcome. Moreover, the features assigned to an algorithm come from humans, making every feature a human decision. Bias in the operation of AI can be defined as an "anomaly in the output of AI systems due to the prejudices and/or erroneous assumptions made during the system development process or prejudices in the training data, so the results from the AI system cannot be generalised widely" (Estévez Almenzar et al. 2022). As it follows from this definition, the biased operation of AI systems can follow from inappropriately collected data sets and from inappropriate or incorrect choices made by humans when making data set choices.

Bias in the data set happens when its representativeness is impaired, and it has been sorted, cleaned and assembled poorly. The problem starts with the inappropriate selection of the source of data, or a faulty collection process, or when a data set of sufficient quality cannot be assembled. The data set will be biased when the data source is prejudiced, for example it is affected by data omission, data inflation or data misrepresentation. These problems can be prevented with the use of data science analytics that can statistically control collection errors and measure the depth and breadth of data sources (Miller et al. 2022). However, bias needs to be investigated and controlled in the entire life-cycle of an AI system, starting with data sampling, which may only use clear and unprejudiced data, the model-building process, which should discover stereotypes, and the use of the system, which should control prejudiced expressions. These all involve human decisions or human supervision.

Further examples of data bias include reporting bias, when data subjects under-report or report selectively the information available. This can be caused by reliance on media publications when gathering data, the use of English as the language of the data, the use of professional jargon, or the pre-selection of data having regard to the expected outcome (Richards and Onakpoya 2019). Reporting bias can be remedied when exceptions are filtered, or extremely positive or negative answers are ignored when collecting data. Implicit bias occurs when the data subject is not consciously aware of his or her prejudices, for instance against certain people or certain groups of people. It is relatively easy to establish, and it can be remedied by excluding the cause of the prejudice (e.g., cultural identity) when establishing the data set. Expert bias occurs when experts are affected by entrenched beliefs and not by objective evidence, and can be avoided by peer or non-peer reviews of the data set (Eastman and Rix 2022). We can talk about under-coverage bias, when the data set is not fully representative and some features are underrepresented or missing. The fairness of a data set depends on whether all features are represented and these features—both of protected and unprotected groups—have an equal probability of receiving a positive outcome (Balayn et al. 2021).

When building an AI system, there is always human intervention; a human will make the decision about what algorithms to use for what purposes. Human choices can be biased, including the fundamental choice of how to create a data set that will model reality. The data set will only be a model and will never have the objectivity of reality (Coeckelbergh 2020). Therefore, all AI systems carry the risk of bias that follows from human intervention. Automation bias creates further problems as over-reliance on automated systems can lead to incorrect decisions made by humans and can reduce human vigilance in searching for and processing information (Strauß 2021). This can undermine the designing of AI systems and human controls over them. In principle, data science methods can mitigate the risk of bias. The developer can ignore problematic variables, for instance variables relating to groups of protected people. They can also balance data sets with measures that exclude an unfair composition of data. Algorithms can be improved by weighting biased data or focusing supervised learning models on a certain subset of the data set. Algorithm assurance can help data curation and de-biasing when the training data variables are measured differently for fair classification (Spindler 2020).

7 Data Ethics

In the documentary film, Social Dilemma, people working in technology openly discuss the goals of technology companies. The goals they identify include increasing technology application usage, making sure that users return and bring more users with them, and developing a business model which makes as much money as possible. The film gives a very honest picture of the technology ecosystem, which people—users, citizens etc. —are supposed to trust. In her book, Gry Hasselbalch (2021) discusses the deep intersections between digital technologies and human society, and talks about how big data and AI create global 'socio-technical infrastructures' that criss-cross different cultures and different legal systems. She also claims that the ethics of data is rooted in cultures of data, which are created by data scientists, technology designers and operators, end users of technologies, and lawmakers. This means that in order to create coherent data ethics, we need to reconcile a multiplicity of values and interests represented by a highly diverse group of actors. The interests and values linked to data include the interests of the values of the developer team, the user business entity or non-profit organisation, and the individual end-user.

The construction of data ethics which is suitable for big data and AI involves further complications. Hasselbalch (2021) argues that the ethics of data must incorporate and address the power relations embedded in the socio-technical infrastructures of big data and AI. The aim is to create an ethics that supports and sustains a 'human-centric distribution of power' in the multi-actor and multi-interest technological realm. As another challenge, it needs to be ensured that autonomous systems operate in a neutral manner, in such a way that they do not superimpose certain values on others. The requirement of AI neutrality follows from the earlier debate about computer neutrality, which aimed to tackle the problem that code can never be trusted as neutral as it is built following choices made by humans according to their particular values (Hasselbalch 2021). In his book, Coeckelbergh (2020) examines the critical questions of whether we can regard machines as moral agents and whether they are responsible for their actions. From an ethical perspective, this possibility cannot be dismissed because machines take actions and make decisions, and there are moral consequences of their activities. He argues that machines can cause very real harm to human values and rights, and they can redistribute resources and wealth in ways that lead to social disagreement. However, the moral responsibility of machines (AI systems) faces significant hurdles (Coeckelbergh 2020). On the one hand, they lack consciousness, will, intention, and emotions; they can only do what people tell them to do. On the other, controlling machines and maintaining an element of human responsibility may be technically impossible, as machines operate at high speed and humans will not have a chance to interfere.

AI systems, as things that exist by craft and not by nature, should be treated as products (Kerrigan 2022). However, this does not mean that ethics and morality cannot be designed into their operation. Legal rules formulating ethical and moral requirements of technologies can impose ethics-by-design obligations. The EU's General Data Protection Regulation (GDPR) (European Parliament and Council 2016) is a measure that imposes data-protection-by-design, and through them data-ethics-by-design, obligations on AI systems. However, the governance of data ethics requires more than compliance with data protection rules. It includes 'processes, procedures, cultures and values' that are designed to ensure the highest standards of behaviours when developing AI systems which aim to 'maintain public trust and ensure that such systems are developed for the public benefit' (Winfield and Jirotka 2018). Achieving these outcomes may require a combination of tools, such as adopting and publishing an ethical code of conduct, organising ethics training for all staff, undertaking an ethical risk assessment for all new products, and demonstrating the transparency of development processes (Winfield and Jirotka 2018).

8 Regulation and Legal Liability

The EU has developed a complex policy framework and strategy in the field of digital technologies and AI for the next decade (European Commission 2023a). As part of this strategy, the EU aims to become a global technology and industrial leader in 'trustworthy AI' (European Commission 2020a). Key actions include the promotion of PP collaboration, the building of research capabilities, enabling developers to test their products, connecting services and AI solutions on marketplaces, and funding innovative ideas (European Commission 2024). However, the European AI sector must conform to the requirement of trustworthiness. The latter requirement received a comprehensive definition in the Ethics Guidelines for Trustworthy Artificial Intelligence of the EU's High-Level Expert Group on AI (HLEG 2019). It was equated with respect for fundamental rights and values, such as human dignity, individual autonomy, democracy, the rule of law, basic human rights, the no harm principle, fairness, and transparency. The EU did not stop at establishing fundamental ethical principles for AI systems, and it pressed forward proposing legal regulation that can ensure the trustworthiness of AI (Kerrigan 2022).

Arguably, the broader, ethically-focused legal regulation of AI was unavoidable for the EU. Article 2 of the Treaty on the European Union puts the rule of law as the EU's central value, which then presents the EU a regulatory agenda that includes guaranteeing accountability, transparency and legal certainty, requires that fundamental rights and equality are protected, and makes guaranteeing the right to judicial protection an important component of any legal framework. The deployment and proliferation of AI systems in the public and private domain risk undermining these principles (Binchy 2022), which puts the EU on course for developing the world's first AI regulation. The EU's regulatory policy on AI placed 'human-centric' AI at the centre of its endeavours (European Commission 2020a and 2020b). The EU's AI Act (European Commission 2021) aims to achieve that objective using multiple regulatory means. First, the measure provides a definition of AI systems, thus reducing legal uncertainty. Developers can rely on this definition and determine whether the rules of the AI Act apply to their product. According to this definition, an AI system is software developed using specific techniques to generate outputs, such as content, predictions, recommendations or decisions concerning human-defined objectives, thereby influencing the environment in which they interact. The general regulator definition is supplemented by an itemised list of technologies (Annex 1), which can be extended by the European Commission. The list includes technologies, such as supervised or unsupervised machine learning and deep learning methods, logic programming, a knowledge base, an inference engine, an expert system, statistical approaches, and estimation methods.

The AI Act (European Commission 2021) is a measure of risk regulation. The risks it is aiming to address are not the risks of a general software product, but the risks of a software-hardware-platform solution that is capable of autonomous decision-making. It can collect data real-time and learn during its operation. Therefore, the risks of AI systems are higher than those of normal software development and deployment. The AI Act regulates these risks by distinguishing different risk categories which necessitate different risk management approaches. It distinguishes between prohibited AI practices, solutions with high-risk AI systems, and low-risk AI products. In the case of high-risk AI systems, it requires from developers the introduction of a risk management system, the use of data governance practices, the keeping up-to-date of documentation and records, the ensuring of human oversight, guarantees of accuracy and system stability, guarantees of cybersecurity, the introduction of quality management and system logging frameworks, and the making of information available to end-users. High-risk AI systems must also be registered in the public EU database. Compliance with these regulatory requirements will be monitored by so-called conformity assessment bodies at the service provider's request, or alternatively by the internal compliance mechanisms of the service provider. The so-called notifying authorities can authorise conformity assessment bodies to carry out their checks. Notifying authorities are national agencies that are granted their monitoring and enforcement powers by the designating regulations adopted by the Member States under the AI Act.

Legal liability for AI systems is an issue that is distinct from regulating AI risks and AI risk management tools. As explained earlier, it concerns imposing liability in law for the human interventions (decisions, controls and inactions) that take place in the life-cycle of the technology. One of its main problems is that the life-cycle involves actions and interventions by a high number of people in different roles, which makes legal relations complex and the determining of liability a very difficult task. In particular, it needs to be established whether responsibility and liability can be distributed among the different actors, and which actor (developers, manufacturers, deployers, end-users etc.) will bear liability for specifically which action or output. In principle, data controllers can be made liable for failing to de-bias data before transferring the data to an automated system. Similarly, product developers are liable for their failure to control bias in a model. Manufacturers have product liability if they sell an AI product that causes harm to consumers. The EU made a limited contribution to regulating liability for AI system in its 2022 proposal for a directive on AI liability (the AILD) (European Commission 2022a). The proposal aims to harmonise national rules regarding access to evidence (i.e., the code and the documentation) on the operation of the AI system in a national court proceeding in a liability case and the burden of proof in such cases.

The requirement of transparency of the data used follows from the GDPR (European Parliament and Council 2016). However, explainability and the right to information of data subjects do not cover the entire model. Only the logic, the purpose and the expected results need to be revealed, as well as why a particular result was produced using the model. The AI Act (European Commission 2021) provides that, as required by the principle of accountability, when the AI developer cannot explain why the system yielded the particular result it did in the case of a problem, it may be necessary to turn to the database, examine and verify it in its status when it was established and made available for the purpose of training. Developers, when they start the development process, may thus need to decide whether database files are preserved and kept as retrospective evidence of the training process. Such a choice may not be entirely compatible with GDPR requirements, and the conflicts between the GDPR and the AI Act's explainability requirement will need to be examined and resolved in future cases.

Under Article 22 of the GDPR, the data controller must take appropriate technical and organisation measures, and is responsible for keeping data management records up-to-date. He or she is also responsible for troubleshooting and reporting data protection incidents. When there are joint or multiple controllers of the data, and the contractual arrangements between them have been inappropriately settled, these obligations may give rise to legal disputes and unclear arrangements for liability. Therefore, when an AI application is sold for deployment, the developer—acting prudently—must ensure that precise contractual or other arrangements are put into place to determine the responsibility of the joint controller, as well as the tasks and responsibilities of the data processor. These arrangements must also determine the procedural protocol and the relevant deadlines to be followed in the event of an incident. The same GDPR provision requires that data subjects (customers) have the right not to be subject to a decision based solely on automated data processing or profiling, when that decision would significantly affect them or have legal consequences for them. Therefore, developers must ensure that deployers of the AI system introduce such an opt-out feature.

AI system developers are subject to further EU regulation. The Data Act (European Parliament and Council 2023) was introduced to set up a European Data Space for the European data industry, allowing them to secure the data necessary for their operation, and to initiate data flow in B2B and B2G directions. The Data Governance Act (European Parliament and Council 2022a) enables the recycling of data from the public sector and allows data altruism when sharing data voluntarily. It also calls for investing in trusted data intermediaries. There are, however, a number of open questions regarding the operation of the European Data Space. It is unclear why data holders would want to share data, for example in B2G relationships when data is covered by business secrecy, or what quality of data data holders are likely to share. It is also likely that the advantages of the European Data Space will materialise for larger market players, as they accumulate larger datasets. Online platforms using AI systems are subject to the Digital Services Act (European Parliament and Council 2022b) and the Digital Markets Act (European Parliament and Council 2022c). They are subject to requirements of automated content moderation, consumer protection, external audit and risk assessment. The electronic networks servicing the data economy are subject to EU cybersecurity regulation. The proposed Cyber Solidarity Act (European Commission 2023b) will set up a European Cybersecurity Shield, and introduce emergency and incident review mechanisms. The Cyber Resilience Act (European Commission 2022b) will introduce harmonised marketing rules for products or software with a digital component, basic cybersecurity requirements governing the planning, design, development and maintenance of such products, and an obligation to provide duty of care for the entire lifecycle of such products.

9 Conclusions

In this Chapter, we examined the general question whether the EU can live up to the promise of developing an 'algorithmic society' that is competitive in the global technological market. We observed that it has chosen its own particular way of building an AI society and industry: its policy actions and regulation aim specifically to build public trust in AI systems and their applications by putting the human at the centre of the technology. In this way, the EU expects the emergence of an AI industry that is more attractive to users globally than its competition, and is socially, politically and economically sustainable and stable in the long term. However, setting the general approach and objectives for policy does not guarantee success. AI-powered solutions may strengthen the position of already dominant market participants, and their consumers will face huge problems because of information asymmetries. At the same time, small competitors will have to address significant market barriers, such as access to reliable, traceable and sufficiently large data sets at an acceptable cost. Otherwise, they will not be able to compete with technology giants.

From a strategic perspective, the regulatory gamble of the EU may actually pay off. It has now developed a complex network of regulation, including the GDPR, the AI Act, and the rules on liability and cybersecurity, that determine the conditions of access to the European technology market and pose restrictions on what kind of AI systems, trained using what kind of data, and developed in what kind of development processes, may be offered for deployment and use there. When a non-EU developer wants to enter the lucrative European market, it must comply with the EU's human-centred vision of the technology. However, there is still a long way to go, and much depends on how robust compliance and its oversight and enforcement will be. The audit frameworks will still need to be developed, insurance for the harms of the technology still needs to emerge, and there is a need for a compensatory framework (a fund) when harm is caused but liability—because of the difficulty of proof—cannot be attributed to one individual in the development chain. The EU technology sector—at the level of start-ups and smaller participants—also needs robust further development. Computational capacity must be supported by hardware and/or cloud-based technology, sandbox facilities for training data must be established, and secure server capacity must be provided. There is also need for massive mentoring programs, networking and community-building projects, both cross-border and national. Without these, technology giants will continue to dominate the market.

References

Balayn A, Lofi C, Houben G-J (2021) Managing bias and unfairness in data for decision support: a survey of machine learning and data engineering approaches to identify and mitigate bias and unfairness within data management and analytics systems. VLDB J 30:739–768. https://doi.org/10.1007/s00778-021-00671-8

Bartneck C, Lütge C, Wagner A, Welsh S (2021) An introduction to ethics in robotics and AI. Springer

BBC (2015) Google apologises for photos app's racist blunder. https://www.bbc.com/news/technology-33347866

Binchy E (2022) Advancement or impediment: Ai and the rule of law. The institute of international and European affairs, Dublin. https://www.iiea.com/images/uploads/resources/Advancement-or-Impediment-AI-and-the-Rule-of-Law.pdf

Chen H, Gomez C, Huang CM et al. (2022) Explainable medical imaging AI needs human-centered design: guidelines and evidence from a systematic review. npj Digit Med 5:156. https://doi.org/10.1038/s41746-022-00699-2

Coeckelbergh M (2020) AI ethics. MIT Press

Council of the European Union (2023) Council of the European Union, general secretariat, analysis and research team (ART): predictions for 2023. https://www.consilium.europa.eu/media/61584/predictions-2023-external.pdf

Criddle C (2020) Facebook sued over Cambridge analytica data scandal. https://www.bbc.com/news/technology-54722362

Eastman N, Rix K (2022) Bias in expert witness practice: sources, routes to expression and how to minimise it. Bjpsych Advances 28(1):35–45. https://doi.org/10.1192/bja.2021.19

Estévez Almenzar M, Fernández Llorca D, Gómez E et al (European Commission, Joint Research Centre) (2022) Glossary of human-centric artificial intelligence. Publications office of the European Union. https://data.europa.eu/doi/10.2760/860665

European Commission (2018) Artificial intelligence for Europe. COM(2018) 237 final

European Commission (2020a) White paper in artificial intelligence—a European approach to excellence and trust. COM(2020) 65 final

European Commission (2020b) A European strategy for data. COM(2020)66 final

European Commission (2021) Proposal for a regulation laying down harmonised rules on artificial intelligence. COM(2021) 206 final

European Commission (2022a) Proposal for a directive of the European parliament and of the council on adapting non-contractual civil liability rules to artificial intelligence (AI liability directive). COM(2022) 496 final

European Commission (2022b) Proposal for a regulation of the European parliament and of the council on horizontal cybersecurity requirements for products with digital elements and amending regulation (EU) 2019/1020. COM/2022/454 final

European Commission (2023a) Europe's digital decade. https://digital-strategy.ec.europa.eu/en/policies/europes-digital-decade

European Commission (2023b) Proposal for a regulation of the European parliament and of the council laying down measures to strengthen solidarity and capacities in the Union to detect, prepare for and respond to cybersecurity threats and incidents. COM(2023) 209 final

European Commission (2024) Communication from the commission to the European parliament, the council, the European economic and social committee and the committee of the regions on boosting startups and innovation in trustworthy artificial intelligence. COM/2024/28 final

European Parliament and Council (2016) Regulation (EU) 2016/679 of the European parliament and of the council of 27 April 2016 on the protection of natural persons with regard to the processing of personal data and on the free movement of such data, and repealing directive 95/46/EC (general data protection regulation), OJ L 119, 4.5.2016, pp 1–88

European Parliament and Council (2022a) Regulation (EU) 2022/868 of the European parliament and of the council of 30 May 2022 on European data governance a (data governance act), OJ L 152, 3.6.2022, pp 1–44

European Parliament and Council (2022b) Regulation (EU) 2022/2065 of the European parliament and of the council of 19 October 2022 on a single market for digital services (digital services act), OJ L 277, 27.10.2022, pp 1–102

European Parliament and Council (2022c) Regulation (EU) 2022/1925 of the European parliament and of the council of 14 September 2022 on contestable and fair markets in the digital sector, OJ L 265, 12.10.2022, pp 1–66

European Parliament and Council (2023) Regulation (EU) 2023/2854 of the European parliament and of the council of 13 December 2023 on harmonised rules on fair access to and use of data (data act), OJ L, 2023/2854, 22.12.2023, ELI: http://data.europa.eu/eli/reg/2023/2854/oj

Hasselbalch G (2022) Data ethics power. Human Approach Big Data AI era. Edward Elgar Publishing

Hill K (2012) How target figured out a teen girl was pregnant before her father did. https://www.forbes.com/sites/kashmirhill/2012/02/16/how-target-figured-out-a-teen-girl-was-pregnant-before-her-father-did/?sh=2147fa046668

HLEG: High-Level Expert Group on Artificial Intelligence (2019) Ethics guidelines for trustworthy AI. https://digital-strategy.ec.europa.eu/en/library/ethics-guidelines-trustworthy-ai

Hunt E (2016) Tay, microsoft's AI chatbot, gets a crash course in racism from Twitter. https://www.theguardian.com/technology/2016/mar/24/tay-microsofts-ai-chatbot-gets-a-crash-course-in-racism-from-twitter

Jägare U (2022) Operating AI: bridging the gap between technology and business. Wiley

Lazer D, Kennedy R (2015) What we can learn from the epic failure of google flu trends. https://www.wired.com/2015/10/can-learn-epic-failure-google-flu-trends/
Kerrigan C (2022) Artificial intelligence. Edward Elgar Publishing, Law and regulation
Mahajan PS (2021) Artificial intelligence in healthcare. MedMantra LLC
Matheson R (2019) Identifying artificial intelligence "blind spots". https://news.mit.edu/2019/artificial-intelligence-blind-spots-0124
Miller E, Kishi R, Raleigh C, Dowd C (2022) An agenda for addressing bias in confict data. *Nature Scientific Data*, *9*(593), https://doi.org/10.1038/s41597-022-01705-8.
Nield D (2022) AI can predict people's race from x-ray images, and scientists are concerned. https://www.sciencealert.com/ai-can-predict-people-s-race-from-medical-images-and-scientists-are-concerned
OECD: Organisation for Economic Co-operation and Development (2019) Recommendation of the council on artificial intelligence. https://legalinstruments.oecd.org/en/instruments/OECD-LEGAL-0449
O'Neil C (2016) Weapons of math destruction. Crown Publishing
Pasquale F (2015) The black box society. Harvard University Press, The secret algorithms that control money and information
Reuters (2018) Amazon ditched AI recruiting tool that favored men for technical jobs. https://www.theguardian.com/technology/2018/oct/10/amazon-hiring-ai-gender-bias-recruiting-engine
Richards GC, Onakpoya IJ (2019) Reporting biases. In Catalog of bias 2019. www.catalogueofbiases.org/reportingbiases
Schiff D, Borenstein J (2019) How should clinicians communicate with patients about the roles of artificial intelligent team members? AMA J Ethics 21(2):138–145
Spindler C (2020) Algorithm assurance. In: Christi S, Bartoletti I, Leslie A, Millie SM (eds) The AI book. The artificial intelligence handbook for investors, entrepreneurs, and fintech visionaries. Wiley
Strauß (2021) Deep automation bias: how to tackle a wicked problem of AI? Big Data Cogn Comput 5(2):18–10. https://colab.ws/articles/10.3390%2Fbdcc5020018
Winfield AFT, Jirotka M (2018) Ethical governance is essential to building trust in robotics and artificial intelligence systems. Philos Trans A Math Phys Eng Sci. 376(2133):20180085. https://doi.org/10.1098/rsta.2018.0085
Zanzotto FM (2019) Human-in-the-loop artificial intelligence. J Artif Intell Res 64. https://doi.org/10.1613/jair.1.11345
Zicari RV et al (2021) Co-design of a trustworthy AI system in healthcare: deep learning based skin lesion classifier. Front Hum Dyn 3 Article 688152. https://doi.org/10.3389/fhumd.2021.688152

The manufacturer's authorised representative in the EU is Springer Nature Customer Service Centre GmbH, Europaplatz 3, 69115 Heidelberg, Germany. If you have any concerns regarding our products, please contact ProductSafety@springernature.com

Printed and bound by CPI Group (UK) Ltd, Croydon, CR0 4YY
30/09/2026
02225239-0012